Eng[d] by W. G. Jackman

John A. Dix.

SPEECHES

AND

OCCASIONAL ADDRESSES.

BY

JOHN A. DIX.

VOL. I.

NEW YORK:
D. APPLETON AND COMPANY,
443 AND 445 BROADWAY.
1864.

RIVERSIDE, CAMBRIDGE:
STEREOTYPED AND PRINTED BY H. O. HOUGHTON.

TO MY WIFE.

You have known for several years my intention to collect and publish for preservation and reference the speeches which I delivered on the leading questions of the day, while representing the State of New York in the Senate of the United States. They form the greater part of the material of these volumes. I have added several occasional addresses and a few of the numerous official reports made by me during my connection with public affairs. This collection, designed chiefly to make those who are to come after us, acquainted with the part I have borne in the national movement during a quarter of a century of extraordinary activity and excitement, I dedicate to you, as an imperfect acknowledgment of the intelligent and devoted coöperation which you have lent me in all the vicissitudes and labors of my life.

John A. Dix.

CONTENTS OF VOLUME I.

SPEECHES IN THE SENATE.

SPEECHES IN THE SENATE.

THE OREGON QUESTION.

FEBRUARY 18 and 19, 1846.

The Territory on the northwest coast of America, west of the Rocky Mountains, known as Oregon, and long in dispute between the United States and Great Britain, was, by a convention between the two countries, concluded on the 20th October, 1818, made free to the vessels, citizens, and subjects of both, for the period of ten years. This agreement was continued in force and indefinitely extended by the convention of 26th August, 1827. In consequence of collisions between the people of the two countries within the disputed Territory, resolutions were introduced into the Senate, in February, 1846, requiring the President to give notice of the abrogation of the last-mentioned convention, in accordance with one of its stipulations. A portion of the senators were in favor of adjusting the controversy by adopting the 49th parallel of latitude as the boundary, leaving to Great Britain the territory north of it; and the others of insisting on the abandonment by Great Britain of the whole country as far north as 54° 40′, from which line northward the title of Russia had been acknowledged by both the parties to the pending dispute. Mr. Dix, while asserting the title of the United States to the whole Territory derived from the discoveries and occupation of Spain, was nevertheless in favor of the compromise line of 49°, which had been offered to Great Britain in previous negotiations.

The question was settled by the adoption of that parallel as the boundary line, under a treaty negotiated by Mr. Louis McLane, and ratified by the Senate at the same session in which the debate took place.

In entering into the debate on the question under consideration, I feel constrained to differ in opinion with two distinguished senators who have preceded me, in relation to the manner in which the discussion should be conducted. I allude to the Senator from Ohio,[1] who opened the debate, and the Senator from Delaware,[2] who followed him. Both took the ground, and with equally strong language, that the title to Oregon ought not to be drawn into this discussion; but for totally different reasons: the Senator from Ohio, because the time for discussing it had gone by; and the Senator from Delaware, because the time for discussing it had not arrived. With the unfeigned respect which I entertain for both senators, I dissent from their opinions with great diffidence of my own. But I am constrained to regard the question of our rights in Oregon as one on which the propriety of the measures proposed peculiarly and eminently depends. What is the proposition before the Senate? It is, to give to Great Britain the notice of twelve months, by virtue of which the treaty between her and the United States, stipulating that the Territory of Oregon shall be free and open to the people of both countries, is to be abrogated and annulled. We cannot disguise the fact that this is a measure of the most decided character, and involving the most important consequences. What is it, sir, but a declaration that the Territory of Oregon, after the expiration of twelve months, shall no longer be open to the subjects of Great Britain? It is the first step towards the assertion of our right of empire and domain in Oregon. I can see it in no other light. I shall support it. But I cannot assent to the propriety of adopting a measure of such magnitude, without saying a single word in illustration of our title to the Territory, over which we are thus preparing to assert our paramount rights. I do not feel at liberty to take such a step, denying summarily all right in others, or abstaining from the assertion of any right in ourselves.

I propose, therefore, as a preliminary of action on my own part, to look at our title to Oregon, — not for the purpose of defining it with critical precision, but so far as

1 Mr. Allen. 2 Mr. J. M. Clayton.

to state the general grounds on which it rests. And I am disposed to take this course, not only with a view to justify the vote I intend to give, but for the further purpose of correcting extreme misconceptions, both at home and abroad, on a few points of vital consequence. No purely American question has, perhaps, excited a stronger interest in other countries; and I doubt whether any other has been so greatly misrepresented. The same misapprehensions exist at home. The public press, for the last few weeks, has been teeming with essays disparaging the Spanish title, on which our own, in some degree, rests. I am unwilling either to pass by these statements in silence, or to meet them with summary declarations of right. It is natural that senators who have been long on this floor, and who have already borne a part in the discussion of this question, should feel differently. But for myself, having never even listened to a debate on the subject, — a subject until recently entirely new to me, — I feel bound to state the grounds on which I act. This is what I propose to do, — not by the analysis of any particular treatise, nor by the examination of any particular view of the subject, but by exhibiting some of the historical facts on which the Spanish title and our own rest. I shall endeavor to perform this duty in the plainest manner, adhering rigidly to the subject, and, if possible, without addressing a single word to prejudice or passion.

The region which now constitutes the Territory of Oregon was seen, and a part of its coast reconnoitred, — I will not say explored, — half a century after the discovery of America. In consequence of its remoteness from the course of trade which was opened by the voyages of Columbus, the supposed rigor of its climate, and the certainty derived from the expeditions sent out from Mexico, that it contained no sources of wealth like those by which Spain had been enriched in the more southern portions of this continent, it remained, for more than two centuries and a half, without any permanent settlement by civilized men. During this long period, Spain constantly asserted her right of proprietorship in it by virtue of discovery, and had formed temporary establishments in its neighborhood from time to time. During the half century which succeeded, it was frequently visited by ships of other nations, by accident, for purposes of exploration, or for objects of commerce, and thus there arose a number of claimants to the right of sovereignty and domain. The claims of Russia have been adjusted with Great Britain. She holds, by the acquiescence of the latter, the whole northwest coast of America north of latitude 54° 40′, as far back as the first range of highlands; and, by virtue of a convention between her and us, we have agreed to form no settlements north of that parallel. The southern line of Oregon we hold to be fixed, by the settlement of the boundary line between the United States and Mexico, at 42°. The territory in dispute has, therefore, a coast of twelve parallels and two thirds of latitude, running back into the interior to the Rocky Mountains; and the United States and Great Britain are the only claimants to the right of proprietorship in it.

Before I proceed to examine their respective claims, it may be proper, as the subject has been referred to on this floor, briefly to state the conditions under which, by the usage of nations, a right of property in lands uninhabited, or occupied by wandering tribes, may be acquired.

The basis usually relied on to support a right of this nature is discovery; but it is a ground of right which becomes untenable, unless followed by an actual occupation of the discovered territory. If a title is not perfected by occupation, a second discoverer may appropriate the territory thus neglected by the first. But this must be upon reasonable evidence of the intention of the first discoverer not to take possession of it. If a second discoverer were to seize upon and appropriate the discovered territory before the first had time to form an establishment within it, such an act of interference would be regarded as an unwarrantable intrusion, which the latter might justly resist. On the other hand, if the first discoverer neglects within a reasonable time to take actual possession of, to form settlements in, or make some actual use of the regions he has discovered, the law of nations will not acknowledge in him any absolute right of property in or sovereignty over it, even though he may have set up monuments or memorials of his discovery at the time it was made. Such is the spirit of the rules in relation to the discovery and occupation of uninhabited territory, as stated by writers on international law. It is certainly not easy to lay down any invariable rule in respect to the time within which, or the circumstances under which, a title by discovery must be perfected by occupation. The rules and maxims of international law are but a practical application of the principles of universal equity and justice; and in the settlement of questions of this nature, the real objects and intentions of the parties are to be sought for in a reasonable interpretation of their acts. I believe, however, the doctrine may be fairly deduced from the whole body of the law on this subject, that rights by discovery remain good until superseded by rights of occupation. With regard to Great Britain, I think I may safely say that her practical rule pushes this doctrine farther. She resists all attempts by others to acquire rights by occupation in territories which she has discovered, and thus renders her own rights by discovery perpetual. Lieutenant Broughton, in the armed tender Chatham, discovered the Chatham Islands, in 1791, after parting company with Vancouver, on their way to the northwest coast.[1] She has not occupied them until recently; and I am not sure that there is now anything more than a whaling establishment on them; but she insists that no other power shall occupy them, because it would be injurious to her settlements in New Zealand, which are nearly five hundred miles distant from them.

I propose now to see what acts have been performed in

[1] See *Vancouver's Journal*, Book I. chap. 11.

respect to Oregon by different nations; or, in other words, to examine the nature of the discoveries which have been made, and the establishments which have been formed in that region, applying to them as I proceed the principles I have concisely stated.

The first discoverer of any part of the northwest coast of America north of, or in immediate contiguity with, the boundary between us and Mexico, was Ferrelo. He was the pilot of Cabrillo, the commander of an expedition fitted out in Mexico in 1543, fifty-one years after the discovery of San Domingo by Columbus. Cabrillo died on the voyage, and Ferrelo succeeded to the command. He examined the coast from the Santa Barbara Islands, in latitude 34°, to the 43d parallel of latitude; but the latter part of his voyage was made, I believe, without landing, and by a mere inspection of the coast from his vessel. In 1535, eight years before this exploration was made, possession had been taken of California by Fernando Cortes, in the name of Spain, and an establishment had been formed in 24° of north latitude. This establishment was kept up for several years; and, in the mean time, the Gulf of California to its northern extremity, with the western coast as high as 38° north latitude, had been explored. These explorations, and the establishments formed in carrying them on, were all made in pursuance of a settled purpose on the part of Spain to extend her dominion over the uninhabited territory on the northwestern coast of America. The discoveries to which these explorations led were, therefore, not accidental. The expeditions were fitted out for the single object referred to. In the prosecution of this design, it is true, the most arrogant and absurd pretensions were set up by Spain in respect to the exclusive navigation of the Pacific; but these must not be permitted to prejudice her just claims to portions of the continent washed by its waters, on the ground of discovery and occupation, and the declared purposes she had in view.

The next navigator who appeared on the northwest coast

was Sir Francis Drake. He left England in 1577, on a predatory expedition against the dominions of Spain in the Pacific. In 1579, after having accomplished his object, and carried devastation and terror into the unprotected Spanish settlements on the coast, he landed in 38° north latitude, in a bay supposed to be that of San Francisco, and passed five weeks in repairing his vessel. He took possession of the country, and called it New Albion. It is pretended that Sir Francis Drake followed the coast as far north as 48°; but the best authorities fix the northerly limit of his examination, which was a mere inspection from his vessel, at 43°, — the supposed boundary of Ferrelo's inspection more than a quarter of a century before. As the British negotiators have abandoned Drake's expedition as a part of the basis of their claim, I will not dwell upon it, excepting to add that his examinations were accidental; they were not made in pursuance of any purpose of exploration or settlement; they led to the discovery of no new territory; and they were not followed up by an actual occupation of the soil. For two centuries no claim to territorial rights, that I am aware of, was set up by Great Britain on the ground of Drake's pretended discoveries.

The next explorer was the Greek pilot, Juan de Fuca, who was sent to the northwest coast in 1592, thirteen years after Drake, by the Viceroy of Mexico, for the purpose of discovering the imaginary Strait of Anian, supposed, at that day, to connect the north Pacific with the north Atlantic Ocean. In the prosecution of his voyage he entered an extensive inlet from the sea, as he supposed, between the 47th and 48th parallels of latitude, and sailed more than twenty days in it. Such is his own account as detailed by Michael Lock; and it accords, as well as his descriptions, so nearly with the actual nature of the localities, that it is now generally conceded to be substantially true; and his name is conferred by universal consent on the strait between the 48th and 49th parallels of latitude. Spain had thus made discoveries on the northwest coast before the close of the sixteenth century as far north at least as the 48th degree of latitude; and the nature of the explorations, from their extent and the settled purpose in pursuance of which they were made, excludes all claim of discovery by others down to that period of time.

In 1603, Vizcaino, a distinguished naval commander, under an order from the King of Spain, made a careful survey of the coast of California to Monterey, in the 37th parallel of latitude; and he also explored the coast as far north as the 43d parallel, giving names to several bays and promontories as he advanced. During the seventeenth century, at least seven different attempts were made by the Spaniards to form establishments in California; but, from the hostility of the natives and other causes, these attempts failed, so far as any permanent settlement is concerned, excepting the last, which was made in 1697. But, within sixty years from this time, sixteen principal establishments were formed by the Jesuits on the western coast of America, between the Gulf of California and Cape Mendocino, one of which was in the bay of St. Francisco, near the 38th degree of latitude. During the whole period from the landing of Fernando Cortes in California, and the latter part of the eighteenth century, Spain had uniformly asserted her title to the northwest coast of America, and had, from time to time, made efforts not only to extend her discoveries there, but to perfect her right of empire and domain by permanent establishments.

In 1774, Perez was ordered by the Viceroy of Mexico to proceed to 60° north latitude, and explore the coast south to Monterey, and to take possession, in the name of the King of Spain, of the places where he should land. He succeeded in reaching the 54th parallel, within two thirds of a degree of the northern boundary of the disputed territory, whence he returned along the coast to

Washington's Island, as it was called by Captain Gray, or Queen Charlotte's Island, as it was afterwards named by the British navigators. In latitude 49° 30′ he entered a capacious bay, where he remained for some time, trading with the natives, — the same bay, beyond all question, which was four years afterwards called King George's Sound, by Captain Cook, and is now known as Nootka Sound.

The next year, (1775,) Heceta sailed as far north as the 48th degree of latitude, and explored the coast south, filling up the outline which Perez had left incomplete. He had previously landed at 41° 10′, and erected a cross, with an inscription setting forth that he had taken possession of the country in the name of his sovereign. In latitude 46° 17′ he discovered a rapid current outward from the land, opposite to an opening which he immediately pronounced to be the mouth of a river. From him it was first called the Entrada de Heceta, and afterwards the river St. Roc. He made repeated attempts to enter it, but was constantly baffled by the violence of the current. This is now conceded to have been the mouth of the river Columbia, which was discovered and entered by Captain Gray, of Boston, seventeen years afterwards.

During the same year the coast was also explored from the 56th to the 59th degrees of latitude by Quadra (y Bodega) and Maurelle, who erected crosses in testimony of their discoveries. On their return, they visited the coast at the 47th degree of latitude, and explored it from the 45th southwardly to the 42d.

It will be perceived by these details, which I have deemed it necessary to state with some particularity, that, previous to 1778, the year in which Captain Cook visited the northwest coast, the Spaniards had examined it with great care and perseverance from 37° to 49° 30′. They had also examined it from the 54th to the 59th parallels, and visited it at intermediate points. And in these explorations they were wholly without competitors, excepting on the part of some Russian navigators, who had made discoveries north of the 56th parallel, and Drake, who had visited the coast at the 38th. During the two centuries which intervened between the expedition of Drake and the third voyage of Cook, no attempt had been made, nor any design indicated, on the part of Great Britain, to avail herself of any pretended claim by virtue of the transient visit of the former to the coast; while Spain constantly asserted her right to it by virtue of previous and subsequent discoveries. And in California and its neighborhood she had, after repeated efforts, succeeded in effecting the permanent occupation of the country, which was her earnest object,—an object which no other power during that long period had even in contemplation.

The third voyage of Captain Cook, undertaken in 1777, gave the first indication of a desire on the part of Great Britain to appropriate such parts of the northwest coast of America as she considered open to settlement, and subject them to her dominion. He was instructed to take possession, in the name of the King, of convenient situations in the countries he might discover that had not been already discovered or visited by any other European power. In 1778 he landed at Nootka Sound, in 49° 33′ north latitude, where he remained nearly a month, trading with the natives and refitting his vessel. I believe this was the only point within the Territory in dispute at which Captain Cook landed; and it is proved by its latitude to be the same bay which Perez discovered four years before, and in which he passed some time, like Captain Cook, trading with the natives. The subsequent explorations of the latter were made farther north—I believe he did not see the coast south of 55°—with a view to the discovery of a passage between the Pacific and Atlantic oceans; and they have no bearing on the question under discussion.

The explorations of Captain Cook gave no title whatever to Great Britain on the score of discovery—the only place where he landed having been previously visited by Perez. Besides, if she had gained a contingent right of possession by virtue of his explorations, she did not proceed to perfect her title by a formal occupancy. The neglect of Great Britain to take actual possession of Nootka Sound, even if she had gained a contingent right by discovery, is conclusive against any claim on her part to a right of property in it. For eight or nine years the British flag was not once unfurled there, as I can learn, although the place had, in the mean time, been visited by navigators of other nations; and it was not until several years later still that it was even entered by a public armed vessel of Great Britain; and then, not until the Spanish Government had taken formal possession of it.

In 1787, Berkeley, an Englishman, in the service of the Austrian East India Company, saw the Strait of Juan de Fuca, but without attempting to enter it. In like manner, Meares, a lieutenant in the British navy, though in the service of a Portuguese merchant, and sailing under the flag of Portugal, sent a boat a few miles into the strait in 1788, having learned from Berkeley that he had rediscovered it the preceding year. Meares also explored the coast in the vicinity of the mouth of the Columbia River, and came to the conclusion, to use his own language, that "no such river as that of St. Roc exists, as laid down in the Spanish charts."[1]

As the transactions in which Meares was engaged, on the northwest coast, are intimately connected with the claim of Great Britain to a right of joint occupancy in respect to Oregon, I trust it will not be deemed superfluous if I examine them somewhat in detail.

Before making the explorations above referred to, Meares had landed at Nootka Sound, and left a party to build a small vessel. He had, for a trifling consideration, obtained the grant of "a spot of ground" from Maquinna, the king of the surrounding country, to build a house for the accom-

[1] *Voyages, &c.*, John Meares, Esq., p. 168.

modation of the party. The occupation was avowedly for a temporary purpose; and he had stipulated with Maquinna to restore the possession to him, when he (Meares) should finally leave the coast.[1] In the autumn of the same year, he left Nootka Sound with his vessels, one of which wintered in China, and the two others in the Sandwich Islands. I should have before observed that he arrived at Nootka Sound with two vessels, the Felice and the Iphigenia; and the third, the Northwest America, was built there during the summer. In the mean time, the Columbia and the Washington, two American vessels from Boston, entered the sound and passed the winter; and, from all the testimony relating to the subject, there is no doubt that the lot occupied by Meares was abandoned, or restored to Maquinna, in pursuance of the agreement between them. During all this time, it is to be recollected, Meares was sailing under the Portuguese flag; and it is a curious fact that he carried with him instructions to repel by force any attempt on the part of Russian, Spanish, or English vessels, to seize him, or carry him out of his way. He was further instructed, in case he was successful in capturing his assailant, to send the vessel to China, to be condemned, and the crew to be tried as pirates;[2] and yet, sir, notwithstanding he was sailing under a foreign flag, with orders to treat his Britannic Majesty's subjects as pirates, in case they molested him, the British Government does not scruple to found its title to Oregon on his voyage!

Though the vessels of Meares sailed under the Portuguese flag, and under the name of a Portuguese subject, he as-

[1] "Maquinna had not only most readily consented to grant us a spot of ground in his territory, whereon a house might be built for the accommodation of the people we intended to leave there, but had promised us also his assistance in forwarding our works, and his protection of the party, who were destined to remain at Nootka during our absence."—*Voyages, &c.* by John Meares, p. 114.

"The chief was also requested to show every mark of attention and friendship to the party we should leave on shore; and, as a bribe to secure his attachment, he was promised, that when we finally left the coast, he should enter into full possession of the house, and all the goods and chattels thereunto belonging."—*Ib.* p. 130.

[2] Appendix to Meares's *Voyages*, papers No. 1.

serted, in his memorial to Parliament, that the parties in interest were British merchants. I desire to state the whole truth, and therefore I give a fact I have not seen noticed. At page 173 of his "Voyages," it will be seen that he took possession of the Straits of Juan de Fuca, in the name of the King of Great Britain, in July, 1788. But, independently of the objection to claims founded upon the transactions of an individual, who, under the most favorable view that can be taken of him, had sought the protection of a foreign flag to perpetrate frauds on the revenue laws of China, this unauthorized act of taking possession under such a flag was preceded many years by similar formalities on the part of the Spanish navigators, under express orders from their sovereign. The twofold character which Meares united in his person certainly gave him manifest advantages, both as a trader and a discoverer. He was a Portuguese captain when defrauding the revenue laws of China for the benefit of British subjects, and a British lieutenant when encroaching on the territorial rights of Spain, for the benefit of the British sovereign.

On the 6th of May, 1789, Martinez, a Spanish naval commander, with two public armed vessels, entered Nootka Sound, with instructions to assert and maintain the paramount rights of Spain to the place and to the adjacent coasts. The Iphigenia and the Northwest America, two of Meares's vessels, had returned from the Sandwich Islands, still sailing under Portuguese colors, and arrived in the sound on the 20th of April, sixteen days before Martinez. The Northwest America sailed eight days afterwards on a trading voyage, and the Iphigenia was a short time subsequently seized by Martinez, on the ground that her instructions were hostile to Spain. She was, however, soon restored, and continued to trade under Portuguese colors,—a fact which shows conclusively that no claim can justly be set up by Great Britain on the basis of the voyage of Meares to Nootka, and his temporary establishment there.

The Northwest America was also seized, for reasons not directly connected with any question of sovereignty, and was employed for nearly two years in the Spanish service.

In the month of June, 1789, two vessels, the Argonaut and Princess Royal, sailing under British colors, arrived at Nootka, and were seized by Martinez. It is unnecessary to enter into the details of this transaction. It is sufficient to say that it led to an animated discussion between the governments of Great Britain and Spain, in respect to their rights in the Pacific and the western coast of America, which, for several months, threatened to produce a war between the two countries, but which was finally terminated in October, 1790, by the Treaty of the Escurial, or the Nootka Sound Convention, as it is more frequently denominated with us. Before the negotiations were concluded, both vessels were voluntarily released by the Spanish authorities in Mexico.

As the Nootka Sound Convention constitutes an essential ingredient in the claim of Great Britain, it will be necessary to advert to such of its provisions as are made the foundation of her title to the qualified exercise of sovereignty which she asserts over the northwest coast of America, and to consider them in connection with the circumstances under which they were framed. The articles which relate particularly to the question under discussion are the 1st, 3d, 5th, and 6th.

The first article provides that —

"The buildings and tracts of land situated on the northwest coast of the continent of North America, or on the islands adjacent to that continent, of which the subjects of His Britannic Majesty were dispossessed about the month of April, 1789, by a Spanish officer, shall be restored to the said British subjects."

The third article provides, that —

"In order to strengthen the bonds of friendship, and to preserve in future a perfect harmony and good understanding between the two contracting parties, it is agreed that their respective subjects shall not be disturbed or molested, either in navigating or carrying on their fisheries in the Pacific Ocean, or in the South Seas, or in landing on the coasts of those seas in places not already occupied, for the purpose of carrying on their commerce with the natives of the country, or of making settlements there; the whole, subject, nevertheless, to the restrictions specified in the three following articles."

The fifth article provides that —

"As well in the places which are to be restored to the British subjects by virtue of the first article, as in all other parts of the north-western coast of America, or of the islands adjacent, situate to the north of the parts of the said coast already occupied by Spain, wherever the subjects of either of the two Powers shall have made settlements since the month of April, 1789, or shall hereafter make any, the subjects of the other shall have free access, and shall carry on their trade without any disturbance or molestation."

The sixth article relates to the coast of South America; but it has an importance in containing a definition of the erections which may be made, confining them to such as may serve the purposes of fishing; and the provisions of the third article are expressly declared to be subject to the restrictions in "the three following articles," one of which is the sixth.[1]

[1] On the 1st of March, 1825, Colonel Benton made an able speech in the Senate of the United States in favor of the occupation of the Oregon (Columbia) River. In this speech he examined the Treaty of the Escurial, (the Nootka Sound Convention,) and insisted that it was proved by its terms to be "a treaty of concession, and not of acquisition of rights on the part of Great Britain"; and "that the permission to land and to make settlements, so far from contemplating an acquisition of territory, was limited by subsequent restrictions to the erection of temporary huts for the personal accommodation of fishermen and traders only." These positions were enforced in his argument by a reference to the assertions of Mr. Fox, and the admissions of Mr. Pitt, when the Nootka Sound controversy was under discussion in the British Parliament. The following are some of the passages to which he referred: —

"Mr. Fox said: What, then, was the extent of our rights before the convention, (whether admitted or denied by Spain was of no consequence,) and to what extent were they now secured to us? We possessed and exercised the free navigation of the Pacific Ocean without restraint or limitation. We possessed and exercised the right of carrying on fisheries in the South Seas equally unlimited." "This estate we had, and were daily improving; it was not to be disgraced by the name of an acquisition. The admission of part of these rights was all we had obtained. Our right before was to settle in any part of the south or northwest coast of America not fortified against us by previous occupancy; and we were now restricted to settle in certain places only, and under certain restrictions. This was an important concession on our part. Our rights of fishing extended to the whole ocean; and now it was limited and to be carried on within certain distances of the Spanish settlements. Our right of making settlements was not, as now, a right to build huts, but to plant colonies if we thought proper. Surely these were not acquisitions, or rather conquests,

I now proceed to state certain facts in respect to this convention, and to draw from them conclusions at which I have arrived with some diffidence. The facts I shall endeavor to present with a rigid regard to accuracy. If my conclusions are erroneous, the better judgment of the Senate will correct them; and I shall have the consolation of reflecting that my errors — if they shall prove such — have led to the discovery of truth, which I am sure is the great object of every senator on this floor.

The first article was practically inoperative, from a total misapprehension of the facts which it supposed. There is no evidence that subjects of his Britannic Majesty had been dispossessed of buildings or tracts of lands in April, 1789, or at any other time, by a Spanish officer. In the message of the British King to Parliament, and in the earnest discussions between the two countries in respect to the seizure of the British ships, I find no mention of such dispossession. When Vancouver was sent out, in 1792, to receive possession of the buildings, &c. to be restored, none could be found excepting those erected by the Spaniards. No building occupied by British subjects remained at Nootka in 1789, when Martinez arrived there; and it was denied by the Indians that any tracts of land

as they must be considered, if we were to judge by the triumphant language respecting them, but great and important concessions." "By the third article we are authorized to navigate the Pacific Ocean and South Seas, unmolested, for the purpose of carrying on our fisheries, and to land on the unsettled coasts for the purpose of trading with the natives; but after this pompous recognition of right to navigation, fishing, and commerce, comes another article, the sixth, which takes away the right of landing, and erecting even temporary huts, for any purpose but that of carrying on the fishery, and amounts to a complete dereliction of all right to settle in any way for the purpose of commerce with the natives." — *British Parliamentary History*, Vol. XXVIII. p. 990.

Mr. Pitt, in reply, did not deny the accuracy of this construction of the treaty as to settlements and erections. But he maintained "that, though what this country (Great Britain) had gained consisted not of new rights, it certainly did of new advantages. We had before a right to the southern whale-fishing, and a right to navigate and carry on fisheries in the Pacific Ocean, and to trade on the coast of any part of North-west America; but that right had not only not been acknowledged, but disputed and resisted; whereas by the convention it was secured to us, — a circumstance which, though no new right, was a new advantage." — *Ib.* p. 1002.

This subject has recently been further illustrated in a close and well-reasoned argument by Mr. Owen, of Indiana, in the House of Representatives.

had been ceded to British subjects. In fact, there were no traces of the occupancy which the article supposed. The only pretence of a cession of territory of which there was any evidence, was the right acquired by Meares, while acting in the name of a Portuguese citizen, and sailing under the flag of Portugal, to occupy temporarily a very small lot, which he himself admits he had agreed to restore when he should leave the coast.

After a long controversy on this subject between Vancouver and Quadra, the Spanish commander at Nootka, the former departed without receiving any restitution of buildings or lands, and the subject was referred to their respective governments. In 1796, Captain Broughton arrived at Nootka, and found the place unoccupied.[1] He nowhere states that he was sent out with instructions to adjust the difficulty. But he says he was informed, by letters left with Maquinna, the Indian king, that "the Spaniards had delivered up the port of Nootka, &c. to Lieutenant Pierce, of the marines, agreeably to the mode of restitution settled between the two courts." But there is no proof of such restitution. The only authority relied on to show such a restitution, is one recently produced by the "London Times." I allude to De Koch, Vol. I. page 126. He says:

> "The execution of the convention of the 28th October, 1790, [the Nootka Convention,] experienced some difficulties which delayed it till 1795. They were terminated the 23d of March of that year, on the spot itself, by the Spanish Brigadier Alava and the English Lieutenant Poara, who exchanged declarations in the bay of Nootka; after which the Spanish fort was destroyed, the Spaniards embarked, and the English flag was planted there in sign of possession." [2]

[1] See his *Voyage of Discovery to the North Pacific Ocean*, p. 50.

[2] See *Histoire Abrégée des Traités de Paix*, &c., par M. de Koch, continué, &c., par F. Schoell.

"L'exécution de la convention du 28 Octobre, 1790, éprouva, au reste, des difficultés qui la retardèrent jusqu'en 1795. Elles furent terminées le 23 Mars de cette annee, sur les lieux mêmes, par le Brigadier Espagnol Alava, et le Lieutenant Anglois Poara, qui échangèrent des declarations dans le golfe de Nootka même; apres que le fort Espagnol fut rasé, les Espagnols s'embarquèrent, et le pavillon Anglais y fut planté en signe de possession."

De Koch has the reputation of being accurate; but there is certainly one error in his statement. There was no such name as Poara in the British Registers of that year. He doubtless meant Pierce.

In opposition to this testimony of a foreign writer, we have the assertion, twice repeated, of the British historian, Belsham, that the Spanish flag at Nootka was never struck, and that the place was virtually relinquished by Great Britain.[1] If any restitution was ever made, the evidence must be in the possession of Great Britain. Señor Quadra, in 1792, offered to give Vancouver possession, reserving the rights of sovereignty which Spain possessed. There may have been a restitution with such reservation; but if there is any evidence of a restitution, why has it not been produced by the British negotiators, or at least referred to? Where are the declarations mentioned by De Koch as having been exchanged? Why, I repeat, has the evidence not been produced? Probably because, if there is any such evidence, it must prove a conditional and not an absolute surrender, — such a surrender as she is unwilling to show, — a surrender reserving to Spain her rights of sovereignty. If there was a restitution, and she possesses the evidence of it, she probably secretes it, as she secreted the map of the Northeastern Territory with the red line, because it would have been a witness against her. When Vancouver went

[1] "It is certain, nevertheless, from the most authentic subsequent information, that the Spanish flag flying at the fort and settlement of Nootka was never struck, and that the whole territory has been virtually relinquished by Great Britain, — a measure, however politically expedient, which involves in it a severe reflection upon the minister who could permit so insidious an encroachment upon the ancient and acknowledged rights of the Crown of Spain." — *Belsham's History of Great Britain*, Vol. VIII. pp. 337, 338.

"But though England, at the expense of three millions, extorted from the Spaniards a promise of restoration and reparation, it is well ascertained, *first*, that the settlement in question never was restored by Spain, nor the Spanish flag at Nootka ever struck; and, *secondly*, that no settlement has even been subsequently attempted by England on the Californian coast. The claim of right set up by the Court of London, it is therefore plain, has been virtually abandoned, notwithstanding the menacing tone in which the negotiation was conducted by the British administration, who cannot escape some censure for encouraging those vexatious encroachments on the territorial rights of Spain." — *Ib.* Appendix, pp 40, 41.

out in 1792, he carried an order from the Spanish Government to the commander at the port of St. Lawrence (Nootka) to restore the buildings and districts or parcels of land which were "occupied" by the subjects of Great Britain at Nootka and Port Cox, and of "which the English subjects were dispossessed." Quadra refused to execute it. No occupation — no dispossession was proved. The treaty did not name Nootka nor Port Cox. Quadra considered, doubtless, the occupation and dispossession as facts to be proved. Though the treaty was absolute in its terms, its execution depended on a contingency assumed to have happened, — a contingency to be shown. In the absence of any such proof, we have a right to insist on the evidence of a restitution, full, formal, unconditional, absolute. Broughton, in 1796, says the restitution was made agreeably to the mode "settled between the two courts." This was a mode settled on the reference of the subject to the two governments after the refusal of Quadra to surrender Nootka to Vancouver. Vancouver, in his "Journal," Vol. VI. page 118, says that on the 12th September, 1794, Señor Alava told him at Monterey that the matter had been adjusted by their respective courts "*nearly* on the terms" which he (Vancouver) had repeatedly offered to Quadra. Even this statement, coming from Vancouver, shows that there was a new agreement between the courts. What was the agreement? We have a right to call for its production.

Such was the practical execution of the first article of the Nootka Sound Convention. One fact is undeniable. Great Britain never occupied Nootka. From 1796 to the present day, no attempt has been made to reoccupy it by civilized men. Captain Belcher, a British naval officer, visited the place in 1837, while making a voyage round the world. In his "Narrative," page 113, Vol. I., he says: —

"No vestige remains of the settlement noticed by Vancouver, nor could I discern on the site of the Spanish battery the slightest trace of stones employed for building. The chiefs pointed out where their houses stood, and where the potatoes grew, but not a trace remains of a European."

The third article, besides stipulating for an unmolested enjoyment of the right of navigating and fishing in the Pacific and South Seas, and landing on the coast, conceded in express terms to the subjects of both nations the right to form settlements in places not already occupied; but this right was subject to the restrictions of the three following articles, one of which was to limit its exercise to the parts of the coast, or the islands adjacent, north of the parts already occupied by Spain. It had, by the terms of the compact, no application whatever to parts of the coast of North America south of the places occupied by Spain at the time the treaty was made. The important question arises, what was the most northern point occupied by Spain in 1790? This became a matter of disagreement between the Spanish and British authorities at a very early day after the Nootka Sound Convention was formed. Vancouver claimed not only the whole of Nootka Sound, but also Port Cox, south of it; and he insisted, to use his own phraseology, that "the northernmost spot on the Pacific coast of America, occupied by the Spaniards previous to the month of May, 1789, was the Presidio of San Francisco, in latitude 37° 48′." Now, it will be observed that an attempt was made to give to the Nootka Sound Convention a construction wholly unwarranted by its terms. Vancouver endeavored to fix the month of April, 1789, as the time when the question of the most northern occupation of Spain was to be settled. The language of the convention, in respect to the right of forming settlements, is, "north of the parts of the said coast already occupied by Spain"; fixing the time, according to every just rule of construction, at the date of the treaty, the 28th of October, 1790. This construction is strengthened by the fact, that a subsequent article concedes the right of forming temporary establishments on the coast of South America, south of parts "already occupied" by Spain, and referring indisputably to the date of the treaty. The words "already occupied" are the same in both articles, and they must be considered as referring to the same period of time.

The question then recurs, what was the most northerly point occupied by Spain in October, 1790, at the conclusion of the treaty?

Martinez, as has been seen, took possession of Nootka Sound on the 6th of May, 1789, and immediately landed materials and cannon for building and arming a fort on a small island at the entrance of Friendly Cove. In November he returned to St. Blas, and, in the spring of 1790, Captain Elisa took his place. A permanent establishment was formed, vessels were sent out on exploring expeditions, and, during the negotiations between Vancouver and Quadra in 1792, the Spaniards were in possession of houses and cultivated lands. Vancouver again found them in possession in 1793, under Señor Fidalgo, and in 1794, under Señor Saavadra, and the post was maintained without interruption until 1795.[1] By turning to page 336, Vol. II., of "Vancouver's Journal," a view of the Spanish establishment at Friendly Cove, on Nootka Sound, will be seen, from a sketch taken on the spot by one of Vancouver's party, in September or October, 1792; and it exhibits ten

[1] Vancouver arrived at Nootka Sound on the 20th May, 1793, and found the Spaniards in possession. He says: "An officer was immediately despatched on shore to acquaint Señor Fidalgo of our arrival, and that I would salute the fort if he would make an equal return; this was accordingly done with eleven guns." —*Vancouver's Journal,* Vol. III. p. 422.

Vancouver arrived at Nootka Sound on the 5th of October, 1793, and, to use his own words, "the usual ceremonies of salutes, and other formalities, having passed, accompanied by Mr. Puget, I waited on Señor Saavadra, the commander of the post."—Vol. IV. p. 289.

Vancouver arrived at Nootka Sound on the 2d September, 1794, and found Brigadier-General Alava in command. He left without resuming the negotiation which he had commenced with Quadra, in 1792. On the 12th November, 1794, he was informed by General Alava, at Monterey, where they met, that instructions had been sent to adjust the matter in an amicable way, and nearly on the terms which he (Vancouver) had repeatedly offered to Señor Quadra in September, 1792. But of this, as has been seen, there is no satisfactory evidence. — See Vol. VI. p. 118.

roofed buildings, with several enclosures of cultivated land. It also exhibits, totally distinct from these lands and buildings, a cove adjoining, and a reference to it, stating that it includes "the territories which, in September, 1792, were offered by Spain to be ceded to Great Britain." This was the site of the hut occupied by Meares, and the Spanish commander refused to make a formal and absolute surrender to Great Britain of any other land.

Thus it is established, by proof not to be impeached, that the Spaniards were in the occupation of a post at Nootka Sound in 1790, when the convention was negotiated and concluded; and I submit, therefore, whether this must not be regarded as the southern limit of the region within which the right of forming settlements, recognized or conceded by the convention, was to be exercised. This point was strenuously and perseveringly insisted on by Quadra in his negotiation with Vancouver, and with obvious justice. To use Vancouver's own language, page 342, Vol. II., of his "Journal," Quadra observed that "Nootka ought to be the last or most northwardly Spanish settlement; that there the dividing line should be fixed, and that from thence to the northward should be free for entrance, use, and commerce to both parties, conformably with the fifth article of the convention; that establishments should not be formed without permission of the respective courts; and that the English should not pass to the south of Fuca." Such was Quadra's construction of the treaty; and he uniformly refused to make any formal surrender of territory or buildings, excepting the small cove referred to. Nootka Sound is midway between the 49th and 50th parallels of latitude; and south of this point, if Quadra's position was well taken, Great Britain could claim no right by virtue of the convention, though it were still in force.

That Great Britain would have had the right, under the convention, at any time during its continuance, to form a temporary establishment on any part of the northwest coast, north of the Spanish post at Nootka, will not be disputed; though it would have been subject to the right of free access and trade reserved to the subjects of Spain. But she neglected to assert her right. She formed no settlements in pursuance of the convention; and, in 1796, Spain, by declaring war against her, put an end to the treaty, agreeably to the acknowledged principle of international law, that the permanence of treaty stipulations can only be secured by express agreement, and that, without such an agreement, they cease to be binding on the occurrence of hostilities between the contracting parties, unless there is something in the nature of the questions settled which is, of necessity, permanent and final. Having failed, then, to make any settlement on the coast from 1790 to 1796, all rights conceded by the convention ceased with the declaration of war, by which it was terminated. From that time forth, Great Britain stood in precisely the same relation to Spain as though the convention had never been formed; and, in order to establish any claim she may advance to territorial rights on the northwest coast, she must resort to those general rules founded upon discovery and occupation which were briefly adverted to at the commencement of my remarks.

I will not discuss the question whether the Treaty of the Escurial was revived by the Treaty of Madrid, in 1814. I consider it put at rest by the able argument of the American negotiator, Mr. Buchanan.

Let me now revert to the progress of discovery and exploration, which I was briefly sketching, and which was interrupted by the events of the Nootka Sound controversy.

In 1789, the American sloop Washington, commanded by Captain Gray, who afterwards discovered the Columbia River, entered and sailed fifty miles in the Strait of Juan de Fuca. Meares, in his narrative, describes a voyage by the Washington entirely through the strait to the north of the islands of Quadra and Vancouver, and thence into the

Pacific. If such a voyage was ever made, it must have been under Captain Kendrick, who was, at another period, in the command of that vessel; for Gray, when he met Vancouver in 1792, said it was not made by himself. But, be this as it may, it is certain that the Washington was the first vessel which penetrated the strait beyond its mouth after its discovery by De Fuca. A subsequent examination was made in 1790, as high as 50°, by order of the Spanish commander at Nootka Sound; so that its shores were well known in their general outlines before the examinations made by Vancouver two years afterwards.

In 1792, Vancouver arrived on the northwest coast, with instructions to examine and survey the whole shore of the Pacific from the 35th to the 60th parallel of latitude, and particularly to examine "the supposed Strait of Juan de Fuca," through which the sloop Washington is reported to have passed in 1789, and to have come out again to the northward of Nootka." He passed the mouth of the Columbia River, which he considered as an opening undeserving of "more attention," and came to the conclusion that, between the 40th and 48th parallels of latitude, the rivers which had been described "were reduced" (I use his own words) "to brooks insufficient for our vessels to navigate, or to bays inapplicable, as harbors, for refitting." On the 29th of April, he met Captain Gray, in the ship Columbia, from Boston, and was informed by him that he had "been off the mouth of a river in the latitude of 46° 10′, where the outset or reflux was so great as to prevent his entering for nine days." And Vancouver adds: "This was probably the opening passed by us on the forenoon of the 27th, and was apparently inaccessible, not from the current, but from the breakers that extended across it." (Vol. II. p. 43.) Notwithstanding this communication by Gray, Vancouver, relying on his own examinations, still remained of the opinion (and he so records it) that, "if any inlet or river should be found, it must be a very intricate one, and inaccessible to vessels of our burden, owing to the reefs, broken water," &c.; and he concludes that he was "thoroughly convinced" that he could "not possibly have passed any safe navigable opening, harbor, or place of security for shipping on this coast, from Cape Mendocino to the promontory of Classet," the entrance of the Strait of Fuca.—(Vol. II. pp. 58, 59.)[1]

[1] The following extracts from *Vancouver's Voyage* illustrate more fully the positions assumed in the text:—

"On the south side of this promontory was the appearance of an inlet or small river, the land behind not indicating it to be of any great extent; nor did it seem accessible for vessels of our burden, as the breakers extended from the above point two or three miles into the ocean, until they joined those on the beach nearly four leagues further south."—*Vancouver's Journal*, Vol. III. p. 34.

This he states to be in 46° 19′.

"The sea had now changed from its natural to river-colored water; the probable consequence of some streams falling into the bay, or into the ocean to the north of it, through the low land. Not considering this opening worthy of more attention, I continued our pursuit," &c.—*Ib.*

"The several large rivers and capacious inlets that have been described as discharging their contents into the Pacific, between the fortieth and forty-eighth degrees of north latitude, were reduced to brooks insufficient for our vessels to navigate, or to bays inapplicable, as harbors, for refitting."—*Ib.* p. 40.

"He [Captain Gray] likewise informed them of his having been off the mouth of a river in the latitude of 46° 10′, where the outlet or reflux was so strong as to prevent his entering for nine days. This was probably the opening passed by us on the forenoon of the 27th, and was apparently inaccessible, not from the current, but from the breakers that extended across it."—*Ib.* p. 43.

"The thick, rainy weather permitted us to see little of the country. Yet we were enabled to ascertain that this coast, like that which we have hitherto explored from Cape Mendocino, was firm and compact, without any opening into the Mediterranean Sea, as stated, in latitude 47° 45′, or the least appearance of a safe or secure harbor, either in that latitude or from it to Cape Mendocino, notwithstanding that, in that space, geographers have thought it expedient to furnish many."—*Ib.* p. 44.

Vancouver states that his inquiries had been lately employed under the most favorable circumstances of wind and weather, and that the surf had constantly been seen from the masthead. He then adds: "The river Mr. Gray mentioned should, from the latitude he assigned to it, have existence in the bay south of Cape Disappointment. This we passed on the forenoon of the 27th; and, as I then observed, if any inlet or river should be found, it must be a very intricate one, and inaccessible to vessels of our burden, owing to the reefs and broken water which then appeared in its neighborhood. Mr. Gray stated that he had been several days attempting to enter it, which he was unable to effect in consequence of a very strong outlet. This is a phenomenon difficult to account for, as, in most cases, where there are outlets of such strength on a seacoast, there are corresponding tides setting in. Be that, however, as it may, I was thoroughly convinced, as were also most persons of observation on board, that we could not possibly have passed any safe navigable opening, harbor, or place of security for shipping on this coast, from Mendocino to the promontory of Classet; nor had we any reason to alter our opinions, notwithstanding that theoretical geographers have thought proper to assert, in that space, the existence of arms of the ocean communicating with a Mediterranean sea and extensive rivers, with safe and convenient ports. These ideas, not derived from any source of substantial information, have, it is much to be feared, been adopted for the sole purpose of giving unlimited credit to the traditions and exploits of ancient foreigners, and to undervalue the laborious and enterprising exertions of our

Only eight days after parting with Vancouver, Gray discovered Bulfinch's Harbor, between the mouth of the Columbia and the Strait of Fuca, and remained three days in it. On the 11th May, 1792, the day after he left Bulfinch's Harbor, he saw, to use his own words, "the entrance of our desired port," and in a few hours was anchored in "a large river of fresh water," as he terms it, to which he gave the name of the Columbia. He remained in the river nine days, and sailed, as he states, more than twenty miles up the channel from the bar at its entrance. Thus was verified the conjecture of Heceta, who, seventeen years before, saw an opening in the coast, which on the Spanish maps was called the river St. Roc. Meares and Vancouver had asserted, in the most positive manner, their conviction that no such river existed; yet, when the fact was clearly ascertained by Captain Gray, who had given copies of his charts to Quadra, the Spanish commander at Nootka, Vancouver, having procured copies from the latter, sent Lieutenant Broughton to examine the river, and take formal possession of it. Broughton not only performed both these services, but, for the purpose of earning for himself the reputation of a discoverer, he labored, in his account of his expedition, to rob Captain Gray of the merit of discovering the river, by the unworthy device of drawing a distinction between the bay in which it debouches and the upper part of the stream. Public opinion has rejected this unmanly attempt; and Captain Gray is admitted by all fair-minded men to have been the first person who entered the river and solved the doubt which had long prevailed with regard to its existence, while Vancouver, twelve days before the discovery, had not hesitated to deny, on the strength of his own

own countrymen in the noble science of discovery." — *Ib.* p. 59.

Captain Gray, it appears, had also made discoveries as high as the northern boundary of the territory in dispute, and even beyond it. Vancouver says: "He had also entered another inlet to the northward, in latitude 54° 30′, in which he had sailed to the latitude of 56°, without discovering its termination." — *Ib.* p. 43.

This was probably what is now known as the Portland Canal. I have not alluded to this fact in the text, though it rests on Vancouver's report of Gray's statement.

personal examination, made "under the most favorable circumstances of wind and weather," to use his own language, that any such great river existed. This attempt on the part of Broughton is the more unmanly, from the fact that he actually entered the mouth of the Columbia with the aid of Gray's chart. I am disposed to acquit Vancouver, in a great degree, from all participation in the odium of this act. The account of the examination of the Columbia by Broughton, contained in "Vancouver's Journal," though in the language of the latter, is, in fact, a report made by Broughton, the commander of the party, as may be seen by reference to the "Journal," Vol. III. p. 85. Vancouver more than once recognizes Gray distinctly as the discoverer of the Columbia. At p. 388, Vol. II., he expresses the hope that he may be able, in his route to the southward, to "reëxamine the coast of New Albion, and particularly a river and a harbor discovered by Mr. Gray, in the Columbia, between the 46th and 47th degrees of north latitude, of which Señor Quadra had favored me with a sketch." At p. 393, same volume, he says he directed that "Mr. Whidbey, taking one of the Discovery's boats, should proceed in the Dædalus to examine Gray's Harbor, said to be situated in latitude 46° 53′, whilst the Chatham and Discovery explored the river Mr. Gray had discovered in the latitude of 46° 10′."

The explorations of Vancouver, though they resulted in a minute and critical examination of the shores of the Strait of Fuca, led to the discovery of no new territory; and it is a singular fact, that, while this naval officer of Great Britain, himself an accomplished navigator, furnished with all the means of making scientific investigations, was pursuing the examinations which were the great purpose of the expedition, Captain Gray, in a trading vessel, and in the prosecution of commercial objects alone, discovered the only two important openings, the Columbia River and Bulfinch's Harbor, on the northwest coast, from the 40th to the 48th parallel of latitude, where Vancouver, after the most critical survey, had discovered none.

It is indeed an extraordinary circumstance that the existence of all the great inlets in the coast, to which Great Britain now lays claim on the ground of discovery, was strenuously denied by the navigators in her public service, until those inlets were discovered and made known by others. We have seen what Vancouver said in relation to the coast between the 40th and 48th parallels of latitude. On the 22d of March, 1778, Captain Cook was in latitude 48° 15′, inspecting the coast. The Promontory of Classet, (or Cape Flattery, as he denominated it,) the southern cape at the entrance of the Strait of Juan de Fuca, was in full view, and but a few miles distant. Hear what he says in relation to the strait: —

"It is in this very latitude where we now were that geographers have placed the pretended Strait of Juan de Fuca. But we saw nothing like it; nor is there the least probability that any such thing ever existed."—*Cook's Third Voyage*, Vol. II. p. 263.

Now, however, Great Britain claims the whole strait and the adjoining country by Vancouver's discovery, though he himself admits (as we shall see) that the Spaniards had surveyed and mapped a portion of it before he arrived on the northwest coast.

In the letter of the British plenipotentiary, Mr. Pakenham, of the 29th of July last, the following passage will be found at p. 67, documents accompanying the President's Message: —

"In 1792, Vancouver, who had been sent from England to witness the fulfilment of the above-mentioned engagement, [the restitution of buildings, &c. at Nootka, which, as has already been seen, were not to be found,] and to effect a survey of the northwest coast, departing from Nootka Sound entered the Straits of Fuca; and after an accurate survey of the coasts and inlets on both sides, discovered a passage northwards into the Pacific, by which he returned to Nootka, having thus circumnavigated the island which now bears his name. And here we have, as far as relates to Vancouver's Island, as complete a case of discovery, exploration, and settlement, as can well be presented, giving to Great Britain, in any arrangement that may be made with regard to the territory in dispute, the strongest possible claim to the exclusive possession of the island."

To repel this assumption, the grounds of which the distinguished British plenipotentiary appears not to have sufficiently investigated, Mr. Buchanan briefly referred to previous examinations by the Spaniards. I now proceed to show, by Vancouver himself, that the assumption is entirely unsustained by the facts.

In the first place, let me correct an error into which Mr. Pakenham has fallen at the outset, in saying that Vancouver, "departing from Nootka Sound," surveyed the Straits of Fuca, circumnavigated the island which bears his name, and then returned to Nootka. Sir, Vancouver had never seen Nootka Sound when he surveyed the Straits of Fuca. He entered the straits on the 29th of April, the evening of the day he met Captain Gray, and proceeded immediately to survey them, as may be seen by his "Journal," Vol. II. pp. 40, 52. He arrived at Nootka for the first time on the 28th of August, four months afterwards (p. 334, same volume). This correction is only important as repelling the inference which might have been drawn from the fact, if it had been as stated by Mr. Pakenham, that Vancouver had been previously established at Nootka, and had departed from it, as from a regular station, on a voyage of exploration to the Straits of Fuca.

But there are more important errors to be corrected.

While Vancouver was surveying the Strait of Fuca, and the extensive inland waters connected with it, Galiano and Valdes, two Spanish officers sent out from Nootka Sound, were engaged in the same service. The two parties met on the 22d of June, about the middle of the strait, near Point Gray, above Frazer's River, and proceeded together northerly, uniting their labors, and surveying its shores to a point near the extremity of the island of Quadra and Vancouver, between the 50th and the 51st degrees of north latitude, where they separated. And here I desire to call the special attention of the Senate to the "Journal" of Vancouver, who states that Señor Galiano, who spoke a little English, informed him "that they had arrived at Nootka on the 11th of April, from whence they had sailed on the 5th of this month," (June,) "in order to complete the examination of this inlet, which had, in the preceding year, been partly surveyed by some Spanish officers, whose chart they produced." Observe, sir, the inlet (*i. e.* the Strait of Fuca), about latitude 50°, partly surveyed and mapped a year before Vancouver came on the coast. Vancouver then continues (Vol. II. p. 210): —

"I cannot avoid acknowledging that, on this occasion, I experienced no small degree of mortification in finding the external shores of the gulf had been visited, and already examined a few miles beyond where my researches during the excursion had extended, making the land I had been in doubt about an island; continuing nearly in the same direction about four leagues further than had been seen by us, and by the Spaniards named Favida [Feveda]."

By turning back to p. 204, Vol. II., it will appear that Vancouver's examination terminated at 50° 6′ north latitude; so that the Spaniards, before his arrival, by his own acknowledgment, had examined the Strait of Fuca to a point north of that parallel; and by turning to p. 249, Vol. II., it will be seen that, on parting with Señor Galiano, the latter furnished him with "a copy of his survey and other particulars relative to the inlet of the sea, which contained also that part of the neighboring coast extending northwestward from the Straits of De Fuca, beyond Nootka, to the latitude of 50° 3′, longitude 232° 48′."

What, then, becomes of this complete "case of discovery, exploration, and settlement," in respect to Quadra and Vancouver's Island, and the Strait of Fuca? It is proved by Vancouver himself that the Spaniards had partially surveyed and mapped the shores of the strait as high as 50° a year before he arrived on the coast. And if we turn to his "Journal," Vol. II. p. 339, it will be seen that Galiano and Valdes arrived at Nootka on the 1st of September, three days after him, by a "route through Queen Charlotte's Sound," round the northern point of the island, "to the southward of that which we had navigated," and of course following its shores more closely than he. "The strongest possible claim to the exclusive possession of the island," to use Mr. Pakenham's language, is not, therefore, as he asserts, in Great Britain, but, as shown by Vancouver himself, it was in Spain then, and is in us now.

But, sir, I have a word to say in relation to the whole subject of Vancouver's explorations.

It would seem that the Spaniards, in the autumn of 1793, had become distrustful of Vancouver's objects in the survey of the northwest coast. At the Bay of St. Francisco, although he had everywhere before been treated with a civility by the Spaniards for which his "Journal" abounded in expressions of gratitude, he was subjected to restrictions which he denominates "unexpected, ungracious, and degrading." On his arrival at Monterey on the 1st of November, the Spanish commander, Arrillaga, declined holding any verbal communication with him, but addressed to him questions in writing as to the objects of his voyage; to which Vancouver promptly replied —

> "That the voyage in which we were engaged was for the general use and benefit of mankind, and that, under these circumstances, we ought rather to be considered as laboring for the good of the world in general than for the advantage of any particular sovereign, and that the Court of Spain would be more early informed, and as much benefited by my labors, as the kingdom of Great Britain."—Vol. IV. p. 309.[1]

[1] The correspondence between Vancouver and Señor Arrillaga, as reported by the former, though too long to be inserted here, is well worth a perusal. On landing, Vancouver called on the Spanish commandant, and was preparing to state his reasons for having entered the ports under his government, when, as he says, "he [Señor Arrillaga] stopped me from proceeding further, and begged that the subject might be referred to a written correspondence, by which mode he conceived matters would be more fully explained." In the afternoon a Spanish officer went on board Vancouver's vessel, and delivered him two letters from the Spanish commandant. "The tenor of these letters [says Vancouver] being very different from what my conversation with Señor Arrillaga had given me reason to expect when I visited him at the Presidio, I was reduced to the necessity of sending him the next day (Saturday, the 2d) a full explanation of the objects of our voyage, and of the motives that had induced me to enter the ports under his jurisdiction." The substance of this explanation is given in the extract in the text, denying the intention of laboring "for the advantage of any particular sovereign." And it was so satisfactory that, as Vancouver says, "On Monday, the 4th, I received a letter from Señor Arrillaga in reply to my letter, in which he was pleased to compliment me upon my ingenuousness," &c.

Here is the confession of Vancouver himself, that there was no intention of interfering with the territorial rights of Spain, and that no special advantages were sought for by Great Britain. It is the highest evidence, the evidence of contemporaneous exposition, against the claims of the British plenipotentiary, and it demolishes the whole fabric of the British title, so far as it is built on Vancouver's explorations.

While on this part of the subject, I desire also to call the attention of the Senate to the manner in which the Oregon question has been discussed in the British Parliament by some of the most distinguished members of both branches of that body. I wish to do so for the purpose of correcting great inaccuracies, and also for the purpose of showing how imperfectly the subject appears to be understood by those who, from their elevated positions, are under the strongest moral obligations to possess themselves of the truth, in order that the public mind of Great Britain may not be misled and inflamed on their high authority.

In the House of Lords, on the 4th of April last, immediately after the reception of the President's inaugural speech, the subject was brought forward by the Earl of Clarendon, not in the usual form of a call on her Majesty's Ministers for information, but in pursuance of a notice which he had given on the preceding day of his design to invite the attention of the House to the question. In the course of his remarks, he undertook to give a sketch of the claims of Great Britain and the United States to the Territory of Oregon. I shall, in respect to the former, quote his own words from the "London Times," a source to which we may confidently look for an accurate report of his Lordship's remarks.. I shall confine myself strictly to the question of title in all I have to say in reference to these debates, avoiding carefully all allusion to the offensive language with which they were in some instances connected: —

"In the first place, my Lords, if priority of discovery could constitute title, our claim would be unquestionable; for Sir Francis Drake, when he first visited that country in 1558, found all the land unappropriated, and took possession of it, giving it the title of New Albion. I do not mean to say that this constitutes a claim; but owing, subsequently, to a seizure of British vessels at Nootka, and to a dispute which arose in consequence, it was arranged by the Treaty of the Escurial that the subjects of the contracting parties should not be molested in fishing and making settlements in parts not hitherto occupied. In 1792, the country adjacent to the Columbia River was taken possession of by Cook, and was explored in 1813 by the Northwestern Company, now called the Hudson Bay Company, who established themselves in Port St. George, under the government of British laws, continuing to the present day, and being the first establishment in that country of a lawful and national character, and recognized as such by foreign States."

In the paragraph I have read, there are numerous errors in the statement of facts, and I must ask the indulgence of the Senate while I point some of them out.

1. Sir Francis Drake arrived on the northwest coast of America in 1579, and not in 1558, as stated by Lord Clarendon, making a difference of twenty-one years in point of time. If this error of date, which may possibly be typographical, were the only one, I should not have troubled the Senate with any reference to it. But there are graver misapprehensions in this statement. It will be seen, that, though Lord Clarendon does not venture to refer to Sir Francis Drake's visit to the northwest coast as constituting a title of itself, he presents it as evidence of "priority of discovery." Sir, that navigator can, in no just sense, be said to have visited the disputed Territory of which Lord Clarendon was speaking. The Territory commences at the 42d parallel of latitude, and runs north to 54° 40′. Sir Francis Drake landed at 38°. He sailed along the coast north of this parallel, according to the best authorities, only as high as 43°. Nor can his visit, in any just sense, be regarded as a discovery. The country, including the Bay of St. Francisco, where he landed, was previously known. It had been seen thirty years before as high as the 43d parallel by Ferrelo, who was sent out by the Viceroy of Mexico for

the express purpose of exploring and extending the dominion of Spain over it; and it was taken possession of at or near the very point where Drake landed, and at various others, long before the Government of Great Britain claimed any right of possession, growing out of this pretended discovery, and the visits of her navigators to the northwest coast.

Besides, Drake's expedition was in the nature of a piratical enterprise, and not an enterprise of legitimate warfare. England and Spain were at peace. It is true, the two sovereigns, Elizabeth and Philip, were engaged in secret plots against each other, — the former by fomenting disturbances in the Low Countries, and the latter by setting on foot rebellions in Ireland; but it was several years later before these intrigues broke out into the open hostility, of which the chief incident was the destruction of the Invincible Armada. (Sir, the contradiction of terms is the work of history, not mine.) Yet Elizabeth, after Drake's return to England, on the application of the Spanish ambassador complaining of his piracies, restored a portion of the booty he had taken, and by this restitution admitted the unlawfulness of his expedition. It is only necessary to look into Hume to see in what light it has always been viewed by the eye of legitimate history. Sir, it should need some boldness, one would think, to set up a claim even to "priority of discovery" on the basis of a transaction like this.

2. Lord Clarendon states that the country adjacent to the Columbia River was taken possession of in 1792 by Captain Cook. Sir, Captain Cook never saw the Columbia River, nor landed in the immediately adjacent country. His visit was to Nootka Sound, on the island of Quadra and Vancouver, separated from the continent by the Strait of Fuca. His voyage is referred by Lord Clarendon to the year 1792. It was, in fact, made in 1778, fourteen years before the Columbia River was entered or even certainly known to exist. Ten years after Cook's voyage to the coast, Meares, on whose explorations the British Government

partially rests its title, reported he could say with certainty, no such river as the St. Roc (the Columbia) existed. Four years later still, Vancouver, after a most careful examination of the coast, came to the same conclusion, as we have seen. Sir, Lord Clarendon evidently confounded the voyage of Cook with that of Vancouver, without an accurate reference to either.

3. It is equally erroneous to say that the Northwest Company explored the country in 1813, and established themselves in Port St. George. Explorations had been made, first by Lewis and Clarke, military officers in the service of the United States, and then by Thompson and others, in the service of the British and American fur companies. But no particular explorations, I believe, were made in the year referred to. The stock and property of the American Company at Astoria were sold to the Northwest Company in that year; but the place was restored to the United States in 1818, and no attempt was made by the Government of Great Britain to extend its laws over any part of the Territory until 1821, eight years after the time at which Lord Clarendon represents Astoria as being under the government of British laws, having the character of a national establishment of Great Britain, and recognized as such by foreign nations. Sir, it has never possessed such a national character, nor been so recognized. If his Lordship had taken the trouble to look at the statement of the British commissioners, (Messrs. Huskisson and Addington,) in 1826, he would have found they distinctly denied that it was a "national possession" or a "military post" in the hands of the Americans; and they endeavored to show by argument that it was not such in the hands of the Northwest Company after its purchase. Its restoration to us in 1818 is incompatible with the assumption that it has such a national character now. The assumption is equally inconsistent with the conditions of the treaties between Great Britain and the United States, which virtually

preclude such an exclusive exercise of sovereignty on her part as to give any establishments made by her subjects a character of nationality. Nay, sir, it is inconsistent with the claims of Great Britain herself, whose commissioners, in 1826, expressly renounced all pretensions to a right of exclusive sovereignty over any portion of the Oregon Territory. It is difficult to fancy a paragraph of as many words so replete with error as the one on which I am commenting.

I regret to say that the subject was presented to the House of Commons with, if possible, still greater misrepresentations, and from an equally distinguished source; though I might not have felt myself called on to notice them, but for their connection with the incidents I have been examining, and particularly the question of title.

The subject was introduced into the House of Commons by Lord John Russell, much in the same manner as it was presented to the House of Lords, — not in the shape of a call for information, but in the nature of a protest against some of the positions taken by the President in his inaugural speech. This gentleman is a distinguished member of the Whig party, a member of a former ministry, and was recently called on by her Majesty to form another, but did not succeed. I will now read to the Senate that part of his Lordship's remarks which relates to the discovery of the Columbia River, one of the principal historical facts on which the United States rest their claim to the Oregon Territory: —

"Now, it appears that Captain Vancouver was sent out by the British Government to discover the line of coast, and to take possession of certain parts laid down in his instructions; and here we come to another part of the claims of the United States, — to a part of their claims where they put in their claim to discovery upon a transaction which I will now proceed to relate. It appears that a merchant vessel, called the Columbia, under a Captain Gray, discovered an inlet, which was supposed to be an inlet of a river. It appears that, after some days, in the month of May, 1792, passed partly at anchor and partly in endeavoring to ascertain the limits of that bay, this vessel sailed out again into the Pacific Ocean. There is a very clear account given by

Captain Gray, the commander of that vessel, that, 'after some days, he says, 'we thought we had found a channel, but found we were mistaken. There is no channel in the part which we endeavored to penetrate, and therefore we must return.' Shortly after this, Captain Vancouver arrived on the coast. He not only went into the same inlet, but he sent his lieutenant — a Lieutenant Broughton — to discover the river, and to go in a boat to a distance up the river. Lieutenant Broughton was more successful than Captain Gray. He actually discovered the entrance of the Columbia River. He went up it in his boat several days, to the distance, I think, of some ninety or one hundred miles. He discovered the territory surrounding it. It was agreed that the river should be called by the name of Columbia, and Lieutenant Broughton returned to his ship. But Captain Vancouver took possession of that river, the coast adjacent, and the Nootka Sound, in the name of his Majesty the King of England. (Hear, hear!) Then, sir, there was something of valid title."

I confess it was with equal regret and surprise that I read this statement of a transaction which has become matter of history, and in respect to the facts of which there is no reasonable ground for serious misconception. I have looked in vain for the quotation Lord John Russell professes to make from Captain Gray. There is no such statement in the only account which I have seen given by the latter of the discovery of the Columbia River, — the certified copy of his log in the State Department. His Lordship goes on to state that Vancouver shortly after arrived on the coast, and not only went into the inlet, but sent in Lieutenant Broughton, "who actually discovered the entrance to the Columbia River." Now, the Senate will observe that, in order to sustain this most unauthorized assumption, almost all the important facts relating to the discovery of the Columbia River — facts shown by Vancouver's own "Journal" — are kept out of view: the meeting of Gray with Vancouver on the 29th April, 1792, five months previously, near the Strait of Fuca; the information given by Gray to the latter of the discovery of the river, and of his unsuccessful attempts to enter it; the incredulity of Vancouver, and his continued conviction that no such river existed; the return of Gray to the river, his success in entering it; the arrival of Vancouver at Nootka, where he obtained copies of Gray's charts left with Quadra, by the aid of which Vancouver was enabled to find the stream, and send up his lieutenant, Broughton, to explore it. I say, sir, all these material facts are suppressed — I trust not intentionally — to sustain the unfounded assumption that Broughton was the discoverer of the Columbia. But it is worthy of remark that Mr. Falconer, a respectable British writer, who has recently published a pamphlet on Oregon, and who wrote about the time Lord John Russell spoke, admits that Gray was the first person who noticed the Columbia River after Heceta, and concedes the discovery to the latter. Happily, the historical facts are too well authenticated to be permanently misunderstood. They were so well known at the time, that even the rivalry — not to say the detraction — of the day conceded to Gray the merit of the discovery, by designating the river by the name he gave it, — the name of the vessel that first entered its waters. In regard to the attempt to restrict Gray's discovery to the bay or mouth of the river, it is only necessary to say that the settlement at Astoria is universally admitted to be on the Columbia River. Is it not so, sir? It is designated "the settlement on the Columbia River," in the despatch of Earl Bathurst directing it to be restored to us in 1818, as well as in the act of restoration. Now, sir, Captain Gray ascended the river, not only as high as Astoria, which is ten miles from the Pacific Ocean, but at least six miles above it, according to Broughton himself. Look at the map of Oregon on your table, by Captain Wilkes, and you will find Gray's Bay, so named by Broughton,[1] on the north side of the Columbia, and higher up than Astoria. According to Gray's own log, he anchored, the day he discovered and entered the river, ten miles above the entrance, and, three days after, he sailed twelve or fifteen miles higher up. He must, therefore, have been from six to

[1] See *Vancouver's Journal,* Vol. III. p. 92.

fifteen miles above the site of the settlement at Astoria. What, then, becomes of the attempt of Broughton, revived by British statesmen, not negotiators, (no negotiator at this day would so risk his reputation,) to restrict Gray's discovery to the mouth of the stream?

Lord John Russell's statement is equally erroneous in other particulars, — erroneous in saying that Vancouver entered the Columbia, or the inlet, — erroneous in saying that he took possession of Nootka Sound. His vessel, the Discovery, did not pass the bar at the mouth of the Columbia River; he did not take possession of Nootka; Quadra refused to make a formal surrender of anything but Meares's Cove, which he would not accept; and the formality of taking possession of the Columbia River was performed by Broughton, after Vancouver had left the coast, much in the same way as it had been done years before by the Spaniards, who were the first discoverers and explorers of the country. I repeat, and I say it with regret, that, besides the errors in point of fact, the leading and material circumstances connected with the discovery of the Columbia River are kept out of view. I do not expect British statesmen to produce arguments in favor of the American title; but when they undertake to refer to historical facts, resting on their own authorities and in their own possession, they are bound to state them with accuracy. Sir, we may excuse illogical deductions from admitted data; we may look with indulgence on differences of opinion in regard to the same facts, knowing, as we do, our liability to be biased by prejudice or by too partial views of personal or national interest. But, for an omission of essential circumstances in the discussion of an important national question, — a discussion entered upon voluntarily, for the purpose of enlightening the public mind of a nation, — there can be no apology, even though it arise from the want of a sufficiently careful examination of the subject. On the Oregon question, it is well known that great excitement existed at the time in Great Britain and the United States,—an excitement which exists still, though happily somewhat abated,—an excitement which needs, perhaps, but little provocation to break out into open hostilities; and no man who appreciates as he ought the calamities which would flow from an interruption of the amicable relations existing between us should be willing to incur the responsibility of misleading the public judgment of either country; or, if he does misdirect it, he should at least have the consolation of reflecting that it was through erroneous deductions, and not a misstatement of facts fairly within his knowledge.

The misrepresentations to which I have alluded are the more to be regretted for the reason, if I do not err, that they constitute almost the only views of the subject which reach the great mass of the British people. In this country, statements of both sides of great national questions are equally diffused. Look at our newspapers, and they will be found filled with the diplomatic correspondence between the British and American plenipotentiaries. The letters of Mr. Pakenham are published with those of Mr. Calhoun and Mr. Buchanan, and are as widely circulated. All read, compare, and judge them. It is not so in Great Britain. As a general rule, the British side of the question only is presented to the British public. Nor is it the official argument of the Government, drawn up by the diplomatist, under a sense of his responsibility to the criticism of other nations and the general judgment of mankind. No, sir. It is more frequently the "tirade" of the politician, by which the public mind of Great Britain is made to pronounce judgment upon great questions of international right and duty.

These misrepresentations are still more to be regretted, because they constitute the basis of the statements which find their way to the continent. Through "Galignani's Messenger," the echo of the British press, they are translated into French, and widely circulated, poisoning the whole public mind of the Continent, and exciting prejudice against us.

I will only add that the Earl of Aberdeen in one House, and Sir Robert Peel in the other, adverted to these statements in a manner which, though not altogether unexceptionable, was in general dignified and statesmanlike; and it is earnestly to be hoped that the better feeling which now exists between the two countries may continue unabated, and lead to a settlement of the question on terms honorable to both.

I feel that I owe an apology to the Senate for this long digression. I trust it will be found in the consideration, that the inaccuracies I have endeavored to point out did not go to the world with the mere weight of an ordinary legislative debate, but with all the evidences of deliberation and arrangement, and therefore calculated to be more dangerous in propagating error.

[It was now three o'clock, and Mr. DIX gave way to a motion of Mr. SEVIER, that the Senate adjourn.

The Senate accordingly adjourned.

THURSDAY, *February* 19, 1846.

Mr. DIX was about to resume his remarks, which he had not concluded at the hour of adjournment yesterday, but yielded the floor to

Mr. J. M. CLAYTON, who said he desired an opportunity to offer a few remarks relative to an allusion made to him by the Senator from New York,[1] in the opening of his speech yesterday. He is reported to have said: —

"In entering into the debate on the question under consideration, I feel constrained to differ in opinion with two distinguished senators who have preceded me, in relation to the manner in which the discussion should be conducted. I allude to the Senator from Ohio,[2] who opened the debate, and the Senator from Delaware,[3] who followed him, not now in his seat. Both took the ground, and with equal peremptoriness, that the title to Oregon ought not to be discussed, but for totally different reasons: the Senator from Ohio, because the time for discussing it had gone by; and the Senator from Delaware, because the time for discussing it had not arrived. With the unfeigned respect

[1] Mr. Dix. [2] Mr. Allen. [3] Mr. J. M. Clayton.

which I entertain for them, I dissent from their opinion with great diffidence of my own."

As the Senator said, he (Mr. C.) was temporarily absent from his seat, but came in a few minutes after the Senator had made that remark. He had mistaken his (Mr. C.'s) position. When he had the honor of addressing the Senate on the 12th instant, he did object to the discussion of the title in open session, but he avowed distinctly at the time his perfect willingness to enter at any moment on that discussion in executive session. He did not mean to say, nor did he think that he was generally understood at the time as meaning to say, that he objected to the discussion of the question at that very moment. On the contrary, he thought that he expressed his willingness to go into it then, if his associates in the Senate wished to do so, — but in executive session. And he begged the Senator to recollect the reason which he assigned why the discussion should be so conducted. He said that, if the question were to be settled by treaty between the two governments, the remarks made in open session were calculated to prejudge, and must necessarily prejudge, the question which would arise upon the treaty. He thought then, and he thought so still, that, if the question were to be settled in that manner, great danger might arise from these public discussions, because it would be recollected that it took but nineteen of them to defeat any treaty; and if the discussion became extended, as was very likely, there was danger that nineteen senators might become so committed before the whole country in regard to the title, and differing from the Executive, why, then, was it not obvious that their consideration of the treaty would be seriously trammelled? On the other hand, he thought then, and thought still, that if discussed in executive session no such difficulty could occur; no man would be then committed before the country. But open discussion was attended with the danger of so many men committing themselves on some parallel of latitude different from that presented in the treaty.

If the Senator would pardon him a few moments longer, he would make a single reference to a remark which fell from the honorable Senator from Indiana.[1] He seemed to apprehend that there was greater danger of strangling Oregon in that chamber than elsewhere. How so? He (Mr. C.) could not possibly comprehend that. If the title to Oregon be clear, — if it be such a title as the country could stand up for and fight for, — it was one that would bear discussion in executive session as well as anywhere else; and the only difference was, that it would be much more safely discussed in executive session than in open session. The honorable Senator, however, at the conclusion of his eloquent address, seemed to apprehend that if the Senate took the

[1] Mr. Hannegan.

responsibility of discussing this question in secret session, perhaps some Caius Gracchus might drive us from our seats, and forcibly expel our President from his elevated seat.

Mr. HANNEGAN. If the Senator from Delaware will allow me, I will restate what I uttered in this particular, and a misreport of which was given in both the "Union" and "Intelligencer," so gross as to be ridiculous.

Mr. J. M. CLAYTON yielded the floor, when

Mr. HANNEGAN said that the language he uttered was, that the withdrawal of so momentous a question from the public eye for secret deliberation and discussion, to be followed — as perchance it might be — by a silent and sudden death of the measure, in direct violation of the will of three fifths of the American people, would be a most serious, if not a melancholy hour in the history of the country. It might prelude the entrance of some Caius Gracchus into that hitherto consecrated chamber, whose heart, big with the fires of freedom, and roused by such an outrage upon public rights, would lead him to address the mighty tribunal without, and, by this simple change of attitude, (here Mr. H. pointed to the doors of the Senate, and raised his hands to the galleries,) turning from that venerated chair, reverse thenceforth the cherished forms of this body, impair its dignity, and destroy its lofty and commanding attitude.

Mr. CLAYTON was glad to hear that explanation.]

Mr. DIX then proceeded with his remarks, and said: —

I beg the Senator from Delaware to be assured that nothing would give me more pain than to misstate any senator on this floor; and I accept with great pleasure the explanation which he has made. I desire also to say, in justice to him as well as to the Senator from Ohio, that I did not use the term "peremptoriness" in referring to the manner in which they had insisted that the question of title ought not, in their opinion, to be discussed. I said they had taken the position in equally strong language.

I now resume the consideration of the important question on which I had the honor to address the Senate yesterday; and in doing so I cannot withhold the expression of my sense of the kind indulgence which has been extended to me. I will endeavor to afford the Senate a substantial proof of that sense of obligation on my part, by bringing my remarks to a close in the briefest possible period of time.

The historical sketch which I was making of the discoveries and establishments in Oregon, when the Senate adjourned yesterday, ended with the year 1792.

The discovery of Bulfinch's Harbor and the Columbia River by Gray, and the explorations of Galiano, Valdes, and Vancouver, in the Strait of Fuca, in that year, terminated the series of maritime discoveries in the disputed territory, which had commenced two centuries and a half before. From that time to the present, nothing has been done on the coast but to fill up the smaller details of the great outline completed by the labors of these navigators.

In the same year, (1792,) Mackenzie, leaving Fort Chippewyan, on the Athabasca Lake, in the 58th parallel of latitude, and nearly midway between the Atlantic and Pacific oceans, proceeded westward to the Rocky Mountains, where he passed the winter. The next spring he resumed his journey, struck the Tacoutche Tessee, (now Frazer's River,) in the 54th parallel of latitude, and descended it some two hundred and fifty miles. He then continued his course to the west, and reached the Pacific in north latitude 52° 20′, — about a degree north of the island of Quadra and Vancouver. Frazer's River, which takes its rise near the 55th parallel of latitude, was for nineteen years supposed to be the northern branch of the Columbia; but, in 1812, it was ascertained by Frazer to debouch in the Strait of Fuca, at the 49th parallel of latitude. It waters the district of country immediately west and north of the valley drained by the upper branch of the Columbia. This district is a part of the great section of the northwest coast, bounded on the east by the Rocky Mountains, and on the west by the Pacific, of which the main channels of access had been laid open by previous discoveries.

In 1804, Captains Lewis and Clarke set out on their expedition to Oregon; and, in 1805, after incredible hardships and labors, they established themselves on the north side of the Columbia River, near its mouth, and subsequently on the south side, and passed the winter there. In the spring of 1806, they commenced their journey homeward, and reached the Mississippi in the fall of that year, having travelled over 9000 miles. This expedition was fitted out under the direction of the Government of the United States, and executed by officers in its service at the public expense. It was undertaken on the recommendation of the President, communicated in a message to Congress in 1803. One of its objects was to examine the country watered by the Columbia River, which had been discovered by a citizen of the United States; and it resulted in a survey — necessarily cursory — of the main southern branch of the river, of the principal stream to its mouth from the junction of the latter with it, and of a portion of Clarke's River, which empties into the northern branch between the 48th and 49th parallels of latitude. This was the first exploration of the Columbia made subsequently to 1792, when it was ascended by Gray, its discoverer, some twenty miles, and five months after by a detachment from Vancouver's party, under Broughton, about one hundred miles, from its mouth.

It is also to be considered that the expedition of Lewis and Clarke was undertaken immediately after the cession of the Territory of Louisiana to the United States by France, — a Territory admitted to include all the country drained by the Mississippi and its tributaries to their head-waters. It was also the understanding at the time, that it was separated from the British possessions in North America by the 49th parallel of latitude, extended westward from the Lake of the Woods indefinitely. Mr. Monroe, in a paper presented to Lord Harrowby in 1804, at London, stated that it had been so settled by commissaries appointed by France and England under the Treaty of Utrecht; and the statement was not impugned or objected to. I am aware that a doubt has recently been raised as to the fact of such a line having been agreed on; but, after nearly a century and a half, it is questionable whether an arrangement which had been acquiesced in [Colonel BENTON here added — "and acted on"], as having been made by the competent authority at the proper time, can be denied, even though no authentic record of the meeting of the commissaries can be found.[1] Other persons were employed by the Government to survey the southern portions of Louisiana; and these contemporaneous expeditions must be regarded by the world as a public manifestation of the intention of the United States to assert all the rights she might justly claim, by discovery or otherwise, to the sovereignty of the country between the Mississippi and the Pacific Ocean.

In 1806, Mr. Frazer, an agent of the Northwest Company, formed an establishment on Frazer's Lake, in the 54th parallel of latitude; and this was the first establishment ever made by British subjects west of the Rocky Mountains.

In March, 1811, the Pacific Fur Company, of which John Jacob Astor, of New York, was the principal, formed an establishment at Astoria, on the south bank of the Columbia River, about ten miles from its mouth, having first established themselves on the north bank; and this was the first settlement ever made on the Columbia, or in the territory watered by that river or its tributaries, excepting two temporary establishments, in 1809 and 1810, formed also by American citizens, which were soon abandoned in consequence of the difficulty of obtaining provisions, and other embarrassments. The Astoria Company also formed an establishment in 1811, on the Okanagan, a tributary entering the Columbia on the north side, between the 48th and 49th parallels of latitude; and in 1812, another near it on the Spokan, also a tributary of the great river.

In 1813, the Pacific Company, in consequence of the embarrassments growing out of the war of 1812 with Great Britain, sold "its establishments, furs, and stock in hand," (including the posts on the Okanagan and the Spokan,) to

[1] See an elaborate examination of the question in *Greenhow's Oregon*, p. 276.

the Northwest Company; and a few days afterwards the British sloop-of-war Raccoon arrived, took possession of the place, and hoisted the British flag.

By the Treaty of Ghent, ratified by us in 1815, it was stipulated that "all territory, places, and possessions whatsoever taken by either party from the other during the war, or which may be taken after the signing of this treaty, excepting only the islands hereinafter mentioned, shall be restored without delay."

In compliance with this stipulation, the establishment at Astoria was restored to the United States. The compliance was full, unconditional, and without reservation of any sort. No claim was set up by Great Britain in her written communications with the United States on this subject, at the time of the restoration, in respect to any right of sovereignty or domain in the territory thus restored. The British Minister at Washington had, it is true, a year before objected to the restoration, on the ground that the place had been purchased by the Northwest Company, and that it had "been taken possession of in his Majesty's name, and had been since considered as forming part of his Majesty's dominions." The objection was virtually abandoned by the restoration; and as the place was restored without a written protest or reservation, the ground of the objection may be regarded as having been considered wholly untenable by those who took it. In this transaction, as in all others relating to the Territory of Oregon, the Government of the United States maintained, in clear and unequivocal terms, its right of sovereignty. In its instructions to Captain Biddle in 1817, it directed him to proceed to the mouth of the Columbia, and there "to assert the claim of the United States to the sovereignty of the adjacent country, in a friendly and peaceable manner, and without the employment of force." This order he executed on the 9th of August, 1818, by taking formal possession of the country on the river. The formal restoration of Astoria was made on the

6th of October, 1818; and, in fourteen days afterwards (on the 20th October), a convention was agreed on by the United States and Great Britain, containing the following article: —

"ART. 3. It is agreed that any country that may be claimed by either party on the northwest coast of America, westward of the Stony Mountains, shall, together with its harbors, bays, and creeks, and the navigation of all rivers within the same, be free and open for the term of ten years from the date of the signature of the present convention, to the vessels, citizens, and subjects of the two powers; it being well understood that this agreement is not to be construed to the prejudice of any claim which either of the two high contracting parties may have to any part of the said country, nor shall it be taken to affect the claims of any other power or state to any part of the said country; the only object of the high contracting parties in that respect being to prevent disputes and differences among themselves."

On the 6th of August, 1827, the main provisions of the foregoing article were renewed by the following convention: —

"ART. 1. All the provisions of the third article of the convention concluded between the United States of America and his Majesty the King of the United Kingdom of Great Britain and Ireland, on the 20th of October, 1818, shall be, and they are hereby, further indefinitely extended and continued in force, in the same manner as if all the provisions of the said article were herein specifically recited.

"ART. 2. It shall be competent, however, to either of the contracting parties, in case either should think fit, at any time after the 20th October, 1828, on giving due notice of twelve months to the other contracting party, to annul and abrogate this convention; and it shall, in such case, be accordingly entirely annulled and abrogated, after the expiration of the said term of service.

"ART. 3. Nothing contained in this convention, or in the third article of the convention of the 20th October, 1818, hereby continued in force, shall be construed to impair, or in any manner affect, the claims which either of the contracting parties may have to any part of the country westward of the Stony or Rocky Mountains."

On the basis of these two treaties the relations of the two countries in respect to Oregon now rest; and, in order to ascertain what are the rights of the contracting parties to the territory in dispute, we must revert to the year 1818, the time when the first agreement was made; for if, as has been seen, nothing contained in the treaties can prejudice in any manner their respective claims, no acts done since, by settlement or otherwise, can create, in respect to the territory in question, any rights which did not exist then.

This position was taken with characteristic vigor and brevity by the distinguished Senator from South Carolina,[1] sitting before me, in a note dated the 3d of September, 1844, and addressed to Mr. Pakenham, while the Senator was acting in the capacity of a negotiator.

Sir, I wish to be distinctly understood on this point, for the reason that the Hudson's Bay Company, in which the Northwest Company has been merged, has for several years been extending its establishments; and because, in the negotiations between the British Government and ours, it has been once, at least, if not more than once, intimated by the former that British subjects had interests there which it was bound to protect. These establishments have been made with full knowledge of the stipulations of the conventions entered into between the two countries; and on no ground, even the ground of equity, can any claim be set up on the basis of these newly-created interests. To agree to suspend the settlement of the controversy, and then to draw from acts done by one of the parties during the suspension new arguments in favor of its own side of the question, is not only repugnant to every rule of fairness, but it is a violation of the letter as well as the spirit of the agreement, and tends to the defeat of the very object in view in making it.

Let us see, then, what discoveries had been made, and what establishments formed, in 1818. Those of Spain were paramount to all others. She had visited and explored the whole coast from California, where she had permanent establishments, to the most northerly line of the territory in dispute. She had discovered the Strait of Juan de Fuca, and formed an establishment within it, I think, in 1792.

[1] Mr. Calhoun.

She had discovered Nootka Sound, and established herself there. And she was strengthened in her claims to the absolute sovereignty of the country by its immediate contiguity to California, of which she had the undisputed and undivided possession, with the exception of two temporary establishments by the Russians, between the Bay of St. Francisco and Cape Mendocino, which were made to facilitate their trade in furs, and by permission of the Spanish Government. It is true she had not kept up her establishments north of Cape Mendocino; but no others had been formed in the same localities; and her rights of discovery, therefore, were not superseded by rights of occupation on the part of other nations in any portion of the territory in dispute, excepting so far as they may have been derived from the American and British establishments, to which I am about to refer.

The United States had discovered the Columbia River, and ascended it, at the time of the discovery, to the distance of twenty-five miles from its mouth. They had also discovered Bulfinch's Harbor, between the Columbia and the Strait of Fuca. They had examined the country watered by the Columbia and some of its tributaries, and formed establishments within it at four different periods: in 1809, 1810, 1811, and 1812; the most southerly near the mouth of the Columbia, and the most northerly between the 48th and 49th parallels of latitude. Spain claimed to have discovered the Columbia seventeen years before Gray entered it; but, in 1821, she ceded all her rights to the country north of 42° to the United States, by treaty, and thus gave us a title to the territory watered by the river, which Great Britain ought never to have questioned. By virtue of the same act of cession, her entire right to the coast became vested in us.

In the course of the public discussions in respect to Oregon, the United States has been charged with dishonor and bad faith in setting up a claim to that Territory, first, by discovery, through the agency of her own citizens; and, secondly, by cession of the rights of Spain. For, as has been said, if the first ground was tenable, she could not, without inconsistency, set up a claim on the second, because she had virtually denied the second by assuming the first as the basis of her right. But, sir, is it not quite possible for two nations to possess rights by contiguity, or to acquire them by discovery, neither perfect, but capable of being rendered so by a merger of both in one? Great Britain herself claims a right of joint occupancy with the United States in Oregon; and she will certainly not deny that a cession of her right to us, or ours to her, would create a perfect title to the country, without affording cause for any imputation of dishonor to either.

Great Britain, in 1818, had surveyed the Strait of Fuca, after its outlines were known; but she had made no discoveries on the coast which were not comprehended within the boundaries of the great districts previously known and visited. She may have had establishments in the valley of the Columbia; but if so, I have not been able to ascertain the fact. She had discovered Frazer's River, which empties into the Strait of Fuca at the 49th parallel of latitude; she had traced it from its source to its mouth; she had formed an establishment on it near the 54th parallel; and it only remains to settle by the testimony of facts the geographical relation which this river and its valley bear to the river and valley of the Columbia.[1]

1 There is no reasonable ground to doubt that the Spaniards discovered the mouth of Frazer's River; but the locality did not appear to me to be so distinctly settled as to authorize me to assume it as a fact in the text. On referring to *Vancouver's Journal*, Vol. II. p. 187, it will be seen that he passed the mouth of the river without discovering it, it being then, as it is said to be now, nearly masked by a shoal extending northwardly from Cape Roberts about seven miles. Cape Roberts is the southern point of the river, and it is intersected by the 49th parallel of latitude. At page 212 of the same volume, it will be seen that, after meeting Galiano and Valdes near Point Gray, (a few miles north of the river,) as he states at page 209, Vancouver says: "I showed them the sketch I had made of our excursion, and pointed out the only spot which I conceived we had left unexamined, nearly at the head of Burrard's Channel; they seemed much surprised that we had not found a river said to exist in the region we had been exploring, and named by one of their officers Rio Blancho, in compliment to the then prime minister of Spain; which river these gentlemen had sought thus far to

I pass by, as unconnected with the question for the reasons I have assigned, all settlements made subsequently to 1818 by the Hudson's Bay Company, on which Great Britain has conferred large and most important powers in respect to the country west of the Rocky Mountains. Indeed, these establishments rest upon no legal concession, even by herself, which confers any right of domain. The Hudson's Bay Company has a mere right of exclusive trade with the Indians, without the privilege of acquiring any title to the soil in Oregon; and in this respect the privileges of the Company differ materially from those conferred on it in relation to the territory it possesses upon Hudson's Straits.

I also pass by, as idle, the formalities of taking possession of the country by Broughton on the Columbia, and Vancouver in the Strait of Fuca,—formalities a long time before performed in numberless localities by the Spaniards; especially as those of the British navigators were unaccompanied by actual settlement and occupation, and were in direct violation of a treaty which those officers were sent out to execute.

I have endeavored, Mr. President, in the first part of my remarks, to maintain the Spanish title to the northwest coast of America. The attempts which have been made to disparage it as antiquated and obsolete, are founded upon partial and illiberal views of the subject. It is unnecessary to say to you, sir, or the Senate, that antiquity is the highest element of title, if the chain can be traced down unbroken and entire to our own times. The Spanish title to the northwest coast is almost coeval with the voyages of Columbus. It is consecrated by discovery, as high as the 43d parallel of latitude, by the lapse of more than three centuries; as high as the 48th, by the lapse of two centuries and a half; and as high as the 54th, by the lapse of more than seventy years. Sixty years ago it stood undisputed and unimpeached by any

no purpose." There can be no doubt that this was Frazer's River, as there is no other stream in the region Vancouver "had been exploring."

antagonist claim or pretension to territorial rights. It was confirmed and perfected by occupation, as high as 49° 30′, half a century ago. During the succeeding twenty years, it was not superseded by rights of occupation on the part of other nations, unless it be to the limited extent I have stated. During the last thirty years, all rights have been suspended by treaty arrangements between the only two powers who can, with any face, set up a claim to the exercise of sovereignty over the territory to which it attaches. In the consideration of national interests in territorial possessions, it is a narrow view to bind down sovereign States to all the rigorous technicalities of private tenures. Great principles of national right, viewed liberally, and applied according to the proclaimed intentions of the parties, are the only guides worthy of statesmen or governments in the settlement of questions of sovereignty over the unoccupied portions of the earth we inhabit. The object of Spain, in respect to the northwest coast, was settlement, — permanent occupation. The object of Great Britain was commerce, traffic, transient occupation. Tested by the principles I have stated, I cannot hesitate to consider the Spanish title to the northwest coast of America, which has of late been so much disparaged, as vesting in us rights which are unimpeachable.

I said, at the commencement of my remarks, that one of my objects was to defend the Spanish title by stating the historical facts on which it rests. I have performed the task which I allotted to myself. I will only add that, with what I have said, I am content to leave the whole question where it now is, in the hands of the Administration, relying on its firmness and its sense of rectitude to sustain our just rights, and to respect the just rights of others.

So conscious is Great Britain of the invalidity of her title, that she does not venture to assert a right to the exclusive sovereignty of any portion of the Territory. In 1826, she claimed only a right of joint occupancy, in common with other powers; but denied the right of exclusive dominion in the United States. While insisting that she was entitled "to place her claims at least upon a parity with those of the United States," she has constantly refused to divide the Territory at the 49th parallel of latitude, the boundary between her and us from the Lake of the Woods to the Rocky Mountains, — a line which would have severed the coast, and the country in immediate contiguity with it, into two parts so nearly equal as to leave her no reasonable ground, even on the score of an equitable division, for the continuance of a controversy. Her desire for territorial extension in this quarter is for the purpose of establishing her colonial dominion over districts of country bordering on us, and confining our settlements within narrower limits. Our contest for territorial rights, which we consider indisputable, has no object but to enable our citizens to extend themselves to our natural boundary, — the Pacific. Her interest is remote and contingent; ours is direct and certain. Hers is the interest of a State in a distant country which she wishes to colonize; ours is the interest of a country in its own proper territory and settlements. She is not content with subjecting to her sway the fertile and opulent regions of the East; but she comes now thousands of miles across the ocean to dispute with us the dominion of the uninhabited wilderness, and curtail the area for our expansion. With the least disposition on her part to listen to the suggestions of reason and justice, this question would long ago have been settled on the fair and honorable terms of compromise, — nay, sir, on the terms of concession, — which we have more than once proposed.

I am sure that, in the course of our Government in relation to Great Britain, in our negotiations, and in the treaties which have been formed between us, no evidence will be found of a desire on our part to encroach on her rights, or to adjust any of the questions which have arisen between us on other terms than those of justice and liberality. The settlement of the northeastern boundary — one of the most delicate and difficult that has ever arisen between us — affords a striking evidence of our desire to maintain with her the most friendly understanding. We ceded to her a portion of territory which she deemed of vital importance as a means of military communication between the Canadas and her Atlantic provinces, and which will give her a great advantage in a contest with us. The measure was sustained by the constituted authorities of the country, and I have no desire or intention to call its wisdom in question. But it proves that we were not unwilling to afford Great Britain any facility she required for consolidating her North American possessions, acting in peace as though war was not to be expected between the two countries. If we had cherished any ambitious designs in respect to them; if we had had any other wish than that of continuing on terms of amity with her and them; this great military advantage would never have been conceded to her.

On the other hand, I regret to say, that her course towards us has been a course of perpetual encroachment. But, sir, I will not look back upon what is past for the purpose of reviving disturbing recollections. Yet I am constrained to say, that, in respect to Oregon, I consider her legislation as a virtual infraction of the Conventions of 1818 and 1827. By an Act of Parliament passed in 1821, she has extended the jurisdiction, power, and authority of her courts of judicature in Upper Canada over the whole Indian territory in North America, "not within her own provinces, or within any civil government of the United States," and of course embracing the Territory of Oregon. She has given them cognizance of every wrong and injury to the person and to property, real or personal, committed within the Territory; and has declared that every person whatsoever (not British subjects alone, but every person whatsoever) residing in it shall be amenable to these courts. Nay, sir, she has authorized the Crown to establish courts within the Territory itself, with power to try criminal offences not punishable with death, and also civil causes to a limited amount, I believe £200, about $1000. She has thus assumed to exercise over this Territory one of the highest attributes of national sovereignty,—that of deciding upon rights of property, and punishing violations of the criminal laws she has extended over them. She could hardly have asserted a more absolute sovereignty than she has done by this unqualified extension of her laws and the jurisdiction of her courts over a territory in which she admits that she has no other right but that of a joint occupancy. I am aware that she has disavowed the intention of enforcing her criminal laws against citizens of the United States. But if Senators will turn to the documents accompanying the President's Message, they will see that the Hudson's Bay Company has a much more summary method of disposing of American citizens, who establish themselves on the north side of the Columbia, in the neighborhood of its settlements. Their condition will not be bettered, if this exemption from the operation of the British statute is to be exchanged for a forcible process of ejection without law.

Under these circumstances, what is the duty of the United States? As I do not intend to intrude myself on the attention of the Senate again, without absolute necessity, on any question relating to Oregon, I desire to say now that I shall vote for the notice to terminate the Convention of 1818, continued in force by that of 1827,—a convention which Great Britain treats as recognizing a right of joint occupancy, but which has in reality been for her an exclusive occupancy of the whole territory north of the Columbia. I am in favor of extending the authority of our laws and the jurisdiction of our courts over the Territory; and in doing so, I would, while the Convention is in force, specially except British subjects, and direct them, when charged with infractions of our laws, to be delivered up to the nearest British authorities. I would make this reservation for the express purpose of preventing, as far as possible, a conflict of jurisdiction, and to avoid all cause for imputing to us a disregard of treaties, or a desire to produce collision or disagreement of any sort. And in order to facilitate the extension of the authority of the Union over our fellow-citizens in that remote district of our country, and to remove, as far as possible, the obstacles to a more free and efficient intercourse between us and them, I would establish at once a chain of military posts, with competent garrisons and armaments, from the remotest navigable waters which flow into the Mississippi, to the eastern face of the Rocky Mountains, stopping there so long as the Convention continues in force. Duty, honor, policy — all demand these measures at our hands; and I trust they will be executed with promptitude and decision.

Will these measures produce war? I cannot believe that they will. I cannot believe it, because they furnish no just ground of provocation. The right to give the notice is reserved by treaty. The right of extending our laws over Oregon is a right similar to that which Great Britain has already exercised for a quarter of a century. The establishment of a chain of posts to the Rocky Mountains wholly within our own territory, invades no right in others. It has been inferred from an expression in a public document, that there is danger of an immediate war, and that a sudden blow may be struck. Sir, I cannot believe it. A war waged against us on account of any one or all of the measures referred to, would be a war of plain unmixed aggression. No nation, in the present age, could embark in such a contest without drawing down upon herself the condemnation of all civilized communities. She would find herself opposed and restrained by public opinion, which, in our day, rules the conduct of nations more powerfully than the arm of force. I hold, therefore, immediate war to be out of the question. Nor can eventual war take place, unless the assertion of our just rights shall be forcibly resisted. But I will not venture to pass judgment on what the future may bring forth. Collisions may grow out of these measures—

collisions ripening, through influences and events which we may be unable to control, into open warfare. I should deeply deplore such a result. The interests of humanity, great principles of political right, self-government, freedom, individual rights, all suffer when the voice of the law is silenced by the tumult of war. "*Inter arma silent leges*," is an adage, of the truth of which history has furnished too many fatal proofs. I would do much to avert such a calamity. I would do anything not inconsistent with the public honor, to avoid a contest which would be disastrous to both parties, no matter what should be its final issue. But beyond this I never can go. And if exemption from war can only be purchased by a surrender of our just rights, I cannot consent to make the purchase. But if war cannot be averted, I trust we shall not commit the great error of undervaluing our adversary. With some opportunity of observing the condition of Great Britain near at hand, I have no hesitation in saying that she was never capable of greater efforts than she is at the present moment. I know that her inordinate distention contains within itself an element of vital weakness. It is not in the order of human society that so extended a dominion should remain long unbroken. But I have not yet been able to detect, in the condition of her body politic, the unerring symptoms of that decay which precedes and works out the dissolution of empires. She has great abuses to struggle against. The Senator from Ohio has well and graphically described them. She has enormous burdens to sustain; but she has great strength to bear them. Her soldiers are not like those of Rome in its latter days, enervated in vigor and relaxed in discipline. You will find them in every quarter of the globe: under the fiery heat of the equator, and amid the frosts of the arctic circle, braving the elements, and setting danger and toil, in every form, at defiance. But, sir, I pretend not, with my narrow foresight, to look into the future. It is possible that her hour may be near at hand.

But we know that the last struggle of the strong man is always the most desperate, and sometimes the most dangerous to the antagonist who has brought him to the ground.

I say this in no spirit of timidity. I say it in a spirit of prudent forecast, with the desire that we may go into the contest, if it shall come, with the assurance that we have to deal with a strong adversary and not a weak one, and that our preparation may be commensurate with the means of offence to which we shall be exposed. I have no doubt of our ability both to defend ourselves and to give back effective blows in return. We were never so strong as we are at the present moment: strong in our position, strong in our means, strong in the spirit and energy of our people. Our defenceless condition has been greatly overstated. We have been told that our coast is denuded. I have heard, whether on this floor or elsewhere I do not know, that there is scarcely a gun mounted for the defence of the commercial metropolis of my own State. There cannot be a greater error. There are hundreds of guns, of heavy calibre, in the city of New York, ready, at the very hour in which I speak, to receive an assailant, and as many more which can be placed in position in an emergency, and this independently of guns afloat. In thirty days I believe the city might be rendered, with a skilful engineer, and with the means which might be placed at his command, prepared — well prepared — against a maritime assault. But, sir, I turn away from all these forebodings of evil. I have confidence in the continuance of peace. I believe the good sense of both countries will revolt at a contest which can bring no good to either, and secure an adjustment of existing difficulties on terms honorable to both. Such is my conviction. But, sir, if I am deceived, then I have only to say, that, while I would be constrained by nothing but overruling necessity to take up the sword, yet, if the necessity shall come, I trust we shall never consent to lay it down until the rights and the honor of the country shall have been fully vindicated.

FRENCH SPOLIATIONS.

APRIL 27, 1846.

On the Bill to provide for the Satisfaction of Claims of American Citizens for Spoliations on their Property committed by the French prior to the Ratification of the Convention with France, of September, 1800.[1]

Having been appointed a member of the Select Committee to which the subject under consideration was referred, and having, after the most careful examination I have been able to give it, come to conclusions adverse to those at which the majority of the committee have arrived, I deem it incumbent on me to state to the Senate the grounds on which my conclusions rest. Nothing but a sense of duty, arising from the position in which I have been placed, would induce me to trespass on the attention of the Senate. I yield my reluctance to take part in the debate, not merely to the fact that I am a member of the committee specially charged with the examination of the subject, but to the consideration that I am one of the minority of the committee, and, therefore, in some degree, bound to assign the grounds of my dissent from the opinion of the majority. I regret that the distinguished Senator from North Carolina, on the other side of the House,[2] who constitutes with myself the minority of the committee, has not undertaken the performance of this duty, assured, as I am, that the Senator's longer experience and greater familiarity with the subject would have enabled him to present it to the Senate much

[1] Delivered on the 27th of April, 1846.

[2] Mr. Mangum.

more satisfactorily than I can hope to do. But the task has devolved on me, and I will perform it to the best of my ability, though fully conscious of the great disadvantage under which I shall labor in following the Senator from Delaware,[1] to whose able argument the Senate had the pleasure of listening on the last two days it was in session.

The Senator commenced his remarks with the observation, that no portion of our fellow-citizens of equal number had less interest in this application than his constituents. No one can appreciate better than myself the enviable position which the Senator occupies in this respect. I wish most sincerely I were in the same position. But, unfortunately, it is quite otherwise. A large amount of these claims is held in my own State, an amount supposed to be equal to one third of the whole; so that, if this supposition were true, and this bill should pass, about seventeen hundred thousand dollars, of the five millions proposed to be appropriated in satisfaction of the claims, would be paid to my constituents. Under these circumstances, it is natural that the subject should have been pressed upon me, not improperly — far from it — but with an earnestness proportioned to the magnitude of the interest at stake. It has been, in some instances, by personal friends for whom I entertain the sincerest regard, and in others, by gentlemen of high standing in the city of New York; — by some who are deeply interested in the claims, and by others who, without any interest in them, believe they constitute a valid demand on the public treasury. I have felt the strongest inducements, therefore, — the inducements of respect and personal regard for some of the claimants, — to take the most favorable view of the subject consistent with overruling considerations of public duty. I have endeavored to do them full justice in my examination of it. I requested them, before I had read a word on the subject, to present their case to me. They did so. I have read all the argu-

[1] Mr. John M. Clayton.

ments on their side of the question: reviews, reports, and speeches; and among others the very able and condensed statement of their case contained in a speech made to the Senate on the 12th of January, 1835, by the distinguished Senator from Massachusetts,[1] who was then, as he is now, the chairman of the select committee appointed to investigate the subject. I have read all these arguments carefully, and with a sincere desire to allow them the full weight to which they are entitled, not only on account of the high sources from which many of them emanated, but from the ability and force with which the subject has been treated.

Having performed this act of justice to the claimants, I felt that I had also a duty to discharge to the public, — a duty to be fulfilled only by a careful examination of the official documents relating to the case. Those documents are contained in the volume I hold in my hand, — a volume of 840 pages, consisting of "A Message from the President of the United States, transmitted to Congress on the 20th of May, 1826, in compliance with a resolution of the Senate; with copies of instructions to the Ministers of the United States to the Government of France, and of the correspondence with said government, having reference to the spoliations committed by that Power on the commerce of the United States anterior to September 30, 1800." I have read this volume, though it is probable that, in the examination of so voluminous a mass of papers, — an examination constantly interrupted by the pressure of other official duties, — much may have escaped me which I ought to have noticed; and it is equally probable that I may not have drawn from the parts which I consider particularly relevant to the subject, the most proper conclusions in all cases. But it has been my aim to do so; and if I have erred in any respect, I will most cheerfully correct my error whenever it shall be clearly pointed out.

[1] Mr. Webster.

Thus far, I have not read a single argument against these claims, either in the form of a speech or a report; and from the best examination I have been able to give to the public documents referred to, and the statement of their own case by the claimants themselves, I have come to the conclusion that the claims do not constitute a just demand upon the public treasury. I will proceed to state the reasons for this opinion.

But, first, I desire to call the attention of the Senate to an argument which has been adduced in their support by the Senator from Delaware, — an argument, I think, best answered by a reference to the manner in which the subject was disposed of for examination when it came before the Senate soon after the opening of the present session. The argument I refer to is this: that in the whole course of the last forty-four years, during which the subject has been before Congress, there have been but three adverse reports, while the favorable reports have been more than twenty. Now, if the Senate will indulge me, I will recall to its recollection the circumstances under which the reference for examination was made. Soon after the session commenced, I presented a memorial, signed by several gentlemen of the city of New York, of the highest respectability, representing a large number of the claimants, and moved that it be referred to the Committee on Foreign Relations, the committee which had, for a series of years, been charged with it. The reference was made. But the Senator from Maine, on my left,[1] immediately rose and presented a similar memorial, and moved that it be referred to a select committee on the distinct ground that a majority of the Committee on Foreign Relations were opposed to the claims, and that the application should be referred to a committee which would present a favorable report. It was also urged in favor of the motion of the Senator from Maine, that this was a claim, and that the Committee on Foreign Relations

[1] Mr. Fairfield.

was not an appropriate one; whereupon a Senator from Mississippi[1] moved that it be referred to the Committee on Claims. But the motion was voted down, for reasons which I have no right to divine, much less to question. The motion of the Senator from Maine was finally sustained by the Senate; and the select committee was very properly constituted by yourself, Mr. President, according to the parliamentary rule that select committees should not be adverse to the subject of reference. I allude to the circumstances in order to repel the inference, which has been drawn from the greater number of the favorable reports on these claims in years past, that this fact constituted an argument in their favor. I cannot so regard it; nor do I think it can be so regarded by any one who considers the circumstances referred to. The same course has probably been pursued in former sessions as in this. When the Committee on Foreign Relations was known to be friendly to the claims, they would naturally be referred to that committee. On the other hand, when the committee was known to be adverse, a select committee would be appointed for the express purpose of procuring a favorable report. Under these circumstances, it seems no longer remarkable that the favorable reports should have been so numerous. One fact was clear: in case the application had been permitted to go to the appropriate standing committee, there would, if his friend from Maine[2] was right, have been one more adverse report. On the whole, therefore, I apprehend that the result of these preliminary investigations is to be regarded not as an argument in favor of the justice of these claims, but as the evidence of a deference on the part of the Senate for established forms and principles of parliamentary proceeding. If it were otherwise, it is quite manifest, that, by the device of sending the application to a standing committee when that committee was known to be favorable, and to a select committee when the appropriate standing committee was known to be ad-

[1] Mr. Speight. [2] Mr. Fairfield.

verse, the merits of the application, according to this test, would every year become more apparent, and we should ultimately have a mass of evidence in their favor that would be irresistible. And here I will leave so much of the argument in favor of these claims as is founded upon the numerical force of reports of committees.

But it is time to look into the merits of the application, and I will do so in the briefest manner possible.

The most ancient treaties to be found on our statute-book are a treaty of amity and commerce, and a treaty of alliance, (I name them in the order in which they were concluded,) between the United States and France; or, to use the language of the treaties, between the United States and his most Christian Majesty. They were executed on the 6th of February, 1778, and they preceded by a few months the earliest treaty on record between us and any of the Indian tribes on this continent. The dissolution of the political connection between Great Britain and the United States had been formally proclaimed to the world nineteen months before; we were engaged in a determined struggle to maintain the independent attitude we had thus taken; and France, by the treaty of alliance referred to, soon became a party to the contest. I say she soon became a party to the contest, because the treaty of alliance was not designed to be carried immediately into full effect. It was in its main stipulations conditional, eventual, prospective; — conditional, on the event of a rupture between France and Great Britain; or, if such a rupture should not take place, then on the termination of the war between Great Britain and the United States. It was not designed to be made public; and when the Congress of the United States, "in a moment of exultation," as Marshall, in his "Life of Washington," says, published it with the treaty of amity and commerce, which was an open treaty, the publication was not approved by the Cabinet of Versailles; and he adds, "that treaty, being only eventual, ought not to have been communicated to the public but by mutual consent."[1] But the condition on which it depended was soon fulfilled, and France became involved in our contest for independence. Of the valuable assistance which she rendered us, it is needless to speak. This portion of our history is not likely to be effaced from our memory, nor, I trust, from the memory of our descendants; and especially all that concerns the gallant Frenchmen, who, like Lafayette, periled their lives and fortunes in our cause. I believe there was then, as now, a strong chord of sympathy between the people of the two countries, which I hope may never be broken. But it is due to the impartiality of history to say, that the Government of France was not so clearly actuated by the purely disinterested motives which have been ascribed to her. The whole history of our negotiations with her in 1777 shows that she had her own interest in view in the part she took in our struggle for independence, and that the encouragement she gave us in the early stages of that contest varied with the varying phases of our fortune. But disinterestedness and generosity, I apprehend, are not the virtues of governments. They are peculiarly and eminently attributes of individual character. They are not even the virtues of men in their associated state; and in the intercourse of nations they dwindle to mere names. I believe the highest qualities to be looked for in the communications of governments with each other, are justice and courtesy.

The Senator from Delaware has referred to the epoch of these treaties as "the darkest hour in our whole Revolutionary struggle." I have not been accustomed so to consider it. They were concluded immediately after the campaign of 1777. I have always regarded this as the great campaign of the war, and the period which succeeded, notwithstanding the embarrassments and sufferings it brought, as one of strong confidence in the ultimate success of the contest for independence. The Senator has drawn a striking picture of the privations and sufferings endured by the American army

[1] Vol. I. p. 237.

at Valley Forge; and I will not say that it is over-colored. But as a picture of the epoch, it seems to me incomplete. I certainly think the Senator has thrown in all the shadows, and left out all the lights — nay, I will say, the brilliant colors — which equally belong to a true picture of that period. I will, with the permission of my honorable friend from Delaware, borrow his canvas, and add what I consider the omitted parts. The Senator from Delaware commenced his sketch with the battle of Brandywine, which was fought on the 11th of September. I will only go about four weeks farther back. I will commence with the 16th of August, when Colonel Baum was defeated at Bennington by Stark. Colonel St. Leger, with his Indian allies, was driven from Fort Stanwix and the Valley of the Mohawk on the 22d August, after the bloody battle of Oriskany. Burgoyne, on the 13th October, — more than a month after the battle of Brandywine, — surrendered at Saratoga, with one of the best-appointed armies Great Britain ever had on this continent; and an American historian has denominated his surrender "the hinge on which the Revolution turned." Sir Henry Clinton had failed in his attempt to coöperate with the army of Burgoyne by the Hudson River, and had returned to the city of New York; and Washington, though laboring under the greatest disadvantages, with an army vastly inferior in numbers to that of his adversary, and ill-provided with the munitions of war, had, by a series of masterly movements and well-contested engagements, neutralized, to a considerable extent, the operations of General Howe in the Middle States. The British general had succeeded in occupying Philadelphia, and made it his winter-quarters; but when the intelligence reached Paris, Dr. Franklin said, (and the saying, I believe, became a by-word on both sides of the Atlantic,) that Philadelphia had taken General Howe. History had pronounced the operations of that general barren victories; and these were almost the only shadows on the face of the campaign. Nearly everywhere else fortune had sided with the Americans. The campaign was, with these and some other trifling exceptions, a series of successes, — decided, marked, brilliant successes. They electrified the friends of the Revolution at home and abroad, as the intelligence of the alliance between France and the United States, according to the eloquent description of the Senator from Delaware, electrified the army of Washington. The United States, alone and almost unaided, had achieved these great successes, and they had placed the establishment of their independence, in the eyes of the world, beyond all reasonable doubt. It was at this juncture that the treaty of amity and commerce, and the treaty of alliance, were concluded between France and the United States. She came to our aid, not because she thought us in the depths of distress, but in the hour of victory, when our triumph seemed no longer doubtful; and unless the testimony of all history is to be discarded, these treaties, but for the successes of 1777, might never have been formed. I do not say this for the purpose of withholding from the Government of France any merit which may justly be claimed for it in siding with us. It was doubtless actuated by an enlightened view of the interest of that kingdom; and it would have been too much to expect it to take part with us in a matter so grave as that of a dissension between the colonies of a European power and the parent State, until it was quite manifest that the resistance would be successful.

These treaties have become connected with the claims under consideration, and the claimants would have us believe inseparably connected with them. I differ totally with them in opinion; and in order to explain the difference between us, it will be necessary to advert to the nature of the treaties, between which and the claims before us this connection is supposed to exist.

The treaties were designed, as their titles import, to establish and regulate commercial relations between the two countries, and to form an alliance for purposes of defence. The essential object of the treaty of alliance was to maintain the independence of the United States. Its stipulations were not limited to the contest then in progress. They were only to take full effect on the contingency I have already referred to. They were designed to extend far beyond that contest. They expressly guaranteed forever, on the part of France, the liberty, sovereignty, and independence of the United States in government and commerce; and on the part of the United States, the possessions of the crown of France in America. The stipulations of the treaty of alliance were reciprocal, creating mutual advantages, and holding out the promise of reciprocal aid. The treaty of amity and commerce was of the same character, embracing common provisions for the mutual benefit of the contracting parties. I desire to state thus distinctly the nature of these treaties, in order that it may be kept steadily in view in the sequel. In the language of an American historian, they placed the two countries "on the footing of the most perfect equality and reciprocity"; — the treaty of amity and commerce, by conferring reciprocal commercial advantages, and the treaty of alliance, by rendering the establishment of our independence more easy and certain, by the expulsion of Great Britain from a large portion of this continent, diminishing the strength of a dangerous rival of France, and opening a new and vast field to her commerce and a valuable market for the products of her industry. The amicable relations thus established between the United States and France survived the war of the Revolution, and continued uninterrupted until 1793. On the 28th of January of that year, France declared war against Great Britain, and both these powers were soon engaged in a series of unprovoked and unwarrantable depredations on our commerce. As early as the 9th of May, but little more than three months after the declaration of hostilities, France, by a decree of her National Convention, under the pretext that Great Britain had seized our vessels laden with provisions and carried them into her ports, taking the provisions for her own use at her own price, and committed other violations of neutral rights, formally declared that the French people were "no longer permitted to fulfil, towards the neutral powers in general, the vows [wishes] they have so often manifested for the full and entire liberty of commerce and navigation."—I refer to page 43 of Senate Document No. 102, 19th Congress, 1st Session; and all my references, unless otherwise expressed, will be to this volume. — The decree then authorized French ships of war to arrest and carry into the ports of the Republic neutral vessels, laden wholly or in part either with articles of provisions belonging to neutral nations and destined to an enemy's port, or with merchandises belonging to an enemy; the merchandises to be confiscated, and the provisions to be paid for according to their value in the place to which they were destined. On the remonstrance of the Minister of the United States, complaining of the decree as a violation of justice and good faith in respect to vessels of the United States, (pages 41 and 44,) this decree was declared, on the 23d of May, not to be applicable to them. On the 28th of the same month it was again made applicable to them, so far as to place in a state of provisional sequestration property seized under the decree of the 9th (page 46). On the 1st of July, vessels of the United States were again exempted from its operation (page 50); and on the 27th of July, it was again applied (pages 50 and 161); and I do not find that it was ever afterwards removed.

When this decree was made, France, by the treaty of amity and commerce with the United States, which was still in force, had stipulated that free ships should make free goods, or, in other words, that the property of an enemy in the ship of a friend should be exempt from seizure and confiscation. She had also specified by the same treaty the articles which should be treated as contraband of war, and liable to seizure when bound to an enemy's port; and from this specification provisions were expressly excluded. I will not say that I regard the seizure of provisions, with the promise of payment, equivalent to treating them as contraband; but, taken in connection with the other parts of the decree, I consider the conduct of France an open and palpable repudiation of the treaty of 1778; and it was subsequently followed by more flagrant violations of her engagements. The vessels of the United States were seized, detained, condemned, and confiscated, under the most unjustifiable pretexts, until in July, 1796, (page 149,) she proclaimed, by a resolve of her Executive Directory, the principle of treating neutral vessels, as to confiscations, searches, and captures, in the same manner as the English were allowed to treat them. The practical effect of this doctrine was, to make the example of Great Britain her own guide and her justification in depredations on our commerce. The infraction of the treaty of amity and commerce with us, under the decree of the 9th of May, preceded any act, or certainly the knowledge by France of any act, on our part in respect to the belligerents, to which she could take exception. It was equally unprovoked and unjustifiable.

On the 22d of April, 1793, the President of the United States, General Washington, issued his celebrated Proclamation of Neutrality, (page 248,) the chief object of which was, to advise the citizens of the United States that we were at peace with the belligerents, to warn them against committing acts of hostility, and to point out the risks they would incur by carrying contraband articles to the ports of either. On the very day this proclamation was issued, the Government was informed that Citizen Genet, as Minister from France, had landed at Charleston, (page 54,) and shortly afterwards that he was engaged in fitting out privateers to cruise against British vessels. He claimed this right by virtue of the 22d article of the Treaty of Amity and Commerce, which denied to foreign privateers, under commissions from powers at war with France or the United States, the right to fit out ships in the ports of either; alleging that this denial of a right to others was a virtual concession of it to France. This interpretation of the article was uniformly denied, and all attempts to give it effect resisted by the United States. The article is in these words: —

"ART. 22. It shall not be lawful for any foreign privateers not belonging to subjects of the Most Christian King, nor citizens of the said United States, who have commissions from any other Prince or State in enmity with either nation, to fit their ships in the ports of either the one or the other of the aforesaid parties, to sell what they have taken, or in any other manner to exchange their ships, merchandises, or any other lading; neither shall they be allowed even to purchase victuals, except such as shall be necessary for their going to the next port of that Prince or State from which they have commissions."

Citizen Genet also claimed, under the 8th article of a convention between the United States and France, executed in November, 1788, defining the duties and privileges of consuls, the exclusive right of deciding, through the consulates established by France in the United States, whether vessels taken by her cruisers were lawful prize or not. This was virtually claiming for the French consulates the powers of courts of admiralty to be exercised within the jurisdiction of the United States. This assumption was also denied by us. We did not claim the right of trying in our courts the validity of captures made on the high seas by France; but we denied the right of France to determine such questions within the United States, insisting that they belonged to the sovereign of the captor, and that resort must be had to his courts. We did, however, claim that the United States were bound to protect vessels within their own waters; and where captures were made by French cruisers within our jurisdiction, that it belonged to the United States to punish these violations of our sovereignty, and to restore the property thus illegally captured. The cogency of this reasoning will be best understood from an examination of the article, which is as follows: —

"ART. 8. The consuls or vice-consuls shall exercise police over all the vessels of their respective nations, and shall have on board the said vessels all power and jurisdiction in civil matters, in all the disputes which may there arise; they shall have an entire inspection over the said vessels, their crew, and the changes and substitutions there to be made. For which purpose they may go on board the said vessels whenever they may judge it necessary. Well understood that the functions hereby allowed shall be confined to the interior of the vessels, and that they shall not take place in any case which shall have any interference with the police of the ports where the said vessels shall be."

Another claim on the part of Citizen Genet was, that the 17th article of the treaty gave the armed vessels of France the privilege of sending their prizes into the United States, and selling them free of duty, though, as Mr. Jefferson said, the privilege of selling prizes in the United States was not given at all. But the whole groundwork of the claim was shown by Mr. Jefferson to be untenable, by asserting and maintaining the construction that the 17th article was intended only to confer the right of sending their prizes, in the first instance, wheresoever they pleased, without paying duty, and of departing to some other place named in their commissions within the jurisdiction of their sovereign, where the validity of the capture was to be finally adjudged. The article is in the following words: —

"ART. 17. It shall be lawful for the ships of war of either party, and privateers, freely to carry whithersoever they please the ships and goods taken from their enemies, without being obliged to pay any duty to the officers of the admiralty or any other judges; nor shall such prizes be arrested or seized when they come to or enter the ports of either party; nor shall the searchers or other officers of those places search the same, or make examination concerning the lawfulness of such prizes; but they may hoist sail at any time, and depart and carry their prizes to the places expressed in their commissions, which the commanders of such ships of war shall be obliged to show; on the contrary, no shelter or refuge shall be given in their ports to such as shall have made prize of the subjects, people, or property of either of the parties; but if such shall come in, being forced by stress of weather, or the danger of the sea, all proper means shall be vigorously used, that they go out and retire from thence as soon as possible."

Citizen Genet also complained, that, by the adoption of the principle that free ships make free goods, in the treaty of 1778, France could not take out of vessels of the United States property belonging to the subjects of Great Britain, then her enemy; while the commercial intercourse between the United States and Great Britain being regulated by no such treaty-stipulation, but being subject to the rule of international law, as it was understood at the time, that enemy's property may be taken in a neutral bottom, Great Britain might take out of vessels of the United States property belonging to the citizens of France; and he insisted that we were bound to prevent it. Mr. Jefferson replied, by asserting the principle of the law of nations as before stated, and insisting that the inconvenience to France, if there was any, resulted from the fact that the treaty-stipulation between her and the United States was an exception to the rule, and that she had no just cause to complain of an agreement to which she had voluntarily consented.

I refer to these complaints of Citizen Genet as the earliest evidences of the dissatisfaction with which France regarded the position of neutrality taken by the Government of the United States. She complained of us as having violated the engagements into which we had entered by the treaties of 1778, and made our refusal to comply with her requisitions the pretext for her depredations on our commerce. But we have seen that the first infraction of those treaties was committed by herself, through the decree of the 9th of May, 1793, before she knew we had taken such a position of neutrality; and I believe it to be difficult for any one, who examines carefully the able expositions made by Mr. Jefferson and Mr. Randolph, of our obligations arising under those treaties, to charge us with any violation of our engagements. On the other hand, the spoliations committed by France on our commerce were in open and palpable violation of the stipulations of the treaty, — so much so, that she did not always even pretend to excuse them, except by the pretext of her necessities.

I will not detain the Senate by entering into a detail of these aggressions, perpetrated at last without even a color of justification, and in disregard of the most persevering and earnest remonstrances on the part of the United States. It suffices to say, that they commenced in 1793, and continued, with occasional intermissions, till 1800. During much of this period, France, it is true, protested that she had no unfriendly designs in respect to the United States, and that she was willing to make reparation where it was justly due. But these protestations, instead of palliating her conduct, served but to aggravate and give point to her depredations. I desire to say, in reference to all these aggressions, that they were committed during a period of political agitation in France, which shook the fabric of society to its foundation, and that they are to be regarded, in some degree, as the fruit of the disturbed order of things under which they occurred.

The treaty of November, 1794, between the United States and Great Britain, (commonly called Jay's Treaty,) gave new offence to France. She complained that we had abandoned in that treaty the principle that free ships make free goods; that, in the stipulations relating to contraband of war, a rule had been adopted different from that contained in our treaty of 1778, with her; and that we had thus violated the principles of reciprocity, which we were bound to observe towards her. The answer to this complaint was, that in this treaty we had adopted, in the two particulars referred to, the rules of law recognized by civilized States; and that we had specially stipulated that nothing contained in it should be construed to impair our obligations to other Powers under preëxisting treaties.

On the 11th of December, 1796, Mr. Monroe, our Minister to France, after presenting his letter of recall, and the credentials of his successor, Mr. Charles Cotesworth Pinckney, to the Executive Directory, was notified that the Directory would "no longer recognize nor receive a minister plenipotentiary from the United States, until after a reparation of the grievances demanded of the American Government, and which the French Republic has a right to expect." (Page 150.)

On the 11th February, 1797, two months afterwards, the Secretary of State of the United States wrote to Mr. Pinckney, who was then in Amsterdam, not being permitted to reside in France, (pages 158 and 159,) that the spoliations on our commerce by French cruisers were daily increasing; that every just principle was set at defiance; that, "if their acts were simply the violation of our treaty with France, the injuries would be comparatively trifling; but their outrages extend to the capture of our vessels, merely because going to or from a British port; nay, more, they take them when going from a neutral to a French port." (Page 154.)

By a decree of the Executive Directory, dated March 2, 1797, (page 160,) a series of orders was adopted, by which the treaty of amity and commerce of 1778, between France and the United States, was virtually abrogated in all the leading particulars which had constituted the groundwork of her complaints against the United States. She annulled the agreement that free ships should make free goods, by declaring enemy's property in neutral vessels lawful prize. She annulled the stipulation that certain articles only should be contraband, by adding new ones to the list. And in other particulars she either annulled express stipulations in the treaty of 1778, or introduced new rules entirely subversive of them. Among other innovations was that of requiring what she denominated a *rôle d'équipage*, or crew's list, agreeably to an ordinance, nearly, if not quite, as ancient as the marine ordinances of Louis XIV., issued in 1681. In default of such a list a vessel was declared to be a good prize.

It is worthy of remark that these orders were issued the day before General Washington's term of office, as President of the United States, expired. He had occupied that high station during the whole period of our difficulties with France. He was responsible for all the acts of our government towards her down to that period of time; and in the early stages of our dissensions with her, Mr. Jefferson had filled the office of Secretary of State, and had given to the treaties of 1778 the interpretations of which she complained as a violation of our engagements with her, and as a justification of her aggressions upon us. I will certainly not assume that the course of our government was right merely because it was directed by these distinguished statesmen and patriots; but the fact that they had so large a share in the transactions of that day is sufficient to make me hesitate long before I will call in question the wisdom or justice of the public measures, in respect to our difficulties with France, at a period so remote from our own times. And I cannot overlook the consideration, that, if there was any injustice, any ingratitude, any breach of good faith, any violation of treaties with France, down to this period of time, when our diplomatic intercourse with her was suspended, Washington, the upright President and the friend of Lafayette, was responsible for it.

The Senator from Delaware has cited, with great emphasis, a circular letter of Mr. Jefferson, as Secretary of State of the United States, for the purpose of charging on our government the obligation of paying the indemnities claimed for spoliations. I think this letter will be found, on examination, neither to have been extraordinary as a public act, nor to have created any liability on the part of the government, which was not fully discharged. The letter was written on the 27th August, 1793, and will be found at page 216. It began by stating, that, "complaint having been made to the government of the United States of some instances of unjustifiable vexation and spoliation committed on our merchant-vessels by the privateers of the Powers at war, and it being possible that other instances may have happened of which no information has been given to the government," he had it in charge to say, that "due attention would be paid to any injuries they might suffer; and that, on their forwarding well-authenticated evidence of the same, proper proceedings would be adopted for their relief." And it added the expression of the confidence of the government in the just and friendly dispositions of the belligerent powers.

It is a well-known fact that there were at the time numerous complaints; and the government not being able with convenience to correspond with all the complainants, probably adopted this method of inviting them to present the evidence of their injuries, that redress might be sought through the customary channels of diplomatic intercourse; and it held out the same assurance of aid in cases of future wrong. It looked not merely to the future, but to the past also.

By referring to page 253, it will be seen that President Washington, in his Annual Message in December, 1793, referred to this circular in the following terms: —

> "The vexations and spoliations understood to have been committed on our vessels and commerce by the cruisers and officers of some of the belligerent Powers appeared to require attention. The proofs of these, however, not having been brought forward, the description of citizens supposed to have suffered were notified, that, on furnishing them to the Executive, due measures would be taken to obtain redress of the past, and more effectual provisions against the future."

These assurances, as we shall see, were redeemed by the government to the extent of its ability. They were given under a generous confidence in the justice of the belligerents. The government was justified in entertaining this confidence, at least in respect to France. On the 27th of September, 1793, a month after the circular was written, Citizen Genet (page 226) wrote to the Secretary of State, giving him the strongest assurances of the friendly disposition of the French government, and informing him that the decree of the 9th of May had been modified by an exception in favor of American commerce, although at this time the decree of the 27th July, reviving that of the 9th of May, had been in force two months.

Our confidence was abused, but the government will surely not be held responsible for the bad faith of foreign powers. The whole extent of its responsibility, under this circular, which, as we have seen, was designed chiefly to notify the merchants to present evidence of their claims to indemnity, was that of seeking the redress of the injuries complained of in every just mode; and this responsibility, as I shall show hereafter, was met and discharged.

I desire to impress the fact on the Senate, that, as early as 1793, the treaty of 1778 was virtually annulled and abrogated by France. It was so in 1797, as far as it could be by her own act. It required only the act of the other contracting party to work a complete abrogation of it; and, as we shall see, this act was not long wanting.

I also desire to note here that the decree of the 2d of March, 1797, was characterized by the Secretary of State, in that year, "as a palpable violation of our treaty with France, which the Directory, without our participation, undertook to modify, professedly to make it conform to our treaty with Great Britain," (page 406; see, also, page 163.) And, in his Message to Congress in December, 1798, the President denounced another law of France, (pages 375–377,) passed in January of that year, in relation to the capture and condemnation of neutral vessels, "as an unequivocal act of war on the commerce of the nations it attacks," (page 429.)

Having thus shown that France had avowedly assumed to

modify the treaty of amity and commerce of 1778, so far as she held that it was not in accordance with the stipulations of our treaty with Great Britain, and that she had virtually abrogated it by an utter disregard of her engagements with us, I will now proceed to show by what measures her violation of the treaty was met on our part. I shall not trouble the Senate with a detail of all the acts passed by Congress to meet the extraordinary emergency produced by the legislation of France, but shall merely refer to the general tenor of the most important. A series of such laws will be found, commencing on the 28th of May, 1798, and ending in February, 1800. By an act of 28th May, 1798, the capture of the armed vessels of France, found hovering on our coasts for the purpose of committing depredations on our vessels, was authorized; by an act of 13th June, 1798, the commercial intercourse between France and the United States was suspended; by an act of 25th June, 1798, the merchant-vessels of the United States were authorized to arm, to repel by force any attempt by French cruisers to search, restrain, or seize them, to subdue and capture such cruisers, and to recapture any vessels of the United States which such cruisers may have taken; by an act of 28th June, 1798, the forfeiture, condemnation, and sale of captured vessels, and the distribution of the proceeds, were provided for, as well those captured by vessels belonging to citizens of the United States as by our public armed vessels; by an act of 9th July, 1798, the public armed vessels of the United States were authorized to capture on the high seas any armed French vessel; and the President was authorized to grant commissions to private armed vessels, with the same authority to subdue, seize, and capture any armed French vessel, as the public armed vessels of the United States possessed.

To crown these acts of open hostility, the United States were, by an act of Congress of the 7th July, 1798, declared to be of right freed and exonerated from the stipulations of the treaties and of the Consular Convention, "heretofore"

— I quote the language of the act — "concluded between the United States and France." These were the treaty of alliance and the treaty of amity and commerce of February, 1778, and the Consular Convention of November, 1788. On referring to the act of the 7th July, 1798, it will be seen that the declaration of our government, that we were freed from the stipulations of the treaties, was put upon the distinct ground of their infraction by France.

I will not argue the question whether a nation, bound to another by treaty-stipulations, has, under circumstances like those in which the United States were placed, the right to declare those stipulations void. Such a right — a right to be exercised with prudence and wisdom, and under a strong sense of obligation to the dictates of justice — seems to me to be inherent in the very constitution of sovereign States, responsible to no common superior. And if any one doubts its existence, I will refer him to Vattel, Book 2, c. 13.

I have already shown that the treaty of amity and commerce had been avowedly modified by France on her own separate action, and against our earnest and persevering remonstrances; and that it had been virtually abrogated by a system of flagrant depredations on our commerce, not only in violation of the express stipulations of that treaty, but against the received principles and rules of international law. I hold, therefore, that the treaties existing between France and the United States in 1793, when their differences commenced, were terminated by the acts and declarations of both parties. The declarations of France were less comprehensive than those of the United States; her acts were open, palpable, and direct. The declaration of the United States was full and unequivocal. She pronounced herself freed and liberated from the obligation of the treaties; and she acted in conformity to the declaration.

But if any doubt remains as to the fact that the treaties had ceased to be of any obligation, it appears to me it must be dissipated by a reference to the hostile acts to which I have referred. The two countries were, for all essential purposes, in a state of war. The public armed vessels of the United States met those of France as enemies, captured them, brought them within our jurisdiction, and, by regularly authorized judicial processes, they were condemned and sold, and the proceeds of the sale distributed among the captors. Private armed vessels, under a like authority, were scouring the ocean, capturing the armed vessels of France, and bringing them in for condemnation. I am aware that this state of hostilities was not preceded by any general declaration of war, and that it was confined, by the acts of Congress referred to, within certain specified limits. But it was not the less a state of open hostility. And though it was denied that it was technically war, I apprehend that a man of that day, who had been told, in the face of the surrounding circumstances, that the United States were at peace with France, would, to say the least, have been somewhat surprised at the information. It was a state of hostility so nearly resembling actual war, that it could only be terminated by a convention or treaty. The parties could never otherwise have resumed their ancient peaceful and friendly relations. And when the French Ministers, at the opening of the negotiation in 1800, (page 584,) required that "the armed ships of the United States should no longer attack the ships of the Republic," our Ministers replied (same page) that they were not authorized even to give assurances on this point, "otherwise than by incorporating them in a treaty."

I repeat, that I consider the treaties of 1778 abrogated by both the contracting parties: first, by declarations, partial on the one side, and full on the other; and, second, by the acts of both, — by an avowed disregard, by an open violation of the stipulations of those treaties on one side, and on the other by authorized, declared acts of hostility, which were not distinguishable from acts of war. And, with the sincere respect I entertain for the opinion of the Senator from Delaware, I cannot but regard the abrogation of the treaties to have been as effectual as though it had been done by mutual consent.

Previous to this entire disruption of the amicable relations of the two countries, Messrs. Pinckney, Marshall, and Gerry, who were sent out as Ministers to France in 1797, had, to use the language of one of our official documents, "been refused a reception, treated with indignities, and finally driven from its territories." (Page 561.)

I will now take up the transactions between the two countries when negotiations were resumed, and see in what light they regarded their relations to each other.

Early in 1799, Oliver Ellsworth, Patrick Henry, and William Vans Murray — the latter being then Minister at the Hague — were appointed Envoys Extraordinary and Ministers Plenipotentiary to France, but with a distinct intimation to the French government that they would not be sent out until we were assured that they would be received. The assurance was given; William R. Davie was appointed in place of Patrick Henry, who declined; and in March, 1800, they reached Paris.

I desire to state, in order to do justice to the subject, one of the strong points on which the claimants rely. In the instructions to our Ministers, they were directed to inform the Ministers of France "that the United States expect from France, as an indispensable condition of the treaty, a stipulation to make to the citizens of the United States full compensation for all losses and damages, which they shall have sustained by reason of irregular or illegal captures or condemnations of their vessels and other property, under color of authority or commissions from the French Republic or its agents." (Page 562.)

These claims to indemnity, which were large in amount, I cannot find that the French government ever unconditionally recognized, at any stage of the negotiation; and the diplomatic correspondence which ensued between our Ministers on the one side, and the French Ministers — Messrs. Joseph Bonaparte, Fleurieu, and Roederer — on the other, was conducted with a good deal of adroitness and pertinacity. The latter, with a view to avoid the payment of indemnities to citizens of the United States for spoliations, set up a claim to the restoration of the ancient treaties, (page 581.) Indeed, they claimed that the treaties of 1778 had never been abrogated; and that, if France indemnified citizens of the United States for a violation of those treaties, the United States should acknowledge the treaties as then existing, and thus give France the benefit of the stipulations they contained. The Ministers of the United States insisted, on the other hand, that the treaties had been dissolved by the acts of both parties (page 612); that the act dissolving them could not be recalled (page 592); and that we were under no obligation to renew them.

The first proposition of our Ministers at the commencement of the negotiation was, "to ascertain and discharge the equitable claims of the citizens of either nation upon the other." (Page 581.) The French Ministers replied, by saying that the first object should be to determine "the regulations and steps to be followed for the estimation and indemnification of injuries for which either nation may make claim for itself or for any of its citizens." — (Same page.) Our Ministers, in their answer, objected to the claims which either nation might make for itself, (page 582,) because they understood the French Ministers to refer to a restoration of the treaties. The French Ministers reasserted their national claims (page 583); and at page 591 it will be seen that they declared, that, when they acknowledged "the principle of compensation," it was "as a consequence of ancient treaties." The position thus taken by the French Ministers at the very threshold of the negotiation I have not found that they abandoned, either during its progress or at its close.

Throughout the negotiation, then, it appears that the French Ministers pertinaciously coupled the restoration of the ancient treaties with the mutual payment of indemnities, (page 641.) To use their own words: "Either the ancient treaties, with the privileges resulting from priority and the stipulation of reciprocal indemnities, or a new treaty assuring equality without indemnity." (Page 618.)

There is no doubt that the position taken by the French negotiators, and adhered to with obstinacy, as our Ministers said in one of their communications, and the final surrender of the treaties and of mutual claims to indemnity, give to the transaction on its face the appearance of an agreement between the parties to set off the one against the other. But I believe that a careful investigation of the matter will show that it was so in appearance only, and not in fact. To place the matter in its true light, we have only to separate the subjects of dispute from each other: first, the treaties; and, second, the indemnities mutually claimed. I assume these to be the only subjects of disagreement. I assume the position deliberately, and with full knowledge that a different classification had been made, viz: first, the treaties; second, our claims for spoliations; and third, the claims of France under the treaties and otherwise. I reject this classification, because the two last items were embraced in the general designation of "indemnities mutually claimed," and because, if the third item was a proper one, then it would have been proper for us to add a fourth by setting up our claims under the treaties as an offset to hers, as the expense of equipping fleets and arming to defend our commerce against her aggressions. She did not claim, as I can find, any indemnity on account of the non-execution of the guaranty contained in the treaty of alliance. We always insisted that the *casus fœderis* had not occurred. We insisted that the war between France and Great Britain was an offensive war on the part of the former, and that the execution of the guaranty could only be claimed in the case of a defensive war. Indeed, I have not been able to find that she called on us to execute it. Her real claim was to a recognition of the treaties, and especially the treaty of commerce. In respect to any claims to indemnity on her part under the latter, it is only necessary to refer to Mr. Jefferson's expositions, to see how groundless they would have been.

The Senator from Delaware stated that France had claimed from us a compliance with the stipulation of the treaty of alliance, by which we had guaranteed to her the possession of her West India islands; and he referred to a letter from Mr. Genet, at page 231, and to another letter from Mr. Adet, Mr. Genet's successor, (page 354,) to prove that she had called on us to execute the guaranty. I am constrained to say that these references of the honorable Senator do not appear to sustain the position, as, I think, the Senator will himself admit on a more careful examination of the subject. Mr. Genet's letter bears date the 14th of November, 1793, and the following is the paragraph alluded to: —

> "I beg you to lay before the President of the United States as soon as possible the decree and the enclosed note, and to obtain from him the earliest decision either as to the guaranty I have claimed the fulfilment of for our colonies, or upon the mode of negotiation of the new treaty I was charged to propose to the United States, and which would make of the two nations but one family."

It will be perceived that this request is in the alternative, and, by a reference to Mr. Genet's preceding letter, that he is speaking of new commercial arrangements with the French colonies under new regulations adopted by France. Not one word will be found in reference to an armed defence of those colonies. In no one of Mr. Genet's previous letters will any claim by the government of France, as I believe, to the execution of the guaranty in the treaty of alliance be found. On the contrary, there is abundant evidence to show that its execution was not designed to be claimed. By referring to page 55, it will be seen by Mr. Jefferson's statement that Mr. Genet, less than six months before this letter was written, declared to Mr. Jefferson himself, to the President, General Washington, and at a public meeting of the citizens of Philadelphia, that "France did not expect that we should become a party to the war" between her and Great Britain. By referring to page 84, it will be seen that Mr. Monroe, our Minister to France, in a letter dated the 15th September, 1794, nearly a year after the date of Mr. Genet's letter, said that the French Republic "had declined calling on us to execute the guaranty"; and at page 78 it will be found that Mr. Monroe, in June, 1794, was instructed, in case the execution of the guaranty was demanded, to refer the French government to our own.

By reference to page 97, a letter from the Secretary of State of the United States to Mr. Randolph will be found, dated the 1st of June, 1795, stating that we had not, nor, as he said, "have we yet been required to execute the guaranty"; and this, it is to be remembered, was nearly two years after Mr. Genet's letter was written.

The facts to which I have referred show, as I think, that France did not design to call on us to execute the guaranty of her West India possessions; and we insisted that we were not bound to execute it. She had clearly not called on us previously to 1796, if the declarations of our own government are to be credited; and her principal West India islands were subdued in 1794 by Sir John Jervis, afterwards Lord St. Vincent: a title conferred on him on account of his masterly defeat of the Spanish fleet off the cape of that name. If we had been called on to execute the guaranty subsequently to 1794, it must have been to reconquer these islands; and it is well known that, by the treaty of Amiens, all the West India possessions of France were stipulated to be restored to her, with the exception of Trinidad. I will not speak of an execution of the guaranty subsequently to 1796; for with what face could we be called on for the purpose by France, when she was engaged in the most flagrant depredations on our commerce?

I now refer to Mr. Adet's letter of the 15th of November, 1796, which will be found at page 354, and which, I think, I was not mistaken in saying had been cited to show that we had been called on to fulfil by force the guaranty of her West India islands to France. Mr. Adet commences his letter by claiming, "in the name of American honor, in the name of the faith of treaties, the execution of that contract, which assured to the United States their existence, and which France regarded as the pledge of the most sacred union between two people, the freest upon earth." He then proceeds to state the grievances of which the Government of France complained, discussing in an elaborate manner the various subjects of disagreement between the two countries, the interpretations given to the 17th and 22d articles of the treaty of amity and commerce in respect to privateers and prizes, the mission of Mr. Jay, the treaty he negotiated with Great Britain, and other kindred subjects. On the 365th page will be found a recapitulation of these grievances by Mr. Adet, as the result of the statement I have just given, and no reference will be found to the guaranty of the West India islands. The only reference I have been able to find to these islands is a general one, near the close of the letter, (page 367,) in which the United States are charged with allowing "the French colonies to be declared in a state of blockade, and its citizens interdicted the right of trading to them"; and this reference I cannot regard as a call on the United States then, or as the evidence of a previous call, to execute the guaranty, — the question I suppose to be at issue.

Mr. Jefferson's letter to Mr. Madison, in April, 1794, to which the Senator from Delaware referred, (see volume 3 of his Works, page 303,) was written at Monticello, and it certainly expresses the opinion that we ought, at a proper time, to interpose and declare that the French West India islands should rest with France. But would Mr. Jefferson have expressed the same opinion a few years later, when our difficulties with her had ripened into open hostility? It is not to be believed. At page 400 of the same volume, a letter will be found from him to Samuel Smith, dated August 22, 1798, in which he says both France and England "have given, and are daily giving, sufficient cause for war"; and at page 425 of the same volume, in another letter, dated March 12, 1799, he says, (though expressing the belief that France had sincerely desired peace,) "The atrocious proceedings of France towards this country had wellnigh destroyed its liberties." Both these letters were written while he was Vice-President of the United States, and while he was taking an active part in the political concerns of the country.

I do not regard this question of any very material consequence so far as it concerns the claims under consideration; but it has been referred to as the evidence of a breach of faith on the part of the United States, and I felt it due to the subject to present the facts I have stated, leaving to the Senate to draw its own conclusions from these facts.

Let us return a moment to the treaties of 1778. They were, as we have seen, treaties for the mutual benefit of the parties. The treaty of amity and commerce contained stipulations of reciprocal advantage. France placed a higher value on the advantages secured to her than we on those secured to us; but this does not affect the nature of the treaties. Their fundamental purpose was mutuality. In renouncing or abandoning them, both parties renounced substantial benefits. In renouncing the treaty of amity and commerce, we lost the benefit of the stipulation that free ships make free goods, — a great principle, for which we had been contending from the foundation of our independence,— and were thrown back upon the more rigorous principle of the international rule, as then asserted, understood, and acted on, that enemy's goods may be taken in neutral bottoms. (Page 624.) We also lost the benefit of the stipulation concerning contraband articles, which were placed by the treaty on a more liberal footing than they would have been if governed by the existing usages of civilized States. France lost some benefits also; but the advantages on the one side under the treaty of amity and commerce may be considered as fairly counterbalancing those on the other. The treaty of alliance contained mutual guaranties; and these were considered beneficial both to us and France. In the instructions to Messrs. Pinckney, Marshall, and Gerry, they were directed to propose an exchange of these guaranties for specific succors; — the United States to furnish a moderate sum of money, or quantity of provisions, when the *casus fœderis* (a defensive war) should occur, and France a like sum of money, or an equivalent in military stores or clothing. (Page 457.) The same view of the subject was taken in 1800 by the American Ministers, who proposed, in case the treaties were revived, that the guaranty should be specific and the succors equal. (Page 633.) I cite these views to show that the treaties were considered as conferring reciprocal benefits and imposing mutual burdens, and that, in renouncing them, the advantage gained was not wholly on the part of the United States. The latter, it is true, were unwilling to reassume the obligations imposed by the treaties, from an earnest desire to avoid alliances which should involve us in wars waged by the great powers of Europe against each other; and the American Ministers offered at one time to pay eight millions of francs (about a million and a half of dollars) as a consideration for not reviving them, — (page 629,) — not as a consideration for getting rid of existing obligations, but for not reviving old ones. But this proposition was a part of a series of offers, embracing an adjustment of all the subjects of dissension, — offers which were not accepted by France because they were considered too advantageous to us. Indeed it was made by the American Ministers with extreme reluctance, even in connection with propositions for our benefit, and from their great desire, to use their own words, "to terminate, without further loss of time, the present negotiation." The offer was made, too, with a distinct recorded declaration by the American Ministers, almost contemporaneous with it, that, if "the guaranty between France and the United States did in fact contemplate succors, they must have been principally for the latter [the United States], who might need them, rather than for the former [France], who was evidently competent to protect herself." (Page 633.)

From the whole course of the negotiation, it is manifest that the treaties were considered as imposing mutual obligations,—not mutual in name merely, but in effect; and I have been able to discover nothing in the history of the negotiation to justify the inference that the United States intended, by finally treating without exacting indemnity for all our claims on France, to offset indemnities to the obligations imposed on her by the treaties, and to assume the payment of the indemnities ourselves. The French negotiators endeavored to set them off against each other, for the reasons I have already assigned; but the justice of such a set-off was never acceded to by the United States. On the contrary, the American Ministers virtually refused to set them off against each other; and they refused, also, to assume the payment of indemnities by the United States.

After a long negotiation, a convention was concluded on the 30th of September, 1800. The second article, which related exclusively to the treaties and to the indemnities, I will read to the Senate.

"The Ministers Plenipotentiary of the two parties, not being able to agree at present respecting the treaty of alliance of the 6th of February, 1778, the treaty of amity and commerce of the same date, and the convention of the 14th of November, 1788, nor upon the indemnities mutually due or claimed, the parties will negotiate further on these subjects at a convenient time; and until they may have agreed upon these points, the said treaties and convention shall have no operation, and the relations of the two countries shall be regulated as follows." (Page 683.)

The third article provided for a mutual restoration of public ships taken before or after the exchange of ratifications.

The fourth article provided for a mutual restoration of property captured, and not then definitively condemned, or which might be captured before the exchange of ratifications.

The fifth article provided for the payment of debts contracted by either nation with individuals of the other, or by the individuals of one with the individuals of the other, or the prosecution of the payment, as if no misunderstanding had existed. But this article was declared not to extend to indemnities claimed on account of captures or confiscations.

The effect of the second article of the convention was to postpone all further negotiation in respect to the treaties and indemnities named in it to a future day.

The Senate of the United States ratified the convention, after expunging the second article, and limiting the duration of the convention to eight years.

Bonaparte, as First Consul, accepted and ratified the convention, as amended, (page 685,) with a proviso, that, by the retrenchment of the second article, "the two States renounce the respective pretensions which are the object of the said article."

On the submission of the convention, as modified by France, to the Senate, it was declared by a vote of that body, on the 19th of December, 1801, that they considered it fully ratified.[1]

The questions which arise from the facts I have stated are: —

1st. Whether the engagement contained in the second article of the convention to negotiate at a future day, in respect to the treaties and indemnities, secured to the United States any advantage in respect to claims for spoliations?

[1] *Executive Journal,* Vol. I. p. 398.

2d. Whether the United States, by expunging the second article, released any claims to indemnities which had been so distinctly recognized by France as to make the United States legally or equitably responsible for their payment to her citizens? And,

3d. Whether the United States, by assenting to the proviso inserted in the ratification by France, renouncing the respective pretensions which were the object of the second article, imposed on herself any obligation to pay the indemnities claimed by her citizens on account of spoliations.

1st. The first question appears to be satisfactorily answered by the whole history of the correspondence between the Ministers by whom the convention was negotiated. The French negotiators uniformly refused to acknowledge the claim of the United States to indemnities, excepting upon a concession of what they professed to regard as important advantages to France by a recognition of the treaties of 1778. The Ministers of the United States refused to accede to these demands. In other words, they refused to secure to the United States the acknowledgment of these claims on the conditions insisted on by the French negotiators. It was a question with them, not of recognizing existing obligations, but reviving obligations which had ceased to exist; and this they declined to do. They refused to purchase the payment of indemnities at the price demanded by France. The result of a fruitless negotiation was, to leave the whole controversy where it was when the correspondence commenced; and if the convention had been ratified without expunging the second article, there is no reason to suppose that a negotiation at a future day would have led to any other issue. On the contrary, I do not see how any one can rise from a perusal of the volume I hold in my hand with the slightest impression that a renewal of the diplomatic correspondence between the two governments would have resulted more favorably to us. The American Ministers state, in substance, in their letter giving a history of the negotiation, that the real object avowed by the French Ministers was to avoid indemnities (pages 632 and 643); that a promise to pay them at a remote period might as easily prove delusive as it would be reluctantly made; and that such a promise could only be obtained by an unqualified recognition of the treaties, the future operation of which could not be varied in any particular for any consideration or compensation whatever. It is not reasonable to suppose, under such circumstances, that any subsequent claim to indemnities in a future negotiation would have had any other result.

2d. The suppression of the second article was a release of the parties from the obligation of further negotiating at a convenient time in respect to the treaties and indemnities, leaving them precisely where they were in respect to the claims or pretensions which were the object of the article. It is not possible to ascertain now what was the object of the Senate in expunging this article. The injunction of secrecy has been removed from the votes, but the debates have not been preserved; and it appears that the American Minister, Mr. Murray, who was appointed to exchange the ratifications, was "perfectly in the dark on the views of the Senate in suppressing the second article." This was his own language. But it is quite clear that the omission of the second article in negotiating the convention would have left the parties, in respect to the matters contained in the article, entirely uncommitted as to their future course; and its suppression did no more. Thus far no claims on France had been released, and no obligations assumed by the United States.

3d. The proviso inserted by Bonaparte in ratifying the convention after its modification by us, and our assent to the terms of the proviso, appear at first view to have changed the position of the parties in respect to the claims or pretensions which were the object of the second article. Those claims or pretensions were in terms renounced. But it is quite clear that the Senate of the United States did not regard the renunciation as changing the state of the question; they did not consider a new ratification necessary; they declared that they considered the convention "fully ratified." Would they have made such a declaration if they had considered the insertion of the proviso as creating new liabilities on either side, or discharging old ones? It is difficult to believe so. Mr. Jefferson spoke of it as "a clause declaratory of the effect given to the meaning of the treaty"; and he authorized Mr. Madison to say that he did not regard it as anything "more than a legitimate inference from the rejection by the Senate of the second article." (Page 703.) Mr. Livingston, our Minister to France, spoke of it as intended "to remove ambiguities"; not to give a new effect to the treaty, but to explain its true meaning and intent. (Page 731.)

Besides, there was no formal offset of the advantages claimed by France as resulting to her from the treaties against the advantages to result to us from a recognition of the indemnities claimed. Down to the termination of the negotiation, and, indeed, to the final exchange of ratifications, such a set-off of one to the other was only inferable, as I think, from the connection of the two subjects, for an interested purpose, by the French Ministers. (Pages 641, *et seq.*)

The Senator from Delaware has referred to the opinions of distinguished individuals, favoring the idea that the United States intended to release France from the payment of these indemnities, in consideration of being herself released from the obligations of the treaties. I will examine two of the most important.

Mr. R. Livingston, who went out to France as Minister near the close of the year 1801, said (page 704) he considered "as a dead loss" "the sacrifices we had made of an immense claim, to get rid of the guaranty contained in the treaty of alliance." And again, in a letter to the French Minister of Exterior Relations, he said: —

> "It will, sir, be well recollected by the distinguished characters who had the management of the negotiation, that the payment for illegal captures, with damages and indemnities, was demanded on one side, and the renewal of the treaty of 1778 on the other; that they were considered as of equivalent value, and that they only formed the subject of the second article." (Page 717.)

Mr. Livingston had taken no part in these negotiations; and it has been satisfactorily shown that there was no formal exchange of pretensions, arising under the treaties on the one side, and claims arising from spoliations on the other. On the contrary, the benefits and the burdens under the treaties were mutual, as well as the claims to indemnities. I will proceed to show, by official documents, that Mr. Livingston was entirely in error in saying that claims for indemnities on our side, and the treaties on the side of France, were considered by the negotiators of equivalent value. Indeed I have already proved, by the testimony of our Ministers, that they considered the prospect of obtaining a recognition of our claims as delusive. (Page 643.) But there is stronger evidence on this point. Mr. Murray, on the 1st of October, 1800, the day after the convention was executed, speaks of the indemnities as "impossible" [hopeless]. (Page 661.) On the 2d of July, 1801, he speaks of our claim to indemnities "as not worth a quarter *per centum*." (Page 676.) On the 3d August, 1801, he says: "If the Senate meant, as I hope, to consider indemnities as worth nothing, then the business, I presume, is closed;" and in the same communication he alleges "the absolute want of value in the prospect of indemnities" as a reason for accepting the proviso inserted by Bonaparte, renouncing all pretensions on both sides under the second article. How, then, can it be said that the negotiators considered the treaties on one side, and the indemnities on the other, as of equivalent value? The testimony proves precisely the contrary: that they considered our claims to indemnities as of no value, or at least hopeless; and such was probably the opinion of the Senate in abandoning them.

I now come to an opinion, which I will admit to be much more formidable if it has been properly interpreted by the advocates of the claims under consideration. I allude to the letter of instructions from Mr. Madison to Mr. Pinckney, our Minister to Spain, in February, 1804. Mr. Madison said that "the claims from which France had been released were admitted by France, and the release was for a valuable consideration, in a correspondent release of the United States from claims on them." (Page 795.)

I should certainly hesitate to call in question so high an authority as Mr. Madison in any statement relating to a matter directly in issue, which he (Mr. M.) had fully investigated; and I do not intend now to question this statement in the sense in which it ought, as I believe, to be understood. The only points of any importance in this statement are: first, that our claims "were admitted by France"; and, second, that they were released, and that "the release was for a valuable consideration, in a correspondent release of the United States from certain claims on them." It is to be borne in mind that Mr. Madison's reference to the subject was for the purpose of sustaining a position taken by our government in a negotiation with a third power, years after the convention of 1800 was concluded; and some allowance is to be made for strength of expression. With regard to the first point, I have said that there never was, as I could find, after the war-measures adopted by us in 1798, an unconditional admission by France of our claims for spoliations. She assented to the principle of mutual compensation for injuries, but with a distinct assertion of her claim to a recognition of the treaties. It was only on the condition of such a recognition that she was willing to inquire into the claims of both parties for injuries, national as well as individual, with a stipulation of mutual indemnity. This, I believe, was the extent of her admission, and it was a very qualified one. With regard to the second point, — the release, — if Mr. Madison intended to say, that, in the adjustment of our difficulties with France, there were mutual claims which were mutually abandoned, no exception could be taken to his statement. And certainly, in any other sense, it would neither accord with the facts I have stated, nor with the declarations of the negotiators themselves. When converted into a sanction of the idea that there was a set-off of indemnities claimed by the United States against our treaty-obligations to France, and into an argument in favor of the position that we were bound to assume the payment of these indemnities, it made Mr. Madison's statement entirely inconsistent with what our negotiators said and did, and with the inferences fairly to be drawn from his own subsequent conduct, as I will endeavor to show hereafter. And I will add here, that I have not been able to find a word in any of Mr. Madison's writings, or those of Mr. Jefferson, countenancing the idea that these claims constitute a just demand against the government.

I do not much like to deal in technicalities. I prefer, as a general rule, to rely on the deductions of common sense, and on maxims so simple and so universally received as to make their application plain to the most ordinary understanding. But I cannot forbear to say that a release for a valuable consideration and a set-off seem to me, in this instance, convertible terms. A set-off implies an unqualified admission of claims on both sides, and a mutual agreement to balance the one against the other. I find, in this case, none of these unquestionable evidences of an exchange of equivalents, — no unqualified admission of our claims for spoliations by France, — no unqualified admission by the United States of treaty-obligations to her, — and no agreement to set them off against each other. On the contrary, we expressly denied the treaty-obligations, and France expressly refused to inquire into indemnities, except on condition of receiving from us the very admission we declined to make.

I regard this case, under all its aspects, as one in which the parties had mutually abandoned their respective pretensions. But if it be assumed that there was a set-off, I shall, without admitting the assumption, insist that it was not of indemnities on one side against treaty-obligations on the other, but of indemnities against indemnities, treaty-obligations against treaty-obligations, — mutual, if not equal, — not bargained for, one against the other, as an exchange of equivalents, but relinquished, renounced, abandoned, on either side, from the utter hopelessness of obtaining a recognition of them on the other. Such seems to me to be the only legitimate conclusion from the whole history of the negotiation, and such was the language of the proviso by which the pursuit of these "respective pretensions" was "renounced."

That there was an abandonment of claims on France for spoliations committed on our commerce, I have never denied. There was a similar abandonment of claims on her part, on account of captures made by us during the hostilities which existed between May, 1798, and the conclusion of the convention of 1800. But whether the United States are, in legal or equitable obligation, bound to satisfy the claims thus abandoned on our part, is the question which we are called on to decide. On this point I have not the slightest doubt. I believe there is no instance in the history of our diplomacy in which the satisfaction of injuries has been so zealously or faithfully pursued. For five years, from 1793 to 1798, we pursued it by negotiation, — earnest, urgent, persevering negotiation. When all peaceful means had failed, we resorted to force. Fleets were equipped, blood was shed, and the physical power of the country was vigorously put forth, to compel redress. For all practical purposes, it was war. The two countries, for interested objects on both sides, chose to commence negotiations on the basis of peace, though, before they closed, they had approached nearly to a war-basis. But the facts remained unaltered. The American Ministers pronounced it to be "war, or that peculiar state of hostility in which they are at present involved." (Page 634.) On another occasion they said, "Doubtless the congressional Act authorizing the reduction of French cruisers by force was an authorization of war, limited indeed in its extent, but not in its nature." (Page 642.) Nay, sir, the president of the French commission, when treating with our Ministers, said, "that, if the question could be determined by an indifferent nation, he was satisfied such a tribunal would say that the present state of things was *war* on the side of America, and that no indemnities could be claimed." The other two commissioners made similar declarations. (Page 633.) And in like manner Mr. Jefferson, in a letter to Samuel Smith, of the 22d August, 1793, (page 398, third volume of his works,) says, "It is true, then, that, as with England we might of right have chosen either war or peace, and have chosen peace, and prudently, in my opinion, so with France we might also of right have chosen either peace or war, and we have chosen war." But call it what you will, it was a resort to force — the last resort of republics as well as kings — to procure a redress of wrongs; and it vindicates our government from all imputation of neglect or want of zeal in the performance of its duty.

In the negotiations which succeeded this state of hostility, all the energies and all the appliances of diplomacy consistent with honor were employed to procure a recognition of the claims of our citizens on France. To a certain extent these efforts were successful. A portion of the claims was recognized, and subsequently paid, under the convention of 1803. A portion remains unsatisfied; but I have endeavored to show that the United States — first, by negotiation, second, by a resort to force, and, third, by another recourse to negotiation — has acquitted herself of all obligation to respond to those, the satisfaction of whose claims she unsuccessfully labored to effect. I will not detain the Senate by entering into an analysis of the different classes of these claims, separating those which are alleged to be unsatisfied from those for which indemnity has been paid. I will not stop to inquire how far these claims may have been well- or ill-founded; to speculate on the chances there may have been, when the testimony was fresh, of reducing them within reasonable limits; or to consider the danger now, after the lapse of more than forty years, of showing injuries which might never have been clearly proved before the power of sifting evidence was seriously weakened, if not utterly lost. These are considerations of so serious a nature as to call on us to pause and ponder well the consequences of throwing these demands on the public treasury. But I rest my opposition to the application for legislative relief on the broader grounds I have stated.

The Senator from Delaware accounted for the neglect of our government to recognize these claims when first presented to Congress by the peculiar state of the public finances in 1801, and for thirty years afterwards. But I apprehend that the state of our finances at a period subsequent to 1801 will be found, in connection with other circumstances, one of the strongest arguments against this application. Mr. Madison was Secretary of State from 1801 to 1809. Mr. Jefferson, who was familiar with the origin and progress of our difficulties with France, and conducted the diplomatic correspondence of our government in respect to them for some time after they broke out, was President of the United States during the same period, — from 1801 to 1809. In 1807, the first report was made in Congress in favor of these claims, — for I cannot agree with the Senator from Delaware that Mr. Giles's report in 1802 was a favorable one. In his Annual Message of 1807, Mr. Jefferson reports a surplus in the treasury of eight millions and a half of dollars. In his Annual Message of 1808, he reports the enormous balance of nearly fourteen millions, of which only about five were required to meet public engagements, leaving again a disposable surplus of about eight millions and a half; and, in connection with this balance, he refers to probable future surpluses, when the freedom of commerce should be restored, and asks whether they shall be permitted to "lie unproductive in the public vaults?" Such was our financial condition in 1807 and 1808. Sir, is it credible, if Mr. Jefferson and Mr. Madison had believed this claim a valid demand on the government, that it would not, through these distinguished individuals, who exercised a controlling influence in Congress, have been recognized and paid? If, with these men at the head of the government, — men familiar with the history of the times, — when the transactions themselves were recent and well known, — with an overflowing treasury, — with millions, in fact, remaining without any specific object, — if, under all these circumstances, the claims were not acknowledged, with what propriety can we be asked to acknowledge them now, after the lapse of more than forty years, when the memory of much that is necessary to give to remote transactions their true coloring, and to correct erroneous conclusions in respect to them, may be irretrievably lost? Sir, there is no safety in such cases but to rest on the contemporaneous judgment of those who had every motive to consider and judge them fairly, and who possessed all the information necessary to make their decision just.

And finally, sir, I am compelled to differ with my honorable friend from Delaware (if he will permit me so to designate him) in the opinion that the government of the United States is in honor responsible for these claims. A government is undoubtedly bound to protect its citizens in their persons and in their property, to the extent of its ability, both from internal and external injuries. It is bound to seek, by all just and feasible methods, a redress of such injuries: if domestic, by a proper application of its authority; if foreign, by negotiation in the first instance, and by force in the second, if the magnitude and enormity of the aggression justify a resort to arms. When it has done all this, it will have performed its duty. If it cannot succeed in obtaining redress, it must be deemed fairly exonerated from all liability to its own citizens when it has made all the efforts it is capable of putting forth for the purpose. Sir, I know of no principle by which a government, after extraordinary efforts to procure a redress of injuries, or an acknowledgment of the claims of its citizens on a foreign State, is bound to assume the satisfaction of those claims because its efforts have proved unsuccessful. If this principle is to be adopted and acted on, we should go back to the ten years which preceded the War of 1812, and satisfy our citizens for spoliations committed on them during peace by Great Britain. We demanded indemnity for these spoliations in negotiating the treaty of Ghent. Our Ministers were repeatedly instructed on the subject. We presented our claims to the British commissioners, and we abandoned them when we found them hopeless. Or, to use the language by which the claim before us is sought to be enforced, these indemnities were "released" to Great Britain "for the valuable consideration" of peace. We should, according to every principle of equity, satisfy these last claims first. Under the convention of 1803 with France, our citizens were paid nearly four millions of dollars on account of claims on France prior to 1800. Under the convention of 1831, they received over four millions and a half more for spoliations subsequently to 1800. In all, we have obtained from France by negotiation, and paid to our citizens, about eight millions and a half of dollars. From Great Britain I am not aware that we have obtained anything, since the treaty of 1794, on account of claims for spoliations, notwithstanding the aggravated injuries she has committed on our citizens, excepting for abducted slaves under the treaty of Ghent. But I hold that the government of the United States is exonerated, in both instances, by a faithful and zealous discharge of its duty, — first, by negotiation, and, second, by a resort to force.

THE WAREHOUSE SYSTEM.

I.

Propositions to establish a warehouse system, under which goods imported into the United States from foreign countries might be stored without payment of duty until withdrawn for consumption, had been for several years before Congress. The bills making provision for the purpose were long and complicated, embarrassing the discussion and endangering the success of the measure by complexity of detail. To avoid these difficulties, Mr. Dix introduced a bill securing all the objects in view by a simple amendment of a single section of an Act then in force, and it passed through both Houses and became a law at the same session. The speech which follows was intended to explain the bill, and was delivered on the 19th of June, 1846.

Mr. President: The bill under consideration was reported to the Senate from the Committee on Commerce, under a resolution instructing them to inquire into the expediency of establishing a warehouse system, and giving them authority to report by bill. The committee having charged me with the introduction of the bill, it devolves on me to explain its provisions, to point out its objects, and to show in what respects it modifies existing laws.

The bill is designed by the committee to respond affirmatively to the inquiry they were instructed to make. It is true, it does not provide specifically for the establishment of a warehouse system; but it aims to accomplish all the objects of such a system, by extending the provisions of existing laws in relation to the storage and final disposal of imported merchandise. They have given it the greatest possible simplicity in form. They have not deemed it expedient to recommend a complex system. They have aimed to introduce no principles wholly new or untried. They have made the system they propose conform as nearly as practicable to the provisions of existing laws. They have founded it on enactments now in force and in daily and familiar operation, — enactments of which the meaning and application have been settled by construction and practice. The bill consists of an amendment of a single section — the 12th section — of the act of the 30th of August, 1842, commonly called the tariff act. It is almost a transcript of that section and the thirteenth. The amendments, though important, are all comprised within the compass of a few lines. Thus, Senators will perceive that the proposed measure will be presented for their consideration in the most simple shape, and that the examination which the importance of the subject demands may be carried on, without embarrassing their attention by complexity of details.

The first observation which I deem it proper to make in connection with the general policy of the measure is, that the warehouse system is actually in existence, though on a very narrow basis, and in a very imperfect form. Indeed, I believe there has been no period from the foundation of our revenue system when it was not in operation in some shape or other, and under certain limitations.

It will, in fact, be necessary, in order to show to what extent it is in force, to go back to the general revenue act of the 2d March, 1799, "to regulate the collection of duties on imports and tonnage."

The 56th section of that act, which is still in force with some modifications, provides, that, after the expiration of fifteen working-days from the time prescribed for reporting a vessel, if any goods shall be found on board, other than such as were reported for entry in another collection district, or some foreign port, they shall be taken possession of, and stored under the order of the collector. The same section also provides, that, after five days' notice to the collector, any goods may be so taken and stored, with the consent of the owner or consignee, or the master of the vessel. By the act of 3d March, 1821, the time allowed for unlading vessels exceeding three hundred tons burden is extended from fifteen to twenty working-days; and by a proviso in the 56th section of the act of 1799, which I am now examining, the fifteen working-days originally allowed may be extended by the collector fifteen days more for vessels laden with salt or coal.

The act of 1799, like all the early acts regulating the collection of duties, gave a credit to the importer where the duties chargeable on imported merchandise exceeded a certain amount. If the duties did not exceed fifty dollars, they were required by that act to be paid in cash; and by the act of the 14th July, 1832, cash payments were exacted for duties not exceeding two hundred dollars. On all sums exceeding these amounts, the importer took the goods and gave his bond, payable at periods varying from three to twelve months, according to the nature of the merchandise and the countries from which it was imported. This was the general system. There was an exception in the case of teas, which were allowed to be deposited in stores agreed on by the importer and inspector of the revenue, — bonds without sureties being taken, in double the amount of the duties, payable in two years. And there was also a general provision authorizing collectors to receive goods in deposit, by way of securing the payment of duties, as a substitute for sureties on bonds. For instance, if the importer preferred not to give sureties, he was allowed to give his own bond and take his merchandise, depositing with the collector a sufficient quantity to insure the payment of the duties on the whole.

Under the system of credits thus established, there was no strong inducement to place goods in store pursuant to the provisions of the 56th section of the act of 1799. Such as were found on board vessels after the time specified for unlading, were usually small in quantity and not of great value. Under the proviso of the 56th section, which I have referred to, authorizing goods to be received in store after five days' notice, with the consent of the owner, I believe it was, and still is, the practice for vessels in haste to enter on the return voyage, and especially packets, to be put on what is called the five days' order, for the purpose of unlading and sending their cargoes to the public stores without waiting for them to be appraised, weighed, measured, and gauged.

Goods thus deposited were, by the provisions of the 56th section, permitted to remain in store for the term of nine months, unless the duties chargeable on them became payable in a shorter period; and in this case a sufficient quantity was allowed to be sold to realize the duties when they were due. The residue was to be sold at the end of the nine months, with the addition of one month prescribed for advertising them. So that, with the nine months allowed for retaining goods in store, one month for advertising, twenty days for unlading, and unavoidable delays, it rarely happened that goods charged with duties payable in nine months were sold in less than a year. Before goods were sold, they were required to be appraised by two or more reputable merchants, and the proceeds of the sale, after deducting the duties and charges, were paid into the treasury of the United States for the use of the owner, upon proof of his right to receive them.

Such was the warehouse system as it existed under the earliest revenue laws. The system of credits established by the same laws, and the limited time for the deposit of merchandise, rendered it of no great practical importance as an instrument of commerce. I call it a warehouse system, though it may be deemed unworthy of the name, as its object was, chiefly, the convenience of the commercial community.

The 12th section of the act of the 30th August, 1842, requires the duties on all imported merchandise to be paid in cash. The act of 1799 required duties to be paid, or secured to be paid, before a permit for landing them was granted. But, in order to ascertain what the duties were, it was necessary, as a general rule, to cause the goods to be weighed, gauged, measured, and sometimes sent to the public stores to be appraised. The necessity of the case, therefore, established this construction of the law, which has existed from the earliest period, — that its requirements are sufficiently complied with if the importer pays the duties regularly ascertained, or secures them when estimated, before he obtains possession of the goods on which they are charged. This practice exists, and must always exist, under any system of cash duties. It existed when the cash system was partial, when it was made universal, and it exists still. Under the cash system, then, the duties must be paid or deposited before the goods go into the possession of the owner. Under the credit system, the owner obtained possession of his goods on giving his bond for the payment of the duties at a future day.

The 12th section of the act of 1842, after exacting the payment of duties in cash, provides, that "in all cases of failure or neglect to pay the duties, on completion of the entry," the goods "shall be taken possession of by the collector, and deposited in the public stores." When so deposited, they are to be kept at the charge and risk of the owner; and if the duties are not paid in sixty days, (or ninety days if imported from beyond the Cape of Good Hope,) the goods, or a sufficient amount to pay the duties, are required to be sold at auction, after an appraisement by the general appraisers. If the owner does not claim the residue, they are to be redeposited, and disposed of under the 13th section of the same act, the provisions of which I shall explain. The time of advertising before a sale is prescribed by the Treasury Department, and has been fixed at thirty days, as under the act of 1799.

Such is the warehouse system, if it can be so called, existing under the 12th section of the act of the 30th of

August, 1842; and it will be perceived that it differs from that established by the act of 1799 in many essential particulars.

1. By the act of 1842, the maximum time during which goods are allowed to remain in store before a sale to realize the duties is reduced from nine months to sixty or ninety days.

2. Under the act of 1799, the appraisement was required to be made by two or more reputable merchants. Under the 12th section of the act of 1842, no special appraisers are named, and it is, therefore, construed to intend the general appraisers, — the official persons appointed under the general law. The appraisement is accordingly made by them.

3. Under the act of 1799, all the goods were to be sold at the end of nine months. Under the 12th section of the act of 1842, only a sufficient quantity is to be sold, at the end of sixty or ninety days, to pay the duties, charges, and interest.

4. Under the 56th section of the act of 1799, the overplus of the proceeds of the sale, after paying the duties and charges, was to be paid into the treasury of the United States, for the use of the owner. Under the 12th section of the act of 1842, the residue of the goods, after selling a sufficient quantity to pay duties, interest, and charges, is to be delivered to the owner, if claimed by him; or if not claimed, to be redeposited in store.

5. The act of 1799 required an inventory and appraisement of the goods before a sale. The act of 1842 requires, in addition, that distinct and printed catalogues descriptive of the goods, with the appraised value annexed, shall be distributed among the persons present at the sale, and a reasonable opportunity given to purchasers to inspect the quality of the goods. These additional requirements are of great importance. Under the old system, these sales were ordinarily mere package sales. The officers of the

customs and persons in their confidence might know all about the goods to be sold, while the purchasers could know very little about them, thus opening a wide door to collusion and fraud.

There are other differences of minor importance not necessary to be specified.

The 13th section of the act of 30th August, 1842, differs materially from the 12th, and is, in its general provisions, more analogous to the 56th section of the act of 1799. The appraisement is required to be made by two or more respectable merchants, and all the goods are required to be sold. This section, at first glance, appears to have been specially framed for the purpose of finally disposing of all unclaimed goods, in whatever manner they may have found their way into the public stores; but, by a construction of the Treasury Department of the 11th July, 1845, it is decided to embrace only such goods as are redeposited in store under the preceding section, after a partial sale to realize the duties, or such as are liable for charges of storage, &c. The time during which goods may remain in store under this section is fixed by the 56th section of the act of 1799, which is in this respect unrepealed, and the sales accordingly take place once in nine months.

In all cases, both under the acts of 1799 and 1842, there is a provision for the speedy sale of perishable goods: a provision equally important to the government, in order that the duties may be realized before the goods become worthless, and to the owner, who may not always know that his goods are in store, and who might, without such a provision, lose their entire value.

I have thus stated the provisions of existing laws in relation to the storage and final disposal of imported goods in all cases of a failure or neglect to pay the duties chargeable on them, and of goods unclaimed by the owners within the time limited for retaining them in store. A comparison of the act of 1799, in respect to the storage of goods, with the act of 1842, will show the latter to be much more stringent in its provisions. It diminishes the time during which the goods are allowed to remain in store from nine months to sixty and ninety days, and it exacts interest on the duties from the date of the entry of the goods on which they are chargeable.

The tariff act of 1842 introduced the most thorough revolution in this department of the revenue system of the United States which has been known since the foundation of the government, by abandoning the old plan of giving credit for duties, and requiring them to be paid in cash for the largest as well as the smallest sums. The old system gave a credit for duties, without exacting interest during the period for which the credit was granted. Under the act of 1842, if there is a failure or an omission to pay the duties on imported merchandise on the completion of the entry, interest is charged from the day the duties accrue, and the importer pays it with the duties when he claims the goods; or if, in default of voluntary payment by the importer, a sale takes place, the interest is added to the duties, and the amount, together with the charges for storage, &c., is realized from the proceeds of the sale.

I desire to say here, Mr. President, to avoid misapprehension, that I am aware of the provision in the tariff act of 1833, or the Compromise act, as it is called, requiring duties to be paid in ready money; but this provision did not go into effect until the 1st of July, 1842; and by the same act all duties were reduced to twenty per cent. on the same day, while the more liberal provisions of the act of 1799, in respect to the storage of goods, if I am not mistaken, remained in force. I also desire to say that I have not overlooked the partial provision in the act of 1832, requiring duties on woollens to be paid in cash, or, if stored, exacting interest on the duties.

The introduction of cash payments for duties, though I

believe it is generally conceded to have operated favorably as far as the Government is concerned, so much so that few, if any, are desirous of disturbing it, at least by reinstating the old system of credits, bears heavily on the mercantile interest in comparison with the latter. The forbearance of payment by the Government was, in practice, equivalent to a cash capital for the merchant to the amount of the duties during the time for which the credit or forbearance of payment was granted. It was, unquestionably, a valuable mercantile facility for those who had the benefit of it, and the discretion to employ it judiciously. But it had its public inconveniences, and it was very properly abolished. It was, however, foreseen and foretold at the time the change was made, that great hardship would be likely to result from it, unless provision was made for storing goods for a limited period, and forbearing during that period to exact the payment of the duties. But it is a singular fact, and one which is not easily to be accounted for on any principle of public utility or convenience, that, when the extraordinary and violent transition took place from credits to cash payments, the maximum time during which merchandise was allowed to remain in store, before a sale to realize the duties, instead of being enlarged, as one would suppose it should have been, or at least continued as it then existed, was actually reduced, as has been seen, from nine months to one third of that period, and for most merchandise to a still shorter time. The change took place, too, at the very moment when the rates of duty were enormously increased on a large class of imports from twenty per cent., the maximum under the Compromise act of 1833. The stringent measure of cash payment was rendered more stringent by a simultaneous increase of the rates of duty, and by depriving the importer, to a great extent, of the facility of placing his goods in store, if the importation should find him unprepared to pay the duties in cash. This privilege, which, under the system of credits, was of no great practical benefit in extensive operations, would, under the system of cash payments, have been a facility of considerable value to importers of moderate means, and would have enabled them to contend, in a limited field at least, with large capitalists, who, if general opinion be true, have now engrossed, in a great measure, the business of importation, and will continue to do so, under existing laws, from their ability to furnish readily the means of meeting the payment of duties in cash on large cargoes. Still, if the time allowed for merchandise to remain in store under the act of 1799 had not been diminished, it would have been too limited to accomplish all the objects anticipated from a warehousing system, especially so far as such a system may lead to the storage of goods for exportation.

I will now state wherein the bill before the Senate proposes to amend existing laws, pointing out as I proceed in what respects it will change the practical operation of the present system; and I shall conclude by a brief summary of the advantages expected to result from it. I have already said that the bill is, with the exception of a few amendments, a transcript of the 12th and 13th sections of the act of 30th August, 1842; and in stating and explaining the amendments, I shall cover all the ground which is new.

The first amendment proposed is, to allow goods to remain in store for a period not less than two, nor more than three years, as Congress may determine, instead of sixty and ninety days, with the privilege of withdrawing them at any time during that period on the payment of duties and charges. This amendment embraces two new provisions: 1st, an extension of the time during which goods are permitted to remain in store; and, 2d, a remission of the interest now exacted on the duties from the date of the entry to the time of withdrawing from the public stores the merchandise on which they are charged. These provisions are so distinct in character that it will be necessary to consider them separately.

1. *As to the extension of time.* — The Senate will perceive that the number of years during which the bill proposes to allow goods to remain in store is left in blank. I will, at a proper time, move to fill the blank with three years, though I am not authorized to say that I shall be sustained in this motion by the judgment of the committee. There are, in my view of the subject, some strong considerations in favor of selecting that period of time. It is the period fixed by the British system, which has been in successful operation for more than forty years; and it may be reasonably supposed that, after so full a trial, it has been selected from considerations of its convenience for commercial purposes. But it is not for this reason alone. The term of three years is the period during which imported goods may, under existing laws, be entered for exportation with the privilege of drawback; and the term thus fixed in one case would seem to indicate a proper limitation in the other; especially as storing goods for exportation will, in all probability, become a very important and extensive branch of business, if this bill should become a law. Should the Senate be of the opinion that the term of three years is too long, and that a shorter period is dictated by any urgent considerations of public convenience or utility, I can only say that I shall submit cheerfully to its better judgment, but with the strong hope that a less time than two years will not be thought of, as I am fully persuaded that it is the least which would be sufficient to accomplish effectually the objects in view. Commercial and financial reactions are not supposed ordinarily to run their course in much less time; and if that period is allowed for goods to remain in store, the owner will be able to avoid the inconvenience and loss on the one hand of reëxporting them unnecessarily, and, on the other, the sacrifice of throwing them upon the domestic market when the demand is limited, or the ability to purchase impaired by derangements in the pecuniary or mercantile transactions of the country.

2. *As to the remission of the interest.* — Interest is now exacted on the duties from the date of the entry of the merchandise on which they are charged to the time when the duties are paid. The proposed amendment proceeds upon the principle of requiring the owner or importer of foreign merchandise to pay the impost when the merchandise is wanted for consumption. If he pays the duties on the entry, and is compelled to keep the goods on hand because he cannot sell them advantageously or without loss, the government has the use of the money paid for the duties, though the merchandise has not been used for the benefit of the owner, while the latter is also paying or losing interest on the amount of the duties he has advanced to the government. In like manner, if a merchant imports goods, pays duties on the entry, and is compelled to keep the goods on hand, they become constantly enhanced in cost, not only by an accumulation of interest on the purchase-money, but of interest on the duties. Cases of this description are undoubtedly of frequent occurrence; and I advert to them for the purpose of showing the injustice, the illiberality, not only of exacting the payment of duties before the merchandise on which they are chargeable is required for consumption, or before the importer can make any advantageous use of it, but of exacting interest on the duties also. The government, by so doing, derives a profit from the merchant without any corresponding benefit to the latter. Under the system of credits, coeval with the foundation of the government, the merchant was allowed to take his goods into his own possession, by giving security for the payment of the duties, without interest, at a future day; and during the period allowed for the credit to run he could always dispose at least of a sufficient amount of the goods to meet the payment of his bonds. It was, as I have already said, a most valuable pecuniary facility to the mercantile community, though having an inherent tendency to run into excess, and to stimulate and extend injuriously the operations of

business. The remission of interest on the duties, from the entry of goods to the time when the duties are paid, does not, strictly speaking, extend a facility to the importer or merchant. It merely abstains from imposing a burden, — from exacting what is unreasonable and unjust, — a profit to the government without any corresponding advantage to him. It allows him to take his goods from the public stores when he wants them, by paying the charges of storage, &c., and the duties, without exacting interest on the latter for the period the goods have been in store. The principle seems so obviously just that I will not pursue the argument further.

It may be proper to add, however, that the system of cash payments proceeds upon the principle of requiring the importer to pay the duties when the merchandise goes into his possession; and this is the only material point in which it differs from the old system of credits. The non-exaction of interest on the duties does not affect this principle. Imported goods, as long as they are deposited in store, are a security to the government for the payment of the duties chargeable on them. The payment of the impost is exacted when the goods are withdrawn, and go into the importer's possession; and thus the great principle on which the system of cash payments proceeds is preserved inviolate.

The observations I have made are confined to the policy of extending the period of time during which goods are allowed to remain in the public stores, without calling for the payment of duties, and of allowing them to be withdrawn for consumption, or domestic use, on paying the charges and the duties without interest. These points embrace the whole of the first proposed amendment.

I proceed now to the second amendment, which is to allow goods at any time during the period limited for keeping them in store to be taken out for reëxportation on the payment of all charges. This amendment is a substitute for that part of the existing revenue system which exacts two and a half per cent. on the amount of the duties paid by the owner of the merchandise when he imports it, and refunded to him when it is reëxported. The government, in other words, in refunding the duties to the importer, retains two and a half per cent. of the amount for its own use. The amount retained was originally one per cent., as may be seen by a reference to section thirty-one of the act of 31st July, 1789, and section fifty-seven of the act of the 4th August, 1790. An addition of one quarter per cent. was made by the act of March 19, 1798, as a substitute for certain stamp-duties on debentures, which were repealed by the same act; and by the act of 30th May, 1800, an addition of two and a half per cent. was made for the same purpose; so that the amount retained was at one time three and three quarters per cent. But these provisions were all superseded by the tariff act of 1816, which reduced the deduction to two and a half per cent. In 1829 all deduction was abandoned; and from that time until 1842, the whole amount of the duties paid on the importation of foreign merchandise was refunded on its exportation. But now, by the 15th section of the act of 30th August, 1842, the amount of the deduction is fixed at two and a half per cent., except in the reëxportation of foreign refined sugars, in which case the amount retained is ten per cent. on the duties paid. The amount thus deducted by the United States in paying back the duties received on foreign merchandise in case of its reëxportation was originally, as is perceived, very small (but one per cent.); and the two second acts to which I have referred — adding two per cent. and three quarters to the amount as a substitute for stamp-duties on debentures — show that the object was to indemnify the government for the inconvenience and expense to which it was subjected. But the object is directly or indirectly shown by all the early laws as well as the early reports in respect to the revenue system.

Under existing laws there is no very perceptible want of equity in this exaction, for the reason that it does not take the form of a direct payment to the government. But under the proposed bill, and with the extension of the period allowed for keeping goods in store, the exaction of a payment equal to the same proportion of the amount of duties chargeable on them in all cases, without reference to the time during which the goods have been stored, would be illiberal and impolitic. The exaction was not designed as a source of revenue to the government, much less as a discouragement to the reëxportation of imported goods. Its purpose was what I have stated, to indemnify the government for the inconvenience and expense of administering the system of debentures. Under any other view of the subject it could only be considered as an unreasonable imposition on commerce, and especially that branch of commerce in which the country is so deeply concerned — the carrying trade.

The bill under consideration proposes to lay aside this exaction entirely, returning to the more liberal provisions of former laws; and, as a substitute for it, to require only the payment of the actual charges and expenses incurred while the goods are stored. By this provision, the interest of the government will be fully protected, and the charges paid by the importer will bear a just proportion to the time he has enjoyed the benefit of the legal provision under which his goods have been held in store. Under the proposed system, the exaction, if it were continued, would become a mere premium paid to the government for the privilege of exporting foreign merchandise for which there was no demand at home.

If the exaction were, as it now is, in the shape of a deduction by the government from duties actually paid, its true character would be less apparent than when the exaction takes the form of an actual payment by the importer on an estimated amount of duties which the government has never received. The last case would always occur under the proposed system, if it should be adopted, as the goods would lie in store without any payment of duties; and, in case of reëxportation, it would be necessary to assume as a basis the amount of the duties which the merchandise would have paid if it had been entered for domestic consumption, and to exact from the owner the payment of a given proportion of that amount as a charge for the privilege of reëxporting it. Such a charge is deemed an illiberal imposition on commerce; and the bill therefore proposes to allow merchandise, during the time it is permitted to remain in store, to be withdrawn for exportation, under the existing legal provisions in respect to drawbacks, upon a payment of actual expenses, including the customary charge for storage.

The third amendment is one on which only a single remark is necessary. The 12th section of the act of 1842 provides for a sale of such quantities of the goods deposited in store as shall be necessary to pay the duties, and directs the goods unsold to be restored; and if unclaimed for nine months, they are liable to be sold for storage, under section thirteen of the same act, after the expiration of that period. The proposed amendment, for obvious reasons, contemplates one sale of all the goods at the expiration of the period allowed for keeping them in store, and adopts the requirements of section thirteen in respect to the formalities of the sale, and the payment of the surplus of the proceeds into the treasury of the United States for the use of the owner. The propriety of making a final disposition by sale of all goods which have been stored for the term of two or three years, in case this period shall be fixed, is too manifest to need illustration.

Another provision, which is entirely new, requires a passing notice. Perishable goods are required to be sold forthwith, as under existing laws; but with them are classed, for the purpose of an immediate sale, gunpowder, fire-crackers, and explosive substances. The danger in large cities from the accumulation of such substances, especially when deposited in the same stores with property of great value, is of such a nature as to demand some effectual preventive. They are not imported in large quantities; and there will be no individual hardship, in the few instances in which a compulsory sale is likely to take place, at all comparable with the risk which would be incurred by the public in admitting them to the benefit of the warehouse system.

I believe I have now stated the general provisions of the proposed bill, and pointed out the amendments it makes in existing laws. They may be briefly summed up thus: —

1. Merchandise may be deposited, and remain in store two or three years, instead of sixty or ninety days, before selling it for the purpose of realizing the duties.

2. Merchandise may be withdrawn from store, at any time during the two or three years, for domestic use or consumption, on the payment of charges and duties, without exacting interest on the latter from the date of the entry.

3. Merchandise may be entered for exportation at any time during the two or three years, on the payment of actual charges and expenses.

These are the leading provisions of the bill. It has been a ruling consideration in framing it to divest it of all complexity. It has been thought proper to put it in the most simple form possible, and to rely mainly for carrying into effect the new provisions it contains on regulations to be framed by the Treasury Department. These may be accommodated to unforeseen circumstances, and exigencies may thus be met which might be without a remedy for a time, if all the details of the plan were at the outset to be regulated by legal enactments. The Secretary of the Treasury is, therefore, authorized to make such regulations, not inconsistent with the laws of the United States, as may be necessary to give full effect to the provisions of the act. As the plan is tried, and its defects or its benefits become fully disclosed, the details may be all placed upon the permanent footing of legal regulation. It is believed that the course suggested will be deemed reconcilable with the most scrupulous considerations of prudence, when it is remembered that there is little in the plan which is absolutely new, or which may not be accomplished by a mere extension or a broader application of existing provisions of law.

I shall now detain the Senate but a moment, in stating some of the principal benefits anticipated from the changes proposed in the existing revenue system.

The first and greatest benefit to the commercial interest is the relief it will afford from the present system of exacting the payment of duties in cash, on the completion of the entry of merchandise. In one sense it may be contended, when compared with the present system, that it is an extension of a credit to the importer for the duties until he can effect a sale of his goods. Strictly speaking, it is but abstaining from an unreasonable exaction; and it is divested of all risk to the public, as the goods will never be permitted to go into the possession of the owner until the duties are paid. It will relieve him from the great hardship, which is common under the present system, of being forced to sell a portion of his goods, and sometimes in an overstocked market, for the purpose of raising the money to pay the duties. It will enable him to pay the duties as he has the opportunity of disposing of his goods for consumption, instead of being compelled to borrow money, or sell his merchandise at a loss, to raise it; and it will enable men of moderate means to enter into competition with large capitalists, who, as I have already said, monopolize to a great extent the business of importation, through their ability to command money to meet the payment of duties in cash. The proposed change is entirely consistent with the principle and the object of cash payments; and by preventing forced sales of goods to raise money for the payment of duties, it will often avoid an overstock of the domestic market with foreign merchandise, to the prejudice of the importer, by compelling him to sacrifice his property, and of the producer of domestic goods of like character, by depressing prices. If we consider also that it will be likely to enlarge the circle of competition in the business of importation, — not to augment the aggregate amount of imports for consumption, but to divide it among a greater number of persons, — it will not be difficult to perceive that the mercantile interest must be greatly benefited by the change.

The second benefit, though perhaps not second in importance, to be anticipated from the proposed measure, is the stimulus it will be likely to give to the carrying trade, by making our ports of entry *entrepôts* for the productions of all countries. Under the present system, if imported merchandise is entered for exportation, the duties are not refunded until after the exportation has actually taken place. Thus, if an importer, having brought merchandise into the country for the domestic market, and having paid the duties, finds at the end of one, two, or three years no demand for it at home, and is compelled to reëxport it, he will have lost during that period the use of the money he has paid for the duties, and he is taxed in addition two and a half per cent. on the whole amount so paid as a premium to the government for the privilege of sending his goods to a foreign market. No better scheme could be devised either to glut the domestic market by forcing the importer to throw his merchandise into it at any price it will command, or, on the other, to discourage navigation by taxing the reëxportation of foreign merchandise which is not wanted at home. Under the proposed plan, foreign merchandise will be allowed to be freely deposited in store, and to be reëxported as freely, with no other imposition than the payment of actual expenses of storage, &c. One of the certain consequences of such a system must be to accumulate in our maritime towns a variety of the products of other countries, where our vessels can make up assorted cargoes for foreign markets. This facility has led to the deposit in British ports of merchandise designed for reshipment to the southern portions of this continent, and, indeed, to all quarters of the globe. The value of foreign merchandise deposited in the warehouses of Great Britain is estimated at two hundred and fifty millions of dollars. The proposed plan would have the same result here, if like effects are to be expected from like causes. The deposit of even a considerable portion of such a quantity in value, made up, as much of it doubtless would be, of goods suitable to the South American and Pacific markets, could not fail to benefit and extend our navigating interest, — one of the most valuable in peace, and the most important of all others to so commercial a community as the United States as a means of defence in war. That our carrying trade would be vastly increased; that shipbuilding would be stimulated; that many foreign markets would be supplied, wholly or in part, by us with merchandise now furnished from the warehouses of Europe; that the industry of our seaports would be put in greater activity; that the commercial transactions of the country would be facilitated; and that a healthier competition would be created in the business of importation, can hardly be doubted. Such, at least, is the opinion of the mercantile community; and so believing, it is natural that they should look with great interest to the concurrence of the Senate in a measure which appears to them so intimately connected with the prosperity of the country.

And finally, Mr. President, if uniform prices and steady markets are, as we are taught to believe, advantageous to the producing classes, the manufacturing interest, next to the commercial, is likely to be most benefited by the proposed measure, through supplies of merchandise near at hand, ready to meet sudden and unusual demands, thus preventing a transient scarcity from becoming the basis of speculation, and furnishing an additional safeguard against those derangements which are always the most injurious to steady industry.

Mr. Dix then proceeded to suggest and explain certain amendments to the bill, which he intended to propose at a future stage of the discussion.

II.

AFTER the preceding explanatory speech, Mr. Huntington, of Connecticut, spoke at length in opposition to the bill, although his speech was never published except in the form of an outline. The following speech in reply was delivered by Mr. DIX on the 9th July, 1846.

MR. PRESIDENT: It was my intention to reply to the Senator from Connecticut[1] on the day after he addressed the Senate; but I have been prevented by a variety of circumstances over which I could exercise no control. With the lapse of time which has intervened, (now more than a week,) his remarks have lost something of their freshness; and I may not be able to follow his argument as closely as I might have done if I could have had an opportunity to respond at an earlier day,—especially as I have been, for a considerable portion of the intervening time, absent from the city, and in no condition to examine his arguments. It would now be in vain, if I were to undertake to follow him from the beginning to the end of his able and well-considered speech. I shall not attempt it. But I desire so far to tax the indulgence of the Senate as to notice the objections he has made to the details of the bill under consideration, to examine a few of his leading arguments against the general policy of the measure, and to point out what I consider grave misapprehensions with regard to certain commercial facts which have an essential connection with the subject.

His objections to the details of the bill came first in the course of his argument, and I shall take them up in the order in which they were presented to the Senate.

But I desire to notice, in the first place, a preliminary remark of the Senator. He did me the honor to say that

[1] Mr. Huntington.

he considered me capable of drawing this bill, — a compliment for which I beg him to accept my thanks, though I did think he took from it much of its value when he added that, in his opinion, such a bill ought not to receive the sanction of the Senate. He said, also, that he considered me capable of drawing a bill on any subject: in this he conceded to me entirely too much merit. And he concluded by saying that, if he had not felt this assurance, he would have supposed the bill, from his view of its probable operation, to have been drawn by some large capitalist, or the factor of some foreign manufacturer. Now, I beg to assure my honorable friend from Connecticut that no person of the description referred to by him had any agency in the matter. The person to whom I was principally indebted for suggestions in respect to it, before it was prepared for presentation to the Senate, was one of those "regular dealers" in New York, who, according to the Senator, have no interest in a warehouse system, — who neither desire nor can afford to use it, — a gentleman of intelligence and information, and who is now a member of the convention engaged in revising the constitution of the State. But I can assure the Senator that the gentleman to whom I allude deems the measure of the utmost importance to those who, under the present system, have not the means of entering into competition with large capitalists, and believes that it will have a salutary influence upon the commercial prosperity of the country.

I proceed now to notice the objections the Senator has taken to the details of the bill: —

1. The first objection, as I understood it, was, that in depositing merchandise in store no invoice was required, no appraisement was necessary, nothing, indeed, to show the nature of the merchandise, or the amount of the duties chargeable on it. If the Senator will refer to the amendments I have proposed, he will see that all these objects are effectually accomplished. The importer of foreign merchandise is required "to make entry" for warehousing it, "in

such form, and supported by such proof, as shall be prescribed by the Secretary of the Treasury." To make entry of merchandise has a specific and well-known meaning in the operations of the custom-house. It involves the necessity of an invoice, and a compliance with a variety of well-digested forms. Nor is this all. Another amendment provides that the duties and the charges on merchandise deposited in store shall be ascertained "on due entry thereof." The duties cannot be ascertained without weighing, gauging, measuring, or appraising the merchandise. Thus it will be seen that a compliance with all the forms of proceeding which are required in the payment of the duties on the entry of merchandise is to be rigidly exacted when it is deposited in store.

2. The next objection is, that if goods are burnt while in store, the government will lose the duties. Now, sir, I ask if the government should exact duties in such a case? Is it not enough that the importer or owner should lose his merchandise? Have not the duties usually been remitted in such cases? I suppose this to have been the practice; and certainly it is opposed to every principle of liberality, and even of fairness, to exact duties on merchandise which has never come into the home market for domestic consumption.

3. The Senator says, if merchandise deteriorates while in store, the government will lose the whole amount, or at least a portion of the duties, and that they will be calculated on the reduced value. In this he is entirely mistaken. The duties, as I have already said, are to be ascertained on the entry for warehousing the merchandise. They will be calculated on its full value; and if it becomes perishable, the officers of the customs will cause it to be sold forthwith under the provision relating to perishable goods, and thus realize the duties before the merchandise becomes worthless.

4. The Senator is of the opinion, that, under the provisions of this bill, merchandise may be taken out of store

and reëxported in any quantity, however small. The bill is not so intended, nor do I think it can properly receive such a construction. If he will look at the twenty-ninth line, he will see that a compliance with the requirements of existing laws, in relation to the exportation of merchandise with the benefit of drawback, is necessary. It must, therefore, be exported in the original packages. But if there is any doubt on this subject, a verbal amendment will be all that is required to remove the objection.

5. With regard to the necessity of a bond to pay the duties, there is good ground for a difference of opinion. It is to be remembered that the goods are to be in the possession of the collector, or, in other words, in the possession of the government. They are a perfect security for the payment of the duties. Why, then, exact a bond? If it be thought expedient, there certainly can be no valid objection. Under the British system no bond is required, if the goods are deposited in the public stores, and are in the possession of the Crown. When the goods are deposited in warehouses belonging to individuals or companies, a bond is required, not usually from the owner of the goods, but a general bond from the owner of the warehouse, stipulating that the goods deposited with him shall be exported, or the duties paid in full.

6. With regard to the danger of a clandestine removal of goods, — another objection urged against the bill, — the answer is, that the danger must be very slight, as the goods will be, as those now deposited in store are, in possession of the custom-house officers. There is, I believe, no provision by law now for the punishment of such offences. But if experience shall show the necessity of such a provision, it can at any time be made. Indeed, I will not object to such an amendment of the bill, if it be thought advisable.

7. With regard to the provision exonerating the master of a vessel from all claim of the owner of merchandise, which has been sold by the collector for the non-payment

of the duties, I will only say that it is copied verbatim from the tariff act of 1842, that it is in constant practice, and no difficulty is known to have resulted from it.

8. It is also objected that if goods are once withdrawn from the public stores, and the duties paid, they can never afterwards be reëxported, or, in other words, that foreign goods can only be reëxported from the stores. Sir, this is an entire misapprehension. All the laws relating to debentures will be left in full force. If an importer or owner of merchandise deposited in store withdraws it, and pays the duties, he may at any time, within the period allowed by law, reëxport it with the benefit of drawback. The existing provisions of law will, in this respect, remain untouched. But in case of reëxportation under such circumstances, a deduction of two and a half per cent. will be made on refunding the duties.

9. It is said, also, that goods may be withdrawn in the smallest quantity for home consumption, and that the public stores will become mere retail shops. It is certainly very unlikely that any such result will follow. No merchandise can be withdrawn without a permit from the collector, and this permit must be paid for. The inconvenience and expense will, in ordinary cases, constitute sufficient obstacles to the withdrawal of minute quantities of merchandise. But if gentlemen think it material, the objection can readily be removed by a proviso that no merchandise shall be withdrawn from store in less quantities than in an entire package, bale, box, or cask.

These, as I understand them, are the objections made to the details of the bill; and I am sure it will afford the Senator pleasure to find, on a more critical examination of the subject, that there is not one of them which is not either groundless, or which may not be removed by the most simple amendment.

I will only say, in conclusion, in respect to the details of the bill, that it has been subjected to the rigid scrutiny of some of the most intelligent individuals in the revenue service, — some now in commission, and others who have become familiar with the operations of the system, through long experience in prominent situations. All these gentlemen concur in the opinion that it will be adequate to the objects it has in view, and that it is sufficiently guarded against abuse. But should experience point out necessary changes, it will always be easy to make them.

I come now, Mr. President, to a portion of the Senator's remarks which will require a somewhat extended and critical examination. When this bill was first called up for consideration, I alluded incidentally, in my explanation of its provisions, to the British warehouse system, and to the influence it had exerted upon the commercial prosperity of Great Britain. I did not say, nor did I intend to intimate, that the plan proposed by the bill under consideration was copied, in any degree, from the British system. On the contrary, I had, throughout my remarks, kept steadily in view the idea that it was founded upon our own laws regulating the deposit of merchandise in the public stores, and that the objects it had in view were to be accomplished by an enlargement and more extended application of the provisions of those laws. In his reply, the Senator referred to the British system, comparing the plan proposed by the bill under consideration with it, and in his references to the operation of the former he came to conclusions to which I cannot yield my assent.

I have no printed report of the Senator's remarks, and, speaking from very hasty and brief notes of his topics, I may inadvertently misstate him. I trust I shall not; but if I do, I beg him to be assured that no one will regret it so much as myself.

I understood one of his first remarks, in relation to the British warehouse system, to be, that it was designed to extend the commerce of Great Britain, and to depress the trade and shipping of other countries. I cannot concur with him in all respects, though not differing with him entirely as to its design; and I shall endeavor to show that its effect has not been to exclude foreign shipping from a participation in the commerce of the British empire.

Its design, as I have always understood, was chiefly to remove great commercial inconveniences, arising from the necessity of paying duties in cash on the entry of merchandise. These inconveniences are stated by McCulloch to have been: —

"1. That the merchant, in order to raise funds to pay the duties, was frequently reduced to the necessity of selling his goods immediately on their arrival, when, perhaps, the market was glutted.

"2. That the duties having to be paid all at once, and not by degrees, as the goods were sold for consumption, their price was raised by the amount of the profit on the capital advanced in payment of the duties.

"3. That competition was diminished in consequence of the greater command of funds required to carry on trade under such disadvantages; and a few rich individuals were enabled to monopolize the importation of those commodities on which duties were payable.

"4. That the system of paying cash on the entry of merchandise had an obvious tendency to discourage the carrying trade.

"5. That it prevented the country from becoming an *entrepôt* for foreign products; and hindered the importation of such as were not immediately wanted for home consumption, and thus tended to lessen the resort of foreigners to the markets of Great Britain, inasmuch as it became difficult, or rather impossible, for them to complete an assorted cargo."

These are the reasons assigned by McCulloch for establishing the system; and it is curious to observe how closely this enumeration of inconveniences describes those under which our own commerce labors.

In the "Yearly Journal of Trade" for 1845, — a work which has been published for twenty-three years, and which, I believe, may be safely referred to as authority in matters touching the commercial system of Great Britain, — I find the following passages in some preliminary remarks in relation to warehousing: —

"Antecedently to the present century, a system of restraint and prohibition pervaded the administration of our maritime and revenue affairs, producing inconvenience to the merchant and detriment to commerce. Much of such inconvenience arose from the circumstance of the import duties being required to be paid on the landing of goods, amounting frequently to many thousand pounds. Such was more particularly the case during the late war, when the usual regularity of commercial transactions was much interrupted, and the merchant, at times, called upon on the unexpected arrival of a ship for a large advance of duties. This gave rise to a system of deferring payment, by allowing goods to be secured in warehouses or other approved places under the locks of the crown, and to be taken out as might suit the convenience of parties, the payment not being called for until the goods were taken out. Hence, in 1803, the establishment of the general warehousing system."

"The principle upon which the warehousing act was founded was, that goods, upon being taken out, either for home consumption, for exportation, or removal coastwise, should be subject to the like conditions as when first imported. This was then deemed a prodigious boon; such it unquestionably was."

Such was the design of the system. It had no direct connection with any consideration of policy in respect to the trade or shipping of foreigners. It was a matter purely of domestic interest, framed exclusively for the benefit of the commerce of Great Britain, — not to depress the commerce of other countries. Indeed, by referring to her statutes, it will be seen that foreign vessels are permitted to carry into her ports, and to warehouse for exportation, articles prohibited to be introduced into the kingdom for home use.

Its effect has not been to discourage the participation of foreign shipping in the commercial intercourse of Great Britain with other nations. On the contrary, foreign tonnage enters to a very remarkable extent into her foreign trade.

In connection with this subject I will proceed to state some of the principal modifications and relaxations of her ancient anti-commercial system, which have taken place within the last half-century. For this purpose I will again refer to the last-named work, in which the changes are better and much more briefly stated than they would be if given in my own words: —

"The opening of the East India trade to private individuals stands foremost in the list of modern alterations in our commercial code. That this trade was almost exclusively confined to the East India Company since the year 1595, during the reign of Queen Elizabeth, is well known.

"The first general warehousing act was passed in 1803. The leading feature of the warehousing act is to defer the payment of duties formerly due to the king at the time of importation, and to allow goods to remain, under certain regulations, in warehouses, or other places, until it may suit the parties to remove them either for exportation or home consumption."

"In the year 1824, an entirely new principle was introduced into the economy of our foreign trade, and which affects in no slight degree the interests of some of our staple manufactures.

"This principle is to abolish, as far as practicable, the prohibitions on import and bounties on export.

"A system of reciprocity in our intercourse with foreign nations has been recently adopted. The ships of those kingdoms that choose to avail themselves of the advantages, may now enter British or Irish ports upon the same terms as ships of the United Kingdom; and, on the other hand, our vessels may enter into the harbors belonging to those foreign nations upon the same terms as if built and navigated by their own countrymen."

Among the most important of these changes are the privileges granted by the reciprocity treaties, to which the writer refers. I confess I was somewhat surprised, when I came to look into the subject, to see their number and the liberal nature of their stipulations. I find that Great Britain has arrangements with twenty-three independent States relating to the trade with the United Kingdom, and nineteen relating to the trade with her possessions abroad. Some of these arrangements rest upon treaties of a very liberal character, and others upon orders of council issued by virtue of a statute authorizing the sovereign to concede certain privileges in consideration of like concessions from the States to which they are granted. I will read to the Senate a few stipulations from two of the treaties, in order that the subject may be better understood.

From a convention of commerce and navigation with Sweden and Norway: —

"*Duties, &c.* — British vessels entering or departing from the ports of the kingdoms of Sweden and Norway, and Swedish and Norwegian vessels entering or departing from the ports of the United Kingdom of Great Britain and Ireland, shall not be subject to any other or higher ship-duties or charges than are or shall be levied on national vessels entering or departing from such ports respectively.

"*Vessels and Goods.* — All goods, whether the production of the kingdoms of Sweden and Norway, or of any other country, which may be legally imported from any of the ports of the said kingdoms into the United Kingdom of Great Britain and Ireland in British vessels, shall, in like manner, be permitted to be so imported directly in Swedish or Norwegian vessels; and all goods, whether the production of any of the dominions of his Britannic Majesty, or of any other country, which may be legally exported from the ports of the United Kingdom in British vessels, shall, in like manner, be permitted to be exported from the said ports in Swedish or Norwegian vessels. An exact reciprocity shall be observed," &c.

From a treaty of commerce and navigation with the Netherlands: —

"*Duties of Customs, Privileges, &c.* — No duty of customs or other impost shall be charged upon any goods, the produce of one country, upon importations by sea or by land from such country into the other, higher than the duty or impost charged upon goods of the same kind, the produce of, or imported from, any other country; and her Majesty the Queen of the United Kingdom of Great Britain and Ireland, and his Majesty the King of the Netherlands, do hereby bind and engage themselves not to grant any favor, privilege, or immunity, in matters of commerce and navigation, to the subject of any State which shall not be also, and at the same time, extended to the other subjects of the other high contracting party, gratuitously, if the concession in favor of that other State shall have been gratuitous; and, on giving, as nearly as possible, the same compensation or equivalent in case the concession shall have been conditional."

By referring to the "Yearly Journal of Trade," for 1845, page 45, it will be seen that Great Britain has reciprocity treaties with fifteen independent States, granting to each other, mutually, the "benefits of the most favored nation." The stipulations above quoted are, therefore, applicable to all the fifteen States.

What has been the result of these international commercial arrangements? It is one of which I must confess I was not apprised, though other Senators may be more familiar with the subject, and the statement may give them no surprise. In the year 1841, (I cannot find the returns of a later year,) the foreign shipping engaged in the commerce of Great Britain bore a greater proportion to her own tonnage than the foreign shipping engaged in the commerce of the United States in the year 1845 bore to our own tonnage. These details I shall give more at length at a subsequent stage of my remarks.

Great Britain has thus adopted the maxim, which it is to be hoped may become universal, — that national prosperity is to be sought for, not in unnecessary restrictions, not in commercial conventions framed with a view to obtain exclusive advantages by subtlety and address, but through the better and more enlightened policy of securing mutual privileges by a liberal application of the principle of reciprocity.

In the commercial intercourse of foreign nations with her colonial possessions, she still maintains, to some extent, a system of restriction. A vessel from any country may carry to her colonies a cargo, the produce of that country, and carry away from those colonies a cargo to any country not a British possession, but not from one British possession to another.

But it is time to return to the details of the British warehouse system. The Senator stated that it was a restricted system. I disagree with him. I shall prove it to be an exceedingly liberal system, not only in respect to the number of warehousing ports, but in respect to the articles allowed to be warehoused. It was established in 1803, on a very limited scale as to the favored articles, and for the port of London alone. It now embraces sixty-eight ports in England, twenty-three in Scotland, and eighteen in Ireland, — in all, 109. In most of the large ports, goods in general may be warehoused; in the smaller ports, particular goods only. London in the southeast, Bristol in the southwest, and Liverpool in the northwest, are privileged for all goods which may be legally imported; and Hull, in the northeast, for the same, with a single class of exceptions. These ports are admirably situated for distributing the products deposited with them to all portions of the kingdom. Stand at Leicester, which lies in the very centre of England, and draw a circle around you which shall pass through one of these ports, and it will touch or graze all the others. There is not a single point in England distant in an air line more than one hundred and fifty miles from some of these ports, excepting the Land's End in Cornwall, which may be two hundred from Bristol. The Senator from Connecticut, if I did not misunderstand him, represented these four ports as the only ones to which a liberal scale of privilege in respect to warehousing had been applied. Sir, my honorable friend is behind the age. He is about up to the era of George IV., or possibly the fourth William. I say it in no offensive sense. He will properly appreciate this disclaimer when I frankly acknowledge that a few days ago I was in the same predicament with him. I have fortunately fallen upon more recent information, and I am happy not only to have advanced myself, but to be able to bring him up with me to the point at which things now stand. Falmouth, in Cornwall, has been made a warehousing port for all goods, with the single exception of silks. Southampton, about midway from the Land's End to the Straits of Dover, is largely privileged. Manchester has recently been made, by act of Parliament, a warehousing town for consumption only. It is an inland place, as we all know, and therefore not fit for warehousing for exportation. I find in the list of warehousing ports twelve privileged for "all goods," with certain specified exceptions. In short, the system, as to ports, has been and is in a constant course of extension.

Let us now see, sir, what goods may be warehoused. On this point I regret to be at variance with the Senator from Connecticut. In looking into the British statutes, I find the number of absolute prohibitions extremely small. They are as follows, and may be seen by reference to 3 and 4 William IV. c. 52: —

1. Goods prohibited on account of the package in which they are contained, or the tonnage of the vessels in which they are laden; as cigars in packages of less than one hundred pounds, or in vessels of less than one hundred and twenty tons burden.

2. Gunpowder, arms, ammunition, or utensils of war.

3. Infected hides, skins, horns, hoofs, or any part of any cattle or beast.

4. Foreign playing-cards, without the name of the maker, &c.

5. Counterfeit coins or tokens.

6. Books first composed, or written, or printed, and published in the United Kingdom, and reprinted in any other country.

7. Copies of prints engraved, etched, drawn, or designed in the United Kingdom.

8. Copies of casts of sculptures, or models, first made in the United Kingdom.

9. Clocks or watches prohibited to be imported for home use.

All other articles prohibited for home use may be imported and warehoused for exportation, and in foreign vessels, except from British possessions.

The list of prohibitions has been diminished since the statute above referred to was enacted. A few years ago all goods from China were prohibited to be warehoused, unless imported in British ships. The China trade, since 1834, has been thrown open to individuals, excepting in the single article of tea. Now, it would appear that teas may be warehoused for exportation, though imported in foreign vessels and brought from any place.[1]

[1] See *Customs, Revenue Laws, and Regulations*, by Lowe, Sherlock, & Richards, p. 118.

We differ also as to the extent of the authority conferred on the commissioners of the treasury. The Senator said they had power to designate any article which they considerered as interfering with their domestic manufactures, and exclude it from the benefit of the warehouse system; and that the power was frequently exercised. He stated this on the authority of individuals whom he did not name. Now, I desire to ask him whether it is not due to this body, in the discussion of great questions of public policy, to state facts on grounds more definite, and better entitled to consideration, than the authority of individuals not even named; especially when these facts are matters of legal regulation, and may be ascertained by a reference to the statutes in which they are contained? Sir, I believe his informant to be entirely mistaken. The powers of the commissioners, in respect to the matter in issue, are contained in the following section of the act of 3 and 4 Will. IV. c. 57: —

"It shall be lawful for the commissioners of his Majesty's treasury, by their warrant, from time to time to appoint the ports in the United Kingdom which shall be warehousing ports for the purposes of this act; and it shall be lawful for the commissioners of customs, subject to the authority and direction of the commissioners of his Majesty's treasury, by their order, from time to time, to appoint in what warehouses or places of special security, or of ordinary security, as the case may require, in such ports, and in what different parts or divisions of such warehouses or places, and in what manner any goods, and what sorts of goods, may and may only be warehoused and kept and secured, without payment of any duty upon the first entry thereof, or for exportation only, in cases wherein the same may be prohibited to be imported for home use; and also in such order to direct in what cases (if any) security by bond, in manner hereinafter provided, shall be required in respect of any warehouse so appointed by them."

Many of the articles to be warehoused are fixed by law, as will be seen by reference to the schedules annexed to the statutes regulating the warehouse system. Over these I infer, though I may be in error, that the commissioners exercise no control. I find some of the ports selected by statute, — Manchester, for instance. Can the commissioners, by their order, close any port so selected against warehousing, or exclude from the warehouses in such port any article the law allows to be deposited in them? I cannot believe it. This would be to exercise a power beyond the law and subversive of it. But if it exists, I cannot find that it has been exercised. The true authority of the commissioners of the treasury, I apprehend, is to regulate, arrange, and control, within the legal limitations. They may enlarge the system by designating new ports; the commissioners of the customs, under their authority and direction, may carry out the details of these extended arrangements; and all such orders may be revoked. But it is only necessary to look into the history of the system, and compare different periods, to see that it has been in a course of regular extension, both as to ports and merchandise. On this point I will not further enlarge.

It has been stated, on the other side, that foreign manufactures intended for home consumption in Great Britain cannot be warehoused. I believe this to be a total misapprehension. It is admitted on all hands that foreign manufactures may be warehoused for exportation, and yet I can find no special authority to deposit them for that purpose. If they may be in the warehouses for exportation, they may be for consumption, unless there is a restriction.

I prove foreign manufactures to be in British warehouses, 1st, by the following regulation: —

> "It shall be lawful for the commissioners of customs to permit any stuffs or fabrics of silks, linen, cotton, or wool, or of any mixture of them with any other material, to be taken out of the warehouse to be cleaned, refreshed, dyed, stained, or calendered, or to be bleached or printed, without payment of duty of customs, under security, nevertheless, by bond to their satisfaction, that such goods shall be returned to the warehouse within the time that they shall appoint." — (3 *and* 4 *Will. IV. c.* 57, *s.* 35.)

This regulation obviously applies to foreign manufactures,

as a reference is made to the payment of "duty of customs."

2. On an application to the lords of the treasury, stating some objections to the existing mode of ascertaining the exact number of yards of "foreign woollen cloth warehoused in this country," the application was granted, so far as regards "such bales of woollen cloths as may be warehoused for exportation only."[1]

This order, which bears date in November, 1820, shows that foreign woollen cloths are warehoused; that some are warehoused for exportation only; and, as a necessary inference, some for home consumption.

3. Manufactures of silk, being the manufactures of Europe, may be imported into certain ports and warehoused generally, viz: London, Dublin, Dover, and Southampton. The same manufactures may be imported into other ports for exportation only. I refer to a work on the "Customs, Revenue Laws, and Regulations," published at Liverpool by Lowe, Sherlock, & Richards, officers of her Majesty's customs. The reference will be found at page 115, of the edition of 1842, under the head of "Notes on Importations," where an order of the commissioners of the treasury is cited. This reference shows that European silks may be warehoused both for exportation and consumption, though under certain restrictions as to ports, doubtless for the purpose of guarding against frauds on the revenue. No such restrictions are found in respect to cottons, woollens, linens, or iron. The inference is, that these articles come under the general regulation, and may be freely imported and deposited in store, either for exportation or consumption, at the option of the importer.

4. By referring to Ellis's "Laws and Regulations of the Customs," edition of 1843, vol. 3, page 299, table F, it will be seen that "all goods manufactured of silk," &c., are among the articles allowed to be warehoused. I find the

[1] *Yearly Journal of Trade,* 1845, p. 97.

same articles in the edition of 1842, and I infer that not only silks, but all other manufactured goods not specially excluded may be freely deposited either for consumption or exportation.

5. The same inference may be drawn from the statistical returns of the British empire. I give some details for the year 1836, excepting those relating to silks, which are for the year 1841: —

	Imported.	Exported.	Retained for consumption.
Cotton manufactures·······	£698,253	£556,117	£89,916
Bar-iron ·················	25,034	4,762	18,921
Wool manufactures········	139,796	11,721	128,075
Silk manufactures of Europe	286,747		239,582
Silk manufactures of India ·	526,812		100,505
	£1,676,642	£572,600	£576,999
	$8,383,710		$2,884,995

It is not perceived how these returns can be fully made out without reference to the warehouse operations of the kingdom. They show that foreign manufactures are not excluded, but that they actually enter into the consumption of the country. The duties, indeed, on most articles are quite low, as may be seen by reference to the British tariff. If they are imported in small quantities, it is because they are excluded by the domestic competition in her own fabrics.

It has been stated, also, that on depositing goods in the British warehouses the owner is required to declare whether he deposits them for consumption or exportation, and that the goods are governed by this declaration. Sir, my investigations have led me to an entirely different conclusion. I find no such restriction, except in a special case, which confirms my inference as to the general rule. I proceed to state the result of my examinations. No declaration is required when merchandise is warehoused, whether it is for exportation or home consumption, unless it is merchandise which cannot be imported for home use. In this case, the importer must declare that he enters it for exportation, and the package is marked "exportation." This seems to be the only case in which a declaration is required on warehousing merchandise. The proof is as follows:—

1. The law requires a declaration to be made in this special case. It requires none in any other case. The omission in general to require a declaration, and the exaction of one in the special case, are conclusive proof that none is required except in the special case.

2. The form of the bond, when a bond is required, seems to prove it. The condition of the bond is for the payment of the full duties of importation, or for the due exportation of the merchandise.[1]

3. It appears (see commissioner's order of 1834) that it is the practice in London, "where a part of the original importation has been exported, and a portion entered for home consumption," to charge the duty on a proportionate part, &c. This seems to show that when goods have been warehoused, a part may be exported and a part entered for home consumption. Though not conclusive, it raises the strongest possible presumption that no declaration is required on warehousing.[2]

4. No goods which have been warehoused can be taken out, "except upon due entry" "for exportation, or upon due entry and payment of the full duties payable thereon for home use." This shows that the election is made on withdrawing the goods from warehouse, and not on warehousing them.[3]

Sir, it is extremely unpleasant, to say nothing of the labor, to be compelled to go into this extended examination to show the erroneousness of statements made by gentlemen whose great respectability is vouched by the Senator from Connecticut,—statements made, according to their own representations, after careful inquiry. I will not assert that

[1] *Yearly Journal of Trade*, 1845, p. 259. [2] *Ibid.* p. 251. [3] *Ibid.*

they are wrong. I do not deal in assertions. I give only the result of my researches into the regulations of the system, citing my authorities and leaving to the better judgment of the Senate to correct my conclusions, if they are erroneous. I state the result thus: —

1. All goods of all descriptions, which may be legally imported into the kingdom, may be warehoused, except the enumerated articles before mentioned.

2. Goods prohibited to be imported for home use may be imported, even in foreign vessels, and warehoused for exportation.

3. All other goods, excepting those comprehended in the two foregoing classes, may be imported and warehoused, either for home consumption or exportation, without any declaration, at the time of the entry, whether they are intended for one or the other.

4. The goods which may be so warehoused without a declaration include foreign manufactures.

Such I understand to be the British warehouse system. I have stated the facts above presented on no authority of individuals. I do not regard such testimony as legitimate in the decision of questions of legal enactment or regulation. I have sought for my authority in the laws and statistics of the British empire. If I have misunderstood them, it has been from putting an erroneous construction on the data from which my conclusions are drawn, — data of the highest authenticity.[1]

The history of the warehouse system of Great Britain affords an instructive lesson of the power of prejudice, kept alive by the misrepresentations of interested classes, to defeat and delay the adoption of social improvements and reforms. In 1733, Sir Robert Walpole, a minister of great energy and intellectual power, undertook to introduce the system in

[1] These conclusions were drawn from the statute of the 3 and 4 William IV. It appears that the laws in relation to warehousing were consolidated in the year 1815; but no material alterations were made in them, — nothing to render necessary any modification of the views herein contained.

London on a very limited scale, and I believe in respect to a single article of importation, — tobacco. He was met by the furious opposition of the moneyed capitalists of England, who monopolized that branch of trade through their ability to command the means of paying the duties on the entry. They inflamed the populace by the grossest misrepresentations; the Parliament House was surrounded by mobs, the life of the minister was threatened, and he was compelled to submit to the humiliation of rising on the floor of Parliament and moving such a postponement as was equivalent to a defeat of the measure. It is curious to look back into the history of that period and see with what violence the scheme was denounced, and what baneful effects were predicted as certain to flow from it. I will read to the Senate a few extracts from Smollett's continuation of "Hume's History of England," to show to what extent the unscrupulousness of self-interest can go, and how successful it may be in carrying popular prejudice along with it. It was contended that it would be —

> "Destructive to trade, and dangerous to the liberties of the subject;" "that it would produce an additional swarm of excise officers and warehouse-keepers, appointed and paid by the treasury, so as to multiply the dependents on the Crown, and enable it still further to influence the freedom of elections; that the traders would become slaves to excisemen and warehouse-keepers, as they would be debarred all access to their commodities, except at certain hours, when attended by those officers; that the merchant, for every quantity of tobacco he should sell, would be obliged to make a journey, or send a messenger to the office for a permit, which could not be obtained without trouble, expense, and delay; and that, should a law be enacted in consequence of this motion, it would, in all probability, be, some time or other, used as a precedent for introducing excise laws into every branch of the revenue; in which case the liberty of Great Britain would be no more." — (Vol. V. p. 647.)

These representations prevailed, and the historian adds: —

> "The miscarriage of the bill was celebrated with public rejoicings in London and Westminster; and the minister was burned in effigy by the populace."

Such was the fate of this measure in 1733; and it was not until 1803 — seventy years afterwards — that a successful effort was made to establish it. It has now become the most important branch of the revenue system of Great Britain, facilitating and extending vastly the operations of her commerce. It has made her mercantile interest the most prosperous in the world; and yet it was through the blind and mistaken opposition of the merchants that its adoption was so long delayed.

I repeat, the history of this measure affords an instructive lesson. It is thus that interested classes — or, what is practically the same, classes fancying themselves interested — are sure to be found arrayed against the introduction of salutary reforms; successfully for a time, but overborne at last by the power of truth; never listening to reason and argument, always waiting to be vanquished; planting themselves before the car of improvement until they are in danger of being run over and crushed, and then hanging on behind in impotent attempts to stay its progress.

I now proceed to examine some objections raised by the Senator to the general policy of the measure. I understood him to say that the system of warehousing proposed by the bill would be maintained at the expense of the American importer, and for the benefit of the foreign importer or his consignee. I do not undertake to give his precise language. I state the proposition in general terms. In other words, it is contended that the privilege of storing goods in our seaports for domestic consumption or exportation, at the option of the importer, will have the effect of accumulating in those ports immense masses of foreign merchandise, which will be thrown into the market to the great injury of the domestic producer. But it seems to me that there is a ready and satisfactory answer to the objection. Whether goods are stored in the countries where they are produced, or in our own cities, is of no consequence so far as the question of competition with our domestic products is concerned, unless it can be shown that in the latter case (storing in our own cities) they will be brought into the domestic market at a cost materially less. This, it is believed, cannot be readily shown. Whether stored at home or abroad, the expense of bringing merchandise into the domestic market must be nearly the same. In either case, it has the same processes to perform. It must be transported from the factories or workshops where it is produced to the sea; it must be shipped, carried across the ocean, brought into our ports, and, before it can enter into the domestic market to be sold, the impost or duty must be paid. The charges and exactions are the same in both cases. If it is placed in store here and allowed to remain for a limited period without paying duty, it is in no better condition, so far as cost is concerned, than it would have been if it had been kept in store in the country where it was produced, unless storage here is cheaper, and this is questionable. Whether it will come into the domestic market at all depends on its cost, and the influence of cost on the demand for consumption. As has been seen, the cost will be the same whether it is stored abroad and kept there until it is required for exportation, or whether it is stored here until it is absorbed by the demand for home use. It is undoubtedly true that the proposed remission of the interest now exacted on the duties from the date of the entry until the goods go into the importer's possession will save to the importer or owner the amount of the interest; and I believe it to be difficult to show that there will be any other difference in cost between goods on which the duties are paid on the entry and those which are stored for a limited period without exacting the payment of the duties until they enter into the consumption of the country. There may be, however, another difference, though inconsiderable, if, as I suppose, the privilege of storing goods shall have the effect of enlarging the circle of competition in the business of importation; for, to the extent that the regular dealers purchase abroad, they will save the charges on foreign agencies here. To the present exaction of interest on the duties, I am totally opposed. It is but a means of adding indirectly to the amount of the duties; and I believe it ought, on every just principle, to be abolished, without regard to any plan of storing goods. Still, though I consider the exaction wrong in principle, I do not admit that it adds so materially to the cost of imported merchandise as to give any appreciable advantage to domestic products of a like character in the home market. Nor have I been able to satisfy myself that the measure proposed by the bill under consideration would add much to the public revenue. The Secretary of the Treasury estimates the increase of revenue at one million dollars; and his opinion is entitled to great respect. From his official position, he has within his reach means of information not always accessible to others. It strikes me, however, as a large estimate. At least it is conjectural. But if it shall prove to be accurate, it does not follow that the imported merchandise, on which this increased revenue is charged, will be altogether of those descriptions which come into competition with our own manufactures; and it will, at all events, find a market for an equal amount of our own products. Merchandise will be stored, unquestionably, in very large quantities, for exportation. So far as the importation and reëxportation of this merchandise extends the carrying trade, it will aid the treasury through the increase of the tonnage duties, which are, however, very inconsiderable. The amount of imposts can only be augmented by bringing a greater quantity of foreign merchandise into the home market. Whether this effect shall take place depends on the demand, which can only be increased through a diminution of the cost of foreign merchandise, thus bringing it within the means of a larger class of consumers, or by enabling it to enter on such terms of advantage into competition with our own products of a like character as to expel the latter from the market. Of course, I do not take into consideration the increased consumption arising from an increase of our population. If I am right in my positions, none of the consequences referred to will be realized. The cost of foreign merchandise will not be materially affected by the proposed plan ; and all the apprehensions founded upon such a supposition will prove groundless. But if I am wrong, then the diminished cost of foreign merchandise will be so much gained to the great body of the consumers. In any event, the reduction of cost will only be to the extent of the indirect increase of the duties by exacting interest on them from the date of the entry of the merchandise on which they are charged; and to this extent every principle of common fairness is on the side of the reduction.

The second objection is, that the proposed plan of admitting foreign merchandise to the benefit of the warehouse system will throw the whole business of importation into the hands of foreign capitalists; that foreign manufacturers will have their agents here; that they will fill our seaports with their products, and exercise an unlimited control over the home market. So far am I, sir, from feeling the force of this objection, that I consider it wholly groundless. Foreigners never have had, and are not likely to have, a very large share in the business of importation, taking all our imports together. They send their products here to some extent, and have their agents here to make sales ; but their participation in the business of importing constitutes a very inconsiderable portion of our whole import trade. Indeed, I regard the present system of exacting the payment of duties in cash on the entry of merchandise as much better calculated to throw the business of importation into the hands of large capitalists, native and foreign, than a warehouse system. If a cargo of merchandise worth one hundred thousand dollars is imported, and the duties are thirty per cent., it will require, under the present system, one hundred and thirty thousand dollars to purchase the merchandise and pay the duties on the entry. With the privilege of placing the goods in store without paying the duties, it will require only one hundred thousand dollars to make the importation. The merchandise will be withdrawn in limited quantities, as sales are made, and the duties will be paid on these separate quantities as they are delivered to the importer or owner. In one case, one hundred thousand dollars will suffice for the transaction; in the other, one hundred and thirty thousand dollars will be required. Now, it is quite clear, that, in proportion as the amount of capital required for the importation of merchandise is increased, you diminish the ability of importers of moderate means to make purchases for themselves abroad, and you multiply the chances of making the business of importing a monopoly in the hands of capitalists. They bring merchandise into the country, pay the duties, and compel the regular dealers to purchase them, with the addition of interest on the duties, commissions for agency, &c., — either depriving the merchant of a portion of his legitimate profit, or enhancing the price of the merchandise before it reaches the consumer, and compelling the latter to bear the burden of these intermediate charges. The privilege of storing goods will tend to break up, to some extent, this system of monopoly, by dispensing with the payment of the duties until the merchandise is required for consumption. Merchandise will be more likely to be purchased abroad at the places of production, instead of being procured of agents here, with the commissions and charges of these agencies superadded. A larger number of individuals will be able to make importations under the warehouse system; and whatever tends to withdraw any branch of business from the hands of a few persons, and to divide it among many, cannot but be beneficial to the community.

But admitting the objection to be well-founded, — admitting that one of the consequences of the warehouse system will be to enable foreign manufacturers to place their productions in store here, ready to be introduced at any moment into the home market, — the answer is, that they never can be so introduced without first paying the duties, and that the domestic producer is equally secure, whether they are stored here or abroad. The force of the objection is further weakened by the consideration, that, through the rapid communication between the Eastern and Western continents by steam, a few weeks are all that is necessary now to bring into our market unlimited quantities of foreign merchandise. The home market can only be controlled by a monopoly of the business of importation; and this, if my positions are correct, will not be so likely to occur under a warehouse system as under a system of cash payment on the entry of merchandise.

In connection with this subject, the Senator referred to the extent to which foreigners are now engaged in the import trade of the United States, and, as I think, estimated it too largely. On this point a brief explanation is necessary. I presume it will be admitted that, in making the estimate, we must confine our attention to the city of New York. There are few foreign importers in Boston, Philadelphia, Baltimore, Charleston, or New Orleans, — not enough, if I am well informed, to make any perceptible variation in the estimate. I take it for granted, also, that in the city of New York woollens, cottons, and silks are the chief imports on foreign account. The value of these articles imported into that city in 1845 was as follows: —

Woollens	$8,154,534
Cottons	8,863,973
Silks	8,789,220
	$25,807,727

Every species of manufactures of wool, cotton, and silk is here included.

It is not easy to ascertain precisely to what extent foreign merchants are concerned in these imports. All estimates must be, in a great degree, conjectural. The Senator's estimate is higher than my own. From the best information

I can obtain, I am not satisfied that much more than half is imported on foreign account. But I am disposed to be liberal, and give nearly two thirds, — $17,000,000. The value of the whole amount of our imports in 1845 was, in round numbers, $117,000,000; imported on foreign account, $17,000,000; leaving a balance in our favor of $100,000,000.

Some of these foreign importers have American partners. They hire our dwellings and warehouses, put the industry of our seaports in requisition, contribute in a variety of modes to the wealth of the country, and send abroad the products of our soil and labor.

In illustration of this portion of his remarks, the Senator referred to the statistics of our commerce, to show how much foreign tonnage had increased under the reciprocity treaties, and that a large portion of our commercial intercourse with other nations is carried on in foreign vessels.

It has been a common complaint in past years, and continues to some extent to be so still, that our commerce is going into the hands of foreigners. Looking at our statistical returns, they seem, at first glance, to confirm the impression that the complaint is well founded. But our judgment ought not to be formed on superficial examination. If we go back to the year 1824, (I take the year the Senator has referred to,) we find the tonnage of American vessels, which cleared from the United States, to have been 919,208, and the tonnage of foreign vessels cleared to have been 102,552, or little less than nine to one in favor of ours. In 1845, the American tonnage cleared was 2,053,977, and the foreign 930,275, a little more than two to one in our favor, showing an enormous difference in the proportion of increase. While ours has but little more than doubled, the foreign has increased more than ninefold. This great increase in the foreign tonnage employed in carrying to and from the United States the subjects of commercial exchange would certainly furnish just cause of alarm, if our own tonnage, so employed, had been stationary. But it has been greatly and very rapidly increasing.

During the last four years it has increased more than 500,000 tons, or at the rate of 34 per cent., while the foreign has increased about 180,000 tons, or less than 25 per cent.; so that it may be fairly presumed that the full effect of the reciprocity treaties has been felt. If we compare the proportion in which British and foreign tonnage is employed in the foreign trade of Great Britain, we shall find less cause to be dissatisfied with our own condition in the same respect. I take the year ending the 5th of January, 1841, (I cannot obtain the returns of a later year,) and find the vessels of the United Kingdom "entered inwards" from all parts of the world were 14,370, with a tonnage of 2,807,367,—exceeding ours in 1845 only about 800,000. In the same year, the number of foreign vessels entered "inwards" was 8355 and their tonnage 1,297,840.[1] Thus it appears that the foreign tonnage engaged in the foreign trade of Great Britain in 1840 was nearly equal to one half of the amount of her own tonnage. With us, the proportion of foreign tonnage engaged in our commerce to our own is more than a third, but less than half, and somewhat less than the proportion engaged in the commerce of Great Britain. If we test the relative importance of the commercial transactions in the two cases by the tonnage of all the vessels, we find those engaged in our commerce average 214 tons each,

[1] Since this speech was made, I have found later returns of the commercial statistics of Great Britain, from which the following details are obtained:—

Shipping entered inwards in the United Kingdom from foreign parts.

YEARS.	BRITISH AND IRISH VESSELS.		FOREIGN VESSELS.	
	No.	*Tons.*	*No.*	*Tons.*
1842	18,525	3,361,211	9527	1,291,165
1843	18,987	3,294,725	8054	1,205,303
1844	19,500	3,545,346	8541	1,301,950

By this statement, it will be seen that the tonnage of Great Britain engaged in her commerce with foreign States has increased, notwithstanding her reciprocity treaties, in a greater ratio than foreign tonnage engaged in the same commerce.

while those engaged in the commerce of Great Britain average only 181 tons each.

If we pursue this examination further, we shall find still less cause for concern. We border on the provinces of Great Britain, and a constant intercourse is maintained between them and us in a variety of commercial transactions of comparatively trivial importance, but constituting a large aggregate. This circumstance enables us to account for a fact which, at first sight, strikes us with some surprise, and excites some apprehension. We find the number of vessels that entered the United States in 1845 was 13,723. Of this number 8133 were American, and 5590 foreign. This seems a large proportion; but when we look into the detail, we find that of these 5590 vessels, 4262 — nearly four fifths — are from the British North American colonies, and that their tonnage amounts to 463,748, (about one half the whole amount of the foreign tonnage engaged in our commerce,) or an average of 109 tons each, — generally small vessels, engaged in the minutest operations of trade. These details will be fully shown by House Document No. 13 of the present session, page 213. Turning to page 232, we find the number of foreign vessels that entered the districts of Cape Vincent, Oswegatchie, Oswego, Genesee, Niagara, Champlain, and Sackett's Harbor, was 1627, with an aggregate tonnage of 273,798. These districts are on lakes Ontario and Champlain, and the river St. Lawrence. Add to these entries 67 foreign vessels which entered Cuyahoga, on Lake Erie, and Detroit, on the river of that name, with an aggregate tonnage of 7703, and we have 1694 foreign vessels, with an aggregate tonnage of 281,101, entering our interior lake and river ports, on waters constituting the boundary between us and Upper Canada. These vessels are for the most part steamers, running between the ports on the British side and our own, and stopping at several points in each direction, and always counting one entry and one clearance each trip. Thus it will be perceived that the number of foreign vessels entering the United States from the British North American provinces, after deducting those engaged in the lake traffic, is reduced to 2568, with an aggregate tonnage of 182,647.

By turning again to Document No. 13, page 232, we find 699 foreign vessels entering the district of Passamaquoddy, with an aggregate tonnage of 54,412, or an average of 78 tons per vessel. The district of Passamaquoddy lies upon the confines of New Brunswick; and from its position and the average size of the foreign vessels entering it, they are obviously small craft engaged in trivial exchanges. The aggregate number of foreign vessels from the British North American provinces is now shrunk below 2000. One more reference to the same page of the document, and I shall dismiss this part of the subject. We find 1265 foreign vessels entering the port of Boston, with an aggregate tonnage of 101,491, or an average of 80 tons per vessel. A large portion of these are small craft, schooners and sloops from Nova Scotia and New Brunswick, laden with plaster, wood, and coal. Portland, Gloucester, Salem, and New York have their share of these visitors from the British provinces. The whole of this portion of the foreign tonnage entering the United States is thus accounted for, and the foreign vessels legitimately engaged in our external trade are reduced to 1328.

Throwing entirely out of view the commercial intercourse between the United States and the North American colonies of Great Britain, in the vessels of both, the vessels and tonnage engaged in the commerce of the United States with all other countries would stand as follows: Vessels of the United States, 5267; foreign vessels, 1328; — about four to one. Tonnage of the United States, 1,351,127; foreign tonnage, 446,815; — more than three to one.

To show how fallacious a cursory examination of our commercial statements would prove as a criterion of the trade of the country, it is only necessary to look at the district of Cape Vincent, near the head of the river St. Lawrence, where the lake steamers touch. By the return, (page 236,) 1337 vessels appear to have entered it, with an aggregate tonnage of 331,867, almost rivalling New York in entries and tonnage. By turning to page 240 of the same document, it appears that the tonnage belonging to the city of New York is 550,359, while that of Cape Vincent is 2670. While the revenue collected at New York exceeded eighteen millions of dollars, that collected at Cape Vincent was $779 and a few cents, or about an average of half a dollar for each vessel entered in the district. I exhibit the details of this case to prove how deceptive the returns are when assumed as a criterion of the extent of our commerce. It is only by a careful analysis of them that the truth can be reached and false impressions removed.

One word more on this subject of tonnage. It has been supposed that a large portion of the trade carried on by foreign vessels was circuitous, — that is, that foreign vessels were in the habit of coming here with cargoes not the produce of the countries to which they belonged, and that they were in the habit of departing with cargoes for other countries than those to which they belonged. This is, to some extent, true; but the amount of this circuitous intercourse is much less than has been supposed. I have taken the trouble to look into this branch of our commerce. I have analyzed the commercial tables, for the purpose of ascertaining where the foreign vessels, which enter our ports, come from and where they go when they clear. It has cost some labor, but it is fully repaid by the result. Of 5587 foreign vessels entering the United States in 1845, 5380 came from the countries to which they belonged, and 207 from other countries; and of 5583 which cleared from the United States, 5254 sailed for their own countries, and 229 for other countries than those to which they belonged. Thus it will be seen that the direct trade in foreign vessels between the United States and those countries to which the vessels belong constitutes more than nineteen twentieths of the whole. Throwing the British North American provinces out of the account, the circuitous trade in foreign vessels constitutes less than one sixth of the whole amount of our trade, direct and circuitous, in foreign vessels.

But it is not alone to the number of American and foreign vessels engaged in our foreign commerce that we are to look for the proportion in which they participate in it. We must see also what they carry; and I now proceed to show to what extent the commercial exchanges of the country are carried on in foreign vessels. The statistical facts I shall state are taken from the letter of the Secretary of the Treasury, transmitting the annual report of commerce and navigation, printed as House Document No. 13 of the present session of Congress, — the same document I have already so often referred to. At page 42 it will be seen that the value of the exports of domestic products during the year ending the 30th of June, 1845, amounted to $99,299,776. Of this amount $75,483,123 were exported in American, and $23,816,653 in foreign vessels, — or more than three to one in favor of American vessels. During the same period the value of the exports of foreign products, articles imported into the United States from foreign countries and reëxported, amounted to $15,346,830, of which amount $11,459,319 were exported in American, and $3,887,511 in foreign vessels, — or a little less than three to one in favor of American vessels. For these details I refer to page 95 of the same document. The whole value of our exports, domestic and foreign, was $114,646,606; and of this amount, $86,942,442 were exported in American, and $27,704,164 in foreign vessels, — or three millions and a half more than three to one in favor of the former. This is a respectable proportion, though not so large as is desirable; but our exports constitute only a part of the foreign trade of the country, and that part which can with least propriety be taken as a criterion of the whole, as further investigation will show. It is to the imports rather than to the exports that we must look for the extent of our participation in carrying to and from our own ports the products which make up the foreign commerce of the country. Our imports are chiefly for our own consumption; they are purchased for the most part on our account, and for these reasons they are imported principally, as is naturally to be expected, in our own vessels. Our exports, to some extent, are purchased on foreign account, and they are naturally carried out in foreign vessels in a like proportion.

By referring to page 193 of the same document, it will be seen that the value of our imports for the year ending the 30th June, 1845, amounted to $117,254,564. Of this amount, $102,438,481 were brought in American, and $14,816,083 in foreign vessels, — or nearly seven to one in favor of American vessels. In carrying the articles imported into the country, therefore, there is a very large difference in favor of our own vessels.

Taking the imports and exports together, they amount to $231,901,170. Of this amount, $189,380,923 were carried in American, and $42,520,247 in foreign vessels, — or nearly four and a half to one in favor of the former.

It is a fact worthy of notice, that the value of our imports in foreign vessels has scarcely varied half a million of dollars for any entire year since 1839, excepting in 1842, a year, as all know, of extraordinary depression. With that exception, the lowest amount imported in foreign vessels in any one year since 1839 was $14,260,362, and the highest $14,816,083. The average of our imports in foreign vessels for the last few years — excluding 1842 and the nine months preceding the 30th June, 1843, when the termination of the fiscal year was changed — amounts to $14,534,-978. During the same period, and making the same exceptions, our imports in American vessels varied from $92,-802,352, in 1840, the lowest amount, to $113,221,877, in 1841, the highest amount in the series of years referred to, — a variation of more than twenty millions.

Of our imports in foreign vessels, $7,354,804 are from the United Kingdom of Great Britain and Ireland and her colonial possessions, — or about one half of the whole amount of those imports. Our imports in our own vessels, from the same countries, amounted to $41,123,562, — nearly seven to one in our favor.

If we add to the imports in foreign vessels from Great Britain and her possessions, as above stated, the imports in foreign vessels from the Hanse Towns, amounting to $2,761,048, they will give together an aggregate of $10,-115,854, — leaving only $4,700,229 of imports in foreign vessels to be distributed among all the other countries on the globe with which we have commercial connections. Of this latter amount, a little more than one million comes from France, a little more than half a million from Denmark, Sweden, and Norway, combined, and the residue from some thirty different countries, and in amounts falling short of half a million in each case.

Such is the condition of our import trade, so far as it is carried on in foreign vessels. I see nothing alarming in it. It ministers in various modes to our own industry. The vessels of other nations which find their way to our ports, bringing with them the products of their own soil or the fabrics of their own art, pay tribute to us by augmenting our revenue, purchasing, to some extent, in our ports the supplies they require for their voyages, and carrying back with them the products of our own labor. I am satisfied with the extent to which we participate in this portion of the great system of exchanges we are carrying on with other countries. If our export trade stood upon a footing as favorable, it would leave little else to be desired. Even as it is, taking our exports and imports together, the extent to which foreign vessels participate in the business of carrying furnishes no cause for uneasiness. Nor do I see any reason to apprehend that the future will present a more unfavorable result.

I now resume the examination of objections to the bill, and will dispose of them in the briefest manner. In respect to the necessity of building stores at the public expense, I will only say that during the late administration inquiries were addressed by the Secretary of the Treasury to a large number of individuals, some of them holding offices in the revenue department, and others engaged in mercantile pursuits in our principal seaports. I have examined all the answers I could find; and of eighty-eight there are eighty-four expressing the opinion that suitable stores for warehousing goods may be hired, and only four expressing a contrary opinion. I have looked over the documents in which they are contained in haste, and may have committed mistakes in the enumeration, but I think not to such an extent as materially to impair its accuracy.

An army of officers (said the Senator from Connecticut) will be required to carry on the system, and it will lead to innumerable frauds. Sir, these were some of the arguments against the British system, as will be seen by referring to the extract I have given from Smollett. And if the Senator will permit me, I will remind him that at the close of the last session of Congress he raised the same objections to a bill allowing a drawback of duties on goods transported from the United States to the adjacent British provinces. The bill became a law, and has been most salutary in practice. Not an additional custom-house officer, as I believe, has been appointed under it, nor have I heard any allegation of fraud arising from the more extended commercial intercourse to which it has led. I trust and believe that the apprehensions of my friend from Connecticut will prove as groundless now as they did then.

One of the closing remarks of the Senator was, that there was no analogy between this bill and the act of 1799, in respect to the deposit of goods in the public stores. I differ with him in opinion entirely. I see a strong analogy between them. The Senator said the provision in the act of 1799 was intended to secure the duties on unclaimed goods, and that its object was public, and not the convenience of individuals. Sir, I think he will admit, on further consideration, that he puts too narrow a construction on that act. It applied also to goods deposited in store with the consent of the owner, consignee, or master of the vessel, and authorized them to be received after five days' notice to the collector. The Senator is learned in the law, and I need only remind him of the rule, that, whenever an authority is conferred on a public officer, and the exercise of the authority may be beneficial to third persons, it is his duty, on the application of the parties interested, to act. The term consent must, therefore, be deemed synonymous with request; and such I believe it is in practice; for, as I said when I explained to the Senate the provisions of this bill, vessels in haste to enter on the return-voyage are constantly unladen under the five days' order. Let us pursue this question of analogy a little further. What were the leading provisions in force in 1799 in respect to the storage and reëxportation of foreign merchandise? Storage for nine months, no interest on the duties, and one and one fourth per cent. deduction on the drawback. What are the provisions in force now? Storage for sixty and ninety days, interest at six per cent. on the duties, and two and a half per cent. deduction on the drawback. The bill under consideration is intended to remove the rigors of the present law, and to restore and extend the privileges of the old. Sir, so strong do I consider the analogy between the provisions of the bill under consideration and the provisions of the act of 1799, that I would almost be willing to take the latter, with a mere extension of the time allowed for storing goods, and ask no more.

But, sir, I have trespassed too long on the indulgence of the Senate, and with a brief reference to a single topic I will bring my remarks to a close.

It is said that this is a measure calculated for the exclusive benefit of New York, and appeals were made to Senators from other States to take notice that the bill contained no provision for rewarehousing goods when once deposited in store at the place of importation. In reply to this appeal I wish to say, that, after the bill was drawn, a provision to allow goods to be removed from one collection district to another, in the manner in which they may now be transported for reëxportation, with the benefit of drawback, was suggested by a distinguished Senator from the South, and I assured him that if such an amendment was proposed, I should not object to it.

But, with such an amendment or without it, my sincere belief is, that New York is no more interested in this measure than some other seaports in the Union. She is the centre of commerce now. A warehouse system can make her no more. But I believe its tendency is to make other cities participate, to a greater extent than they do now, in the commerce of the country. Its tendency is to make them depots of merchandise for the supply of the interior districts of which they are respectively the outlets: — Boston, for the New England district, which lies back and north of her, not great in territorial extent, but wonderful in activity and physical power, with a network of railways covering it and connecting it with her; Philadelphia, for the rich interior of Pennsylvania, and the still more western districts which that State has rendered tributary to her by means of the internal channels of communication of which the city is the terminus; Baltimore, Charleston, and Savannah for the interior districts which receive their supplies through those cities; and last, though among the first in importance, New Orleans, with the immense valley of the Mississippi, and the almost boundless regions upon the Missouri, the Arkansas, and the Red rivers, which look to her as their only outlet, and their only point of transshipment, both for their inward and outward trade. I believe these cities, in proportion to their population and commerce, will be as much benefited as

New York by the measure under consideration. They will become depots for the merchandise required to supply the several districts dependent on them, and New Orleans may also confidently look for a large and valuable share of the export trade in foreign products deposited for reëxportation in her warehouses. As Senators from other States have been appealed to, I desire to commend the Senators from Louisiana to an attentive consideration of the commercial statements on their tables. New Orleans sends abroad domestic products to the value of twenty-five millions of dollars. New York sends only about ninety thousand dollars more. Look now to the imports. New York receives seventy millions, New Orleans only seven, — a tenth part. The foreign products, in which the vast export of New Orleans is paid, go first to New York, and the duties are paid there. I ask them to consider these facts, and say whether, under the proposed system, New Orleans may not become the depot for the merchandise required for the consumption of the valley of the Mississippi, and for exportation to South America.

Sir, I did not understand the Senator from Connecticut as intimating that this measure has been urged by myself with any exclusive view to benefit New York. I am sure he knows me too well to suppose that in my legislative capacity I am not actuated by a higher motive than that of endeavoring to shape the legislation of the Union so as to give any undue advantage to mere local interests. When the Senate did me the honor to make me a member of the Committee on Commerce, I considered myself charged, in common with my associates, with the responsibility of looking to the commercial interests of the whole country. I have endeavored to meet that responsibility in a liberal and impartial spirit. I might safely appeal to the other members of the committee to say whether I have busied myself in devising schemes of local benefit for the State I have the honor to represent, — whether I have not discouraged applications from that State in more than one instance, because I believed them not to be made under such circumstances as to render it proper to grant them. It is my duty, doubtless, in conjunction with my colleague, to see, as far as lies in my power, that the interests of New York are not overlooked in our consultations for the general good. That duty I shall endeavor to discharge faithfully and vigilantly. But I trust I shall never be found pressing any local interest of my own State in opposition to the common interests of the whole Union. Such a service I can never consent to perform. My constituents do not expect it of me. They would be the first to pronounce me unworthy of the trust they have reposed in me if they were to find me acting upon grounds so narrow and so subversive of all just principles of legislation. Sir, New York asks no partial exercise of legislative power in her favor. She needs none. She desires only to stand on equal ground with her sister States. Her "claim hath this extent, no more."

In bringing forward this measure, I have been actuated by the single desire of benefiting the commerce of the country at large, of liberating it from some of the restrictions by which it is embarrassed, and of giving it freer and broader scope. I believe these objects may be effected without prejudicing any other interest. I believe the measure proposed is due to every consideration of fairness. I have given it my support under these convictions. I shall defend it to the last. I trust it will receive the sanction of the Senate. If I shall be disappointed, I shall bow, as is my duty, to the judgment of the majority of my associates on this floor. But in such an event, which I will not anticipate, it will be with the assurance, not that the measure is unworthy, but that it would have succeeded if it had been advocated by the mover in a manner at all commensurate with its claims to support.

LIEUTENANT-GENERAL OF THE ARMY.

JANUARY 4, 1847.

Mr. Dix moved that the Senate proceed to the consideration of the bill to appoint a lieutenant-general to command the military forces of the United States during the war with Mexico.

The motion was agreed to, and the bill was taken up accordingly, as in committee of the whole.

Mr. President: The bill under consideration was introduced in accordance with the recommendation contained in the President's special message of the 4th instant. The reasons for asking the appointment of a general to command all our military forces in Mexico were briefly explained in that message. Having introduced the bill as a member of the Committee on Military Affairs, I deem it due to the Senate and to the subject to state the considerations by which I have been governed in giving the measure my support.

Our military operations in Mexico have heretofore been carried on in detached commands, on very extended lines, and in the execution of enterprises not only totally distinct from each other, but at geographical distances so remote as to preclude anything like direct combination between the forces respectively employed in them. These enterprises have all been successful. Santa Fé and Chihuahua have been overrun and occupied by the military forces under General Kearney; the Californias by Colonel Frémont and our naval forces in the Pacific; New Leon and part of Tamaulipas by General Taylor; and Durango by General Wool and General Worth. The whole of northern and central Mexico, as far south as the mouth of the Rio Grande and the twenty-sixth parallel of latitude, is virtually in our possession. The Mexican authority may by this occupation be considered extinct in this extensive district, constituting — if we include Sonora and Sinoloa on the eastern shore of the Gulf of California, from which I believe the Mexican forces are withdrawn — about two thirds of the entire territory of the Mexican republic, and about one tenth of its population. The land forces, by which these acquisitions have been made, are rapidly concentrating upon the southern line of the subjugated territory. Their operations are to be, in some degree, combined, instead of being carried on in separate divisions. General officers, who have heretofore operated independently, are to come together and to act with each other in the accomplishment of common objects. At least four of these generals have the same rank, that of major-general, the highest rank in the service; and precedence among them in their respective arms is, therefore, to be determined by date of commission. In subordinate commands this mode of settling questions of precedence is inevitable, and ordinarily leads to little practical inconvenience. But to permit the right to the chief command over such numerous forces as are now to be combined, and in such extensive operations as are to be carried on, to be determined by mere priority of commission, and not by superiority of grade, is, to say the least, exceedingly undesirable, not only in deference to military principles, but because this very circumstance has often proved unfriendly to united and zealous action, and sometimes has led to the frustration of plans of campaign, and even to defeat, when success would have been certain with proper coöperation on the part of the commander and his subordinates. I might appeal, for the truth of this remark, to our own military history, as well as to that of other countries. I believe I may say, it is a well-settled opinion in respect to military command, and especially in extensive operations, that the chief commander should, if possible, be superior in grade to the other general officers serving under him. The considerations by which the correctness of this principle is supported, are perfectly compatible with the highest patriotism and honor in the persons holding subordinate commands. It is strictly a question of military organization. We may concede to all the purest devotion and disinterestedness; and yet, in the organization of military bodies, and in the preparation of plans of campaign, we should be wanting in ordinary prudence, if we were not guided by those general principles which are calculated to render our arrangements proof, as far as human arrangements can be, against all hazard of failure in their execution. If there is a particular form of organization better suited than any other to give efficiency to the movements of military forces, it is the part of wisdom to adopt it; nor should we be content with a less efficient form, even though we have the fullest confidence in the patriotism and zeal of those who are to take part in the contemplated enterprises. Sir, I have entire faith in the devotedness and gallantry of the officers of our army, and of the volunteers; and no one shall surpass me here in attributing to them the praise, and awarding to them the justice to which they are entitled. I consider the proposed measure entirely consistent with the interests of both arms of the service, which are deeply concerned, though not so deeply as the interests of the country, in giving to the military body, of which they are a part, the most judicious and efficient organization.

Looking to the numerical forces to be moved in combination, they will far exceed any number ever commanded in this country — and I believe I may say in any other, except from accident or some temporary necessity — by a major-general, the highest grade in our service. The proper command of an officer of that rank is a division. A major-general and a general of division are convertible terms. A division consists of two brigades; a brigade consists of two regiments in the regular service, and three in the volunteers. The command of a major-general, therefore, is from four to six thousand men. The force to be employed in Mexico, if our operations are to be carried on with proper vigor, should not fall short of twenty-five or thirty thousand fighting men in the field. It now exceeds twenty thousand. It is sufficient for four full divisions. To permit it to be commanded by a major-general, having no precedence over his associates excepting by the date of his commission, is as inconsistent with military principles as it would be to organize a regiment with three or four majors, and without a colonel, or, in other words, without a head. It is far too large a force to be commanded either by a major-general or a general having no higher rank than others serving under him. Such an arrangement is totally inconsistent with military principles and usages, looking to organization in its narrowest sense. When Napoleon was in command of the army of Italy, after his first successes, the Executive Directory determined to associate with him General Kellermann, one of the best commanders of that day. Napoleon remonstrated against it in a letter written in his usual terse and vigorous style; and he concluded by saying, that one bad general was better than two good ones. Sir, there is great force and truth in the proposition. He intended to intimate that every military body should have a distinct head; and certainly the observation is eminently applicable to cases in which the numerical forces are greatly disproportioned to the rank of the officer commanding them. For these reasons, if there were no others, I should be in favor of the President's recommendation to appoint an officer of higher rank to command our armies in Mexico.

Thus far I have spoken of the proposed measure as connected with sound principles of military organization and command. I desire now to present some considerations of a different nature. Our military commanders in Mexico are operating in an enemy's country of vast extent. They are overrunning provinces, reducing cities and towns, and providing for the security of the subjugated territories under the rules of international law, and according to the usages of civilized States. These are high prerogatives, the incidents of war, having their authority in conventional rules beyond the civil constitution and municipal laws of our own country. It is very desirable that the depositary of these high and extraordinary powers should not only carry with him the requisite military talents, but that he should also possess the experience and the civil qualifications indispensable to enable him to meet his responsibilities intelligently and discreetly. Not only his own government, but all civilized nations have an interest in the maintenance of rules designed to mitigate the asperities of warfare by applying to the conduct of war the principles of humanity and justice. Errors in the application of these rules may involve his own government in embarrassment and reproach. These considerations, I am aware, apply rather to the qualifications of the man than to the rank he may happen to hold. I advert to them only for the purpose of indicating the importance of the position occupied by the commander of our armies in Mexico, and the propriety of extending to the President the broadest field for selection.

In the message of the President, it is recommended that authority be given to appoint a commanding general for our military forces in Mexico, without specifying any rank. The committee, in reporting the bill, propose to confer on him the rank of lieutenant-general, — the grade in other services next above that of major-general, which is the highest in ours. The grade was created in 1798, during our dissensions with the French republic, by an act authorizing the President to raise a provisional army. The office was conferred, by the unanimous vote of the Senate, on General Washington, and was accepted by him, but with the express stipulation that he should not be called into service until the exigency for which the office was created — an invasion of the United States by France — should actually occur. He did not believe it would occur; he was not deceived in this belief; and he never entered on the discharge of his duties, excepting so far as to give advice with regard to the organization of the army. About a year after this grade was created, and a few months before he died, another act was passed, authorizing the appointment of a commander of the army, with the title of "general of the armies of the United States," and thereupon abolishing the office of lieutenant-general. I have not been able to find that the appointment was ever made; and by a return from the War Department, in 1800, General Washington was reported as lieutenant-general, *dead*. According to the analogies of other services, the rank of general is higher than that of lieutenant-general. I have not thought it material to inquire into the object of the second act; but it may have been designed to confer on him a rank as nearly approaching that which he bore in the revolutionary war (that of general and commander-in-chief) as was consistent with the Constitution of the United States, which declares the President to be commander-in-chief of the armies of the United States.

In other services, the rank of lieutenant-general is, I believe, a part, and an essential part, of the military organization. In France, it was formerly conferred on the chiefs of provinces, and the individuals holding it were invested with civil as well as military functions. In modern times, I believe, it has become purely a military title, and it confers a rank intermediate between that of major-general, which is below, and general, which is above it. As the grade next to that of major-general, it seems the proper title, if a higher grade is to be created. On the other hand, though the office of commander of the military forces in Mexico will be purely military, nevertheless, in providing for exigencies which may arise in the occupation of an enemy's territory, — and, let me add, with as little disturbance as possible to the local authorities and the ordinary administration of justice, — his station becomes one of the highest delicacy and importance. If a new grade is to be created, I repeat, the title of lieutenant-general will be admitted to be proper in a strictly military sense, and it is descriptive of the relation in which the commander of the armies in Mexico will stand to the President as commander-in-chief of the armies of the United States under the Constitution. He cannot be in Mexico in person, and he must, therefore, command there by his lieutenant or deputy, by whatever name the latter may be called.

The proposed creation of a new grade in the army, higher than any now known to the service, does not contemplate the creation or delegation of any new authority to the officer who may be appointed to it. He will possess no other powers than those now possessed by our military commanders. The act creating the office limits its duration to the war with Mexico. It is proposed to be created for the extraordinary emergency in which the country is placed, and will cease with it.

I desire it to be distinctly understood that the measure is proposed with a view to the vigorous prosecution of the war; and in this view only I support it. If we were to have a war of posts, or a long and moderate war, the office would be unnecessary, and I should not give it my support. On this point I desire to say a few words more. I concur fully in the sentiments expressed by the Senator from Kentucky[1] at a late session of the Senate, with regard to a vigorous prosecution of the war. I see no alternative but to advance with a competent force, and continue our operations until Mexico shall consent to make peace. Least of all would I approve the policy which has been referred to on this floor, of maintaining our present

[1] Mr. Crittenden.

line of possession, and waiting for peace to come to us. I see in such a policy no beneficial results. On the contrary, I see in it nothing but evil and mischief. I believe it would be a line of war, assassination, and rapine, which neither party would have the ability to put down. It is only a restoration of peace, resting upon the solemn sanctions of a treaty, that can engage either party to treat the perpetrators of outrage with the severity necessary to suppress it. Draw a line across the Mexican territory and place your soldiery there to guard it, and you will be exposed to the danger, so well described by the Senator from Kentucky, of having your own divided forces attacked by the combined forces of the enemy at any point which he may select. Besides, sir, take such a line, and let our present hostile relations to Mexico continue, and you give to individual acts of depredation, in some degree, the sanction of law. You convert a war of communities into a war of individuals, without responsibility, and without restraint, while the hostile feeling between the two countries will constantly grow more embittered by the repetition of acts of violence. Peace alone, uniting the sovereign power of both countries in the maintenance of order, can terminate a state of things disastrous to both, and at war with all the interests of humanity.

I have said that I see no hope but in a vigorous prosecution of the war. I believe that with proper energy it may be brought to a close. The opposition which has been made to us in Mexico has, I believe, come wholly from the army. There has been no uprising of the people, as there would be with us if our soil were to be invaded by a foreign power. There are two reasons why it is so. Our military operations have been carried on chiefly in a sparsely populated country, and the great body of the Mexicans are nearly disarmed. I have a paper before me, published in the city of Mexico, containing an article from Zacatecas, showing a most extraordinary fact. If Senators will look at their maps, they will find the department of Zacatecas, southwest of New Leon, of which Monterey is the chief town, southeast of Durango, and northwest of San Luis Potosi, — lying, in a word, in the very centre of the territory of Mexico. And yet the frontiers of the department and those of Durango are subject to the constant incursions of bands of savages, from twenty, thirty, fifty, to two hundred in number. Let me read an extract from this article: —

"ZACATECAS, *October* 25, 1846.

"In our last number we announced that, besides the one hundred men who had gone out in the direction of the northern frontier of the State, to free the inhabitants from the depredation of the savages, his Excellency the commanding general would go out in person on the first of the next month, with the rest of the force of the sixth regiment of permanent cavalry. But having received the day before yesterday news, which was communicated by extraordinary express from the political chiefs of Sombrerete and Nieves, that a party of savages, whose number they estimated at two hundred, had shown themselves in the neighborhood of Mateo Gomez, Santa Catarina, and other villages in that quarter, his Excellency the commanding general hastened his departure, and yesterday he marched with about two hundred men of the sixth regiment, a detachment of the active battalion, a company of the national guard, and a detachment of artillery of the same guard, with one piece of cannon. Besides, his Excellency has sent orders to the political chiefs of Nieves, Sombrerete, Fresnillo, and others in that quarter, to assemble the militia, as far as the excessive scarcity of arms would permit, and aid the operations of the commandant general. We believe, then, if the savages succeed in attacking the people of the frontier, they will be severely punished."

The same paper contains an account of a fight with the Indians, in Durango, on the 18th of October, in which eleven Mexicans were killed and twenty-four wounded. The scene of these Indian depredations is two hundred miles in advance of our army at Monterey, nearly midway between Saltillo, in Durango, and Santa Ana's head-quarters, at San Luis Potosi. It is an extraordinary fact, as indicating the defenceless condition of the great body of the Mexicans, and from "the excessive scarcity of arms," the militia could only be partially employed. The people, it would seem, are dependent for their protection on the army; and when this is withdrawn, they are again exposed to outrage and depredation from the most insignificant bands of savages.

I will now call the attention of the Senate to two articles of great interest and importance, as connected with the history of the contest in which we are engaged with Mexico, and as casting some light upon the course which it may be incumbent on us to pursue. I have two Mexican papers, published in the city of Mexico about the middle of November, and containing what may be regarded as the manifestoes of the two great parties in that country, put forth in anticipation of the meeting of the extraordinary Congress now in session. The first is the "Monitor Republicano," (the Republican Monitor,) of the 14th of November, 1846, containing, under its editorial head, an article which I will read from the Spanish; and in translating it, as I proceed, I shall endeavor to follow it with literal accuracy, for any deviation from the original would impair its strength: —

"Most weighty are the questions of which the solution belongs to the Congress soon to be convened, and their gravity incalculable. One of the most important is the termination or continuation of the actual war with the United States, a subject on which depends nothing less than our existence as an independent nation.

"The reasons which exist for terminating the war are most powerful; and not less weighty are those which oblige us to continue it. Our situation is truly critical, and immense the responsibility of those who are to decide our fate.

"Our country, weakened by twenty-five years of intestine wars, cannot present the energetic and invincible resistance which are the fruit of peace, of union, and of order in the public administration. Events common to all youthful nations, and which ours has been unable to avoid, have brought us to the condition which we to-day deplore, but from which, unhappily, it is not in our power immediately to escape. The nations of Europe, attentive to their own interests, all incline to favor our enemies, because they consider them stronger, and because from their triumph they anticipate greater advantages for their industry and commerce. Misfortunes, the offspring of the improvidence and weakness of a few men, are attributed to the whole nation, which in this manner has incurred reproaches it was far from meriting. Finally, everything conspires against us, and on all sides the most gloomy perspective presents itself. These, and many other reasons which will readily occur to him who reflects a moment, persuade us of the imperious necessity of putting an end to so great a calamity as that which afflicts us.

"But in what manner can we attain it? What treaties can we make, which will not cover us with opprobrium? These wicked men have usurped our territory, demolished our cities, destroyed our sea-ports, and rendered our shipping useless: they have committed every species of violence upon our citizens, and offered every description of outrage to our country. Can we, without covering ourselves with ignominy, humble ourselves, and yield what they desire, and what will be to us, beyond measure, unfavorable? Mexico has suffered grave injuries from the civil war which has burned without intermission in her bosom; but she will not admit that her sons have lost the noble ardor with which they have always fought to defend their natal soil. All Mexicans, without any exception, are resolved to sacrifice all their interests, and their existence, before they will consent to be the slaves of avaricious adventurers; and this noble decision is the surest pledge of triumph. The smallest, the most insignificant people on earth, are invincible when they combat for their independence. And Mexico, — will she not maintain her dignity? Will she not know how to avail herself of any of the great elements of defence with which nature has endowed her?

"These are powerful motives why we should pursue, at every peril, a most just contest, — a contest to which we are stimulated by the greatest incentives that can be imagined.

"What, then, is the issue of this most important matter? We confess, in good faith, we are unable to foresee; and that only the most mature deliberation of wise and experienced men is capable of bringing to a good termination a question of life or death for Mexico.

"Great, then, should be the circumspection with which the future Congress should proceed, — a Congress which we shall accuse of our ruin, or to which we shall be the debtors for our salvation. Every citizen of those who compose it, when he finds himself in the Hall of the Representatives of the people, should forget every interest, every affection, and keep only in view his country, whose fate he is to decide irremediably."

This, sir, is the declaration of the republican party of Mexico; and I cannot, by any words of mine, add to its force or eloquence. This party I suppose to be far the most numerous and the most patriotic, but kept down by the army, the clergy, and the monarchists. Though their manifesto breathes a noble spirit of patriotism, and denounces us as invaders of the Mexican soil, I think it will not be difficult for an attentive reader to perceive that they are strongly disposed to peace, and that they see nothing but evil to the republic from the military rule of Santa Ana. It is the party with which our negotiations were commenced for an amicable settlement of the Texas question. We have, I fear, lost much of its confidence since the war commenced. We are considered as determined to dismember the republic. The Mexican papers are full of a plan which they attribute to us, of dividing their territory at the 23d degree of latitude, the parallel of Tampico and San Luis Potosi; and while they suppose this to be our determination, it is natural that they should speak of us with asperity. But let it be once understood that we are disposed to settle our differences on just and liberal terms, and I believe there will be no obstacle with them to a pacification. They are now powerless; but it may be that, in the progress of the war, their condition may be reversed, and that, by a wise policy on our part, political results of the highest benefit to Mexico may be secured, and her republican institutions may be established on a more solid and durable foundation.

I will now read to the Senate a paper of a different character, — a paper which may be fairly considered as the manifesto of Santa Ana himself. I find it in the "Diario del Gobierno de la Republica Mexicana" (the Journal of the Government of the Mexican Republic) of Sunday, the 22d November, 1846; but the article is copied from a paper printed at San Luis Potosi, and entitled "La opinion del ejercito," (the opinion of the army,) and doubtless conducted under his supervision. Indeed, it contains a reference to his opinions, which may be regarded not only as authentic, but semi-official: —

"San Luis Potosi, *November* 13.

"The War with the United States. — Public opinion expressed through the press has been continually arraigning our rulers, of all epochs, for the apathy and indifference with which they have viewed the Texas question since the unfortunate event of San Jacinto. From that time the Mexican people knew what would be the consequences of this criminal indifference, and constantly and energetically begged for the restoration of the constitution of 1824, as the only means of recovering, with less difficulty and by force, possession of that vast and rich territory usurped by a small handful of adventurers.

"Unfortunately, the preceding administration, occupied solely with keeping themselves in power, turned a deaf ear to the voice of the people, refusing them even the coöperation of our valiant army in an enterprise which, singly, they could not have accomplished. They feared that the citizens, on receiving arms to revenge the outrages committed upon the nation, would turn them against their rulers, and hurl them from the posts which they held by means of revolutions. In this manner they succeeded in weakening the strength of the people, and putting to sleep their enthusiasm, so as to favor the rapacity of the Americans, who already meditated the annexation of Texas to their States.

"This act of perfidy was verified by a decree of the Chamber of Deputies of the United States; and the reclamations from our government, and the answers to them, were in great part unknown to the people, from whom they were carefully concealed, in order that public opinion might not interfere with measures so little favorable to the interests of the community. Thus have negotiations of the highest importance to Mexico constantly become more complicated, until we now see ourselves invaded, and a large portion of our country occupied, not merely by Texan adventurers, but by the army of the United States, ordered hither without reason, and with perfidious views on the part of that government which aspires to overthrow the independence which we acquired at the cost of so much blood.

"Of all these evils, and of many more sacrifices which have been made, and are still making, by the people to recover the territory of Texas, and that newly occupied, preceding administrations are the cause, and more particularly that of the 6th of December, 1844, which, forgetting its pledges to the nation, confided its arms to a disloyal general, who planned the ruin of our institutions before marching to the frontier to punish, as he was ordered, our invaders. To this administration, we repeat, the country owes the state in which it now finds itself with our perfidious neighbor; and it is responsible for the manner in which our diplomatic relations with that power now remain.

"The negotiations which the minister, Cuevas, commenced with the government of the United States, to terminate the Texas question in an amicable manner, gave reason to the cabinet of that republic to believe that Mexico was feeble, and that they could remain with impunity in the possession of our territories as soon as a part of their army should present itself on this side of the line that divides the two territories. All that has happened, the periodical press, as the most sure organ of public opinion, foretold; and it reproved severely the conduct observed by the cabinet of that period for admitting an envoy of the government of the United States, who came empowered to arrange our difference with the Anglo-Saxon peacefully. This same opinion was manifested by the army of operations, which, under the orders of General Paredes, was in this capital; and there is no doubt that the nation repudiates all accommodation with the American government.

"The best proof which can be given of this fact is, that now when we enjoy liberty, when the nation sees itself governed by the constitution of 1824, and when it has a government of its own, since it is eminently popular, citizens of all classes present themselves full of enthusiasm to offer their services *to make war upon the unjust invader.* In all parts they are contending and disputing the preference to march, and anxiously await the day of battle to avenge the blood of their brethren, shed on the fields of Palo Alto, Resaca, and Monterey.

"NO ACCOMMODATION, cry the people: *No measures of pacification* while these rapacious invaders remain in our territory. These are the sentiments of *our army and of the people,* of our ILLUSTRIOUS CHIEF,—and these will be also the feelings of the sovereign extraordinary Congress, provided its deliberations are governed by *obedience to the popular will.*"

As I have already said, this article is from a paper published at San Luis Potosi, and it may be regarded as the organ of Santa Ana, and as speaking his sentiments. The article was put forth on the 13th of November, about three weeks before the Congress met. It seems, on its face, designed to forestall the deliberations of Congress. It leaves no field for discussion. "No accommodation," is the command of Santa Ana, at the head of fifteen or twenty thousand men. What are we to infer? That, as war will continue him in command of the army, he is unwilling to terminate it? It would certainly seem so; and yet this bold language may be a mere stroke of diplomacy. While assuming an attitude of uncompromising hostility to us, and before his countrymen, it may be that he is secretly in favor of peace. But there is enough, it appears to me, in both manifestoes to counsel us to continue our preparations, and to pursue the war with vigor, standing ready to terminate the contest on just and liberal terms, whenever Mexico shall listen to our overtures.

I have but one word more to say in support of the bill. The President has asked the appointment of a commander of the armies in Mexico, with an increased rank. He believes it to be essential to the proper organization and movement of the army. He believes the success of our military operations may depend on it. Sir, when the public honor and reputation are at stake, I am willing to extend to the administration, on whom rests the whole responsibility of bringing the war to an honorable termination, any reasonable aid it requires. If we deny him the means he asks, and there shall be any failure in the enterprises set on foot, the responsibility will rest, not on him, but on us. While I am never in favor of enlarging unduly the sphere of executive patronage or power, I am in favor of extending to the President, within the sphere of his existing powers, the fullest command of means. It is a necessary incident to the conduct of war to invest him, in this respect, with a large discretion. Be it for good or for evil, we must give him our confidence. It is always possible an Executive may not respond to it as we think he ought. But it is quite clear that he cannot without it hope for a successful execution of his plans. With these impressions, I shall vote for the men and means which may be asked to carry on the war with vigor. I shall vote for such an organization of the army as is deemed necessary to give it the greatest efficiency, so long as I see no salutary principle violated. The honorable Senator from Kentucky[1] expressed the same determination in respect to men and means at a late meeting

[1] Mr. Crittenden.

of the Senate. Sir, no one appreciates the patriotism of that honorable Senator better than myself; and I sincerely wish the confidence in the Executive, which this determination implies, could, consistently with his views of duty, be carried a little farther, — that, while giving to the government all the men and money asked for, he could also vote for such an organization of the army as is deemed necessary to a vigorous prosecution of the war; for means and men avail little without the energy moral and physical of an efficient organization. For myself, I perceive nothing objectionable in the measure proposed. On the contrary, I can readily conceive it to be essential to the successful prosecution of our military operations in Mexico. I believe it to be necessary to a proper organization of the army; and I sustain it with cheerfulness, as a measure which is deemed necessary by the administration to sustain the honor of the country and to insure the success of its arms.

THE THREE MILLION BILL.

MARCH 1, 1847.

On the 8th of August, 1846, the President of the United States sent a message to Congress, asking an appropriation of two millions of dollars to provide for any expenditure which might be necessary for the purpose of settling our difficulties with the Republic of Mexico, with which we were at war. It was well understood that the object was to secure a cession of territory from that republic. A bill making the appropriation was introduced into the House of Representatives on the same day. Mr. Wilmot, of Pennsylvania, offered an amendment, which was adopted, asserting as an express and fundamental condition of the acquisition of territory from Mexico by virtue of any treaty to be negotiated with that republic, that neither slavery nor involuntary servitude should exist in any part of said territory except for crime. This amendment was known as the Wilmot proviso. The bill passed the House on the day it was introduced, and was sent to the Senate late at night. The following day was Sunday. On Monday morning, the day Congress adjourned, the bill was taken up in the Senate, but no vote was taken, Mr. Davis of Massachusetts having spoken against it until the hour of adjournment.

In 1847, a similar bill was introduced into Congress, making an appropriation of three, instead of two millions. On this bill Mr. Dix delivered the speech which follows.

It may be proper to state, with a view to a more correct understanding of the issue presented by the Wilmot proviso, that its advocates sustained it on the distinct ground that, as slavery had been abolished throughout the Mexican republic, the acquisition of territory without prohibiting slavery would, on the theory asserted by the Southern States, lead to its restoration where it had ceased to exist, and make the United States responsible for its extension to districts in which universal freedom had been established by the fundamental law.

Mr. President: I intended to address the Senate on the general subject of the war; but being always more ready to listen than to speak, I have given way to others who were desirous of presenting their views. And I have done so with pleasure, because I knew that they were much more capable than myself of enlightening the judgment of the Senate on the questions before it. I have thought the occasion an appropriate one for recurring to the principles on which our government was founded; of reviewing its progress; of entering into a critical survey of our position as a nation, for the purpose of estimating intelligently our responsibilities to ourselves and others; of seeing wherein our strength consists; and of determining by what course of policy the permanent interests of the country are most likely to be promoted. If I do not mistake prevailing indications, an opportunity may be afforded hereafter for such a review, and one fully as appropriate as the present. I pass by all these grave considerations. I rise for the purpose of saying a few words in respect to the position taken by the non-slaveholding States concerning the acquisition of territory, and the admission of future States into the Union, — a position taken by resolutions passed by the legislatures of nine of these States. This question is presented by the bill passed by the House, and now awaiting the action of the Senate. It has been largely discussed on both sides. New York is one of the States by which resolutions relating to the question have been adopted. Her course, as well as that of other States, has been the subject of censure here. As one of her representatives on this floor, I wish to say something in her vindication, and in reference to the vote I may be called on to give, probably at too late an hour for discussion. And, in the first place, I desire to state what I understand to be the rights of the original parties to the Constitution, in respect to the subject of slavery within their own limits.

The Constitution of the United States recognized the existence of slavery in the thirteen original States, which were parties to that compact. The recognition was not in direct terms, but by force of certain stipulations designed to provide for exigencies which were the consequences of its existence. These stipulations are binding upon all the members of the Union, — as well those which were so originally, as those which have since been admitted into it. Whatever opinions may be entertained with regard to the political or social influences of slavery, the obligation of those who live under the protection of the Constitution to carry out in good faith all its stipulations is too plain to admit of doubt or controversy. It is a solemn obligation, therefore, to leave the States in which slavery exists, unmolested and free to deal with it according to their own interests and conceptions of duty.

Such I understand to be the rights and obligations of the States which were the original parties to the federal compact; and they belong equally to those who have since become parties to it.

I pass to the consideration of admitting new States into the Union, with slavery. Whether an organized State, formed from territory not belonging to the United States, or, in other words, whether a foreign State, shall be admitted into the Union at all, is a problem which may be determined (waiving all questions of constitutional power) upon general considerations of expediency, without regard to the particular conditions on which it is proposed to be received. The admission of Texas is the only case of this kind which has occurred since the adoption of the Constitution. Slavery existed in that republic at the time of the admission, and we did not require that it should be abolished. It is true, the compromise line adopted on the adjustment of the Missouri question was fixed as one of the conditions of the admission. Slavery was prohibited north of 36° 30′ north latitude. But it is equally true, I believe, that there was no settlement then, if there is now, in that part of Texas which lies north of the parallel of latitude referred to. There was no slavery to be abolished. It was an uninhabited wilderness. I believe it to be true, also, that Texas, notwithstanding the fundamental condition on which she was admitted into the Union, — that slavery should not exist above 36° 30′, — has extended to her whole territory, without reservation, the provisions of her constitution in respect to slavery; one of which is, that "the Legislature shall have no power to pass laws for the emancipation of slaves, without the consent of their owners; nor without paying their owners, previous to such emancipation, a full equivalent, in money, for the slaves so emancipated."

The reasonings which prevailed with some of those who voted for the admission of Texas, without further restriction, are all founded on the single fact that slavery existed in that republic. We took it as we found it. The same reasonings, applied to the acquisition of foreign territory in which slavery does not exist, demand that it shall be received as we find it, and that we shall so maintain it as long as it continues to be territory. If it shall at any time thereafter be organized into a State, and admitted into the Union, it is entitled to come in with all the political rights of the original States, and, therefore, free to determine for itself what its forms of organization, political or social, shall be, provided they are not inconsistent with the obligations of the fundamental compact between the States, or with any stipulation or compromise in respect to the territory from which it is formed. If slavery exists when a State comes into the Union, it may be subsequently abolished in such form as the constitution or laws of the State prescribe for expressing the sovereign will or assent. On the other hand, if slavery does not exist when a State comes into the Union, it may be subsequently established by the act of the State, without violating any provision of the federal Constitution. This freedom of action is inseparable from the sovereignty of the State, and there is no authority to control it by federal laws.

I have thus stated what I understand to be the conceded

rights of the States in respect to this subject. I admit, to the fullest extent, the exclusive control of each State over the subject, within its own jurisdiction. I admit the right of the States to be exempt from every species of intermeddling or interference within their own limits. I have always acted in conformity with this admission. I introduced resolutions in the first meeting ever held at the North in opposition to the movements of the Abolitionists. The meeting was held in Albany in 1835, and its proceedings not only met with the approbation of a large portion of the people of the non-slaveholding States of all parties, but I believe they met also with the approbation of the whole South. They were founded upon the principle I have already stated, — perfect freedom in each State, under the guaranties of the Constitution, to determine for itself, without external interference, whether it will abolish, continue, or establish slavery within its own limits.

I return again, for an instant, to the question of acquiring new territory, as territory, belonging to other independent nations. We have done so in two instances, — by the purchase of Louisiana in 1803, and Florida in 1820. Slavery existed in both; and, at the time of acquiring them, no provision was made for abolishing or restraining it. They were, in this respect, taken as they were found. I refer to these cases to show that there has been no interference with slavery, by those who are opposed to it in principle, where it has actually existed, when acquiring new territory, and that they have been willing on such occasions to leave it to the silent influences of the moral and physical causes, which must ultimately determine its limits, both in point of time and geographical extent.

A higher question than any ever yet presented to us is made by this bill. It proposes an appropriation of money to purchase territory from Mexico, — a measure of which I approve. I am in favor of the appropriation and the purchase. I have always been in favor of acquiring California on just terms. Its ports on the Pacific Ocean would be invaluable to us, and they are of little use to Mexico.

By a fundamental law of the Mexican republic, slavery is prohibited throughout its political jurisdiction. I know it has been assumed that slavery exists in Mexico; but I believe it will be found that the assertion has been made without sufficient consideration. It is not denied that slavery is forever prohibited by the constitution of Mexico. The prohibition was, I believe, first proclaimed by President Guerrero, in 1829: it has since been ingrafted upon the constitution. I am aware that barbarous usages, established under the Spanish rule, still continue, and among them some which enforce the collection of debts by personal restraint of the debtor. But they do not exceed in barbarity the laws of some of our States, in which debt was, until very recently, and is perhaps now, treated as a crime, and punished by imprisonment. The old colonial usages of Mexico do no more than to compel a debtor to pay his debt by labor, and give the creditor a control over his person until it is paid. In the city of Mexico, if a common laborer owes money, his creditor may send him to a bakery, and keep him there until he has paid his debt. It is a usage of the place. The *peones*, as they are termed, are common laborers. The term was, I believe, originally derived from Asia. It was in vogue in the early periods of the Spanish dominion in Mexico. In the second despatch of Fernando Cortez to the Emperor Charles V., (the first is not extant,) in the original Spanish, he speaks of his departure from Vera Cruz with fifteen horse, and *trescientos peones*, — three hundred foot-soldiers. The military application of the term is obsolete in Mexico, and it is now applied, I believe, exclusively to common laborers. They constitute, perhaps, a third of the population of the republic. Multitudes of them labor on the large estates (*haciendas*) for their daily bread; and if they become indebted to the proprietor, he may compel them to remain on the estate until they pay him. This is the extent of what is termed slavery in Mexico. It is an arbitrary process of enforcing the payment of debts; and it is decidedly more merciful than imprisonment for debt. It is a usage regulated by colonial laws, which are yet unrepealed, and it must wear out gradually, like all usages which have become incorporated into the social organization of a people, and which are incompatible with its spirit.

I will read a few passages from a Spanish work on Mexico, ("Ensayo Historico de las Revoluciones de Megico," — Political Essay on the Revolutions of Mexico,) which illustrate the condition of that republic in respect to this and other remnants of her colonial dependence. The author (Zavala) speaks of the laboring classes, or *peones*, thus: —

"More than three millions of individuals called suddenly to enjoy the most ample rights of citizenship, from the state of the most opprobrious slavery, without any immovable property, without a knowledge of any art or employment, and without commerce or industry."

The following passages sketch graphically the struggle which is in progress between arbitrary and liberal principles: —

"From the year 1808 to the year 1830, that is to say, in the space of a generation, such a change of ideas, of opinions, of parties, and of interests has supervened, as to overthrow a recognized and respected form of government, and to transfer seven millions of people from despotism and arbitrary power to the most liberal theories. Customs and habits alone, which are transmitted in movements, actions, and continued examples, have not changed; for how can abstract doctrines change suddenly the course of life?

"There is, then, a continual struggle between the doctrines which are professed, the institutions which are adopted, the principles which are established, on the one side, and the abuses which are sanctified, the customs which prevail, the semi-feudal rights which are respected, on the other; between national sovereignty, equality of political rights, the liberty of the press, popular government, on the one side, and between the intervention of an armed force, privileged rights, religious intolerance, and the proprietors of immense estates."

Mexico is still in a state of political transition, passing from an arbitrary to a liberal system, and time will be necessary to enable her to eradicate and heal deeply-seated disorders in her social organization. For more than fifty years after the establishment of our independence, debt was punished as a crime in my own State. How can we expect Mexico, in less than half that period, to cast off all the badges of her colonial servitude? But to return to the point from which I departed, — she has a provision in her constitution prohibiting slavery forever.

Shall the territory we acquire from her come to us with this prohibition, or shall it be made an area for the further extension of slavery? In other words, shall we purchase territory where slavery is now prohibited, and virtually rescind the prohibition? Shall we ingraft slavery upon territory where it does not lawfully or constitutionally exist, using the arms of the Union to conquer, or the treasure of the Union to purchase it? These are the questions presented to us; and the resolutions passed by the legislatures of New York and other non-slaveholding States have anticipated and given them negative answers. The New York resolutions declare, that, "if any territory is hereafter acquired by the United States, or annexed thereto, the act by which such territory is acquired or annexed, whatever such act may be, should contain an unalterable fundamental article or provision, whereby slavery and involuntary servitude, except as a punishment for crime, shall be forever excluded from the territory acquired or annexed"; and they instruct the Senators from the State to "use their best efforts to carry into effect the views expressed in the foregoing resolutions."

This vote of instruction passed the Senate unanimously, the question upon it having been taken separately from the other resolutions. All parties and divisions of party concurred in the propriety of the instruction, and of course in the subject-matter of the resolutions; for it is not to be supposed that any one would vote to instruct Senators to do what he believed wrong. I ought to state, that three votes in the Senate, out of twenty-six, (the whole number,) and nine votes in the House, out of one hundred and five, were cast against the resolution containing the proposed restriction; but I believe all the members who gave these twelve votes, with, perhaps, a single exception, avowed themselves in favor of the principle asserted, though they voted against the resolution, because they objected to the form in which it was presented, or the time selected for passing it. I believe I may safely say, that there is no difference of opinion in the legislature on the subject of excluding slavery from any territory hereafter to be acquired. I have no knowledge of the views of the members, except so far as they may be inferred from the terms of the resolution. I have had no communication, direct or indirect, with any one of them. But it may be reasonably presumed that their conclusions were strengthened by the fact, that, in the territory bordering upon us on all sides, slavery is excluded, and that to receive it without restriction would be, according to the construction of those who oppose restriction, to extend and establish slavery where it is not now permitted to exist. On this question, I believe I hazard nothing in saying, that not only New York, but all the non-slaveholding States, are undivided in opinion.

Mr. President, in the adoption of the resolutions to which I have referred, the non-slaveholding States have taken no new ground. It is older than the Constitution under which we live. It belongs to the era of the Confederation,— to the period of partial organization, which intervened between the adoption of the Articles of Confederation and the establishment of the Federal Government. In 1787, when a government was instituted for the territory northwest of the Ohio river, by the same men, or the associates of the same men, who were the authors of the Declaration of Independence and the framers of the Constitution, they included in the ordinance a provision prohibiting slavery and involuntary servitude. I will read it to the Senate: —

"There shall be neither slavery nor involuntary servitude in the said Territory, otherwise than in the punishment of crimes, whereof the party shall have been duly convicted: *Provided, always,* That any person escaping into the same, from whom labor or service is lawfully claimed in any one of the original States, such fugitive may be lawfully reclaimed, and conveyed to the person claiming his or her labor or service aforesaid."

The proviso in the bill which came from the House is in substance the same.

I have referred to the year 1787 as the period of the adoption of the provision I have read. But it had, in fact, a still earlier origin. It was proposed in 1784 by Mr. Jefferson, but failed for want of the votes of the requisite number of States. The thirteen original States then composed the Confederation; the votes were taken by States, each State counting one; seven States, or a majority, were necessary to carry any question; some questions could only be decided affirmatively by nine votes; and this proposition received the votes of only six States. Maryland, Virginia, and South Carolina, at that time voted against it. North Carolina was divided. Mr. Jefferson of Virginia, the author of the provision, and Mr. Williamson of North Carolina, voted in its favor. The author of the Declaration of Independence and the author of the slavery restriction in the ordinance of 1787 are the same person. The principles proclaimed in the one were doubtless designed by the author to be practically enforced in the other. He stands before the world, as far as the obligations of our social condition permitted, consistent with himself.

The ordinance, of which the provision I have quoted is a part, finally passed in the affirmative in 1787, with a slight modification in its terms. It received the votes of eight States. There was but one vote against it, and that was given by a member from New York, though the vote of the

State was given for it. Georgia, South Carolina, North Carolina, and Virginia unanimously supported it. Much of the Northwestern Territory was then a forest, and in the hands of the fathers of the Constitution its future destiny was placed. They performed their duty under that high sense of conscientiousness and responsibility which seems to have guided all their deliberations in providing for their own government and that of the States then about to spring up in the bosom of the wilderness; and I venture to say that the entire population of that wide-spread territory, now instinct with life, and strength, and freedom, and intelligence, and all the blessings of civilization, looks back with approbation and gratitude upon the conduct of those who gave direction and shape to the political character of the communities it contains.

The non-slaveholding States have, by their resolutions, placed themselves upon the ground taken by Jefferson more than sixty years ago. Circumstances render the position of Jefferson even higher than that now taken by them. Slavery existed *de jure*, if not *de facto*, in the Northwestern Territory in 1787. The ordinance was a virtual abolition of it. The proposition, originally made in 1784 by Mr. Jefferson, was, that after the year 1800 it should cease to exist. He proposed to take sixteen years for its abolition. The ordinance, as it passed, went into immediate effect. The non-slaveholding States only ask, that, in the acquisition of territory now free, slavery shall not be established. In the one case, it was abolished where it existed; in the other, it is only proposed to be excluded where it does not exist.

The course of the non-slaveholding States has been denounced as aggressive. Sir, it has, from the earliest period, been liberal and forbearing. They have acquiesced in all the propositions which have been made from time to time to add southern territory to the Union; they have concurred in appropriating money for the purpose, contributing their own share, and thus bearing a part of the burden of the purchase.

They united in the purchase of Louisiana, in the purchase of Florida, and in the annexation of Texas. They have contributed in these cases to the extension of slavery over a geographical area exceeding that of the thirteen original States, —equal to four fifths of that of the original States and their territories. They have voted for the admission of States from Louisiana and Florida, with provisions in their constitutions not only recognizing slavery, but prohibiting its abolition by the legislative power of those States. They have acceded to all this upon the principle of leaving the States free to regulate this subject for themselves within their own limits. In Texas, slavery existed only nominally. That republic had an area of more than three hundred thousand square miles, according to the boundaries claimed by its congress. Its population, bond and free, when admitted into the Union, did not exceed one hundred and fifty thousand souls. It was, for the most part, unpopulated. Its admission into the Union with slavery was, therefore, a virtual extension of slavery over an area equal to more than half the area of the original thirteen States. We were told that attempts had been made by foreign governments to abolish slavery in Texas, and that the success of these attempts would endanger the domestic tranquillity of the Southern States. The non-slaveholding States were appealed to, on this and other grounds, to unite in the immediate annexation of Texas. They yielded their assent. In all this they have acquiesced. Sir, they have done more: they have contributed to it; for it could never have been accomplished but by the aid of Northern votes. They believe they have fulfilled towards the South every obligation of fraternal duty. And yet they are accused of aggression, because they will not consent to the extension of slavery to free territory.

We have been told by our Southern friends, with few exceptions, that they regarded slavery as a moral and social evil, for which they were not responsible, — an evil forced upon them by foreign rulers during their colonial dependence. It is under this view of the subject that they have been sustained by their friends in the North, not only in the full possession and enjoyment of all their rights over this subject within their own limits under the Constitution, (this is a duty none should be so unscrupulous as to disregard,) but in purchasing slave territory, and establishing slaveholding States. Acquisition has gone on uninterrupted by us, and indeed aided by us, until there is no longer any slave territory on this continent to bring into the Union. We have literally absorbed it all.

The non-slaveholding States are now asked to go further: to purchase free territory and leave it open to the extension of slavery; to extend to free soil and to free communities an evil which our Southern friends have told us was forced upon them against their wishes and consent. The unanimity with which the legislatures of New York, Pennsylvania, Ohio, and other States have acted in reference to this proposition, is but an index to the universal opinion which pervades the whole North and West. They never can give their assent to it. It is regarded by all parties as involving a principle which rises far above the fleeting interests of the day, — a principle which they should not be asked to yield; for by yielding it, they would consider themselves instrumental to the extension of what they believe to be wrong, and what, in their opinion, nothing but necessity can justify.

If the principle by which the non-slaveholding States have been governed in acquiring territory is acquiesced in, this question may be settled in a moment, and without agitation. Let the territory, if any is acquired, be taken as it is found, — with the provision of the Mexican constitution abolishing slavery forever. Apply to it the principle which was applied to Florida and Texas. The non-slaveholding States have never refused to acquire territory with slavery where it actually existed. Let the South not refuse now to take free territory where slavery does not exist, and leave it free.

We are told that slavery must not be excluded from the

territories, because emigrants from the Southern States cannot go there with their property, or, in other words, their slaves, and that this would be "an entire exclusion of the slaveholding States." Sir, I do not so understand it. It is not exclusion to the slaveholder, nor is it exclusion to the free laborer of the South who owns no slaves. The slaveholder who emigrates to territory where slavery does not exist may employ free labor. The free laborer of the South who emigrates to free territory is surely not injured in his condition. It is not so with the free laborer of the North in respect to slave territory. He will not go where he is compelled to toil side by side with the slave. He is as effectually excluded as he would be by a positive prohibition. He will not emigrate with his property to territory open to slaves. The property of the free laborer is in himself, — in his powers of exertion, his capacity for endurance, in the labor of his hands. To him these are of as much value as the property which the master has in his slaves. I am not very familiarly acquainted with the internal condition of the Southern States; but I suppose there is a very numerous class in them, especially in Maryland, Virginia, North Carolina, Kentucky, and Missouri, — I mean the non-slaveholding free laborers, — who will be benefited by providing that territory, which is free when acquired, shall remain free. I think I am not mistaken in supposing this class to be far more numerous in some, if not all the States I have named, than the class holding slaves. Am I mistaken in supposing free labor is a powerful, if not a dominant, interest in the States referred to? Wherever free labor has gone forth on this continent, the forest has bowed before it; towns and villages have sprung up like magic in its track; canals, railroads, and busy industry, in all its imaginable forms, have marked its progress; civilization, in its highest attributes, follows it; knowledge and religion go with it hand in hand. Obliterate everything else, and you may trace its march by the school-house, sowing broadcast the seeds of intelligence, and the spire, "losing itself in air, as if guiding the thoughts of man to heaven." Sir, I speak of free labor everywhere, — in the South as well as the North. Even on the hypothesis of an equality in the claims of free and slave labor, (which I do not admit,) the argument in favor of taking this territory as we find it appears to me unanswerable.

Mr. President, I would not have voted to connect the proviso in the bill passed by the House, and now awaiting the action of the Senate, with any measure for the prosecution of the war. My State would not have desired it. The resolutions of the legislature are in favor of all proper measures for the prosecution of the war. From the commencement of the war, my honorable colleague and myself have sustained all measures recommended by the administration for carrying it on; and, as a member of the Committee on Military Affairs, I have had some share in maturing them. I have voted for the pecuniary means asked for, the number and description of troops which were deemed necessary for the purpose, and a commanding general for the armies in Mexico, with a rank in some degree commensurate with the numerical force to be combined, and moved in combination. I have opposed all propositions to clog military bills with extraneous matter, thus postponing our action upon them at a critical period in the campaign. The bill under consideration is of a different character. It is a proposition to purchase territory. My friend, the chairman of the Committee on Foreign Relations,[1] with his characteristic frankness and directness of purpose, — qualities as honorable in a legislator as they are in a man, — has gone so far as to indicate the extent of the acquisition which, in his opinion, we ought to expect, — California and New Mexico. The object, then, is not in doubt. It is avowedly to acquire foreign territory. Under these circumstances, is it not appropriate to know on what terms

[1] Mr. Sevier.

foreign territory shall become territory of the United States, when on these terms may depend the propriety of applying the public treasure to make the purchase? The legislature of New York so considered it. The questions of time and circumstances were fully discussed before the adoption of the resolutions. The proposition under discussion is not a measure for the prosecution of the war. It was not deemed an indispensable peace measure; for when the pecuniary claims are all on our side, an appropriation of money necessarily contemplates objects beyond that of making peace. I say this in justice to the New York legislature, as well as its Representatives in Congress, who were, with a single exception, unanimous in favor of the proviso. If it shall fail to receive the sanction of the Senate now, it must again arise on any proposition to acquire new territory, and arise in a form in which a decision cannot be avoided. It will be sustained with greater unanimity; for those who now hesitate on the point of time, or from a natural desire to postpone the settlement of embarrassing issues, will be found in its favor.

Whatever doubt may have been entertained heretofore with regard to the necessity of making the declaration contained in the proviso, I think there can be none now. It is distinctly assumed that there is no power under the Constitution to prohibit slavery in the territories. While it is contended that there is power under the Constitution to acquire slave territory, and to introduce slave States into the Union, it is denied that there is any authority to restrain or prohibit slavery in free territory. We have gone on and introduced into the Union all the slave territory on this continent; and when we reach free territory, we are told that the extension of the provisions of the Constitution to it renders it, *ipso facto*, by virtue of the compromises of the Constitution, open to slavery. According to this construction, the extension of our Constitution and laws to any portion of the Mexican territory, either by conquest or peaceful acquisition, overturns the local law, overturns the provision of the constitution of Mexico, which declares slavery to be forever prohibited. Mr. President, is this the true interpretation of the Constitution under which we live? Is it armed with full power to bring slave territory into the Union, but void of all power to bring in free territory and maintain it free? Is this the government, to use the language of Jefferson, our fathers fought for? The construction referred to would establish as a fundamental provision of the acquisition of new territory that it shall be open to slavery, even though free when acquired. Sir, I have not time, at this late period of the session, to discuss this question with the deliberation and care its importance demands. But a future occasion may come, and I will not shrink from the discussion.

I have heard with great regret the dissolution of the Union spoken of in connection with this measure. I can hardly think those who so connect the two subjects are aware of the position in which they place themselves. It is virtually declaring, that, unless we will consent to bring free territory into the Union, and leave it open to the extension of slavery, the Union shall be dissolved. Our Southern friends have heretofore stood upon the ground of defence; of maintaining slavery within their own limits against interference from without. The ground of extension is now taken, and of extending slavery upon free territory. I cannot believe this position will be sustained by the Southern States. It is new ground, and it is taken with avowals which are calculated to spread surprise and alarm throughout the non-slaveholding States.

The course of the non-slaveholding States under these new developments will, I doubt not, be steady and firm. No State will stand by the Union with a more inflexible determination to maintain it than New York, — none will adhere more tenaciously to all the obligations of the Constitution. And yet, sir, none could hope for a higher career of prosperity if the States were to be dissevered. In eighteen years her entire debt, under the provisions of her new constitution, will be paid, and she will be left with an annual surplus income of at least three millions of dollars from her internal improvements, after defraying all the expenses of her government. Standing, as she does, on the line of commercial intercourse between the Atlantic and the great lakes, with the rich and productive States bordering on them, the addition of the custom-house to her internal channels of communication would make her the wealthiest community, in proportion to her population, within the pale of civilization. She would be an empire in herself. But she scorns to enter into an estimate of these advantages. She will not "calculate the value of the Union." She prefers to stand, as she does, on the same footing with the smallest of the States, herself the most populous and powerful, rather than to stand foremost and preëminent in the field of disunion. In whatever manner this question shall be decided, she will be found on the side of the Union, not to resist dismemberment by force, — for disunion is better than intestine war, — but to contribute by her influence and her counsels to uphold the fabric of the federative system.

Mr. President, I regret to hear either disunion or civil war spoken of in connection with this measure. But, I repeat, the former is to be preferred to the latter. In wars waged with foreign countries, deplorable as they always are, there are some moral fruits which atone, in a slight degree, for their accompanying evils. There is the sense of national honor, — the parent of high achievement; the sentiment of patriotic devotion to the country, which shrinks from no labor or sacrifice in the public cause; and the feeling of mutual sympathy and dependence, which pervades and unites all classes in the hour of adversity and peril. Far as they are overbalanced by the domestic bereavement and the public evil which war always brings in its train, they serve to purify the thoughts of something of their selfishness by turning them away from the sordid channels in which they are too apt to run. But civil war has no ameliorations. It is pure, unmixed demoralization. It dissolves all national and domestic ties. It renders selfishness more odious, by wedding it to hatred and cruelty. The after-generation, which reaps the bitter harvest of intestine war, is scarcely less to be commiserated than that by whose hands the poisonous seed is sown. Less, far less than these, would be the evils of disunion.

But, sir, we shall have neither. The interests, the feelings, the good sense of the country, all revolt at internal dissension in every form. If this question shall be decided against the non-slaveholding States, if their voice shall be unheeded, New York will not, for that reason, listen to any suicidal project of dismemberment. No, sir; no. By no agency of hers shall the fraternal bonds which unite her to her sisters be rent asunder. Their destiny, whatever it may be, shall be also hers. Be it for evil or for good, she will cling to them to the last. But I say for her and in her name, — I believe I do not misunderstand her resolutions, — that she can never consent to become a party to the extension of slavery to free territory on this continent. If it is to be extended to new areas, — areas now consecrated to free labor, — the work must be done by other hands than hers; and she must leave it to time and to the order of Providence to determine what shall be the legitimate fruits of measures which she believes to be wrong, and to which she can never yield her assent.

THE WAR WITH MEXICO.

The following speech was delivered on the 26th of January, 1848, in support of a bill to raise an additional military force with a view to retain possession of the territory of Mexico, until she should consent to make peace on terms satisfactory to the United States. The resolutions of Mr. Calhoun, alluded to by Mr. Dix at the commencement of his speech, declared that, "to conquer Mexico, and to hold it either as a province or incorporate it into the Union, would be inconsistent with the avowed object for which war has been prosecuted; a departure from the settled policy of the government; in conflict with its character and genius; and in the end subversive of our free and popular institutions."

Mr. President: It was my wish to address the Senate on the resolutions offered by the Senator from South Carolina,[1] and not on this bill. I should have preferred to do so, because I am always unwilling to delay action on any measure relating to the war, and because the resolutions afford a wider field for inquiry and discussion. But as the debate has become general, and extended to almost every topic that can well be introduced under either, the force of the considerations by which I have been influenced has become so weakened, that I have not thought it necessary to defer longer what I wish to say.

Two leading questions divide and agitate the public mind in respect to the future conduct of the war with Mexico. The first of these questions is, Shall we withdraw our forces from the Mexican territory, and leave the subject of indemnity for injuries and the adjustment of a boundary between the two republics to future negotiation, relying on a magnanimous course of conduct on our part to produce a corresponding feeling on the part of Mexico? There are other propositions, subordinate to this, which may be

[1] Mr. Calhoun.

considered as parts of the same general scheme of policy, — such as that of withdrawing from the Mexican capital and the interior districts, and assuming an exterior line of occupation. I shall apply to all these propositions the same arguments; and if I were to undertake to distinguish between them, I am not sure that I should make any difference in the force of the application. For, whether we withdraw from Mexico altogether, or take a defensive line which shall include all the territory we intend to hold permanently as indemnity, the consequences to result from it, so far as they affect the question of peace, would, it appears to me, be the same.

The second question is, Shall we retain the possession of the territory we have acquired until Mexico shall consent to make a treaty of peace which shall provide ample compensation for the wrongs of which we complain, and settle to our satisfaction the boundary in dispute?

Regarding these questions as involving the permanent welfare of the country, I have considered them with the greatest solicitude; and though never more profoundly impressed with a sense of the responsibility which belongs to the solution of problems of such magnitude and difficulty, my reflections have, nevertheless, led me to a clear and settled conviction as to the course which justice and policy seem to indicate and demand. The first question, in itself of the highest importance, has been answered affirmatively on this floor; and it derives additional interest from the fact, that it has also been answered in the affirmative by a statesman, now retired from the busy scenes of political life, who, from his talents, experience, and public services, justly commands the respect of his countrymen, and whose opinions on any subject are entitled to be weighed with candor and deliberation. I have endeavored to attribute to his opinions, and to those of others who coincide with him wholly or in part, all the importance which belongs to them, and to consider them with the deference due to the distinguished sources from which they emanate. I believe I have done so; and yet I have, after the fullest reflection, come to conclusions totally different from theirs. I believe it would be in the highest degree unjust to ourselves, possessing, as we do, well-founded claims on Mexico, to withdraw our forces from her territory altogether; and exceedingly unwise, as a matter of policy, looking to the future political relations of the two countries, to withdraw from it partially, and assume a line of defence, without a treaty of peace. On the contrary, I am in favor of retaining possession, for the present, of all we have acquired, not as a permanent conquest, but as the most effective means of bringing about, what all most earnestly desire, a restoration of peace; and I will, with the indulgence of the Senate, proceed to state, with as much brevity as the magnitude of the subject admits, my objections to the course suggested by the first question, and my reasons in favor of the course suggested by the other.

I desire, at the outset, to state this proposition, to the truth of which, I think, all will yield their assent: that no policy which does not carry with it a reasonable assurance of healing the dissensions dividing the two countries, and of restoring, permanently, amicable relations between them, ought to receive our support. We may differ in opinion, and perhaps hopelessly, as to the measures best calculated to produce this result; but if it were possible for us to come to an agreement in respect to them, the propriety of their adoption could scarcely admit of controversy. This proposition being conceded, as I think it will be, it follows that, if the measure proposed — to withdraw our forces from Mexico — be not calculated to bring about a speedy and permanent peace, but, on the contrary, if it be rather calculated to open a field of domestic dissension, and possibly of external interference, in that distracted country, to be followed, in all probability, by a renewal of active hostilities with us, and under circumstances to make us feel severely the loss of the advantage which we have gained, and which it is proposed voluntarily to surrender, — then, it appears to me, it can present no claim to our favorable consideration. I shall endeavor to show, before I sit down, that the policy referred to is exposed to all these dangers and evils.

I do not propose to enter into an examination of the origin of the war. From the moment the collision took place between our forces and those of Mexico on the Rio Grande, I considered all hope of an accommodation, without a full trial of strength in the field, to be out of the question. I believed the peculiar character of the Mexicans would render any such hope illusive. Whether that collision was produced in any degree by our own mistakes, or whether the war itself was brought about by the manner in which Texas was annexed to the Union, are questions I do not propose to discuss now; and, if it were not too late, I would submit whether the discussion could serve any other purpose but to exhibit divided councils to our adversary, and to inspire him with the hope of obtaining more favorable terms of peace by protracting his resistance. No one can be less disposed than myself to abridge, in any degree, the legitimate boundaries of discussion. But I am not disposed to enter into such an investigation now. The urgent concern is to know, not how the war originated, not who is responsible for it, but in what manner it can be brought to a speedy and honorable termination, — whether, as some suppose, we ought to retire from the field, or whether, as appears to me, the only hope of an accommodation lies in a firm and determined maintenance of our position.

The probable consequences of an abandonment of the advantages we have gained may be better understood by seeing what those advantages are. I speak in a military point of view. While addressing the Senate in February last, on an army bill then under consideration, I had occasion to state that the whole of northern Mexico, as far south as the mouth of the Rio Grande and the 26th parallel of latitude, was virtually in our possession, comprehending about two thirds of the territory of that republic, and about one tenth of its inhabitants. Our acquisitions have since been augmented by the reduction of Vera Cruz and the Castle of San Juan de Ulua; the capture of Jalapa, Perote, and Puebla; the surrender of the city of Mexico, and the occupation of the three States of Vera Cruz, Puebla, and Mexico, with nearly two millions and a half of souls. It is true, our forces have not overrun every portion of the territory of those States; but their chief towns have been reduced, the military forces which defended them captured or dispersed, their civil authorities superseded, their capital occupied, and the whole machinery of government within the conquered States virtually transferred to our hands. All this has been achieved with an army at no one period exceeding fifteen thousand men, and against forces from three to five times more numerous than those actually engaged on our side, in every conflict since the fall of Vera Cruz.

I had occasion, on presenting some army petitions a few weeks ago, to refer to the brilliant successes by which these acquisitions were made; and I will not trespass on the attention of the Senate by repeating what I said at that time.[1] But I cannot forbear to say, that there is a moral

[1] The reference alluded to is contained in the following extract: —

"I will not detain the Senate by entering into any detailed review of these events with a view to enforce the appeal contained in the petition on the attention. I hope, however, I may be indulged in saying, in justice to those who bore a part in them, that the first conquest of Mexico cannot, as it appears to me, be compared with the second, either as to the obstacles overcome, or as to the relative strength of the invaders. The triumphs of Cortez were achieved by policy, and by superiority in discipline and in the implements of warfare. The use of fire-arms, until then unknown to the inhabitants of Mexico, was sufficient in itself to make his force, small as it was, irresistible. In the eyes of that simple and superstitious people, he seemed armed with superhuman power. Other circumstances combined to facilitate his success. The native tribes, by whom the country was possessed, were distinct communities, not always acknowledging the same head, and often divided among themselves by implacable hostility and resentments. Cortez, by his consummate prudence and art, turned these dissensions to his own account; he lured the parties to them into his own service, and when he prein the contest, the effect of which is not likely to be lost on ourselves or others. At the call of their country, our people have literally rushed to arms. The emulation has been to be received into the service, not to be excused from it. Individuals from the plough, the counting-house, the law-office, and the workshop, have taken the field, braving inclement seasons and inhospitable climates without a murmur, and, though wholly unused to arms, withstanding the most destructive fire, and storming batteries at the point of the bayonet, with the coolness, intrepidity, and spirit of veterans. I believe I may safely say, there has been no parallel to these achievements by undisciplined forces since the French revolution. I am not sure that history can furnish a parallel. As to the regular army, we always expect it to be gallant and heroic, and we are never disappointed. The whole conduct of the war in the field has exhibited the highest evidence of our military capacity. It confirms an opinion I have always held, — that a soldier is formidable in ratio of the importance he possesses in the order of the political system of which he is a part. It establishes another position of vital importance to us: that, under the protection of our militia system, the country may, at the

sented himself at the gates of the city of Mexico, he was at the head of four thousand of the most warlike of the natives, as auxiliaries to the band of Spaniards with which he commenced his march from Vera Cruz. Thus his early successes were as much the triumph of policy as of arms. General Scott, and the gallant band he led, had no such advantages. The whole population of the country, from Vera Cruz to Mexico, was united as one man against him, and animated by the fiercest animosity. He was opposed by military forces armed like his own, often better disciplined, occupying positions chosen by themselves, strong by nature, and fortified according to the strictest rules of art. These obstacles were overcome by his skill as a tactician, aided by a corps of officers unsurpassed for their knowledge of the art of attack and defence, and by the indomitable courage of their followers. With half his force left on the battle-field or in the hospital, and with less than six thousand men, after a series of desperate contests, he took possession of the city of Mexico, containing nearly two hundred thousand inhabitants, and defended by the remnant of an army of more than thirty thousand soldiers. I confess I know nothing in modern warfare which exceeds in brilliancy the movements of the American army from the Gulf to the city of Mexico. I shall not attempt to speak of them in the language of eulogium. They are not a fit theme for such comment. Like the achievements of General Taylor and his brave men on the Rio Grande, at Monterey, and Buena Vista, the highest and most appropriate praise is contained in the simplest statement of facts."

termination of every contest, lay aside the more massive and burdensome parts of its armor, and become prepared, with energies renewed by that very capacity, for succeeding scenes of danger.

Mr. President, the political condition of Mexico has been gradually approaching a dissolution of all responsible government, and of the civil order which constitutes her an independent State. This lamentable situation is not the fruit alone of our military successes. The factions by which that country has been distracted, each in turn gaining and maintaining a temporary ascendency, and often by brute force, lie at the foundation of the social and political disorder which has reigned there for the last twenty years. To most of the abuses of the old colonial system of Spain she has superadded the evils of an unstable and irresponsible government. The military bodies, which have been the instruments of those who have thus in succession gained a brief and precarious control over her affairs, though dispersed, still exist, ready to be reunited and to renew the anarchy which we have superseded, for the time being, by a military government. And this brings me to the first great objection to the proposition of withdrawing our armies from the field.

I have already said that no policy can deserve our support which does not hold out the promise of a durable peace. Nothing seems to me more unlikely to secure so desirable a result than an abandonment of Mexico by us at the present moment without a treaty, leaving behind a strong feeling of animosity towards us, with party-divisions as strongly marked, and political animosities as rancorous, perhaps, as they have been at any former period. Even when her capital had fallen, humbled and powerless as she was, party-leaders, instead of consulting for the common good, were seen struggling with each other for the barren sceptre of her authority. Our retirement as enemies would, in all probability, be the signal for intestine conflicts as desperate and sanguinary as those in which they have been engaged with us, — conflicts always the most disastrous for the great body of the Mexican people, for, on what side soever fortune turns, they are certain to be the victims. You know, sir, there are two great parties in Mexico, (I pass by the minor divisions,) the "federalistas" and "centralistas." The former, as their name imports, are in favor of the federative system; they are the true republican party. With us, in former times, the terms "federal" and "republican" designated different parties; in Mexico, they are both employed to designate the friends of the federative system. The centralists are in favor of a consolidated government, republican or monarchical in form, and are composed of the army, the clergy, and I suppose a small portion of the population. I believe our only hope of obtaining a durable peace lies in the firm establishment of the federal party in power, — the party represented by Herrera, Anaya, Peña y Peña, Cumplido, and others. I understand Herrera has been elected president of the republic; and this is certainly a favorable indication. But, unfortunately, I fear this party would not succeed in maintaining itself, if Mexico were left to herself at the present moment with an embittered feeling of hostility towards us. The military chiefs, who control the army, and who might rally it again for political uses, if we were to retire without a treaty, are for the most part enemies of the federative system, and conservators of the popular abuses, to which they owe their wealth and importance. Nothing could be more unfortunate for Mexico than the reëstablishment of these men in power. It would bring with it a hopeless perpetuation of the anarchy and oppression which have given a character to their supremacy in past years, — a supremacy without a prospect of amelioration in the condition of the Mexican people, — a supremacy of which the chief variation has been an exchange of one military despot for another.

Calamitous as the restoration of this party to their former

ascendency would be for Mexico, it would hardly be less so for us. Relying on military force for their support, their policy would be to continue the war as a pretext for maintaining the army in full strength, or, at least, not to terminate it till peace would ensure their own supremacy. It is believed that these considerations have been leading motives in the resistance they have opposed to us. It is true, the republican party has been equally hostile, so far as external indications show; but the fact is accounted for by their desire to see the war continued until the army and its leaders, the great enemies of the federative system, are overthrown. Undoubtedly the obstinate refusal of Mexico to make peace may be very properly referred to the natural exasperation of every people whose soil is invaded; but there can be little doubt that it has been influenced in no inconsiderable degree by considerations growing out of party divisions, and the jealousy and animosities to which those divisions have given rise. My confidence in our ability to make an amicable arrangement with the federal party, if it were in undisputed possession of the government, arises from the belief that their motives are honest, that they have at heart the public welfare, and that they must see there is no hope for Mexico but in a solid peace with us. My utter distrust of the centralists arises from the belief that their objects are selfish, and that, to accomplish them, they would not hesitate to sacrifice the liberties of the people and the prosperity of the country. But whether I err in these views or not, I feel quite confident I do not err in believing that if our armies were to be withdrawn from Mexico, without a peace, the flames of civil discord would be rekindled in that unhappy country, and burn with redoubled violence. I should greatly fear that the military chiefs would succeed in reëstablishing their ascendency, and that no probable limit could be assigned to the duration of the war. If I am right, our true policy is to stand firm, and, if possible, united, until wiser counsels shall prevail in Mexico, and a disposition shall be shown to come to an amicable arrangement with us on reasonable terms.

The objection I have stated to the proposition of withdrawing our forces from Mexico concerns only the relations which now exist, or may exist hereafter, between the two countries. If there were no other objection, the question might be decided upon considerations touching only their domestic interests and their mutual rights.

But I come to the second objection, — one perhaps of graver import than the first, because it supposes the possibility, if not the probability, of an interference in her affairs by other countries, if we were to retire without a treaty and without commercial arrangements which it would be in our power to enforce. The President alluded to the subject in his annual message at the opening of Congress, and expressed an apprehension of danger from that source. I participate in it. I shall assign the grounds on which it rests; and I only regret that, in stating them with the minuteness necessary to make them fully understood, I shall be compelled to draw much more largely than I desire on the patience of the Senate.

Senators are doubtless aware that the right of intervention in the affairs of this continent was formally asserted in the French Chamber of Deputies, in the year 1845, by M. Guizot, Minister of foreign affairs, as the organ of the government of France. He regarded the great powers on this continent as divided into three groups, namely, Great Britain, the United States, and the states of Spanish origin; and he declared that it belonged to France "to protect, by the authority of her name, the independence of states, and the equilibrium of the great political forces in America." To this declaration, I have thought it not out of place, in connection with the subject under discussion, to call the attention of the Senate; not for the purpose of undertaking the formal refutation, — of which I think the whole doctrine of intervention, as it has been practically enforced in Europe, is clearly susceptible, — but for the purpose of denying it as founded upon any well-established principles of international law, and, if it had such a foundation, of denying its applicability to the political condition of this continent. To enter fully into the examination of this important subject would require more time than it would be proper for me to devote to it. I propose only to pass rapidly over a few of the principal considerations it suggests.

The declaration of M. Guizot was the first public and official intimation, by a European government, of an intention to interfere with the political condition of the independent communities on the continent of America, and to influence by moral, if not by physical agencies, their relations to each other. And if it had been presented in any other form than that of an abstract declaration, not necessarily to be followed by any overt act, it would have behooved us to inquire, in the most formal manner, whether this asserted right of interposition derived any justification from the usages of nations, or from the recognized principles of international law; or whether it was not an assumption wholly unsupported by authority, and an encroachment on the independence of sovereign states, which it would have been their duty to themselves and the civilized world to resent as an injury and a wrong.

Am I in error in supposing this subject derives new importance from our existing relations with Mexico, one of the states of Spanish origin, which M. Guizot grouped together as constituting one of the great political forces of this continent, among which the "equilibrium" was to be maintained? Sir, more than once, in the progress of the war, the governments of Europe have been invoked, by leading organs of public opinion abroad, to interpose between us and Mexico. Is it not, then, appropriate briefly to state what this right of intervention is, as it has been asserted in Europe, what it has been in practice, and what it would be likely to become, if applied to the states of this continent? I trust it will be so considered.

The doctrine of intervention, to maintain the balance of power, is essentially of modern origin. From the earliest ages, it is true, occasional combinations have been formed by particular states for mutual protection against the aggressions of a powerful neighbor. History is full of these examples. Such a coöperation is dictated by the plainest principles of self-preservation, for the purpose of guarding against the danger of being destroyed in detail; and it is founded upon such obvious maxims of common sense, that it would have been remarkable if it had not been resorted to from the moment human society assumed a regular form of organization. These defensive alliances were deficient in the permanence and methodical arrangements which distinguish the modern system of intervention. Hume saw, or fancied he saw, in them the principle of the right of intervention to preserve the balance of power which is asserted at the present day. But it could only have been the principle which was developed; they certainly never attained the maturity or the efficient force of a regular system.

The modern doctrine of intervention in the affairs of other states, which has sprung up within the last two centuries, is far more comprehensive in its scope. It has grown into a practical system of supervision on the part of the principal European powers over their own relative forces and those of the other states of Europe; and though it may, in some instances, have been productive of beneficial effects in maintaining the public tranquillity, it has as frequently been an instrument of the grossest injustice and tyranny. From the first extensive coalition of this nature, which was formed during the long series of wars terminated by the peace of Westphalia, in 1648, down to the interference of Great Britain, Prussia, Austria, and France, in the contest between the Sultan and Mehemet Ali, in 1840, a period of nearly two centuries, — an interference designed, in some degree, to prevent what was regarded as a dangerous protectorate over the affairs of the Porte by Russia, — the exercise of the right has been placed, theoretically, on the same high ground of regard for the tranquillity of Europe and the independence of states. Practically, it has often been perverted to the worst purposes of aggrandizement and cupidity.

If we look into the writers on international law, I think we shall find no sufficient ground for the right of intervention. Grotius, who wrote in the early part of the seventeenth century, denied its existence. Fenelon, who wrote about half a century later, denied it, except as a means of self-preservation, and then only when the danger was real and imminent. Vattel, who wrote nearly a century after Fenelon, and a century before our own times, regarded the states of Europe as forming a political system, and he restricted the right of entering into confederacies and alliances for the purpose of intervention in the affairs of each other to cases in which such combinations were necessary to curb the ambition of any power, which, from its superiority in physical strength, and its designs of oppression or conquest, threatened to become dangerous to its neighbors. De Martens, who wrote half a century ago, acknowledges, with Vattel, the existence of the right under certain conditions, though he hardly admits it to be well settled as a rule of international law; and he limits its exercise to neighboring states, or states occupying the same quarter of the globe. But, according to the last two writers, who have perhaps gone as far as any other public jurists, of equal eminence, towards a formal recognition of the right, it only justifies a union of inferior states within the same immediate sphere of action, to prevent an accumulation of power in the hands of a single sovereign which would be too great for the common liberty.

I am confident, Mr. President, that no one can rise from a review of the history of modern Europe, and from an examination of the writings of her public jurists, without being satisfied that the right of intervention, as recognized by civilized nations, is what I have stated it to be, — a mere right, on the part of weaker states, to combine for the purpose of preventing the subversion of their independence, and the alienation of their territories, by a designing and powerful neighbor; a right to be exercised only in cases of urgent and immediate danger. It is simply a right of self-preservation, undefined, undefinable, having no settled or permanent foundation in public law, to be asserted only in extreme necessity, and, when arbitrarily applied to practice, a most fruitful source of abuse, injustice, and oppression. One clear and certain limitation it happily possesses, — a limitation which, amid all its encroachments upon the independence of sovereign states, has never until our day been overpassed. By universal consent, by the unvarying testimony of abuse itself, it is not to be exercised beyond the immediate sphere of the nations concerned. It pertains rigidly and exclusively to states within the same circle of political action. It is only by neighbors, for the protection of neighbors against neighbors, that it can, even upon the broadest principles, be rightfully employed. When it traverses oceans, and looks to the regulation of the political concerns of other continents, it becomes a gigantic assumption, which, for the independence of nations, for the interests of humanity, for the tranquillity of the old world and the new, should be significantly repelled.

Mr. President, a review of the history of Europe during the last two centuries will bring with it another conviction in respect to the right of intervention, — that no reliance can be placed on its restriction in practice to the objects to which it is limited by every public jurist who admits its existence at all; and that nothing could be so discouraging to the friends of free government as an extension of the system to this continent, if the power existed to introduce it here. Though the combinations it is claimed to authorize may, in some instances, have protected the coalescing parties from the danger of being overrun by conquering armies, the cases are perhaps as numerous in which their interposition has been lent to break down the independence of states, and to throw whole communities of men into the arms of governments to which their feelings and principles were alike averse. The right, as has been seen, (and it cannot be too often repeated,) with the utmost latitude claimed for it by any public jurist, goes no further than to authorize a league on the part of two or more weaker states to protect themselves against the designs of an ambitious and powerful neighbor. In its practical application, it has more frequently resulted in a combination of powerful states to destroy their weaker neighbors, for the augmentation of their own dominions or those of their allies. From a mere right to combine for self-preservation, they have made it in practice a right to divide, dismember, and partition states at their pleasure, — not for the purpose of diminishing the strength of a powerful adversary, — but under the pretence of creating a system of balances, which is artificial in its structure, and, in some degree, incongruous in its elements, and which a single political convulsion may overturn and destroy. Do we need examples of the abuse of the power, — I will not call it a right? They will be found in the dismemberment of Saxony, the annexation of the republic of Genoa to the kingdom of Sardinia, and the absorption of Venice by Austria. There is another and a more aggravated case of abuse to which recent events have given new prominence. In 1772, Russia, Prussia, and Austria, under the pretence that the disturbed condition of Poland was dangerous to their own tranquillity, seized upon about one third of her territories, and divided it among themselves. In 1793, notwithstanding her diminished proportions, she had become more dangerous, and they seized half of what they had left to her by the first partition. Sir, she continued to grow dangerous as she grew weak; and in two years after the second partition, they stripped her of all that remained. In 1815, the five great powers, at the Congress of Vienna, from motives of policy, and not from a returning sense of justice, organized the city of Cracow and a portion of the surrounding territory, with a population of about one hundred thousand souls, into a republic, under the protection of Austria, Russia, and Prussia, with a guaranty of its independence in perpetuity. Russia pledged herself, at the same time, to maintain her share of the spoil as the kingdom of Poland in name and form, with a constitutional government. At the end of seventeen years, in violation of her pledge, she virtually incorporated it, as an integral part, into the Russian empire. The little republic of Cracow was all that remained as a monument of the dismembered kingdom. A year ago, it was obliterated as an independent state by the three great powers of eastern and northern Europe, in violation of their solemn guaranty, and assigned to Austria. The name of Poland, the fountain of so many noble and animating recollections, is no longer to be found on the map of Europe. The three quarters of a century which intervened from the inception to the consummation of this transaction are not sufficient to conceal or even to obscure its true character. The very magnitude of the space over which it is spread only serves to bring it out in bolder and darker relief from the pages of history.

If the United States, in the progress of these usurpations, have not remonstrated against them, and contributed by her interposition to maintain the integrity of the states thus disorganized and dismembered in violation of every rule of right, and every suggestion of justice and humanity, it is because we have been faithful, against all movements of sympathy, against the very instincts of nature, to the principle of abstaining from all interference with the movements of European powers relating exclusively to the condition of the quarter of the globe to which they belong. But when it is proposed or threatened to extend to this continent and to ourselves a similar system of balances, with all its danger of abuse and usurpation, I hold it to be our duty to inquire on what grounds it rests, that we may be prepared to resist all practical application of it to the independent states in this hemisphere.

Mr. President, the declaration of M. Guizot could hardly have been made without the previous approbation of the government of which he was the organ. The same sovereign occupies the throne of France, — the same minister stands before it as the exponent of his opinions. Is the declaration to be regarded as a mere idle annunciation in words of a design never intended to be carried into practice? Let me answer the question by the briefest possible reference to circumstances. France was the coadjutor of England in the attempt to induce Texas to decline annexation to the Union. Failing in this, she attempted to accomplish the same object indirectly, by persuading Mexico to recognize the independence of Texas, on condition that the latter should remain an independent state. These terms were offered to Texas, and rejected. In the year 1844, I believe less than twelve months before M. Guizot's declaration was made, (and the coincidence in point of time is remarkable,) a book on Oregon and California was published in Paris by order of the King of France, under the auspices of Marshal Soult, President of the Council, and M. Guizot, Minister of Foreign Affairs, and written by M. de Mofras, who was attached to the French legation in Mexico. The first part of the work is devoted to Mexico, and certainly contains some remarkable passages. He speaks of the establishment of a European monarchy as a project that had been suggested as the only one calculated to put an end to the divisions and annihilate the factions which desolated that beautiful country.[1] He says, the Catholic religion and family relations

[1] The day after this speech was delivered, Mr. Dix received from a friend in New York, who could have had no knowledge of his intention to speak, much less of the topics he designed to discuss, a translation from a speech delivered to the Cortes of Spain on the 1st of December, 1847, by Señor Olozoga, a man of distinction, and supposed to be the same individual who was a few years since first minister of the crown. By this speech it appears that, as recently as 1846, a year after M. Guizot's declaration was made, and two years after M. de Mofras's book was published, large sums were expended by Spain for the purpose of establishing a monarchy in Mexico, and of placing a Spanish prince on the throne. The close connection of the governments of France and Spain, by the marriage of the Duke of Montpensier, the son of Louis Philippe, to the sister of Queen Isabella, gives additional importance to these developments: —

"No one, either on this floor or else-

with the ancient possessors of the country would be the first conditions required of the princes who should be called to reconstruct there a monarchical government. He then adds: —

"The infantas of Spain, the French princes, and the archdukes of Austria, fulfil these conditions, and we may affirm that, from whichever quarter a competitor should present himself, he would be unanimously welcomed by the Mexican people.

"What, then, are the interests of France in these questions?

"The establishment in Mexico of a monarchy of any description whatever, resting upon a solid basis, should be the first object of our policy; for we know that the instability attached to the actual form of its government brings with it disadvantages for our commerce, and inconveniences for our people."

He adds, that if Mexico is to preserve her republican form of government, her incorporation into the Union of the North would seem more favorable to France than her existing condition, on account of the development of commerce and all the guaranties of liberty, security, and justice, which his compatriots would enjoy; and that England would lose, under such an order of things, what France would gain. Thus, though the dismemberment and absorption of Mexico

where, can deny that the project has been entertained of establishing a monarchy in Mexico, and to place a Spanish prince on the throne. This project, conceived in the time of the Conde Aranda, would have saved our colonies from the sad fate they have suffered; but brought forward on this occasion, it was the most absurd idea that could have been conceived. But we have not only to deplore having excited political animosities and the consequences this has produced in that country, we have also to lament the money lost and thrown away upon Mexican soil. And in order that the Cortes may not believe I am about to make accusations of so grave a character without possessing proofs to corroborate them, I now hold in my hand a statement of the sums expended and drawn from the treasury in Havana in the year 1846, signed by the Señor Navarro as auditor, and Mugica as treasurer. In this statement there is an item which says: 'Paid bills of exchange remitted by the minister plenipotentiary of her Majesty in Mexico for matters belonging to the service, $100,000.' But much greater than this was the authority our minister in Mexico possessed for disposing of the public funds. I do not know whether he has made use of it. I do not even know his name. I suppose he will employ them with scrupulous honesty; but is the Spanish people so bountifully supplied with millions that they can afford to send them to the New World, for the purpose of sustaining political intrigues in that distant region? How many meritorious military men, who have shed their blood for the good of their country, and whose means of support have been cut down to the lowest possible point, might have been aided by these large sums? How much misery might have been alleviated by the money which has been thrown away in this manner? And where do they find authority for squandering millions to foster foreign intrigues?"

by the United States are regarded by M. de Mofras as preferable to the commercial monopoly and the "species of political sovereignty," as he denominates it, which England has exercised in that country, the first object of France, according to him, should be a reconstruction of monarchy in Mexico, with a foreign prince on the throne, and this prince from some branch of the Bourbon family. The opinions contained in this book are not put forth as the mere speculations of a private person. They are the opinions of an agent of the government: the publication is made by order of the king, and under the auspices of his two chief ministers, and so stated in the title-page. I do not mean to hold the government of France responsible for all the opinions contained in that work; but can we believe that those I have quoted, concerning as they do so grave a subject as the international relations of France with Mexico, and of Mexico with the United States, would have been put forth without modification under such high official sanctions, if they had been viewed with positive disfavor? It appears to me that we are constrained to view them, like the declaration of M. Guizot, though certainly to a very inferior extent, as possessing an official character which we are not at liberty wholly to disregard, when we consider the one in connection with the other.

And now, sir, I ask, do not these opinions and declarations, especially when we look to the open and direct interference of Great Britain and France, by force of arms, in the domestic affairs of some of the South American republics within the last two years, furnish a just ground of apprehension, if we should retire from Mexico without a treaty and as enemies, that it might become a theatre for the exercise of influences of a most unfriendly character to us? With the aid of the monarchical party in Mexico, would there not be danger that the avowed design of establishing a throne might be realized? The chances of open interposition are unquestionably diminished by the results of the war;

but I am constrained to believe the chances of secret interference are increased by the avidity imputed to us for territorial extension. Ought not this danger to influence, to some extent, our own conduct, at least so far as to dissuade us from abandoning, until a better prospect of a durable peace shall exist, the advantage we have gained as belligerents? We know, a great majority of the Mexican people are radically averse to any other than a republican form of government; but we know, also, the proneness of a people among whom anarchy reigns triumphant, to seek any refuge which promises the restoration of tranquillity and social order.

Mr. President, any attempt by a European power to interpose in the affairs of Mexico, either to establish a monarchy, or to maintain, in the language of M. Guizot, "the equilibrium of the great political forces in America," would be the signal for a war far more important in its consequences, and inscrutable in its issues, than this. We could not submit to such interposition if we would. The public opinion of the country would compel us to resist it. We are committed by the most formal declarations, first made by President Monroe in 1823, and repeated by the present Chief Magistrate of the Union. We have protested, in the most solemn manner, against any further colonization by European powers on this continent. We have protested against any interference in the political concerns of the independent states in this hemisphere. A protest, it is true, does not imply that the ground it assumes is to be maintained at all hazards, and, if necessary, by force of arms. Great Britain protested against the interference of France in the affairs of Spain in 1823; she has more recently protested against the absorption of Cracow by Austria as a violation of the political order of Europe, settled at Vienna by the allied sovereigns, and against the Montpensier marriage as a violation of the treaty of Utrecht; but I do not remember that in either case she did anything more than to proclaim to the world her dissent from the acts against which she entered her protest. It has always seemed to me to be unwise in a government to put forth manifestoes without being prepared to maintain them by acts, or to make declarations of abstract principle until the occasion has arrived for enforcing them. The declarations of a President, having no power to make war without a vote of Congress, or even to employ the military force of the country except to defend our own territory, is very different from the protest of a sovereign holding the issues of peace and war in his own hands. But the former may not be less effectual when they are sustained, as I believe those of Presidents Monroe and Polk are, in respect to European interference on the American continent, by an undivided public opinion, even though they may not have received a formal response from Congress. I hold, therefore, if any such interposition as that to which I have referred should take place, resistance on our part would inevitably follow, and we should become involved in controversies of which no man could foresee the end.

Before I quit this part of the subject, I desire to advert to some circumstances recently made public, and, if true, indicating significantly the extent to which Great Britain is disposed to carry her other encroachments on this continent, as in every other quarter of the globe. On the coast of Honduras, in Central America, commonly called the Mosquito coast, there is a tribe of Indians bearing the same name, numbering but a few hundred individuals, and inhabiting some miserable villages in the neighborhood of Cape Gracias a Dios, near the fifteenth parallel of north latitude. Several hundred miles south is the river San Juan, running from Lake Nicaragua to the Caribbean sea, a space of about two degrees of longitude, with the town of Nicaragua at its mouth, and a castle or fort about midway between the town and the lake. The lake is only fifteen leagues from the Pacific, and constitutes, with the river San

Juan, one of the proposed lines for a ship-canal across the Isthmus. Great Britain has recently laid claim to the river San Juan and the town of Nicaragua, if she has not actually taken possession of the latter. I have seen a communication from the British consul-general at Guatemala, asserting the independence of the Mosquitoes as a nation. I have also seen a communication from the British consul at Bluefield, on the Mosquito shore, asserting that "the Mosquito flag and nation are under the special protection of the crown of Great Britain," and that "the limits which the British government is determined to maintain as the right of the king of the Mosquitoes" "comprehend the San Juan river." By Arrowsmith's London Atlas, published in 1840, the Mosquito territory covered about 40,000 square miles, nearly as large an area as that of the state of New York; but it did not extend below the twelfth parallel of latitude, while the river San Juan is on the eleventh. I have seen the protest of the state of Nicaragua against the occupation of the town of Nicaragua on the river San Juan, which, as the protest declares, has been from time immemorial in her quiet and peaceable possession. The state of San Salvador, one of the Central American republics, also unites in the protest, and declares her determination, if the outrage shall be carried into effect, to exert her whole power until the usurper "shall be driven from the limits of Central America."

I understand, for I speak only from information, that Great Britain has for some time claimed to have had the Mosquitoes, a mere naked tribe of Indians of a few hundred persons, under her protection.[1] Through her influence, they appointed a king, who was taken to Balize, a British station

[1] *Extract of a Letter from the Supreme Government of the State of Nicaragua to the Supreme Government of the State of San Salvador.*

"A tribe with no recognized form of government, without civilization, and entirely abandoned to savage life, is suddenly made use of by enlightened England for the purpose of planting one of her feet upon the Atlantic coast of this State; or rather, for the purpose of taking possession of the port for communication between Europe, America, and Asia, and other important countries at the point where the grand inter-oceanic canal is most practicable."

on the bay of Yucatan, and there crowned. It is said, also that, on the decease of the king, he was found to have bequeathed his dominions to her Britannic Majesty. It appears to be certain that she has, under this pretence of protection, extended her dominion over an immense surface in Central America; that she has at least one vessel of war, the Sun, commanded by an officer bearing an English name, "Commander Trotter, of the Mosquito navy," as he is styled in a letter written by the British consul at Bluefield; and that she is still further extending herself, against the remonstrance of the Central American states. But these states, besides being physically weak, are distracted by internal feuds; and if the proceedings complained of be not the unauthorized acts of British agents, which Great Britain will disavow, it is hardly to be expected that a usurpation, so unjustifiably consummated, will be abandoned on an appeal to the justice of the wrong-doer. Whether our government should remain quiescent under this encroachment upon near and defenceless neighbors, is a question worthy of consideration. Under any circumstances, it seems to me to afford little assurance of non-interference with the affairs of Mexico, if our forces were to be withdrawn without a treaty.

There is another consideration which ought not to be overlooked. In July last, Lord George Bentinck made a motion for an address to her Britannic Majesty, praying her to take such measures as she might deem proper to secure the payment of the Spanish government bonds held by British subjects. Those bonds amount to about three hundred and eighty millions of dollars, and on about three hundred and forty millions no interest whatever has been paid; and, including this debt, nearly seven hundred and thirty millions of dollars are due to British subjects by foreign governments, — a sum equal to about one fifth of her national debt. He contended, that, "by the law of nations, from time immemorial, it has been held that the recovery of just debts is a lawful cause of war, if the country from which payment is due refuses to listen to the claims of the country to whom money is owing." He quoted authorities to show that the payment of the debt, or the interest on it, might be enforced without having recourse to arms, though asserting the right to resort to force to compel it. He referred to the rich colonies of Spain, and especially Cuba, to show that there was wealth enough in its annual produce and revenue "to pay the whole debt due by Spain to British bond-holders." He referred to the naval force which Spain possessed, to show that there would not be "any very effective resistance," and that "the most timid minister" need not fear it. Having, in the course of his remarks, called the attention of the Minister of Foreign Affairs to the subject, Lord Palmerston, in responding to his call, entered into an extended statement in respect to the foreign debt due to British subjects. He drew distinctions between transactions by one government with another, by British subjects with a foreign government, by British subjects with the subjects of another government, and between debts and acts of injustice and oppression. These distinctions, however, he treated as matters of expediency and established practice. He assented to the doctrine laid down by the noble lord who made the motion for an address, and he said, if it were the wise policy of England to lay down a rule that she would enforce obligations of this character with the same rigor as those of a different character, she would have a full and fair right, according to the laws of nations, to do so. And he concluded by saying that England had not refrained from taking the steps urged by his noble friend, because she was "afraid of these states, or all of them put together"; that it was not to be supposed the British Parliament, or the British nation, would long remain patient under the wrong, and that they had ample power and means to obtain justice.

I pass over the doctrines put forth in the speech of Lord George Bentinck, and sanctioned by Lord Palmerston, though I believe it not perfectly clear that they can be maintained to the full extent by an appeal to any well-established principles of international law. You know, sir, that we have sometimes found British statesmen, even those holding places nearest to the throne, at fault, both in respect to matters of principle and matters of fact, though it is certainly but justice to concede to them the possession of more enlarged views of policy, combined with greater practical talent and tact, than is often to be found in the councils of European sovereigns. I also pass over an offensive allusion to the failure of two or three of the states of this Union to pay their debts, " as a stain upon the national character," (I quote the exact words,) when it is well known that the suspension of payment was temporary, and from overruling necessity; that in most instances resumption has taken place; and that, in all, the most earnest efforts have been made to resume the discharge of their obligations. This imputation was cast upon us at the moment when our people, with one heart, were sending abroad their agricultural surplus to feed the famished population of Ireland, not merely in the way of commercial exchange, but in the form of donations, in shiploads, public and private. And so far as the commercial portion is concerned, I believe our merchants have for months been draining our banks of specie, to send abroad to meet their own pecuniary obligations, while for a time at least they were unable to draw on their debtors in England for the proceeds of the breadstuffs by which her subjects had been fed. But I pass by all this, and come to the important fact that Mexico was among the indebted foreign states enumerated in a report, on which the motion of Lord George Bentinck was founded. What is the extent of her indebtedness I do not know, but I understand about seventy millions of dollars; and I believe it was but recently that the public domain in California was mortgaged to the creditors for a portion of this amount, though the lien is now said to be discharged.

I appeal to honorable Senators to say, with these facts before them, and in view of this public and official assertion of a principle, which, according to Lord Palmerston, the British government has only abstained from practically enforcing through mere considerations of policy, whether, if our forces were withdrawn from Mexico, and that country should become a prey to the anarchy and confusion which has reigned there so long, and which, if renewed, would in all probability become universal and hopeless, — whether, I say, there would not be a temptation too strong to be resisted to reduce the principle thus proclaimed to practice; whether some portion of the Mexican territory might not be occupied as a guaranty for the payment of the debt due to British subjects, and thus another principle be violated which we are committed to maintain? I do not mean to say that this consideration, if it stood alone, should absolutely control our conduct. But as auxiliary to the graver considerations to which I have referred, it may properly be allowed some weight, — enough, sir, perhaps, to turn the scale, if it were already balanced, — though, I think, there is sufficient without it to incline us decisively to the side of continued occupation.

Besides, British subjects have other extensive pecuniary interests in Mexico: they have large commercial establishments, and heavy investments of capital in the mining districts. If the political affairs of that country should fall into inextricable confusion, it is not to be supposed that these great interests will be abandoned by Great Britain; and yet it is extremely difficult to see by what interposition on her part they could be secured without the danger of collision between her and us.

Mr. President, in what I have said in respect to the danger of foreign interposition, I have not relied upon the ephemeral opinions of the day, or on opinions expressed in public journals abroad, however intimately those journals may be supposed to be connected with governments, as the organs of the views which it is deemed advisable to throw out, from time to time, for the public consideration or guidance. I have resorted to no irresponsible sources. I have presented opinions and declarations proclaimed with more or less of official sanction, and, for the most part, with the highest, — I mean the declarations of ministers, speaking for their governments to the popular body, and as the responsible representatives of sovereigns, holding in their own hands the authority to enforce, or attempt to enforce, what they proclaim. How far these declarations, taken in connection with the acts referred to, should influence our conduct, is a question on which we may not all agree. But it appears to me that it would be a great error in statesmanship to treat them as wholly unworthy of our consideration. Jealousy of our increasing power, commercial rivalry, political interests, all combine to give them importance. It is the province of a wise forecast to provide, as far as possible, that these adverse influences shall find no theatre for their exercise. To abandon Mexico would, it seems to me, throw wide open all the avenues for their admittance, — to one power for commercial monopoly, and to the other for political control, — and perhaps impose on us the difficult and dangerous task of removing evils which a proper vigilance might have prevented.

It may be, Mr. President, that we shall have an early peace. I sincerely hope so. In this case, we must withdraw from Mexico; and it may perhaps be said that the dangers I have referred to, as likely to result from our absence at the present moment, may possibly be realized. These dangers, whatever they may be, we must incur whenever she shall tender us a peace which we ought to accept. But there is a wide difference between retiring as belligerents and enemies without a treaty, and as friends under an amicable arrangement, with solemn obligations on both sides to keep the peace. In the former case, probably one of the first acts of Mexico would be to reassemble her army, and her government might fall under the control of her military leaders. In the latter, amicable relations being restored, and military forces being unnecessary, at least to act against us, the peace party would have better hopes of maintaining themselves, of preventing the army, which is now regarded as responsible for the national disasters, from gaining the ascendency, and also of excluding influences from abroad, which would be hostile to her interests and fatal to the common tranquillity of both countries.

In the references I have made to France and Great Britain, I have been actuated by no feeling of unkindness or hostility to either. Rapid and wide-spread as has been the progress of the latter, we have never sought to interfere with it. She holds one third of the North American continent. She has established her dominion in the Bermudas, the West Indies, and in Guiana, on the South American continent. She holds Balize, on the bay of Yucatan, in North America, with a district of about fourteen thousand square miles, if we may trust her own geographical delineations. We see her in the occupation of territories in every quarter of the globe, vastly, inordinately extended, and still ever extending herself. It is not easy to keep pace with her encroachments. A few years ago, the Indus was the western boundary of her Indian empire. She has passed it. She has overrun Affghanistan and Beloochistan, though I believe she has temporarily withdrawn from the former. She stands at the gates of Persia. She has discussed the policy of passing Persia, and making the Tigris her western boundary in Asia. One stride more would place her upon the shores of the Mediterranean; and her armies would no longer find their way to India by the circumnavigation of Africa. Indeed, she has now, for all government purposes of communication, except the transportation of troops and munitions of war, a direct intercourse with the east. Her steamers of the largest class run from England to Alexandria; from Alexandria there is a water-communication with

Cairo, — some sixty miles; from Cairo it is but eight hours overland to Suez, at the head of the Red Sea; from Suez her steamers of the largest class run to Aden, a military station of hers at the mouth of the Red Sea; from Aden to Ceylon, and from Ceylon to China. She is not merely conquering her way back from Hindoostan. She has raised her standard beyond it. She has entered the confines of the Celestial Empire. She has gained a permanent foothold within it; and who that knows her can believe that pretexts will long be wanting to extend her dominion there? Though it is for commerce mainly that she is thus adding to the number and extent of her dependencies, it is not for commerce alone. The love of power and extended empire is one of the efficient principles of her gigantic efforts and movements. No island, however remote, no rock, however barren, on which the cross of St. George has once been unfurled, is ever willingly relinquished, no matter how expensive or inconvenient it may be to maintain it. She may be said literally to encircle the globe by an unbroken chain of dependencies. Nor is it by peaceful means that she is thus extending herself. She propagates commerce, as Mohammedanism propagated religion, by fire and sword. If she negotiates, it is with fleets and armies at the side of her ambassadors, in order, to use the language of her diplomacy, "to give force to their representations." She is essentially and eminently a military power, unequalled on the sea and unsurpassed on the land. Happily, the civilization, which distinguishes her at home, goes with her and obliterates some of the bloody traces of her march to unlimited empire.

Much less has any unkind feeling dictated my reference to France. Our relations with her have usually been of the most friendly character. From the foundation of our government there has existed, on our side, a strong feeling of sympathy in her prosperities and her misfortunes, which no temporary interruption of our friendship has been able to eradicate. There is reason for this feeling: it would not have been creditable to us as a people if it had proved a transient sentiment. She stood forth at a critical period in our contest for independence, and rendered us the most essential service by her coöperation and aid. The swords of Washington and Lafayette were unsheathed on the same battle-fields. Our waters and our plains have been crimsoned with the generous blood of France. The names of Rochambeau, De Grasse, and D'Estaing are identified with our struggles for freedom. They have become, in some degree, American, and we give them to our children as names to be remembered for the gallant deeds of those who bore them. It is not surprising, under such circumstances, that in the survey of the European system we should have been accustomed to regard France as the power most likely, in the progress of events, to become the rival of England on the ocean as she has been on the land; and with a large portion of our people, if the wish has not been "parent," it has, at least, been companion "to the thought." For this reason, the declaration of M. Guizot was considered, independently of all views of right, as peculiarly ungracious, and as a demonstration of feeling totally inconsistent with the ancient friendship by which the two countries have been united. I have never believed it to be in accordance with the sentiments of the French people. And so strong has been my reliance on their right judgment and feeling, that I confess I have thought it not unlikely that an interposition in our affairs, so completely at variance with amicable relations, which ought to be held sacred, might be arrested by a more decisive interposition at home against its authors.

I repeat, I have spoken in no spirit of unkindness either towards Great Britain or France. I desire nothing but friendship with them, — close, cordial, constant, mutually beneficial friendship. I speak of them historically, as they exist and exhibit themselves to the eyes of the civilized world.

Thus far, I have considered the probable consequences of

retiring from Mexico, as they are likely to affect our political relations with her, and possibly with other states. I now turn, for a single moment only, to a different class of considerations, — I mean considerations arising out of our claims to indemnity for injuries. Although the war was not commenced to secure it, this is one of the avowed objects for which it has been prosecuted. Shall we abandon the position we have taken, and leave this object unaccomplished? Shall we not rather retain what we have acquired, until our just claims are satisfied? To do otherwise would be to have incurred an enormous expenditure of treasure and blood to no purpose, — to have prosecuted the war till we had the means of indemnifying ourselves in our own hands, and then voluntarily to relinquish them. Such a course seems to me utterly irreconcilable either with justice to ourselves or with sound policy. If I am not mistaken in the views I have expressed, it would be an abandonment of indemnity without getting rid of the war, on which we must now rely to procure it. These considerations do not apply to the policy suggested by the honorable Senator from South Carolina. He proposes to take indemnity into our own hands, by occupying a portion of northern or central Mexico, and holding it without a treaty. My remarks are only applicable to the policy of withdrawing from Mexico altogether, and leaving the adjustment of differences to future negotiations.

Having thus declared myself in favor of the occupation of Mexico until she shall consent to make peace, I deem it proper to say, in connection with this subject, that I have been uniformly opposed, and that I am still opposed, to all schemes of conquest for the acquisition of territory. In this respect, I concur in what the Senator from South Carolina has said, and for nearly the same reasons. I am opposed to all such schemes, because they would be inconsistent with the avowed objects of the war; because they would be incompatible with justice and sound policy; and because, if successful, they would be utterly subversive of the fundamental principle of our political system, resting as it does on a voluntary association of free and independent states. I have been uniformly in favor of the most energetic measures in the prosecution of the war, because I believed them most likely to bring it to a close. In carrying our arms to the enemy's capital and occupying his territory, I can see nothing inconsistent with the principles of justice or the usages of civilized states. In the prosecution of a war undertaken to procure a redress of injuries, the territories or property of an enemy may be seized for the express purpose of compelling him to do justice. More may be taken than would constitute a fair indemnity for actual injuries, provided it be done with the intention of restoring the surplus when he shall consent to make peace on reasonable terms. It is in this spirit, and with this intention, that my coöperation has been given to the vigorous prosecution of the war. We have a right to insist on a fair boundary; we may exact indemnity for injuries; we may demand indemnification for the expenses of the war, if we please. But here all right ceases; and if, when this is conceded, we have more on our hands, we are bound, on every principle of law and good conscience, to make restitution. It is admitted on all hands that Mexico is incapable of indemnifying us in money. But she may do so by ceding to us territory which is useless to her, which she has not the ability to defend, and which may be useful to us. I have always been in favor of acquiring territory on just terms. The acquisition of California has always appeared to me very desirable, on account of its ports on the Pacific. I have uniformly voted for acquiring it, when the proposition has come before us. I believe, on the first occasion, I was in a minority of ten or eleven. My opinion is unchanged. Indeed, it is confirmed by the fact, that California has, by our military operations, become forever detached from Mexico. If it were to be abandoned by us, its forty thousand inhabitants would undoubtedly establish an independent government for themselves, and they would maintain it, if undisturbed by foreign interference. I take the actual condition of things as I find it, and with an earnest desire to fulfil all the obligations it devolves on us in a spirit of justice towards Mexico and towards the people of California.

I concur, also, in what the honorable Senator from South Carolina has said in relation to the influence of war on our political institutions. No man can deplore it, under any circumstances, more than myself. Independently of the evils which it always brings in its train, there are considerations connected with our political organization and the nature of our social progress, which render it doubly pernicious in its tendencies. The final success of the experiment we are making in free government may depend, in some degree, on a steady maintenance of the spirit of peace, in which our political system had its origin, and in which it has thus far been administered. Great as is our capacity for war, our whole scheme of government is averse to it. The greatest possible economy in expenditure; the least possible patronage in the hands of the Executive; the smallest pecuniary exactions from the people, consistent with our absolute wants; the absence of all demands on the public treasury which call for unusual contributions of revenue or promote excessive disbursements; the exemption of the country from all exigencies which devolve on the legislative and executive departments of the government the exercise of extraordinary powers; — these are the conditions under which the ends of our political organization are most likely to be fulfilled. Sir, none of these conditions belong to a state of war. Extravagant disbursements; extraordinary contributions of revenue, present or prospective, — present, in augmented burdens of taxation, prospective, in the shape of loans and anticipations of income, leading ultimately to taxation; extraordinary powers summarily, and sometimes arbitrarily exercised; — these are the inseparable companions of war; and they are inimical to the very genius of our social system.

There are considerations, which, in my judgment, render a war with Mexico peculiarly unfortunate, and which justify all the efforts we have made to bring it to an amicable termination. We are mutually engaged in carrying out on this continent the experiment of free government, which in all other ages has proved abortive. We are trying it under eminently auspicious circumstances. We have no strong governments around us, founded upon antagonist principles, and adverse in their example and influence to the success of ours. We are sustained by the faculty of popular representation, which was unknown, or at least imperfectly known, to the free states of antiquity, and by force of which we have been enabled to carry out, on geographical areas of indefinite extent, an organization which had previously been deemed applicable only to communities of limited population and territory. It is natural, under these circumstances, that the friends of free government, wherever they are to be found, should turn to us as the last hope of liberal institutions. They look to us for examples of moderation and forbearance in our intercourse with foreign nations, — especially those having forms of government analogous to our own, — and for an exemption from the evil passions which have embroiled the countries of the old world, and involved them, century after century, with brief intermissions, in wars of ambition and revenge. In asserting the superiority of our own form of government, the strength of the argument will be weakened, if we shall be found no more exempt than those which are less popular, from strife and contention with neighboring states. Regarding the success of our institutions as affecting deeply the welfare of our race, and vindicating the competency of mankind to self-government, I have always esteemed it peculiarly unfortunate that any cause of alienation should have existed of sufficient magnitude to induce the two principal republics of the western hemisphere to turn their arms against each other. The cause of liberal government is injured, and far more deeply injured than it has been by the dissension of the republics in the southern portion of the American continent.

These are considerations which it were well for us always to keep in view: in peace, that we may not rush hastily into war; in war, that we may spare no honorable effort for a restoration of peace.

There is yet another consideration of a kindred character. While the monarchies of Europe are at peace with each other, and social improvement is advancing, on the continent at least, with unparalleled rapidity, almost the only wars now waging among neighboring states are between us and Mexico, and between some of the South American republics. I desire, as much as any one can, to see these dissensions composed, and to see these republican states resume the fulfilment of their great mission among the nations, — the maintenance of the principles of political liberty, and the cultivation of the arts of civilization and peace.

In these views I concur with the Senator from South Carolina. But here I am constrained to separate from him. When we come to practical measures, our paths lie wide apart.

It is for the very reasons I have just stated, that I cannot assent to the policy he proposes. I believe it calculated to prolong the war, not to terminate it; to keep alive the spirit of animosity which divides us from Mexico, instead of restoring the friendly relations which ought to exist between us. I am in favor, then, of standing as we are. And, sir, if she shall refuse to make peace, if we must continue in the occupation of her capital and three fourths of her territory, it may be in the order of Providence that we shall, through this very necessity, become the instruments of her political and social regeneration. In the party conflicts which distract her, the means may be found of consolidating her government on a republican basis, of healing her dissensions, and of uniting her to us in bonds of friendship by an exercise of magnanimity and forbearance in the final adjustment of our difficulties with her. I believe even now something of the salutary influence of our presence in her capital and principal seaports begins to be felt. The abolition of transit duties, the reduction of the impost on foreign articles of necessity and convenience, and a freer commerce among the Mexican states, may, if continued, strike a fatal blow at the anti-commercial system by which her people have been oppressed, and the internal abuses by which her rulers have grown rich, — a system of mal-administration not even equalled by that which exists in old Spain. The higher improvement in government, in the arts, and in civilization under all its forms, which distinguishes our own people, may, by force of actual contact, be communicated to the Mexicans, and lay the foundation of an improved social order. Startling as the reflection is, it is nevertheless true, that civilization, and even Christianity, have sometimes been propagated by arms, where they would otherwise have been hopelessly excluded. Thus, the very passions which seem fitted only to desolate human society, may, in the hands of Providence, become the agents of its advancement. Let us, then, hope and trust that the contest in which we are engaged with a neighboring power, deplorable as we all consider it, may be an instrument of social and political amelioration to our adversary.

The Senator from South Carolina has said, in his emphatic language, that we are "tied to a corpse." It is a striking figure, Mr. President, and partakes strongly of the boldness in which the illustrations of that distinguished Senator are always conceived. Mexico is, indeed, prostrate — almost politically inanimate, if you please — under the oppressions which have been heaped upon her, year after year, by unscrupulous rulers. But I should be sorry to believe her beyond the power of resuscitation, even by human means. I do not expect, as our contact with her becomes more intimate, to see her, like the dead body touched by the bones of the prophet, spring, at a single bound, to life and strength. But I hope to see her — possibly through our instrumentality — freed from the despotic sway of her military rulers, and rising, by sure degrees, to the national importance I wish her to possess; — order and tranquillity first, next social improvement and stable government, and at last an honorable rank among the nations of the earth. I contemplate no direct interference with her government, no permanent system of protection to be exercised over it, no alliance with her beyond what may be necessary to secure to us the objects of peace. But I do contemplate a treaty stipulating for commercial arrangements, for protection and security to our own citizens in their future intercourse with her, and no withdrawal of our forces without it; at least, until all chance of obtaining one shall prove hopeless. If we were to retire now, all commerce between her and us would cease and be transferred to our rivals; our frontier would be a line of war, not a boundary between peaceful neighbors; and unless the tide of conquest should be poured back upon her, under the provocations such a condition of our relations would almost necessarily superinduce, no citizen of the United States could be expected, for years to come, to plant his foot on Mexican soil. War dissolves the political and commercial relations of independent states, so far as they rest upon voluntary agreement. It is only by a treaty of peace that they can be revived, or new relations be substituted for the old.

Mr. President, advocating as I do the occupation of Mexico until she shall consent to make peace, it may be incumbent on me to state in what manner I think it can best be maintained. And here I must say, I think the estimates of the effective force in the field have been greatly overstated. I propose no specific plan for adoption. I leave all practical measures in the hands of those to whom they belong. I only purpose to state what suggests itself to my mind as advisable. I think we should find it most advantageous to remain much as we are, excepting to occupy such ports on the Pacific as our fleet may reduce and maintain as commercial avenues to the interior. It may, however, become necessary to occupy San Luis Potosi and Zacatecas, for the protection of the mining operations in those states, and the agricultural districts near the city of Mexico, to command supplies for the army. I should consider an army of twenty-five thousand well-disciplined, effective men, the smallest number adequate to the purpose of maintaining positions, keeping open communications from the coast to the interior, and dispersing the enemy's troops, if they shall be reëmbodied; but, in order to keep up such a force, we should require a nominal organization of at least forty thousand men, with full thirty thousand under pay. Without the general staff, the twenty-five regiments of regulars now in service, and the ten new regiments proposed by the bill, will constitute such a force; and when the latter shall be raised and brought into the field, a portion of the volunteers may be discharged, if it shall be found prudent to do so. Many of the regiments are greatly reduced in numbers, and, as I understand, are anxious to return home. I doubt now whether there are more than twenty-five thousand effective men in all Mexico, though the rolls show over forty thousand.[1] Some of the returns on which the Adjutant-General's report is founded are of as early a date as August last. It will be recollected that last summer, when there was great anxiety in relation to General Scott, statements of the number of his troops were published here. They were founded on the returns in the Adjutant-General's office; and in his official report of the battles before the city of Mexico, General Scott complained that his force had been greatly overstated. He said it had been "trebled" in these returns, if I recollect rightly, and that the army had been "disgusted" by the exaggeration. The returns of the army now should, in like manner, be subjected to great deductions in order to obtain the real effective force. If the ten regiments proposed by the bill are authorized, months will be required to

[1] General Cass, chairman of the Committee on Military Affairs, here said, the Adjutant-General was of opinion that they did not exceed twenty-four thousand.

raise them; they will not, probably, as the chairman of the Committee on Military Affairs has stated, give many more than seven thousand men, and in the mean time the army will become constantly diminished by the casualties of service. For these reasons, and for those given — so ably given — some days since by my honorable friend from Mississippi,[1] I support the bill. I support it for another reason, which has governed me from the commencement of the war: to place at the control of the Executive the men and means deemed necessary to bring it to an honorable termination.

As hostilities are now suspended, the chief province of the army will be to maintain internal tranquillity, support the civil authorities in the execution of the laws, to free the country from the robber and guerrilla bands by which it is infested, and subserve the great purposes of government by affording security to liberty, property, and life, — a security the Mexicans have not often fully enjoyed. The very exercise of these beneficent agencies will tend to disarm hostility towards us with the thinking portion of the population. It will place our armies in a most favorable contrast with hers, which have been scourges, rather than protectors, to their own countrymen. I would, if possible, have no more bloodshed. I would make our armies the protectors, not the enemies, of the Mexican people, and render them subservient to the eradication of abuses, and to the institution of a better civil administration, under Mexican magistrates, abstaining from all interference with the frame of the government, and changing in its action only what, by universal consent, requires to be changed. If this course were to be adopted and steadily pursued, I should earnestly hope its effect would be, at no distant time, to make the capital, under our protection, the centre of an influence which would lead to the reëstablishment of the federative system on a durable basis, and give to that distracted country the settled order which is alone necessary to make her happy and prosperous.

[1] Mr. Davis.

To abandon the city of Mexico would, I fear, put an end to all these prospects and hopes. That city is the political, as well as the financial, centre of the Republic. It is there governments have been instituted and deposed, armies levied, revenue systems devised and carried into execution. So long as we hold it, and control the adjoining districts, I believe nothing but imprudence or mismanagement can raise up a formidable opposition to us. If we abandon it, all the resources of the country, which it commands, will again be at the control of its rulers, to be employed against us in the renewal of active hostilities. Before it was captured, energetic movements seemed to me our true policy. Now that it is in our undisputed possession, our leading object should be to introduce better commercial and financial systems, and let them work out, under our protection, their legitimate results.

Great qualities are necessary in him who is charged with the execution of these delicate and responsible functions. He should have prudence, self-control, a knowledge of civil affairs, of the country, of the people and their character, and, if possible, their language. Established institutions, existing usages, sometimes prejudices even, must be respected. Some of the most disastrous reverses which have befallen armies of occupation have had their origin in violations of the prevailing customs and feelings of the people. To avoid this fatal error, everything depends on the discretion and wisdom of the directing authority.

It may be, that all reasonable expectations will be disappointed; that the hostility of Mexico will prove unappeasable; that she will prefer the political disorganization which now exists to an amicable arrangement with us. If so, circumstances must dictate the course to be pursued when this conviction shall be forced on us. But, sir, let us not adopt such a conclusion hastily. Let us rely on the influence of more rational motives to give us peace.

And now, sir, I submit whether this course had not better

be pursued for a while, if I am right in supposing the temporary occupation of Mexico, under discreet officers, may lead to a stable peace, rather than to withdraw our forces, and leave the adjustment of difficulties to the uncertain chance of a restoration of a responsible government, to be terminated at last, perhaps, by the renewed arbitrament of arms.

I have thus stated with frankness the views I entertain in respect to the future conduct of the war. Notwithstanding the anxious consideration I have given to the subject, they may be erroneous. It is a question of great difficulty, on which differences of opinion may well exist, and on which a mistaken course of policy may lead to the most unpleasant consequences. Whatever faith I may entertain in the soundness of the opinions I have advanced, I certainly should have more, if they were not totally at variance with those of gentlemen possessing, from longer experience, much higher claims than myself to public confidence. But I have not on this account thought proper to withhold them, knowing, as we do, that, from the very contrariety and conflict of thought and conviction, valuable deductions may sometimes be drawn.

Mr. President, I feel that I have already trespassed too long on the indulgence of the Senate; but I am unwilling to close without asking its attention for a very few moments to some considerations connected with our future growth and progress, and with the influence we must, in spite of ourselves, exert over the destinies of Mexico. They are no new opinions: they have been expressed years ago, both in public and private.

Sir, no one who has paid a moderate degree of attention to the laws and elements of our increase, can doubt that our population is destined to spread itself across the American continent, filling up, with more or less completeness, according to attractions of soil and climate, the space that intervenes between the Atlantic and Pacific oceans. This eventual, and, perhaps, in the order of time, this not very distant extension of our settlements over a tract of country, with a diameter, as we go westward, greatly disproportioned to its length, becomes a subject of the highest interest to us. On the whole extent of our northern flank, from New Brunswick to the point where the northern boundary of Oregon touches the Pacific, we are in contact with British colonists, having, for the most part, the same common origin with ourselves, but controlled and moulded by political influences from the eastern hemisphere, if not adverse, certainly not decidedly friendly to us. The strongest tie which can be relied on to bind us to mutual offices of friendship and good neighborhood, is that of commerce; and this, as we know, is apt to run into rivalry, and sometimes becomes a fruitful source of alienation.

From our northern boundary, we turn to our southern. What races are to border on us here, what is to be their social and political character, and what their means of annoyance? Are our two frontiers, only seven parallels of latitute apart when we pass Texas, to be flanked by settlements having no common bond of union with ours? Our whole southern line is conterminous, throughout its whole extent, with the territories of Mexico, a large portion of which is nearly unpopulated. The geographical area of Mexico is about 1,500,000 square miles, and her population about 7,000,000 souls. The whole northern and central portion, taking the twenty-sixth parallel of latitude as the dividing line, containing more than 1,000,000 square miles, has about 650,000 inhabitants, — about two inhabitants to three square miles. The southern portion, with less than 500,000 square miles, has a population of nearly six and a half millions of souls, or thirteen inhabitants to one square mile. The aboriginal races, which occupy and overrun a portion of California and New Mexico, must there, as everywhere else, give way before the advancing wave of civilization, either to be overwhelmed by it, or to be driven upon perpetually contracting areas, where, from a diminution of their accustomed sources of subsistence, they must ultimately become extinct by force of an invincible law. We see the operation of this law in every portion of this continent. We have no power to control it, if we would. It is the behest of Providence that idleness, and ignorance, and barbarism, shall give place to industry, and knowledge, and civilization. The European and mixed races which possess Mexico are not likely, either from moral or physical energy, to become formidable rivals or enemies. The bold and courageous enterprise which overran and conquered Mexico, appears not to have descended to the present possessors of the soil. Either from the influence of climate or the admixture of races, — the fusion of castes, to use the technical phrase, — the conquerors have, in turn, become the conquered. The ancient Castilian energy is, in a great degree, subdued ; and it has given place, with many other noble traits of the Spanish character, to a peculiarity which seems to have marked the race in that country, under whatever combinations it is found, — a proneness to civil discord, and a suicidal waste of its own strength.

With such a territory and such a people on our southern border, what is to be the inevitable course of empire? It needs no powers of prophecy to foretell. Sir, I desire to speak plainly: why should we not, when we are discussing the operation of moral and physical laws, which are beyond our control? As our population moves westward on our own territory, portions will cross our southern boundary. Settlements will be formed within the unoccupied and sparsely peopled territory of Mexico. Uncongenial habits and tastes, differences of political opinion and principle, and numberless other elements of diversity, will lead to a separation of these newly-formed societies from the inefficient government of Mexico. They will not endure to be held in subjection to a system which neither yields them protection nor offers them any incentive to their proper development and growth. They will form independent states on the basis of constitutions identical in all their leading features with our own; and they will naturally seek to unite their fortunes to ours. The fate of California is already sealed: it can never be reunited to Mexico. The operation of the great causes to which I have alluded must, at no distant day, detach the whole of northern Mexico from the southern portion of that republic. It is for the very reason that she is incapable of defending her possessions against the elements of disorder within and the progress of better influences from without, that I desire to see the inevitable political change, which is to be wrought in the condition of her northern departments, brought about without any improper interference on our part. I do not speak of our military movements. I refer to the time when our difficulties with her shall be healed, and when she shall be left to the operation of pacific influences, — silent, but more powerful than the arm of force. For the reason that she is defenceless, if for no other, I should be opposed to all schemes of conquest. Acquisition by force is the vice of arbitrary governments. I desire never to see it the reproach of ours. For the sake of the national honor, as well as the permanency of our political institutions, I desire not to see it. The extension of free government on this continent can only be arrested, if arrested at all, by substituting war for the arts of peace. Leave it to itself, and nothing can prevent the progress of our population across the continent. Mr. Jefferson, with his prophetic forecast, foretold this result forty years ago. He prophesied the peaceful progress of our people to the Pacific. He foresaw them forming new settlements, and, when strong enough to maintain themselves, organizing independent societies, and governing themselves by constitutions and laws analogous to our own. It is true, he believed the area of freedom might be enlarged, advantageously to ourselves and others, without extending to the same broad limits the area of our jurisdiction. It was the progress and the triumph of great principles of political right to which his philosophical mind instinctively turned as to the legitimate aim and boundary of our ambition and desires. Since his day the public mind in this country has greatly outrun his anticipations of our progress. It looks to the extension of our Constitution and laws over regions, which were formerly considered beyond our reach as integral portions of the same system of government. Modern improvements have given great strength to this prevailing sentiment. It is possible by steam-power, if we can succeed in making the proper application of it over so broad a surface, to reach the Pacific Ocean from Lake Michigan, or the Mississippi, in eight or nine days, — a period of time less than that which was required to travel from Boston to Philadelphia, when the Congress of the American colonies first assembled in the latter city. Under these circumstances, the extension of our political boundary so as to embrace all territory we may justly call our own, seems no longer to be considered a questionable policy. If other districts, not now within the territories of the Union, shall found independent governments, and shall desire to unite themselves to us on terms mutually acceptable, it is a question which concerns only them and us, and in which no stranger can be permitted to intrude. When the time comes for the settlement of any such questions, they will doubtless be considered with all the solemnity which belongs to propositions involving the public welfare. To those with whom the decision belongs let us leave them, with the assurance that the wisdom which has governed and guided us so long, will still point out to us the path of liberty, tranquillity, and safety.

One position we have assumed, and I trust it will be maintained with inflexible firmness, — that nations beyond this continent cannot be permitted to interfere with our progress, so long as there is on our part no violation of their rights. I would resist, at the outset, as matter of the gravest offence, all indications of such interference. If the abstract right could be asserted on grounds of international law, there has been nothing in the nature of our extension, or the means by which it has been accomplished, to warrant its application to us. From the formation of our government, for nearly three quarters of a century, military power — brute force — has had no agency in the conquests we have achieved. We have overrun no provinces or countries abounding in wealth. Our capital has witnessed no triumphal entries of returning armies, bearing with them the spoils and trophies of conquest. Our ships have not been seen returning from subjugated districts, freighted with the tributes of an extended commerce. In the extension of our commercial intercourse we have not, like our Anglo-Saxon mother, been seen hewing down with the sword, with unrelenting and remorseless determination, every obstacle which opposed itself to her progress. Our career thus far has been stained by no such companionship with evil. Our conquests have been the peaceful achievements of enterprise and industry, — the one leading the way into the wilderness, the other following and completing the acquisition by the formal symbols of occupancy and possession. They have looked to no objects beyond the conversion of uninhabited wilds into abodes of civilization and freedom. Their only arms were the axe and the ploughshare. The accumulations of wealth they have brought were all extracted from the bosom of the earth by the unoffending hand of labor. If, in the progress of our people westward, they shall occupy territories not our own, but to become ours by amicable arrangements with the governments to which they belong, which of the nations of the earth shall venture to stand forth, in the face of the civilized world, and call on us to pause in this great work of human improvement? It is as much the interest of Europe as it is ours, that we should be permitted to follow undisturbed the path which, in the allotment of national fortunes, we seem appointed to tread. Our country has long been a refuge for those who desire a larger liberty than they enjoy under their own rulers. It is an outlet for the political disaffection of the Old World, — for social elements which might there have become sources of agitation, but which are here silently and tranquilly incorporated into our system, ceasing to be principles of disturbance as they attain the greater freedom, which was the object of their separation from less congenial combinations in other quarters of the globe. Nay, more; it is into the vast reservoir of the western wilderness, teeming with fruitfulness and fertility, that Europe is constantly pouring, under our protection, her human surpluses, unable to draw from her own bosom the elements of their support and reproduction. She is literally going along with us in our march to prosperity and power, to share with us its triumphs and its fruits. Happily, this continent is not a legitimate theatre for the political arrangements of the sovereigns of the eastern hemisphere. Their armies may range, undisturbed by us, over the plains of Europe, Asia, and Africa, dethroning monarchs, partitioning kingdoms, and subverting republics, as interest or caprice may dictate. But political justice demands that in one quarter of the globe self-government, freedom, the arts of peace, shall be permitted to work out, unmolested, the great purposes of human civilization.

Mr. President, I trust there will be nothing in the final adjustment of our difficulties with Mexico to impair, in any degree, the moral of our example in the past. Our course, heretofore, has been one of perpetual exertion to bring about an amicable arrangement with her. I trust we shall persevere in the same course of conduct, whatever unwillingness she may exhibit to come to terms. Entertaining the opinions which I have expressed, I naturally feel a deep solicitude, as an American citizen, that our public conduct should comport with the dignity of the part we seem destined to perform in the great drama of international politics. I desire to see our good name unsullied, and the character we have gained for moderation, justice, and scrupulousness in the discharge of our national obligations, maintained unimpaired. In these, let us be assured, our great strength consists: for it is these which make us strong in the opinion of mankind.

In what I have said concerning the progress of our people over the unpopulated regions west of us, and in respect to our responsibilities as a nation, I trust I shall have incurred no imputation of inconsistency. On the contrary, I trust I shall be considered consistent in all I have said. I regard our extension, as I have endeavored to foreshadow it, to be the inevitable result of causes, the operation of which it is not in our power to arrest. At the same time, I hold it to be our sacred duty to see that it is not encouraged or promoted by improper means. While I should consider it the part of weakness to shrink from extension, under the apprehension that it might bring with it the elements of discord and disunion, as our political boundaries are enlarged, I should hold it to be the part of folly and dishonor to attempt to accelerate it by agencies incompatible with our obligations to other nations. It is the dictate of wisdom and of duty to submit ourselves to the operation of the great causes which are at work, and which will work on in spite of us, in carrying civilization and freedom across the American continent.

In advocating a continued occupation of the cities and territory we have acquired in Mexico until she shall assent to reasonable terms of peace, I trust also that I shall be deemed consistent with myself. Deprecating war as the greatest of calamities, especially for us, I desire to see this war brought to a close at the earliest practicable day. I am in favor of whatever measures are most likely to accomplish this desirable end. I am opposed to an abandonment of our position, —

1st. Because I believe it would open a field of domestic dissension in Mexico, which might be fatal to her existence as an independent state, or make her take refuge in the arms of despotism;

2d. Because it might lead to external interference in her

affairs of the most dangerous tendency both to her and us; and

3d. Because I fear that we should only gain a temporary suspension of hostilities, to be renewed under great disadvantages to us, and with every prospect of a longer and more sanguinary contest.

Mr. President, it is this last consideration which weighs most heavily upon my own mind. I hold it to be indispensable to the public welfare, under all its aspects, that we should have, at the termination of this contest, a solid and stable peace. Unpromising as the condition of things seems at the present moment, my hope still is, that firmness tempered with prudence will give us, not a mere outward pacification with secret irritation rankling within, but substantial concord and friendship, which shall leave no wound unhealed. And, sir, we should be satisfied with nothing short of an accommodation of differences which will enable the country with confidence to lay aside its armor, and to resume the peaceful pursuits to which, by the inexorable law of our condition, we must look for prosperity and safety.

My advice, then, (if I may presume to advsie,) is, to stand firm, holding ourselves ready at all times to make peace, and carrying into our negotiations for that purpose a determination to cement a future good understanding with our adversary, by an adjustment of our differences on terms of justice, moderation, and magnanimity.

MINISTER TO THE PAPAL STATES.

MARCH 21, 1848.

THE motion to strike from the Appropriation Bill the item for a mission to the Papal States, being under consideration in the Senate, Mr. DIX said: —

I VOTED yesterday against the amendment of the Senator from Indiana,[1] proposing a resident minister to the Papal States. I did so, because it was brought forward in opposition to the proposition of the Senator from Missouri,[2] to send out a minister plenipotentiary. If this motion to strike out fails, and the Senator from Indiana moves his amendment again, I shall vote for it; and in stating my reasons, as I propose to do now, without waiting for his motion, I hope it will not be considered out of place if I present some statistical details in relation to the condition of the Papal States.

I desire, in the first place, to say, that I do not regard this as a political mission, unless the term political be understood in its largest sense. Much less do I consider it a religious mission, as the honorable Senator from North Carolina[3] would have us regard it. I consider the Pope, to all intents, as a temporal sovereign. He has been so for the last eleven hundred years. I believe the first territorial possession of the Pope was conferred upon him by Pepin, the father and predecessor of Charlemagne, in the eighth century. It consisted of the Duchy of Rome, or, at that time, more properly called the Exarchate of Ravenna, and was wrested by the King of France from the Lombards, who had overrun northern and central Italy. It extended

1 Mr. Hannegan. 2 Mr. Benton. 3 Mr. Badger.

from the present frontier of Naples, on the Mediterranean, to the mouth of the Tiber, including the Southern Campagna and the Pontine Marshes, and running back to the Sabine and Volscian hills. In the twelfth century, the Countess Matilda, of Tuscany, bequeathed her possessions to the Pope. They embraced the patrimony of St. Peter, on the Mediterranean, extending from the mouth of the Tiber to the present frontier of Tuscany, and the march of Ancona on the Adriatic, with the adjoining district of Spoleto. Large accessions were subsequently made by conquest,— Umbria, Romagna, Perugia, Orvieto, Citta di Castello, Bologna, Ravenna, and other cities and districts of country. In the seventeenth century, the Duke of Urbino abdicated in favor of the Pope; and at a still later period, some further additions were made by arms. Thus, the territorial possessions of the Pope are held, like those of other sovereigns, by succession, donation, and conquest. I consider the territorial possessions of the Church as much the dominions of the Pope as the territorial possessions of Spain are the dominions of her Most Catholic Majesty; and I see no more reason to decline diplomatic relations in the first case than in the last, unless there is, in other respects, a propriety in doing so.

It is true, there is a peculiarity in the form of the Papal government, from the fact that the temporal head of the State is also the spiritual head of the Roman Catholic Church. The Senator from North Carolina very justly remarked, that his chief ministers were ecclesiastics. As is well known, the most important political body in the Roman States is the Sacred College of the Cardinals, who are the princes of the Church. They are seventy in number,—the same in number as the disciples sent out by the Great Founder of the Christian faith to preach the gospel to the world. Six are cardinal bishops, fifty cardinal priests, and fourteen cardinal deacons. I believe the number has been invariable for two hundred and fifty years, though it is not always full. All vacancies are filled by the Pope, who is chosen by the cardinals from their own body. The government is, therefore, an unlimited elective monarchy, or, if you please, a hierarchy, of which the Pope is the head.

The government is administered, under the direction of the Pope, by the Secretary of State, who is a cardinal. He is aided by several departments, bureaus, or boards, the chief of which is the Camera Apostolica, corresponding with our Treasury Department. It is under the charge of the Chamberlain, who is assisted by a number of cardinals and subordinates of different grades. There is also the Buon Governo, charged with the municipal police of the States; the Sacra Consulta, to which is intrusted the civil and political administration of the provinces; and the Sacra Ruota, the great court of appeals in judicial proceedings. There are several more of these boards, of which I do not remember the names or the functions; but they are all under the direction of cardinals. The Chamberlain is the only one of these executive officers who is appointed for life; and the reason for the distinction is, that he administers the government on the death of the Pope for nine days, when a new election takes place; and during that period he has the privilege of coining money in his own name. The Secretary of State, who is the Prime Minister and the confidential adviser of the Pope, besides having the general direction of the administrative functions of the government, presides especially over the Sacra Consulta, or the department for the provinces, — to give it a name suited to its functions.

There is another class of official dignitaries of high rank under the Papal government, — the prelates. They are always of noble birth, but not always in holy orders. There are some two or three hundred of these dignitaries employed in various departments of the government, civil or ecclesiastical. The post of prelate often opens the way to higher preferment, and is next in importance to a membership

32

of the Sacred College. These are the great officers of the government.

Mr. BADGER. Will the Senator allow me to ask him, — for my recollection is not very accurate, and I am taking a great deal of interest in what he is saying, and listening to him with much pleasure,—whether I understand him correctly as saying that these prelates are not always in holy orders? Are they not either in holy orders or else undergoing an ecclesiastical apprenticeship, which involves the design to take holy orders?

I said they were not always in holy orders, and I believe I am not mistaken. They usually, if not uniformly, occupy posts under the government. Some of them are governors of provinces, under the denomination of delegates; and many of them are employed in the executive departments. Some of them become cardinals; but I should not consider it accurate to say of them as a body that they were undergoing an ecclesiastical apprenticeship.

Let me now turn to the political divisions of the Papal States.

The Papal dominions are divided into twenty provinces. The first is the Comarca of Rome. The other nineteen are divided into legations and delegations. The former are six in number, and have each a cardinal to preside over them. The latter are thirteen in number, with prelates as their presiding officers. Each province is divided into communes, with peculiarities of local government.

In the provinces, the legations and delegations have a council, (Congregazione di Governo,) consisting of the Gonfaloniere, or mayor, of the chief town, and from two to five councillors, according to the magnitude and importance of the province. They are named by the Pope, and hold their office for five years. The councillors have no vote; but when they differ in opinion from the presiding officer of the province, their reasons are reduced to writing and sent to the Secretary of State.

Some of the delegations are divided into districts, with governors subordinate to the delegate. Each district is again divided into communes, with their ancient magistrates and councils. These councils are close corporations, the members of which are self-elected, subject to the veto of the delegate, and retain their seats for life. A Gonfaloniere, or mayor, elected from their own body by themselves, presides over them. Of these communes there are some eight or nine hundred, if I remember accurately, with similar forms of administration.

Thus it will be seent hat the whole government is as far removed as possible from popular influence. It is from the centre to the extremities founded and administered upon the principles of a close corporation; and this is its chief peculiarity.

The administration of justice partakes of the nature of the political organization. It is founded on the basis of the *Corpus juris civilis* and the *Corpus juris canonici*, — the civil and canon law. All criminal proceedings are conducted with closed doors, and the testimony taken in writing. The accused is entitled to the aid of an advocate, called the *avvocato de poveri*, (the advocate of the poor,) who is appointed by the Pope and paid by the government. Imprisonment is the chief punishment for crime; fines are rarely imposed; there is no such thing as liberation on bail; and the whole administration of criminal justice is so dilatory that there are always a very large number of persons imprisoned and awaiting their trial.

In all I have said, it will be readily seen how much the present head of the Papal States has to reform, — in the frame of the government, in its administration, and in criminal jurisprudence. There is no participation by the people in the administration of public affairs. In Tuscany, Napoleon introduced publicity in criminal proceedings, and it has survived all succeeding changes of the government. In Rome it is excluded. Whether it was introduced there by Napoleon after the deposition of the Pope and the establishment of the kingdom of Italy, I do not remember, but I have no doubt that it was.

What changes the Pope contemplates, how far he proposes to allow the people to participate in the administration of public affairs through the choice of their own magistrates and the enactment of their own laws, I have until very recently considered doubtful, — nor is the extent of the reform he contemplates very distinctly understood now. It will be recollected that a few months ago he called together a council of delegates from the different provinces. I read his opening address to them with great care, supposing it would contain an outline of the political changes he contemplated. He stated that he had called them together for consultation, which seemed to exclude the idea of legislation; that extravagant expectations had been entertained as to his purposes, and that he intended to transmit to his successors unimpaired the authority he had derived from those who had preceded him. Not long before this annunciation was received, I was invited to attend a public meeting in the city of New York, called to express the general sympahty which was felt in his measures of reform. Not being able to attend, I addressed a letter to the committee of arrangements; and there were several other letters written by gentlemen of distinguished character, and some of them occupying high official stations. Not feeling at that time quite sure of the sequel, I did not indulge in the enthusiastic expressions which some of the letters contained. I endeavored to render the Pope full justice. I desire to do so now. And I must say that the recent intelligence from abroad justifies all the expectations which have been entertained in respect to his contemplated measures of reform. He has already done much for good government in Italy. He arrayed himself boldly at the outset against the influence of Austria, — an influence which, since the general pacification of Europe, in 1815, has been a perfect blight upon the growth and progress of popular freedom. He has resisted fearlessly the designs of that government upon the independence of the Roman people. He has refused to the Austrian troops a passage through his dominions for the purpose of aiding the King of the Two Sicilies in putting down the struggles of the Neapolitan and Sicilian people against the narrow-minded tyranny by which they have been oppressed. He has done more. He has formed a national guard in the Papal States; he has put arms into the hands of the Roman people, and he is preparing them by military exercises for the assertion and maintenance of their own rights. He has, in a word, given an impulse to popular freedom throughout Italy; and it is owing in a great degree to him, that constitutional forms of government have been given to the people of Sardinia, Tuscany, and the Two Sicilies.

The late arrival affords us still more gratifying evidence of his movements. Two papers have been put into my hands, from which I will read brief extracts. The first is from a letter in the "Courrier des Etats Unis," dated in Paris, which I will translate literally: —

> "The reaction of the revolution in Naples has been felt, as I foresaw, in the other parts of Italy. The King of Sardinia and the Grand-Duke of Tuscany have also given to their subjects a constitution, modelled after the French Charter. Pius the Ninth has promised, in a proclamation and in conversation with those around him, something analogous to it. In the mean time, he has changed his cabinet, and has formed a ministry composed almost entirely of laymen. This is a great reform."

The other extract is from the letter of the European correspondent of the "National Intelligencer," published in this morning's paper. I will read it: —

> "The good and conscientious Pope has had misgivings as to his power to grant a reformed constitution to his people, fearing that his doing so would interfere with the oath which he took at his accession to office, to hand down the *temporalities* of his kingdom uninjured to his successors. He submitted his doubts to a council of ecclesiastics learned in such matters, and the result is, a decision that his yielding to the wishes of the people and the spirit of the times will not be an infringement upon his official oath. It is supposed, therefore, that the people of Rome will soon receive a constitution founded on the same principles as those of Naples, Sardinia, and Florence. His Holiness

has advanced a great step, by his employment of well-qualified laymen in high positions in the State, which have hitherto been filled by ecclesiastics. Three vacancies lately occurred, and three liberal-minded laymen succeeded three churchmen. How much does the world owe to Pius IX! His liberal conduct first put the ball of reform in motion: it is not destined to stop until it has regenerated Europe."

Thus it appears that the Roman people are to receive from the Pope a constitutional government. And, what I consider of great importance as a measure of reform, he has already begun to introduce laymen into his political councils. At the general pacification, in 1815, it was understood that the chief ministers of the Pope were to be chosen from the laity. This understanding was violated; and it has been one of the leading causes of public discontent in the Papal States. It has been for a very long period one of the reforms most earnestly sought for; and it may be hailed as the precursor of an ultimate separation of the ecclesiastic and secular branches of the Papal government, by conferring political offices on laymen, and confining churchmen to the exercise of their ecclesiastical functions,—an arrangement favorable alike to the Church and the State, by promoting the purity of the one and the prosperity of the other.

While the Pope has much to reform, he has much to contend against—not only from the opposition of those who are hostile to all progress, but from the embarrassed condition of the finances of the Papal States. Some ten years ago, the revenues were about nine millions of dollars; two millions and a half were derived from internal taxes, chiefly on landed property; about four millions and a half from the customs, excise, &c.; about nine hundred thousand dollars from lotteries, and the residue from miscellaneous sources. Some of these revenues were collected at an enormous expense. The revenue from lotteries, for instance, which yielded nine hundred thousand dollars in the gross, cost about six hundred thousand in the collection, leaving only three hundred thousand in the treasury as an offset to the general demoralization of which they were the cause. In the same year, the expenditures exceeded the revenues about half a million of dollars. Four years ago, I understood the deficiency exceeded a million, and the preceding year a million and a half. From the difficulty of obtaining statistical information, I could not ascertain the amount of the public debt; but from the interest paid on it, amounting to about two millions and a half of dollars, exceeding one quarter of the entire revenue of the Papal States, it must have exceeded forty millions of dollars. It cannot now, I think, be less than fifty millions. It may be much more.

Sir, this is a very heavy pecuniary burden for a small state. The whole superficial area of the Papal States is about thirteen thousand square miles, — less than one third the area of the State of New York; and a population, according to the *raccolta*, or census, of 1833, of two million seven hundred thousand souls, — about the same as the population of New York. While Rome has two hundred and ten inhabitants to a square mile, from the difference in surface, New York has but sixty. The population of the Papal States is very unequally distributed. Only about one third of the surface is cultivated, and a considerable portion is very thinly inhabited. I doubt whether the population has much increased during the last fifteen years. In 1833, the city of Rome had about one hundred and fifty thousand inhabitants; in 1838, it had less than one hundred and forty-nine thousand, — a slight decrease.

The Papal States have some commerce; but little is carried on in her own vessels. There are but two harbors for vessels of any considerable burden, — Civita Vecchia, on the Mediterranean, and Ancona, on the Adriatic. The excellence of both ports is due, in a good degree, to the Emperor Trajan. There were other valuable ports once, but they have become useless for large vessels. Terracina, the ancient capital of the Volsci, was formerly a naval station of great importance; but it is now obstructed by deposits of sand. The Porto d'Anzo, — the ancient Antium, — about midway between Terracina and the mouth of the Tiber, is also obstructed, and nearly useless, from the same cause.

There is but one navigable river in the Papal States — the Tiber. As there have been some allusions to it in the course of the debate, I hope I shall be excused if I make some references also to its condition as to commerce and navigability. It empties into the Mediterranean seventeen miles from Rome. As it approaches the sea, it divides into two channels. On the left arm stood the ancient Ostia. It has long since fallen into ruins, and a modern Ostia stands near it; but, from the unhealthiness of the place, it is almost deserted, and the channel of the river is nearly filled up. The right arm is navigable to the sea. On this channel stood the ancient city of Portus; but only the ruins are now visible, and the modern town of Fiumicino has risen up a mile and a half below. The channel is narrow, deep, and rapid. The description of Virgil, as he makes Æneas first see the Tiber, is still applicable to it. I do not know that I can quote him accurately, but if I do not, there are gentlemen of classical learning on both sides of the Chamber who will correct me: —

> — "fluvio Tiberinus amœno,
> Vorticibus rapidis et multa flavus arena,
> In mare prorumpit."

The description is not inaccurate: with rapid whirlpools, and yellow with earth, it bursts into the sea. The current is so rapid that vessels could only stem it with strong winds; but they are now towed up by steamers. Vessels of small size — among them a steamer — go up to Rome, and at some seasons there is a good deal of freighting done on the river. Indeed, it is navigable for boats to its junction with the Nera, some forty miles above. But from the rapidity of the current near the city and below, deposits of sand are constantly obstructing the passage, and an annual appropriation of money is made to keep it open.

The exports of the Papal States are not large, but they are numerous. They consist of corn, oil, silk, skins, fruits, woad (a substitute for indigo, which grows spontaneously in southern Italy,) hemp, &c. Wool is exported in large quantities to England; and among other exports is tobacco, of which they send abroad annually about three hundred thousand pounds.

They can scarcely be said to have a commercial marine. Some ninety vessels, averaging probably about eighty tons each, constitute the whole, excepting fishing-smacks, and small coasters. There are six merchant-vessels in the city of New York with an aggregate tonnage exceeding that of the ninety merchant-vessels of the Roman States. This, however, we need not regret; for if we can extend our commercial relations with them, we shall do all the carrying, both for them and ourselves.

Agriculture, the basis of all industry, is in a very depressed state, and from peculiar causes. The great peculiarity of the agriculture of the Papal States is the division of the champaign land into immense farms. The Campagna around Rome, called the "Agro Romano," (the Roman field,) the Maremma, extending from the frontier of Tuscany, along the coast, to the southward, and the low lands in other districts, are owned by a few persons. The farms usually contain several thousand acres. The entire Agro Romano, comprising more than one fifth of the Campagna, contains over eight hundred and fifty square miles. This tract is in the hands of about forty farmers, or "Mercanti di Campagna," as they are called. The farms are worked on the "Mezzeria" system, or at halves, under the direction of *fattori*, or stewards, who occupy farm-houses on the land, while the owners live in the cities. The same system prevails in Tuscany, where it has worked tolerably well. In Rome it is thought exceedingly unfavorable to agricultural improvement. Something is attributable to the peculiarity of the Roman plain, in respect to climate and health, which renders it necessary to devote the greater part to grazing. In the winter it is covered with cattle and sheep, — not less perhaps than a million of both, — under the guardianship of shepherds and herdsmen. As the summer advances, the Campagna becomes too unhealthy to be inhabited, and the cattle are driven to the Sabine hills, and even to the mountains of the Abruzzi. When the harvest season arrives, the heat becomes almost intolerable; and multitudes of the laborers, who come down from the mountains to gather the harvest, perish from the fatal effects of the malaria. As soon as the grain is gathered, the Campagna becomes a desert until the summer heats are over. Neither men nor cattle are to be seen. The buffalo, who seem to be proof against the heavy pestilential vapors which the burning sun brings out from the humid earth, are almost the only inhabitants of the deserted plain from June to October.

With this imperfect agriculture, a complete monopoly is given to the rural proprietors by the corn-laws of the Papal States. When the price of flour on the Mediterranean is under $9, and on the Adriatic $8.25 per barrel, the introduction is prohibited. It is the same with wheat. When it is under about $1.40 the bushel on the Mediterranean, or $1.20 on the Adriatic, it is not allowed to be introduced. The operation of this system is to give the entire market to the Roman agriculturist, and, by excluding the cheaper breadstuffs of the Levant and the Austrian provinces on the eastern shore of the Adriatic, to compel the Roman people in some districts, and in times of scarcity, to eat dear bread.

Notwithstanding the depressed condition of the Papal States, there is no country capable of a more rich or varied production; and if the measures of reform now in progress shall be carried out, and the social as well as the political condition of the people be elevated by the abrogation of bad laws, I know no state of the same magnitude which may hope for a higher prosperity.

I have thus, Mr. President, presented some statistical details in respect to the condition of the Papal States, not with the expectation of influencing the vote of any Senator on this floor, but for the purpose of assigning the grounds on which I place my own. I am in favor of establishing diplomatic intercourse with Rome, first, with a view to friendly relations, — the object for which most missions are created; and second, with a view to commerce. I repeat, I do not regard the mission as political, unless that term be understood in its broadest sense; and in this view all missions are political. I consider it our sacred duty to keep aloof from the internal agitations of European states, and from the movements of their sovereigns and people. We must sympathize with everything that is favorable to freedom; but we can do no more. Our rule of action is non-intervention in the political concerns of the eastern hemisphere, and by a rigid adherence to it we may with the more confidence insist on an application of the same principle by European states to the political concerns of the independent communities on this continent. I look, then, first to friendly relations with central Italy.

But I look chiefly to commerce. Depressed as the industry of Rome is, I think something may be done to extend our commercial relations and intercourse with her, and perhaps also with Tuscany, lying on her borders. Great Britain has an immense trade with the Mediterranean. She sends every year fifteen millions of dollars in value of her own products into Italy alone, and probably several millions more of foreign products, which she imports for reëxportation. A portion of this lucrative trade legitimately should be ours; and I think we may obtain it, if we send a discreet and intelligent man to Italy.

I voted for a minister plenipotentiary, as proposed by the Senator from Missouri,[1] supposing it would be followed, if his amendment had prevailed, by a proposition to abolish the

[1] Mr. Benton.

post of *chargé d'affaires* at Naples. The post of *chargé d'affaires* at Turin I would not have touched. Sardinia is distant, and has distinct commercial interests. But we might have sent a minister with full powers to central and southern Italy, to reside a part of the time at Rome, and part of the time at Naples, — an arrangement not unprecedented in diplomatic intercourse with states bordering on each other. I thought, in opening diplomatic intercourse with Rome, it should be done in the mode most acceptable. A minister is accredited to the sovereign of the country to which he is sent, — a *chargé d'affaires* to the secretary of foreign affairs, or the chief executive department. A minister would be on a footing with the diplomatic representatives of the states of Europe, at the Papal Court, — a *chargé* will be inferior in grade and in influence. Rome and Naples are but one hundred and sixty miles apart. Four years ago, a railroad was in a course of construction from Naples to the Roman frontier. It was nearly finished to Capua. Gregory XVI., the predecessor of the present Pope, refused to charter railroad companies. He did not encourage foreign intercourse, social or commercial. Pius IX. is of a totally different temper. He is desirous of promoting in every way facilities for communication, foreign and domestic. He has chartered a company to construct a railway to Civita Vecchia; and another, as I understand, to meet the Neapolitan railroad at Terracina. In two years Rome and Naples will probably be but five hours apart. The arrangement suggested would, therefore, have been convenient as well as proper. But, as the proposition failed, I shall vote for a minister resident.

Before I conclude, I wish to say a few words on the religious question. I have already said, I do not regard this, in any sense, as a religious mission; nor can I conceive that it can be properly so considered. Gentlemen have gone so far as to suppose that it will be repugnant to the Protestant feeling of the country. I cannot believe there is any just ground for such an apprehension. We send a diplomatic representative to the Emperor of China, who claims to be the sole vicegerent of the Supreme Being on earth. We have a minister at Constantinople, and three consuls, salaried officers, exercising diplomatic functions, in Africa,— two in the Barbary States, and one in the empire of Morocco; and the people of all these countries are either Turks, Moors, Arabs, Berbers, or Jews,— all utterly denying the authenticity of the Christian faith. And yet, when we propose to send a diplomatic representative to a temporal sovereign in Europe, it is objected that the Protestant feeling of the country may be wounded, because he is also the head of a most respectable and important branch of the Christian church. Sir, I cannot comprehend this feeling, and I am therefore disposed to doubt its existence. At all events I shall vote for the appropriation, and trust to my Protestant friends for a just appreciation of my motives.

CALIFORNIA CLAIMS.

MARCH 29, 1848.

Mr. DIX addressed the Senate as follows: —

MR. PRESIDENT: The transactions out of which the claims provided for by the bill under consideration arose, were explained yesterday in the brief but very pertinent and lucid remarks of the honorable Senator from Michigan,[1] as chairman of the Committee on Military Affairs, before which the testimony substantiating the case was taken. I hold in my hand the printed document containing this testimony, and before I sit down I will read some portions of it to the Senate, though I may perhaps but present what is familiar to all.

I do not know that any explanation further than that which has already been given by the honorable Senator from Michigan is necessary to vindicate the propriety of passing the bill. The pecuniary obligations, for the discharge of which it provides, were contracted in good faith, for the purpose of subduing the country and of expelling from it the military forces of Mexico. In the execution of these objects, the young and accomplished officer at the head of our troops, Colonel Frémont, exhibited a combination of energy, promptitude, sagacity, and prudence, which indicates the highest capacity for civil and military command; and, in connection with what he has done for the cause of science, it has given him a reputation at home and abroad of which men much older and more experienced than himself might well be proud. That the country will do justice

[1] Mr. Cass.

to his valuable and distinguished services I entertain not the slightest doubt.

The objects accomplished by Colonel Frémont, as subsequent developments have shown, were far more important than those I have referred to. There is no doubt that his rapid and decisive movements kept California out of the hands of British subjects, and perhaps out of the hands of the British government; and it is in this point of view that I desire to present the subject to the Senate. If these transactions stood alone, if they constituted an isolated case, I might not deem it necessary to call attention to them. But as a part of a system to all appearances deliberately entered upon and steadily pursued, it seems to me that they may justly claim a more extensive consideration than would otherwise be due to them.

While discussing the bill to raise an additional military force in January last, I stated some facts in illustration of the encroachments of Great Britain on the southern portion of the North American continent. I alluded particularly to her movements on the Mosquito coast, where she is establishing herself under the pretence of giving protection to an insignificant tribe of Indians, but in reality to gain possession of a territory not only intrinsically valuable on account of its natural products, but doubly so to her on account of its advantages of position. This occupation does not rest upon the ground of an original establishment on territory unreclaimed from its primeval solitude, or even on territory not reduced to actual possession by its first discoverer. It is a portion of the old Spanish dominion in North America, constituting, after the dissolution of the empire of Spain in the western hemisphere, a part of the confederation of Central America, and now an integral part of the states of Honduras and Nicaragua: and if the power of Spain had continued unbroken, this unjustifiable encroachment would not have been heard of. I stated on a former occasion that the territory occupied in the name of the

Mosquito nation by Great Britain contains about 40,000 square miles,—nearly as large a surface as that of the State of New York, — and that she had recently sought to extend her possession by forcible means to the river San Juan de Nicaragua, near the eleventh parallel of latitude, one degree further south than the territory actually claimed as belonging to the Mosquitoes according to her own geographical delineations.

Nearly a century ago some connection existed between Great Britain and the Mosquito Indians; but the territory was abandoned by her under treaty-stipulations with Spain. When the connection was renewed I am unable to say; but I believe the first open and avowed attempt to exercise rights of sovereignty over the territory, through consular agents, was in 1843, when Mr. Patrick Walker was appointed consul at Bluefields; and this appointment was instantly the subject of a protest by at least one of the South American states.

Before I proceed to give the details of this encroachment, I wish to call the attention of the Senate to the position taken by the Executive of the United States, nearly twenty-five years ago, in respect to the future colonization of this continent by European powers.

In the annual message of Mr. Monroe to Congress, in December, 1823, he stated, that, in the discussion of the respective rights of Great Britain, Russia, and the United States, on the northwestern coast of America, the occasion had "been judged proper for asserting as a principle, in which the rights of the United States are involved, that the American continents, by the free and independent condition which they have assumed and maintained, are henceforth not to be considered as subjects for future colonization by any European powers." In the same message it was declared, that we should regard any attempt on the part of European powers to extend their political "system to any portion of this hemisphere as dangerous to our peace and safety." "With existing colonies or dependencies of any European powers," says the message, "we have not interfered, and shall not interfere. But with the governments who have declared their independence, and maintained it, and whose independence we have, on great consideration and on just principles, acknowledged, we could not view any interposition for the purpose of oppressing them, or controlling in any other manner their destiny, by any European power, in any other light than as the manifestation of an unfriendly disposition towards the United States."

The two positions assumed by the Executive of the United States were, —

1. That there must be no further colonization on either of the American continents by any European power; and,

2. That there must be no interference by European powers with the independent states in this hemisphere.

And these declarations were accompanied by the disavowal on our part of all intention to interfere with existing colonies or dependencies of any European power on this continent.

Of the wisdom or policy of these declarations, I have nothing to say; though I must add, that I have always considered the publication of manifestoes, which the government putting them forth is not prepared to maintain at all hazards, as calculated to detract from its dignity and influence.

Mr. Monroe's declarations have not been maintained. They applied to South as well as North America; and during the last five years, the Banda Oriental and the Argentine Confederation have been the theatre of an armed intervention, on the part of Great Britain at first, and ultimately of Great Britain and France, which is almost unprecedented in the history of nations, as a violation of the right of every community to regulate its domestic concerns in its own way, without external interference. I will not detain the Senate by entering into the details of these transactions. Suffice it to say, that, in 1838, in consequence of internal dissensions in the Banda Oriental, or the Oriental Republic of Uruguay, fomented by foreign officers and residents in Montevideo, General Oribe, the President, resigned, and fled to Buenos Ayres, his rival, General Reveira, succeeding to his political post. In 1842, Oribe entered the Banda Oriental, drove Reveira into Brazil, and besieged his general (Paez) in Montevideo, which was subsequently invested by sea by the Argentine fleet. The interposition of Admiral Purvis, commanding the British fleet, when the admiral of the French fleet refused to interfere, on the ground that such interference would violate well-established principles of international law, has had the effect of prolonging for five years a war which would otherwise have been speedily decided, and led to a violation of every rule of international duty, through a further intervention in the affairs of the Argentine Confederation, by the combined fleets of France and Great Britain, under the sanction of their respective governments. Those who desire to know more of these transactions will find a most interesting discussion in the British House of Lords, in the Parliamentary Debates of 1845, Vol. 83, page 1152. In reply to some inquiries proposed by Lord Beaumont, the Earl of Aberdeen made the defence of the Ministry. He was followed by Lord Colchester, who had been at the Rio de la Plata, and who was thoroughly acquainted with all that had taken place. He corrected many of the Earl of Aberdeen's statements; and I think it will be admitted that he left to the Ministry a most unsatisfactory ground of defence. On the principles laid down by Mr. Monroe, it would have been the duty of the United States to interpose for the purpose of protecting the Oriental and Argentine republics from this flagrant invasion of their rights as sovereign and independent states. We have failed to do so, I do not say whether rightly or not; but the impolicy of making declarations which we are not prepared to maintain is strongly exemplified in our inaction.

In the annual message of the President to Congress, in December, 1846, the declarations of Mr. Monroe were reiterated, but the application of the principles he asserted was virtually restricted to the continent of North America. Whatever hesitancy there may be in extending the application further, to this extent its assertion and maintenance at all hazards can afford, it appears to me, no ground for a difference of opinion; and, so believing, it was with great pleasure that I listened to the spirited remarks of the honorable Senator from Delaware [1] on this subject, at the close of the debate on the bill to raise an additional military force. Our own security depends, in no inconsiderable degree, on the tranquillity of the states bordering on us, or in our neighborhood. The interference of European powers in their affairs can have no other effect but to produce distractions dangerous alike to them and to us. We have a right to insist, then, on the principle of non-intervention on this continent,—a principle lying at the very foundation of all national independence,—a principle which cannot be violated without offending against the common welfare and the common interest of the whole civilized world. In connection with this subject, I desire to say that I have always insisted, in the most earnest manner, on the duty of non-interference on our part with the affairs of European states. I consider it the more imperative now, when great political changes are taking place, and when the whole continent of Europe may be convulsed to its centre.

In this view of the subject, the encroachments of Great Britain in North America possess an importance which cannot be exaggerated. I begin with Central America, and shall pass on to California, where we have had recent evidence of a deliberate design to obtain possession of the country, for the purpose of excluding us.

In February last, I received a letter from a friend in New York,—a gentleman of high respectability, extensively

[1] Mr. Clayton.

engaged in commercial transactions, chiefly with Central and South America, and who formerly held a seat in the House of Representatives,—stating that he had noticed my allusion to the affairs of the Mosquito coast, and that he could give me some information on the subject, if I desired it. I immediately made the request, and received from him, about a month ago, a letter, which I will read to the Senate:—

"NEW YORK, *February* 28, 1848.

"DEAR SIR: Your favor of the 25th instant is received. In compliance with your request, I have hastily drawn up the outlines of the information alluded to.

"In August, 1845, Mr. James S. Bell visited New York, and was introduced to me as a person having great commercial advantages at the English settlement of Bluefields, Mosquito nation, Central America, and who desired to form a connection with a house at New York, by which these advantages could be made available for commercial enterprise. Having at that time much business at Balize and Truxillo, I was ready to listen to propositions for increasing my trade with that country, especially to receive the valuable information which I was told Mr. B. could impart. Mr. Bell stated he was the Secretary to the British consulate at Bluefields, which he assured me was really the government *de facto* of the Mosquito nation,—a tribe of dissolute and degraded Indians, whose king, a lad of fourteen, was an inmate of the consul-house, and dependent on that functionary for the necessaries of life; that the Mosquito country had been privately conveyed to the British government, and that that claim, when questioned, could be maintained by a legal title of purchase from the king; that the object of the British government was not only the possession of this territory, which abounded with rich forests of mahogany, and other valuable woods, on the coast, and many miles in the interior on navigable rivers, but *at the proper time* to show, prove, and maintain by force of arms, if necessary, the Mosquito (their own) title to as far south as 10° of north latitude, comprising San Juan and the rich country of Lake Nicaragua, thus securing the best route to the Pacific, as well as by far the most fertile and productive of all that section of Central America; that he (Mr. Bell) had made two visits, accompanied by skilful surveyors and engineers, to San Juan, and thence to the interior, and to the Lake Nicaragua, for purposes of exploration, &c., by order of the government, conveyed privately to Mr. Walker, the consul at Bluefields; that he came to the United States to effect on his individual account a connection with some mercantile house, by which to establish branches at Bluefields and at San Juan, in advance of its becoming a *British port;* that he had received an exclusive grant for the cutting of mahogany on Bluefields river and adjacent coast; that this connection with, and intimate relation to, the consulate at Bluefields, *alias* the Mosquito government, would give him such advantages at San Juan, that he could nearly monopolize the interior trade of that place, and ship to the United States large quantities of spice, indigo, cochineal, hides, &c., in exchange for cotton goods, flour, &c.

"Mr. Bell, by written documents and letters, satisfied me fully of the truth of his statements, which recent events have in part confirmed. I declined the propositions, but another house has accepted them, so far as to engage the services of about thirty men to return to Bluefields with Mr. B. to cut mahogany, one cargo of which has actually been received at this port. Mr. Bell, whilst here, had a large chair made, with canopy, &c., gilded profusely, and covered with damask, which he stated was the *throne* of the king of the Mosquitoes; also, halberds and other paraphernalia of royalty, which he took out with him to Bluefields. At the time, these statements made but little impression upon me; but recent events, particularly your speech, have showed too truly their truth and importance."

In connection with this subject, I will also read a communication furnished me, at my request, by the head of one of the foreign embassies in this city, and addressed, by the British *chargé d'affaires* at Bogota, to the government of New Grenada, setting forth the extent of the British claims. In January last, I furnished other evidence, to the same point, on the authority of the British consul-general at Guatemala. I present this as corroborative, and as of higher authority: —

"British Legation, Bogota, *Sept.* 24, 1847.

"Circumstances having given rise to a question as to the extent of the coast frontier of the kingdom of Mosquito, her Britannic Majesty's government, after having carefully examined the various documents and historical records which exist relative to this subject, have instructed the undersigned, her Britannic Majesty's *chargé d'affaires,* to inform the government of New Grenada that her Majesty's government are of opinion that the right of the King of Mosquito should be maintained, as extending from the Cape of Honduras down to the mouth of the river San Juan.

"The undersigned has likewise been instructed to state that her Majesty's government will not view with indifference any attempt to encroach upon the right or territories of the King of Mosquito, who is under the protection of the British Crown.

"In addressing this communication to his Excellency M. Man. Ancizar, Grenadian Secretary of State for Foreign Affairs *ad interim*, the undersigned begs to assure him of his high and most distinguished consideration.

DANIEL F. O'LEARY."

From the information I have been able to gather, Mosquito has become, for all practical purposes, a British colony. The real head of the Mosquito nation is Mr. Patrick Walker, the British consul at Bluefields. The nominal king of the Mosquitoes is a mere boy, living in his house. The Mosquito nation consists of a few hundred naked Indians,—idle, ignorant, and worthless. Under the pretence of giving protection to this miscalled nation, Great Britain has extended her sovereignty over a district of country nearly as large as the State of New York or Pennsylvania. She has vessels of war, commanded by British subjects, under the name of the Mosquito navy. And, in a word, she has appropriated to herself a part of the territory of Honduras, and is encroaching on the territory of Nicaragua, against the solemn protest of the Central American states. Her objects are doubtless threefold: —

1. To extend her political dominion on this continent;
2. To open new fields for commercial enterprise; and
3. To obtain possession of the most practicable route for a ship-canal across the Isthmus, and thus to control the commercial communication between the two oceans.

This last object is naturally regarded as the most important. The route has been surveyed minutely, thoroughly, by a British engineer, and its practicability ascertained. From the Caribbean sea to Lake Nicaragua, the river San Juan is susceptible of the requisite improvement. The lake is already navigable for vessels of any burden; and from the lake it is less than sixteen miles to the Pacific, with a mean descent of about one hundred and twenty-eight feet. The results of this examination will be found at the end of the first volume of Stephens's work on Central America.

But it is not through her connection with the Mosquito coast alone that Great Britain is extending herself across the continent. Through her establishment at Balize she is penetrating to the very heart of the peninsula of Yucatan. She had at first only a permission to occupy a small district on the coast for the purpose of cutting logwood, and to enjoy the use of a fishery for the subsistence of the persons employed. This permission was given during the Spanish rule in America. It was confirmed in 1783 by the treaty of Versailles, under very cautious restrictions, and slightly extended by the treaty of London in 1786. The sovereignty of Spain over this territory became, by virtue of the independence of her colonies, of which Yucatan was one, vested in Mexico. But the right of Great Britain to Balize, I am told, has not been recognized either by Mexico or Yucatan. She not only continues to hold the coast, but she has extended herself over a district of about fourteen thousand square miles, embracing one of the most valuable portions of Yucatan; and I believe she claims it by conquest. She is within sixty miles of Chiapas, the southern State of Mexico; and her chief establishment is said to be a vast depot of contraband. A fierce contest is now going on between the Spanish and Indian races of Yucatan; and the latter, who were once disarmed and harmless, are now found to be abundantly supplied with powder and firearms, — many of the latter bearing the stamp of the tower of London. When this contest, marked, as all such contests are, by murder, and rapine, and wanton barbarity, shall have exhausted the combatants, both parties may be willing to take refuge in the power, and find tranquillity under the protection, of Great Britain. Sir, this is the usual issue of her intervention in the domestic concerns of other States — those especially in which civilization has made but little progress. This is still more likely to be the result when semi-barbarous tribes are intermingled with civilized races, as in the greater portion of this continent to the south of us, and from numbers or local circumstances approaching an equality with each other in point of strength.

I do not make these statements, Mr. President, for the purpose of exciting feeling here or elsewhere. It is a subject which I desire to see considered with calmness and deliberation; but it is one which deeply concerns us. Our tranquillity, our political comfort, our commercial interests, are all involved in the exemption of neighboring states from domestic dissensions and violence; and we have a right to see that these mischiefs are not promoted by unauthorized interference from abroad. I do not propose to speak of the right of interference in the internal concerns of other states. On a former occasion I said to the Senate all that I desire to say on that subject. But I hold it to be our right and our duty, when we see questionable movements by foreign powers on this continent, either through their constituted authorities or through their subjects, supported by the power of the state, to know what are their objects, and to see that the political independence of our weak and defenceless neighbors is not insidiously subverted, and their territorial possessions wrested from them by unwarrantable encroachment.

One of the peculiarities of the system by which Great Britain has extended herself over so large a portion of the globe is, that she usually acts, in the first instance, by private rather than by public agents. She employs commerce to effect what other governments accomplish by public authority and force. Instead of sending an army or a fleet to take possession of a coast, she sends a trading company. Nothing can be more unsuspicious than the circumstances under which their first lodgment — the germ, perhaps, of a future empire — is made. They only wish some facilities for landing and for shelter while they dispose of their merchandise; they desire to establish a factory (which, in the British acceptation of the term, is a house for traders), and to enjoy some temporary conveniences for traffic. The permission is given, a foothold is obtained, a house is built, and a picket, a ditch, an embankment follow. These simple improvements (to use an American phrase) grow insensibly into a settlement, a fortress, and a colony, and the occupation becomes perpetual. Here are British subjects, British property, and British interests to be protected; the honor of Great Britain is concerned, and it will not permit them to be abandoned. Her East Indian empire, the most vast and lucrative of her possessions, was gained through the agency of a trading company. Through a trading company she gained her first foothold on the northwest coast of America, and obtained for herself in the end some of the best portions of Oregon.

There is another peculiarity in the British system of extension. Colonization is only desired so far as it is coextensive with political sovereignty. She does not labor to civilize or improve where she cannot rule. Commercial interest is the principal, and social improvement the incident in her progress.

Sir, there were two great systems of colonization in ancient times, — those of Greece and Rome, — and each distinct in its character. Greece was actuated by no sordid reference to self in the extension of her people. When she sent out her children to colonize distant territories, she let them go forth independent and free. She did not insist on carrying her political sovereignty along with them, and compelling them to pay a servile obedience to it. She sent them out with her benedictions and her prayers, to enjoy, unshared by herself, whatever prosperity they could earn by their industry and their valor; and it was through these migrations that the foundations of ancient civilization were laid in southern Italy.

Roman colonization was totally different in its character. Rome, indeed, did not encourage colonization out of Italy in the early days of the republic. In its latter days, and during the early period of the empire, she sent out colonies to distant regions, and retained them in dependence on herself. She desired that all the streams of prosperity which emanated from her should be poured back, in enlarged currents, upon their source. It was a vast system of centralization. Under its influence the heart became distended and gorged, while the extremities were left exhausted and cold, and the whole system fell asunder by force of this inequality.

This is the British system of colonization; it has been made more liberal of late, but unless still further relaxed, its fate will be the same. Its great characteristic is dependence on the parent state; its most inflexible formulas, (if I may be allowed the expression,) colonial governments subservient to the Crown, commercial regulations framed with an exclusive, and usually (such is the fatality of all selfishness, individual or national) with a mistaken view to metropolitan interests.

It is not for our advantage that this system should be extended. We desire freedom in commercial intercourse. We do not interfere with any colonial systems, however exclusive, where they now exist. We do not oppose their extension in other portions of the globe. But having no colonies ourselves, desiring none, looking only to an extension by pacific means, and from the operation of natural laws, over the unoccupied districts of country west of us, we have a right to insist that colonial establishments, exclusive in their character as respects commercial intercourse, shutting out the world except the parent state, and dependent on distant governments, shall not be planted in our neighborhood in violation of the rights of defenceless states. I would not make this principle the theme of a declaration or a manifesto. I would have it quietly announced to those whom it concerns, and firmly maintained against all infringement.

Before I dismiss this part of the subject I wish to say that I am not unwilling to concede to Great Britain some merit for what she has done for constitutional liberty in the past, nor am I disposed to deny that her colonial system may in the end lead to results of great value to the cause of civilization. She has, in more than one instance, arrayed herself against the progress of arbitrary government in Europe, and asserted principles which lie at the very basis of all free institutions. Through her colonial possessions she is disseminating throughout the globe the intelligence and the civilization by which she is herself distinguished; and, when the political bonds by which her vast possessions are held together shall be rent asunder, — a day not distant, perhaps, — when the sceptre of her empire shall be broken, the colonies she has planted on every continent and in every sea will become so many centres from which the lights of knowledge and freedom will be radiated to the darker portions of the earth. While advocating a determined resistance to her encroachments, I am willing, nevertheless, to do her this political justice.

Let me now turn to the subject more immediately in hand — the California claims. The propriety of passing the bill providing for the payment of them has been fully shown by the honorable Senator from Michigan. It only remains for me to consider the subject in connection with the particular topic which I have discussed.

By the testimony taken before the Committee on Military Affairs, it appears, —

1. That Eugenio Macnamara, a Catholic priest, made application to the government of Mexico for the grant of land in Upper California, for the establishment of Irish colonies. The first colony was to be established at San Francisco; the second at Monterey; and the third at Santa Barbara; and the number of colonists was not to be less than ten thousand. There is no date to the application; but other documents show it to have been previously to the 19th of January, 1846.

2. The avowed objects of Macnamara were to keep the Californias out of the hands of the Americans, who are represented, in his memorial to the Mexican government,

as an artful and base enemy, and as abhorring the people and the religion of Mexico.

I will read to the Senate some extracts from his original application to the Mexican government. They will be found in the translation at page 19 of the document containing the testimony taken before the Committee on Military Affairs, and in the original Spanish at page 77 of the same document:—

"I, Eugenio Macnamara, Catholic priest and apostolical missionary, take the liberty of submitting to your Excellency some reflections on a subject which at this time attracts much public attention. I allude to the expectations and actual condition of Upper California.

"It does not require the gift of prophecy to foresee, that within a little time this fertile country will cease to be an integral part of this republic, unless some prompt and efficacious measures be adopted to restrain foreign rapacity.

"For this reason I propose, with the aid and approbation of your Excellency, to carry forward this project, to place in Upper California a colony of Irish Catholics. I have a triple object in making this proposition: I wish, in the first place, to advance the cause of Catholicism; in the second, to contribute to the happiness of my countrymen; thirdly, I desire to put an obstacle in the way of further usurpations on the part of an irreligious and anti-Catholic nation. I therefore propose to your Excellency that there be conceded to me an extent of territory on the coast of Upper California for the purpose I have indicated."

I will also read an extract at page 21 from his second application, urging attention to the first. It will be found in Spanish at page 79:—

"Your Excellency will excuse me, that I take the liberty further to demonstrate that no time ought to be lost in this important affair, if it is desired to be realized, since your Excellency knows well enough that we are surrounded by an artful and base enemy, who loses no means, however low, to possess himself of the best territory of this country, and who abhors to the death its race and its religion.

"If the means which I propose be not speedily adopted, your Excellency may be assured that, before another year, the Californias will form a part of the American nation. Their Catholic institutions will become the prey of the Methodist wolves, and the whole country will be inundated with the cruel invaders. Whilst I propose the means of repelling them, my propositions ought to be the more admissible, inasmuch as I have no personal interest in the affair, save the progress of the holy religion of God, and the happiness of my countrymen."

The stigmas cast upon us and upon one of our most respectable religious sects, I regard as designed by Macnamara to minister to the prejudices of Mexico, with a view to the accomplishment of his purposes, rather than as emanating from a conviction of their truth.

3. The grant to Macnamara, after being submitted to the consideration of the Governor of California, was made on the 4th of July, 1846, and comprised about three thousand square leagues, containing, besides the bay of San Francisco, some of the best lands and some of the most important military and commercial positions in California.

4. Macnamara was taken to California in a British sloop of war (the Juno) in June, 1846; a British ship of eighty guns, (the Collingwood,) commanded by Admiral Seymour, followed in July, and Macnamara was taken away in her.

The extract I am about to read from the affidavit of Colonel Frémont will show the connection between Macnamara's movements and those of the public armed vessels of Great Britain. It will be found at page 14 of the document: —

"The fruits of the revolutionary movement thus passed to the United States, and have remained with her ever since. These fruits were very considerable. Besides the peaceable possession of all the northern part of California, and the actual force in the field under the independent flag, which immediately went into service under the United States, there is good reason to believe, and evidence is now at hand to sustain that belief, that the revolutionary movement prevented a design of the Californians to put their country under the flag of the British, and also prevented the completion of the colonization grant of three thousand square leagues to Macnamara, who was brought to California in the British sloop of war Juno in the month of June, 1846. Admiral Seymour, in the Collingwood, of eighty guns, arrived at Monterey on the 16th of July. Macnamara was on board the Collingwood when I arrived at Monterey on the 19th, and was carried away in that vessel. The taking possession of that place on the 7th had anticipated him, and the revolutionary movement had checked the designs of the Californians to place the country under British protection; and also prevented the fulfilment of the great grant to Macnamara, the original papers of which I now have here, to be shown to the committee and to be delivered up to the government."

5. In addition to the Macnamara grants, some of the most valuable missions were sold in May and June, 1846, to British subjects, for very inconsiderable sums, showing an evident design, in case the United States should get possession of the Californias, to keep some of the most valuable districts out of the hands of the government, by converting them, through fraudulent conveyances, into British property.

6. It appears also that a plan was set on foot by the British vice-consul in California, Mr. Forbes, Macnamara, and others, to put that country under the protection of Great Britain, and at the very moment when it was expected that a war would break out between the United States and Mexico. The time, the circumstances, the actors, all indicate a deliberate design to get possession of California, for the purpose of keeping it out of the hands of the United States. The auspices under which a junta was planned and convoked for the purpose of asking the protection of Great Britain are shown by an extract which I will read from the affidavit of Captain Gillespie, of the Marine Corps, and which will be found at page 28 of the document: —

"About this time (June 30) I learned that the junta which was to have assembled at Santa Barbara upon the 15th June, and which had been planned and arranged by and through the agency of Mr. Forbes, the British vice-consul, and an Irish Catholic priest, by the name of Macnamara, had been prevented from assembling in consequence of the rising of the settlers. This junta was proposed for the purpose of asking the protection of England, and of giving an immense tract of land in the valley of the San Joaquin for the settlement of ten thousand Irishmen, to be brought to California under the direction of Macnamara. All this intrigue of British agents was broken up by the timely and prompt operations of the settlers, under the direction of Captain Frémont."

By Lieutenant Minor's testimony, which will be found at pages 43 and 44, it appears that the convention or junta was held, and that a majority were in favor of claiming the protection of England, — a decision naturally to have been expected, when it is considered under what auspices it was convoked. The extracts I am about to read contain also some interesting facts connected with the movements of the British admiral: —

"The undersigned, a lieutenant in the navy of the United States, has the honor to make the following answers to the interrogatories put to him by your honorable committee:

"The undersigned being in command of the southern district of California during the latter part of 1846, was informed by Pedro C. Carilla (and he believes the information thus obtained is founded on facts) that he, the said Carilla, was a member of a junta that assembled at Santa Barbara in June, 1846, for the purpose of declaring the independence of California, and of asking the protection of the United States or Great Britain; that the junta was represented by all of the inhabited portions of California; that a majority of the same were for claiming the protection of England; that their resolves would probably have been executed had it not been for the war and their fears of an armed force, then on the north side of the bay of San Francisco, under the command of Captain Frémont. The undersigned has understood from other sources, entitled to confidence, that a majority of the people of California desired the protection of England. The opinion he thus formed was strengthened by the fact that an English frigate (the Juno) had, about the time the junta met, landed an English subject named Macnamara at Santa Barbara, of whom it was said that he had obtained a grant from the Mexican government of a large and fertile portion of California, embracing the whole valley of the San Joaquin, from its source to its mouth, — a valley, as the undersigned believes, comprising one third of the richest portion of California. The undersigned believes that the British squadron in the Pacific, commanded by Rear-Admiral Sir George T. Seymour, composed then of a larger force than they ever had upon that ocean, were employed in closely watching the movements of the American commodore. Being aware of this fact, Commodore Sloat, when he heard of the first battle on the Rio Grande, got under way in the frigate Savannah, then anchored off Mazatlan, for the ostensible purpose of proceeding to California. An English vessel of war weighed soon after the Savannah, and stood in the direction of San Blas, where it was known the admiral was. After cruising in the gulf two days, the commodore returned to his anchorage off Mazatlan, when another English ship got under way and stood in the direction of San Blas. The undersigned believes that this manœuvre of Commodore Sloat was intended for the deception of the English admiral. On the 8th of June, 1846, the Savannah again made sail, and after a passage of twenty-three days, during which a press of canvas was carried, she arrived at the port of Monterey, in Upper California. The Collingwood, of eighty guns, the flag-ship of Admiral Seymour, entered the harbor on the 15th of July, and the undersigned believes that the admiral was disappointed when he saw the American flag flying on shore."

The testimony of Captain Hensley, from which I will give a brief extract, and which will be found at page 33, fully sustains the statement of Lieutenant Minor: —

"I am a resident in California, where I have resided since the autumn of 1843. In the month of May, 1846, I went to San Francisco, where I met with General Vallejo, one of the most prominent and influential men in Upper California. I understood from him that he had recently attended a convention, composed of General Castro, himself, and five others, delegates from the different districts in California, at which the proposition had been made and debated to separate from Mexico, and establish a government in California, under the protection of some foreign power, believed by us to be England; but, as the general positively stated, the majority was not in favor of placing the country under the protection of the United States, though he himself was. General Vallejo was of course guarded in conversing on so dangerous a subject as this was at that time; but the above is the substance of his remarks, as understood by myself and others who heard them."

The grant to Macnamara is so connected with the movements of the public vessels and public agents of Great Britain as to raise a strong presumption that he was secretly countenanced by the British government. Doctor John Baldwin, whose testimony will be found at pages 46 *et seq.*, states that Macnamara lived in the house of the British consul, or *chargé d'affaires*, in Mexico, and that he understood in that city, in September and October, 1847, a plan had been projected, under the auspices of the British legation, to colonize California with emigrants from Ireland. These facts will be more fully shown by his affidavit, at pages 46 and 47 of the document, from which I will read a single paragraph: —

"I resided in the Republic of Mexico from the year 1822 until 1838, a period of sixteen years, during which I made the acquaintance of many of the leading men of the country.

"I again entered Mexico (city) on the 14th of September, 1847, and remained there until the 1st of November; during that time I made the acquaintance of the priest Macnamara, and from sources entitled to credit I was informed that he had, under the auspices of the British legation, projected a plan to colonize California with emigrants from Ireland. His project had met the approbation of the Mexican government, and he went to California to perfect his plans. In the mean time, it was ascertained that the ulterior views of Macnamara were to promote the interest of the British government and not the Mexican government. A fierce opposition was contemplated by the republican members of Congress, when he should return with his matured plans from California; this resistance became unnecessary in consequence of the conquest of California by the arms of the United States. Macnamara lived in the family of either the British consul or *chargé d'affaires* in Mexico."

I have referred to the connection of Macnamara's movements with the public vessels of Great Britain as presumptive evidence of the connection of the British government with them. I do not inquire whether Admiral Seymour had special instructions or not. From the declaration of Admiral Purvis, in the intervention of La Plata, it is highly probable that British naval officers cruising in distant seas have general instructions "to protect British interests at all hazards," (I believe that is the phrase,) leaving an unlimited discretion to the officer, and giving to the government the advantage of being able to approve or disavow his conduct in special cases, according to its own interest. From all the circumstances connected with the transactions in California, we are constrained to believe that the British naval commander was fully apprised of Macnamara's objects, as well as the design to place that country under the protection of Great Britain, and that he was there coöperating in the one, and ready to coöperate in the other. Indeed, by referring to the testimony of Mr. Loker, at page 39, it will be seen that his arrival there had been talked about and expected with a view "to take possession of California."

I have given, Mr. President, a mere outline of the transactions of British subjects and British agents in California. The leading facts are verified by the affidavits of Colonel Frémont, Captain Gillespie, of the marine corps, Lieutenant Minor, and Midshipman Wilson, of the navy, Colonel Russel, Captain Hensley, Doctor Baldwin, and many gentlemen connected with the civil and military transactions of the Californias after the rupture between the United States and Mexico; and some of the most important circumstances are authenticated by the public records of California which fell into our possession.

It is impossible that the success of these movements should not have brought us into direct collision with Great Britain. We could not have failed to regard them, considered in connection with her proceedings in Oregon, and more recently in Central America, as part of a deliberate design to environ us with her colonies, and especially to shut us out from the Pacific and its extending commerce. From all the facts, we can hardly doubt either that she would have taken possession of the country in her own name, or, what is perhaps more probable, that she would, in the first instance, have taken it under her protection. In this case the drama of the Mosquito coast, the performers only being changed, would have been acted over again. A Californian governor, somewhat above the grade of the king of the Mosquitoes in respectability, but on the same level with him in subservience to the protecting power, would have been put in the foreground, while British subjects would have occupied the country, and gradually reduced it into the possession of Great Britain. Thus shut out from the Pacific, our own people would have been met at the Sierra Madre, or perhaps still further east, and the tide of emigration and settlement would have been turned back upon the Atlantic coast. It is in this point of view that these transactions possess the greatest interest and importance, and that the sagacity, promptitude, and decision of our youthful commander in California, at the time the disturbances broke out, have given him the strongest claims on his countrymen. Any faltering on his part — any hesitancy in acting and in acting promptly — might have cost us millions of dollars and thousands of lives; and it might also have cost us a contest of which the end is not readily foreseen.

THE YUCATAN BILL.

A BILL to take temporary military possession of Yucatan was introduced into the Senate, in pursuance of a recommendation of the President that our naval forces in the Gulf of Mexico should be employed to afford relief to the white population, who were in danger of extermination by the Indians, and to prevent that province from becoming a colony to a European power. The provisions of the bill went far beyond the suggestions of the President. Mr. Dix, in his speech, which was delivered on the 17th May, 1848, opposed the military occupation of Yucatan as provided for by the bill, but advocated the President's recommendations.

MR. PRESIDENT: I said yesterday, when I offered the amendment which you have just announced as the question first to be decided by the Senate, I should be quite willing that the vote should be taken upon it without discussion; but that if the debate proceeded, I should have something to say in support of my motion. I find the whole subject is to be further discussed; and so many inquiries have been addressed to me, by members of this body, in relation to the particular object of the amendment, that I feel myself called on to explain it. I shall, at the same time, avail myself of the opportunity to make some remarks upon the general question. In doing so, I feel that I shall labor under some disadvantage, as I was not present during the first week of the discussion, and have not had time since to read the printed report; so that it is possible I may, in the remarks I shall make, cover ground which has already been better occupied by others.

The question presented to us by the bill we are considering is not in itself a very simple one; and it appears to me that it has been converted, perhaps not unnecessarily, into one of still greater complexity. I shall endeavor, in what I have to say, to divest it of some, at least, of its complications.

The State of Yucatan is distracted by an internal conflict between the different classes of which her population consists. She has applied to us and to other nations for aid; and she tenders her political sovereignty to any power which will take her under its protection. Sir, there can be no higher evidence of the hopelessness of the condition to which she is reduced, and I recollect no other instance, in modern times at least, in which a State has offered to surrender its nationality to a foreign power, for the purpose of being protected against itself. The President has called our attention to the subject in a special message; and I think he would have been indefensible if he had not done so. He submits no proposition to us, but leaves it to the judgment of Congress to determine what measures shall be adopted to prevent Yucatan from becoming the colony of a European power, and to rescue the white race from extermination or expulsion. The Committee on Foreign Relations, in pursuance of the suggestion of the President, has reported a bill authorizing him to take temporary possession or occupation of the country, and providing arms, munitions of war, ordnance, and troops for that purpose.

The first suggestion which occurs to us is, that this is an internal dispute in which, under ordinary circumstances, we could not properly take part. We insist on the principle of non-intervention in the affairs of other independent States. We hold every violation of this principle to be an offence against the common order and the common tranquillity of civilized society. We insist upon its observance by other nations. Our first duty, then, is to observe it ourselves.

Is there anything in the peculiar relations of Yucatan to the United States and to Mexico which would authorize us to interpose and perform a high duty of humanity, without violating the rule I have stated? Upon the solution of this question, the propriety of our interference mainly depends. In my judgment, from the examination which I have been able to give to the subject, the circumstances do warrant our interference in some efficient mode; and I shall be happy if I can succeed in making this conviction as apparent to the mind of the Senate as it is to my own. In attempting to do so, it will be necessary to examine the relhtions, past and present, of Yucatan to Mexico, and the existing relations of both to us.

Yucatan, I believe, was never comprehended in the vice-royalty of Mexico, under the old Spanish dominion — at all events, excepting for purposes of revenue. She was under a separate government, or captain-generalcy, and communicated directly with the court of Madrid. In 1821, she succeeded in establishing her independence without the aid of Mexico; and when the empire was formed under Iturbide, she became united to it under certain conditions. On the fall of Iturbide, and the dissolution of the empire, she again became independent. When the constitution of 1824 was adopted by the United Mexican States, she became a member of the Confederation, with the distinct declaration that her connection with it should continue only so long as that constitution was preserved inviolate. In 1834, when the constitution of 1824 was subverted by Santa Ana, she became independent a third time. But an army was sent against her by Santa Ana, I believe under the command of his brother-in-law; Merida, the capital, was taken; her militia disbanded; some of her principal citizens banished; and she was, in fact, reduced to the condition of a military despotism under the authority of the central government of Mexico. The same attempt was made on Texas, who was happily more successful than her southern sister in repelling it.

This state of things continued until 1840, when Yucatan threw off her subjection, proclaimed her constitution, and was on the point of declaring her independence, when a negotiation was entered into with Mexico, which resulted, in 1841, in a treaty, leaving her a part of Mexico, but with certain separate powers in respect to her constitution and laws, and, I believe, especially in regard to her revenue, which was left independent of the general revenue system of the republic. This treaty, though executed by commissioners on both sides, and agreed to by Yucatan, was never ratified by Mexico; and in 1842 another army was sent into Yucatan: Merida was again invested, Campeachy was bombarded for several months; but, in the following year, the Mexican forces were defeated or withdrawn; and, at the close of 1843, she became again united to Mexico, with some reservations of sovereignty beyond those possessed by the other Mexican states. In consequence of the bad faith of the Mexican government, and the differences that were constantly springing up between them, she declared, on the first of January, 1846, the connection dissolved; and in March of that year, when war between the United States and Mexico was considered imminent, she refused to furnish men and money on the requisition of the Central government. In August, 1846, about two months after the commencement of the war, an extraordinary congress was convoked in Yucatan, chiefly through the influence of the friends of Santa Ana, who was then in Cuba, and by a majority of one vote he was declared to be the President of Mexico. This decree, however, was soon after annulled, and the declaration of the first of January, 1846, was revived and ratified with the popular sanction. From the commencement of the war, therefore, except for the very brief period I have mentioned, Yucatan has maintained an attitude of strict neutrality.

Notwithstanding these repeated changes, I doubt whether the severance of the political relation of Yucatan with Mexico can be considered complete. Her withdrawal from the Union has never been sanctioned by Mexico; nor is it quite apparent that her position, past or present, carries with it the attributes of an effective and unqualified independence. In a qualified sense, indeed, she may be said to have been independent; but we have constantly treated her as a part of the Mexican republic, though abstaining from acts of hostility against her on account of her refusal to take part in the war against us. She complains that, while not considering her as an enemy, we have, nevertheless, not treated her as a friend or a neutral. We have occupied the port of Laguna, in the Island of Carmen,—one of the islands which nearly shuts out Lake Terminos from the southern portion of the Gulf of Mexico. The ground of this occupation, on our part, was, that a trade in contraband was carried on between that port and Tabasco, which was hostile to us, and which borders on Lake Terminos.

Such, then, is the political condition of Yucatan, an integral portion of Mexico, having no active participation in the war against us, and maintaining, for the most part, a strict neutrality. The peculiar relation in which Yucatan stands to Mexico, and to us, undoubtedly complicates the question of our interference in her domestic affairs. We have entered into a treaty with Mexico; and although we are not permitted here to speak definitely with regard to its stipulations, enough has been made public in a legitimate way to show that we are precluded from undertaking any hostile enterprise against any portion of the Mexican territory or people. An armistice has been agreed on, and is now in force, preparatory to the evacuation of the country, in case the treaty is ratified. These facts have become matters of public notoriety, not through the action of this body, but through the acts of the two governments, legitimately performed in execution of the preliminary articles of agreement. Under these circumstances, it appears to me that the military occupation proposed by the bill, even though temporary, may be considered incompatible with a strict construction of the treaty. As I have already said, we have constantly treated

Yucatan as a part of Mexico. The President so considers her in his special message calling our attention to the subject. This being conceded, the stipulations of the treaty are as applicable to her as to any other department or state of the Mexican republic. We can only do in respect to her what we may do in respect to Jalisco, Tabasco, or any other of the Mexican states. Military occupation, in its commonly received sense, implies, if carried out, a displacement or subversion of the existing government. It would be no defence to say that Yucatan voluntarily submits to our power. Should we be authorized, this treaty being in force, to occupy, by military force, the state of Tabasco, for instance, if the local government were willing to submit to us? No, sir. I apprehend that the sanction of the Central government would be necessary to warrant it. In like manner, Yucatan being a part of Mexico, it appears to me that the military occupation of that state by us would require the sanction of the Central government. This rigid construction of the treaty may seem technical and over-scrupulous. Perhaps it is so. But in all matters involving the inviolability of international engagements, the strictest performance of stipulations is not only the part of prudence, but of imperative duty. We should afford no pretence for imputing to us an act of bad faith. Now, it is only to the form of the interposition — to military occupation and its incidents — that I object. And I trust my friend from Indiana, the chairman of the Committee on Foreign Relations,[1] will not adhere to the first section of the bill with tenacity, if he shall be satisfied that there is any other form of intervention which is unobjectionable, and which will, at the same time, accomplish the same end,— which will avoid all pretext for the imputation of violating the treaty, and yet enable us to effect every legitimate object of the interposition. And here I desire to say, that I approve of the second and third sections of the bill, providing arms, munitions of war, and troops, to

[1] Mr. Hannegan.

put an end to the war of devastation in Yucatan. I know nothing more revolting in the history of modern times than the exterminating warfare carried on by the aboriginal against the European races. Neither age nor sex, nor even the sanctity of religion, is respected. The infant is slaughtered at the mother's breast; the priest is immolated at the altar. It is not legitimate warfare; it is cold-blooded, atrocious murder.

So far as we are permitted, by international obligations and by constitutional forms of political organization at home, I am disposed to interfere for the purpose of putting an end to transactions so repugnant to every dictate of humanity, and every principle of civilization. I am willing to vote for the second and third sections of the bill. For the first section I have proposed a substitute, which I will now read: —

Strike out all the first section after the enacting clause, and insert the following: —

"That the President of the United States be authorized to employ the army and navy of the United States to aid in putting an end to the war of devastation in Yucatan, provided the aid hereby authorized be rendered in concurrence with the government of that state."

The difference between the original section and the substitute is this: the former authorizes the President to occupy or take military possession of Yucatan; the substitute authorizes him to employ the army and navy to assist the government of Yucatan in putting an end to the unnatural warfare carried on within that state. In the first case, the government would be virtually superseded; in the second, we should act in conjunction with it. And, sir, if we should decide to act, I should entertain a strong hope that our interposition might be speedily effectual. With the moral power of our victories in Mexico, a discreet officer going there, as much in the capacity of a pacificator as a combatant, might, aided by a small force, be able to restore harmony and peace between the contending parties.

But for the treaty with Mexico and the armistice entered

into with a view to its execution, I think the President would be fully authorized, in the conduct of the war, to do all that is proposed by the bill. It is the peculiar relation in which we stand to Mexico, of which Yucatan is a part, which presents, in my judgment, an impediment to military occupation. As it is, the treaty being in force, I think if we had troops to spare in Mexico, they might be sent into Yucatan by the President, to aid the government in bringing about a termination of hostilities. If the Indians should attack the Mexican settlements in Coahuila or Durango, or any other portion of the republic, does any one doubt that we might detach a portion of our troops in Mexico to aid those settlements in defending themselves, without violating the armistice or the treaty? It would be an act of friendship and of mercy, not an act of hostility; and it is only against offensive operations that the treaty and the armistice are intended to guard. The honorable Senator from Mississippi[1] suggests that the terms of the armistice require that we should interpose, whenever a necessity arises, to protect any part of the Mexican republic from the incursions or attacks of the Indians; that we have so interposed; and he considers it to be applicable to this case. Under this view of the subject, the interposition of Congress is required, rather with a view to provide the President with the means than to confer upon him the authority to act. But in placing the army and navy at his disposal, for a special purpose by law, it seems proper to define the conditions under which they shall be employed. This is done by the substitute, which declares that he shall act with the concurrence of the government of Yucatan. Thus all pretence of violating the treaty or the armistice will be obviated.

Is there any violation of international obligations, so far as they depend on principles of public law, in extending to Yucatan the required assistance? I think not. We are already in the occupation of a portion of Yucatan. Our

[1] Mr. Davis.

fleet has for a long time been in possession of Laguna, and thus commanded a large portion of the coast. We have exercised not only military but political authority there, holding stations, imposing duties, and collecting revenue. Indeed, Yucatan complains that by this very assumption or exercise of authority we have deprived her of her revenues, and diminished her ability to provide against the exigencies in which she is placed. This is one of the grounds on which she appeals to us for succor. She asks us to give back to her in one way the means we have taken from her in another. In this view of the subject, it is as much redress as aid which she seeks.

Sir, I think there is some truth in what she says. But whether that be so or not, the very fact that we are in the occupation of a portion of Yucatan takes the whole case out of the ordinary rule of non-intervention. We occupy one of her seaports under the laws of war. To aid the existing government under such circumstances, in subordination to its own wishes, in restoring tranquillity and putting an end to domestic dissensions, cannot be deemed a violation of the rule that one nation shall not interfere in the domestic concerns of another. Indeed, but for the treaty we might interfere without the consent of the government, having already partial occupation. It is only the obligations arising under it that make such consent necessary at all.

If we were at peace with Mexico and Yucatan, I confess I should very much doubt whether we could, on any consideration of humanity, interpose between parties engaged in intestine conflict with each other, however strong our inclination might be. I will not say that there are not obligations of duty to our fellow-men, which rise above all the restraints of political organization and government. But it must be a very extreme case, which can authorize us, even from motives of humanity, to exercise powers not expressly conferred by the Constitution and laws by which we are governed. Nothing, perhaps, short of an exigency threatening to uproot the very foundations of civilized society, or concerning our own self-preservation, would warrant any other than a strictly constitutional exercise of power. But I see no such embarrassment in this case. Under the laws of war — by virtue of the occupation of one portion of Yucatan — it appears to me that we may perform, in respect to any other portion, every obligation which humanity dictates and enjoins. I have no hesitation, therefore, so far as the right of interposition is concerned, to vote for the second and third sections of the bill, and I am willing to vote for the first section so amended as to make our interposition subordinate to the government of Yucatan, to make it an act of friendship to her, without being an act of hostility to Mexico.

Mr. President, in discussing the bill providing for the satisfaction of certain claims in California, I stated that the Indians in Yucatan were abundantly supplied with arms, and that some of these arms were of British manufacture. I did not intend to intimate that they were furnished by the government of Great Britain, or by agents acting under her direction or authority. I supposed then, as I suppose now, that they were, for the most part, procured from British traders at Balize, in the way of exchange; and I have been confirmed in that belief by an article in a British newspaper published at Kingston, Jamaica, stating that an exterminating war was carried on by the Indians in Yucatan, by means of arms procured from British traders, and condemning the latter for engaging in a traffic which was the source of so much wanton violence and inhumanity.

By another article, taken from the same paper, it appears that a commissioner has been sent from Yucatan to Balize to invoke the observance of treaty-stipulations by Great Britain in respect to the sale of arms and ammunition to the Indians. I will read it to the Senate: —

"The Indians had been waging a destructive war with the white inhabitants of the State of Yucatan, and had destroyed the large villages of Ajomeo and Ychmul, and possessed themselves of almost all the towns to the eastward of Peto and Valladolid. A commissioner has arrived at Balize, Honduras, from Yucatan, to prevent, if possible, the sale of arms or warlike stores to the Indians."

This traffic has been carried on in violation of an ancient treaty with Spain ; and not very ancient either. By the treaty of London, 1786, it was expressly stipulated by Great Britain that she would strictly prohibit all her

"Subjects from furnishing arms or warlike stores to the Indians in general situated upon the frontiers of the Spanish possessions."

Mr. Sierra, in one of his notes to Mr. Buchanan, states that the British authorities at Balize have consented to prohibit the sale of arms and ammunition to the Indians, though he expresses a doubt whether the assurance will be observed in good faith. I should have inferred, from the assurance thus given, that the obligations of the treaty referred to were recognized as of binding force, though the pledge might have been given from motives of humanity. But I find, by an article in the "Times," a newspaper published at Balize, that the British authorities have refused to recognize the obligation of the treaty of 1786. I will read an extract from it, that what I say may not be misunderstood:

"We understand that Mr. Peon has been appointed by the government of Yucatan, on special mission to her Majesty's superintendent, to claim for his government the benefit of the treaty of 1786, entered into between their Majesties, the kings of Great Britain and Spain. In that treaty there is a clause which would appear to bear directly on the existing state of affairs in Yucatan. It is to the following effect."

Here follows the stipulation which I have quoted. The "Times" then continues: —

"We are unable to communicate the grounds on which we learn that her Majesty's superintendent has declined to admit the present applicability of the treaty. It must be, however, known to all, that none of the neighbouring Spanish republics can be properly said to have inherited the rights which the Spanish Crown possessed in this part of the world. As a question of humanity, however, it is much to be desired that all the caution which can be exercised by our merchants should be exercised to prevent powder or arms being sold to the Indians; and, even as a matter of mercantile speculation, we think that it will usually be of more importance to our trade with Yucatan, to aid in reëstablishing order in that province, by refusing to supply the Indians. We subjoin some further remarks, which we have received on this subject."

These remarks are in the nature of a strong appeal to the humanity of the merchants. It does not appear by this article what effort the British authorities at Balize have made, if any, to prevent the sale of arms and ammunition to the Indians. But it does appear, that they deny the obligation of the treaty of 1786. And, certainly, the inference is, that they have not interposed from motives of humanity, and prohibited the traffic; for, if they had, this appeal by a newspaper to the humanity of the merchants would have been superfluous.

Mr. President, it would be a very harsh judgment to suppose that the British authorities at Balize had encouraged this traffic for the purpose of expelling the Spanish race, and thus facilitating the extension of the dominion of their own sovereign. Even if it were for the interest of Great Britain to do so, such a supposition should not be made without the strongest evidence. But, sir, I do not think it unreasonable or harsh to suppose this contest is encouraged by British traders, who have pecuniary interests there, and whose gains might be increased by the expulsion of the Spanish race; for, in that event, the whole peninsula would fall under the dominion of the Indians. British subjects would more readily gain a foothold there: having once gained it, they would be protected by their government; and it would not be surprising to see the protection of Great Britain extended over the Indian population. It appears to me that we cannot doubt such a probability without wilfully closing our eyes against light. This process of extension is in progress at the very moment when we are discussing and doubting it. Let me state a few facts in reference to the settlement at Balize, to which I have already referred. It was first recognized specifically as a British settlement by the treaty of Versailles in 1783, though there is a provision in the tripartite treaty of 1763, (that which terminated the old French war here,) recognizing the right of Great Britain to occupation in that quarter generally. But the treaty of 1783 is the first in which the settlement is distinctly recognized. The right of occupation was given for a specific purpose. It gave only the right to cut logwood, build houses and magazines for the convenience of the workmen and their families, and to enjoy a free fishery for their subsistence on the coast. Great Britain expressly stipulated to demolish all fortifications, if there were any, and to erect no more. The sovereignty of Spain was distinctly reserved. The limits of the territory, in which these advantages were to be enjoyed, were carefully defined. I have traced them on the map, and I find they did not exceed an area of two thousand square miles, if the rivers Hondo and Balize, the northern and southern boundaries, are accurately laid down. By the treaty of 1786 they were extended south to the river Sibun, making, at the utmost, an area of four or five thousand square miles. According to Arrowsmith's "London Atlas," published in 1840, that settlement has an area of fourteen thousand square miles, — three times its original extent. Nor is this all. By the "Encyclopædia Britannica," and Martin's "British Colonies," it is claimed to have an area of more than 62,000 square miles, — a surface exceeding that of the entire peninsula of Yucatan. In what direction it is proposed to extend the settlement, in order to comprehend these sixty or seventy thousand square miles of surface, does not appear. It is left in doubt by the respectable authorities I have named, under the most ungeographical declaration that "the inland boundaries are ill defined," though they were most critically defined by the treaties of 1783 and 1786. With this shadowy boundary, which leaves everything undetermined, excepting on the side of the Bay of Honduras, the sea, where nature has drawn a line, which man cannot make uncertain, it may be defined hereafter according to circumstances. They may be extended north into Yucatan, southwest into Guatemala, or southeast into Honduras, and in the latter case form a junction with the territories of the Mosquito king.

And, by the way, the name of this newly created sovereign reminds me that there are some indications of extension further south, which are not very easily discredited. By the treaty of Versailles, Great Britain stipulated that her subjects should abandon all other portions of the Spanish continent, and retire within the limits of the settlement at Balize. By the treaty of London, she stipulated to evacuate the country of the Mosquitoes *eo nomine* as well as the continent in general, and the islands adjacent, without exception. I believe she did evacuate them, and I am not aware that she has occupied the country of the Mosquitoes again in her own name. But she has done what is equivalent to occupation: she has taken the king of the Mosquitoes under her protection; she has assumed to define the limits of his dominions; she has given notice to the Central and South American governments, that they are not to interfere with those limits; she has sent ships to the coast, and troops into the interior, maintaining the former there under the name of the Mosquito navy. She is encroaching on the Central American states, attacking forts, appropriating territory, and making war on the people. It is only about a month ago, that we learned she had attacked and taken possession of the town of Nicaragua, and killed some seventy or eighty of the Central Americans. She has recently sent black troops there, not only from Jamaica, but from New Providence, on the confines of Florida, to maintain the authority of the Mosquito king, — the chief of a band of naked Indians, himself scarcely more elevated in the social scale than his followers. His throne a sand-hill, his sceptre a reed, his robe a blanket, he puts armies and fleets in motion, speaks to the nations through the mouths of British diplomatists, and invades the territories of neighboring states by sea and land, with

. . . . "royal banner, and all quality,
Pride, pomp, and circumstance of glorious war."

I do not hesitate to say, that so broad a farce as this has never been enacted with so much gravity by a respectable state. It would be a farce under all its aspects, were it not for the encroachments upon the Central American states, of which it is the source. To them it is a matter of the most serious import, and it has met their solemn and repeated protests.

About three months ago I stated, in some remarks on a military bill before the Senate, that Great Britain has recently set up a claim to San Juan de Nicaragua, and I prophesied at that time, from the indications I saw, that she would, at no distant period, take forcible possession of that place. She has done so already. The prophecy has become history, written, like many other transactions of the same nature, in letters of blood. I also stated, that one of the great objects of this extension was, to command a route for a ship-canal across the continent, narrowed there to an isthmus. This route has been critically surveyed and examined from the Caribbean Sea, up the river San Juan, to Lake Nicaragua, from Lake Nicaragua to Lake Leon, and from Lake Leon to Realejo on the Pacific. Surveys, drawings, maps, plans, diagrams, estimates — everything that pertains to and precedes the construction of public works — have been carefully prepared. I believe these evidences and achievements of a high intellectual and social civilization are not pretended to be the work of the Mosquito king; but it would not be surprising if her claim to execute this great enterprise of uniting the two oceans should be asserted in his name, — certainly not more surprising than some other things which have been recently done under the same auspices.

The river San Juan de Nicaragua is one degree south of

the southern limit of the Mosquito territory. According to British maps, that territory extends only to the 12th degree of north latitude. The river empties into the Caribbean Sea at the 11th parallel. But it has recently been claimed that it extends to the 11th, with an intimation, as I understand, that it may possibly extend to the 10th, or even the 9th, which would include a part of Panama.

Before I quit this part of the subject, I will read to the Senate an extract from the "Despatch," another British newspaper, published at Kingston, Jamaica, reciting the grounds on which this claim rests: —

"The differences between the government of Central America and the king of Mosquito are now of some years' standing. The former republic has never acknowledged the sovereignty claimed by King George over any portion of the territory called Mosquito; and on numerous occasions the mahogany cutters engaged with the Mosquito government, for which they paid a toll up the river Roman, have been disturbed, and driven off by the Central Americans. These aggressions led to communications between the council of Mosquito and Downing Street, and resulted, if we were rightly informed, in directions from the Foreign Office, that the boundaries of the Mosquito territory should be traced according to the best existing authorities, documentary or otherwise, and, these being defined, England bound herself to support the integrity of the king's dominions. The result of this survey was to attach the whole of the river San Juan to the dominions of Mosquito, and the flag of King George was consequently, shortly afterwards, formally hoisted at the fort of San Juan."

Such, according to this authority, is the claim of Great Britain to the Mosquito territory, which she expressly stipulated by treaty to evacuate, — a claim resting upon an arrangement with the Mosquito government which has never been recognized by the Central Americans as an independent state, — a government, in fact, alleged to have been established, or rather got up in its present form, by Great Britain herself; and it would seem from this statement, which is sustained by other evidence corroborating it, that she examines documents *ex parte*, traces boundaries, settles them without consultation with those whom they vitally concern, binds herself to support them, and acts accordingly. A more summary execution of the law of force cannot readily be found.[1]

Since the meeting of the Senate this morning, I have received a copy of a notice from the British consul-general in Central America, addressed to the Principal Secretary of the Supreme Government of Nicaragua, in September last. It is translated from the English into Spanish.

[1] It is due to fairness, inasmuch as some of the arguments contained in the text are drawn from constructions put upon treaties and other public records by the Central and South American states, to exhibit the grounds on which Great Britain rests her claim to the authority she is exercising in the country of the Mosquitoes. They are as follows:

1st. "Some time after the conquest of Jamaica by the expedition sent forth by Oliver Cromwell, in 1656, the Mosquito king, with the concurrence of his chiefs and people, placed themselves under the protection of Charles the Second; and the governor of Jamaica, in the name of his sovereign, accepted this union, and promised them the royal protection."

2d. In 1749, a fort was erected by a British force from Jamaica, and the royal flag was hoisted, "thus making a formal publication to all the world, and to the Crown of Spain, that the independent country of the coast was under the direct sovereignty and protection of Great Britain."

3d. "From this time until the conclusion of the war of 1756, the Mosquito shore continued to be a military, federal, protected province of Great Britain."

4th. In 1765, a council of government was appointed, a court of common pleas, &c.

5th. The Mosquito nation was never subjugated by Spain, but always retained its independent character; and "the Mosquito territory is still an independent country, and one over which Spain never had the least control or occupation."

6th. "None of the anarchical states of Central America have any right by occupation, or by recogni ion, to the Mosquito country."

7th. "It is clearly shown in the works of writers well acquainted with the Mosquito shore, such as Dampier, Falconer, Trobisher, Bryan Edwards, Hodgson, and others, that the tribes under the Mosquito kings have been independent ever since the downfall of Montezuma, and have had a recognized territory appertaining to themselves, and governed by laws administered by their own hereditary kings."

These are, in brief, the grounds of the British claim to the protection she is exercising over the Mosquito territory, and more especially "of the proceedings of the British naval forces at St. John's on the Mosquito coast," and they are stated in her own language. The quotations above made are chiefly from Macgregor's "Progress of America," 739 *et seq.*

It is unnecessary to add that some of the material facts are contradicted by the states of Central America.

In respect to the town and river of San Juan de Nicaragua, Great Britain contends that the government of Central America first sent a force down to San Juan, and established a custom-house on the north side of the river, which the Spaniards had never before occupied, in 1836; that it was done without the consent of the king of the Mosquito coast, who had previously granted the territory, where it was established, to a British subject; that the Central American flag did not appear there till 1843; and that the "administrator," or collector of customs, on the application of a British officer, gave a written acknowledgment that he had hoisted the flag by courtesy, and not as of right, and that the port was claimed by the king of Mosquito.

She also states, that the Mosquito authorities have remonstrated against the occupation, and that, these remonstrances having failed, her naval forces have been sent to aid them in taking possession of the place.

I have only had time to look at it so as to see its purport; but I will read it now to the Senate, translating it back into English.

"BRITISH CONSULATE GENERAL,
"*Guatemala*, 10*th September*, 1847.

"*To the Principal Secretary of the Supreme Government of the State of Nicaragua.*

"Sir: Questions having arisen at various periods, with the states of Honduras and Nicaragua, concerning the extension of the maritime frontier of the kingdom of Mosquito, her Britannic Majesty's government, after carefully examining the various documents and historical registers which exist relative to the subject, is of the opinion that the territorial right of the king of the Mosquitoes should be maintained as extending from Cape Honduras to the mouth of the river San Juan; and I am charged to notify the supreme governments of the states of Honduras and Nicaragua, as I have now the honor of doing, that the government of her Britannic Majesty considers that the king of Mosquito has a right to this extent of coast, *without prejudice to the right which the said king may have to any territory south of the river San Juan;* and that her Britannic Majesty's government cannot see with indifference any attempt to usurp the territorial rights of the king of Mosquito, who is under the protection of the British crown.

"I have the honor to be, sir, your obedient servant,
"FREDERICK CHATFIELD.

"Copy: Department of Foreign Relations of the Superior Government of the State of Nicaragua. Mangua, October 14, 1847.
"SALINAS."

It will be seen by this notice, that Great Britain lays the foundation for a claim, in behalf of the Mosquito king, to territory south of the river San Juan, leaving the boundary undefined. This note bears date the 10th of September last. And it is a curious fact, that in an official note, bearing date the 24th of the same month, addressed to the government of New Grenada, no intimation is given of such a claim south of the river San Juan. I read the last-mentioned note while addressing the Senate on the California claims; and the omission is the more extraordinary, as the British government can hardly be unadvised that New Grenada claims, jointly with the Central American states, the coast of the Caribbean Sea, not only to the river San Juan, but as far north as Cape Gracias a Dios. The object of the omission, if it had an object, must be left to conjecture. It may have been accidental, or it may be that Great Britain did not think it advisable to alarm, at that juncture, the most stable of the governments having an interest in the question, by putting forth a claim so well calculated to excite uneasiness.

With these evidences of a fixed purpose of extension and aggrandizement of Great Britain in this hemisphere; with our vivid recollection of the tenacity with which she asserted her claim to territory on our northeastern boundary and in Oregon, — territory remote from her, chiefly valuable because it encroached on us, and curtailed the limits for our expansion; with the still more fresh and vivid recollection of the transactions in California, with a view to obtain a large and valuable portion of that territory for British subjects;[1] with these evidences of a purpose, open and palpable, to extend her own dominion upon this continent, if not to prevent the extension of ours; I am really surprised that any one can doubt she would avail herself of the first opportunity of gaining an ascendency in Yucatan. It borders upon her own settlement at Balize, and is separated from it, according to her own representation, by a boundary "ill defined." Sir, I must say that I know no parallel to this incredulity, excepting in the state of things in Athens, which produced the third philippic of Demosthenes, — in the blindness which would not see an enemy in Philip, when Phocis, and Pheræ, and Elis, and Olynthus, and the two-and-thirty cities of Thrace had fallen into his hands. I do not make the comparison because I fancy any other resemblance between the historical features of that epoch and this. In other respects, the parallel fails. I do

[1] In connection with this subject, I deem it due to fairness to state, that Lord Palmerston has instructed her Britannic Majesty's representative at Washington "to contradict, on all occasions, the unfounded assertion that her Majesty's government has been taking any steps whatever to acquire any footing in California"; and that this instruction came to my knowledge after this speech was delivered.

not wish any member of this honorable body to see an enemy in Great Britain. I do not so consider her myself. I consider her as a friend; I desire that she may continue so, at most a rival in commerce, in the generous competition of industry, and in the extension of civilization and freedom. I do not envy her, or its legitimate possessors, the dominion over the torrid plains of Central America, — that crust of earth parched by a raging sun above, and heated by volcanic fires beneath. Much less do I regard her extension in our neighborhood with apprehensions for our safety. We have long since grown beyond the dimensions in which there was any danger to be apprehended from the extension of other nations upon this continent, no matter how closely they may be brought into contact with us. But I make these statements in order that we may see what is actually in progress, — not because it brings with it any serious cause of apprehension on our own account, but that we may not coldly turn away our faces when weak and defenceless neighbors are invaded and despoiled. For myself, sir, I cannot help seeing in Great Britain a spirit of aggrandizement which is perpetual in its progress, not on this continent alone, but in every other portion of the globe where there is territory unoccupied, and too often where there is territory occupied by those who are too weak to defend it. I believe, also, whether this conflict in Yucatan shall terminate in the expulsion of the Spanish race, or the discomfiture of the aboriginal, that her boundary will be likely to be extended further into the interior. That "ill-defined" boundary may become defined, and with greatly enlarged dimensions.

Mr. President, I have nothing more to say upon this point, excepting that I do not support the bill, because I think the occupation of Yucatan by us is necessary to keep it out of the hands of European powers. I am not sure that I could, except under very extraordinary circumstances, be induced to advocate the military occupation of a country for such a purpose. But if we see movements of foreign powers on this continent, and especially in our near neighborhood, which are suspicious, we have a right to call on them, through the ordinary channels of diplomatic intercourse, to know what are their objects; and if we do not receive frank and satisfactory answers, if we have reason to believe that those objects are in violation of the great principles of international right, or dangerous to our tranquillity, or even our interests, we may properly take such measures of precaution or prevention as the exigency of the case shall require. I do not undertake — indeed it might not be very easy — to assign the precise measure of provocation which would justify resistance on our part, or the extent to which resistance might be rightfully carried. Every emergency must be left to be determined by a wise and considerate regard to its attending circumstances. But of the existence of such a right of resistance on grounds of international law, I do not entertain the slightest doubt.

And here, Mr. President, I must ask the indulgence of the Senate, while I look hastily into the nature and origin of the right. Every sovereign state is to be considered under two aspects: the first concerns its interior relations, the relations which exist between the governing and the governed, or, in other words, between the government and the people; the second concerns its exterior relations, or its relations with foreign states.

The first class only is ordinarily the subject of internal or municipal regulation. The Constitution of the United States, for instance, regulates the relations of the federal government to the states and to the people. It scarcely touches the exterior relations of the country, excepting so far as it declares in what departments the powers of making war, peace, and treaties, and appointing ambassadors, shall vest. Now, it is quite apparent that there is a numerous class of exterior relations wholly untouched by the Constitution, not always regulated by treaty-stipulations. They arise out of the natural rights and obligations of sovereign states, and are regulated by usage, by the general international law which has grown up and become sanctioned by the acquiescence of all civilized communities. One of our vessels, public or private, cannot go ten miles from the land without becoming subject to an international code, not founded upon the internal laws of states, whether organic or administrative, not regulated ordinarily by treaty-stipulations between them, but as old, nevertheless, as the *Consolato del Mare*, and deriving its force from public consent.

These rights and duties are correlative. What one nation is bound to do, any other may call on it to perform. We cannot live in the general society of nations without observing these rules ourselves; nor can we consent that they shall be violated by others, where our safety or interest is concerned. There are obligations of this sort applicable to the land as well as the sea. One of these is, that no nation shall interfere with the internal concerns of another. As a member of the great family of nations, we have a right to insist that this rule shall be observed. In all cases, where the rule or the principle is settled beyond dispute, any member of the general society of nations is as fully warranted in calling upon any other member to respect it as any member of this confederacy is authorized to call upon another to observe the obligations of the fundamental compact. The only question that can arise is one of practical prudence: how far we shall deem it expedient to interpose to prevent a breach of international obligations. I have always contended that, even for this purpose, we ought not to interfere with the movements of European powers, when those movements relate to questions strictly European. And I have insisted, with the same earnestness, that there should be no interference on their part with the internal concerns of the independent states in this hemisphere, and especially in our neighborhood, involved as our interests, political and commercial, are in their tranquillity and exemption from domestic agitations.

If I am asked for the origin of the right on our part to interpose for the purpose of preventing a breach of international obligations, I refer again to the general code by which all civilized states are governed. As to the mode, I have nothing to say. I repeat, every emergency must be determined by the surrounding circumstances in which it is presented. Whether we shall interpose at all, is a question of prudence, a question undoubtedly to be disposed of with the greatest deliberation, when it is proposed to make it the basis of practical conduct.

But I do not put our intervention in this case upon the ground either of resisting unauthorized interference on the part of other nations, or of anticipating and preventing it. I place it upon the peculiar circumstances in which we stand in relation to Yucatan, circumstances which seem to me to impose on us an obligation independently of all considerations even of humanity. We have taken possession of the principal outlet of trade in her chief staple productions, and the principal inlet for the foreign commodities which she received in exchange. We have appropriated her revenue to ourselves. We even went so far as to impose duties on her own products, carried from one of her ports to another, though, as soon as this was ascertained to be the case, directions were very properly given by the President that they should be discontinued. We have thus not only taken her own revenues, but we have imposed on her people new burdens by taxing the transit of articles which were previously exempt from duty. I do not intend to intimate that we have done anything not deemed essential to the successful conduct of the war. In regard to the revenue which we have collected at Laguna, I have endeavored to learn the amount; but I am told that the accounts are kept in connection with other receipts and disbursements, so that time is required to separate them. The Navy Department, however, has been able to ascertain that the amount collected has been between fifty and sixty thousand dollars for a portion of the last year, — the returns for the year not being complete. But this does not show the amount that we have diverted from the treasury of Yucatan. We all know that war is the great enemy of commerce; and it must readily be seen that the effect of our hostile operations in Mexico has been to diminish the ability of Yucatan to meet the exigency in which she is placed. It seems to me, that, if she had no other claim than this, in addition to the consideration that she has been neutral throughout the contest, she might very properly call upon us for aid. If we cannot act from motives of humanity, if we feel constrained to regard this question as one to be determined according to the coldest and most rigid maxims of political prudence, may we not find, nevertheless, in the circumstances I have stated, an appeal to our justice which we cannot readily set aside? I think so; and it is upon this ground chiefly that I place my support of this bill.

In performing this act of justice, it is a grateful reflection that we may also perform an act of humanity; that we are enabled to turn, for the moment, from the painful duty of assaulting towns and overrunning provinces — a duty imposed on us by the prosecution of hostilities with Mexico — to the more congenial office of extinguishing the flames of internal discord, and of reconciling classes which are waging against each other an exterminating war. Sir, I cannot fancy a more striking contrast in the social and political condition of two nations than that which exists between the United States and Yucatan, — in the prosperity and tranquillity of the one, and in the disorder and desolation of the other. The law presides here in her majesty, spreading her broad shield over all. Industry and the arts, helpless infancy, decrepit age, life, liberty, property, all that men possess, and cherish, and hold dear, are protected by the power of a moral opinion, which lies at the foundation of the established order of government and society, and upholds both. If we turn to our Central American neighbor, the whole picture is reversed: law, order, tranquillity, the friendly association of classes and castes, all have perished; the moral and physical ties which render life desirable and human possessions secure have been forcibly rent asunder; towns and villages have been given to the flames, and their wretched inhabitants to the sword; plantations have been ravaged; farm-houses sacked, demolished, burnt; property plundered where it could be carried away, and destroyed where it could not; men, women, and children, driven from their homes, (if, indeed, they are so fortunate as to escape the fury of their remorseless pursuers,) rush to the sea, in the hope of finding some passing vessel which may take them from the blackened and desolated land.

> . . . . " Incendia fumant.
> Muris nulla fides. Squalent populatibus agri,
> Et medio spes sola mari." . . . .

Sir, this is a mere outline of the picture of devastation which Yucatan presents. I would not, if I could, undertake to fill it up with its loathsome and revolting details. I do not draw this sketch, imperfect as it is, for the purpose of making an appeal to the sympathy of the Senate. I only present it for the purpose of adding a final remark.

If honorable Senators shall think with me that it is our right and our duty to interpose; if they shall consent to act in the mode proposed by the bill, or in some other mode, which may seem to them more free from objection; if the effect of our interposition shall be to put an end to this unnatural warfare, to restore peace to Yucatan, to give back her desolated fields and plains to industry and order, and the dominion of law; it will constitute, in the sight of civilization and humanity, a far more ennobling triumph than a dozen victories won for the extension of empire at the point of the bayonet and the cannon's mouth.

A TERRITORIAL GOVERNMENT IN OREGON.

The bill establishing a territorial government in Oregon excluded slavery, by declaring to be valid and operative all laws then existing in the territory. One of these laws expressly prohibited slavery and involuntary servitude, otherwise than for the punishment of crimes whereof the party should be duly convicted. Mr. Davis of Mississippi had, before Mr. Dix's speech was delivered, offered an amendment providing that there should be no prohibition of domestic slavery while the territory remained "in the condition of a territory of the United States." Mr. Dix's speech was delivered on the 26th June, 1848, and the bill was passed on the 12th of August ensuing, with the restrictions and prohibitions of the ordinance of 1787, one of which was an express exclusion of slavery.

Mr. President: During the present session of Congress, propositions have been repeatedly introduced into the Senate involving the question of slavery. I have abstained from all participation in the discussions to which they have given rise, because I considered them as abstract propositions having no direct practical bearing or effect. The measure before us is of a different character. It contemplates an act of legislation; it proposes a law containing provisions to be enforced and to control the inhabitants of a district of country more than two hundred thousand square miles in extent. By this act we are literally laying the foundations of a future empire. It is a subject eminently practical; and therefore I speak.

The questions, to which the discussion of the bill has given rise, are of the highest moment. They concern the power of Congress over the territory belonging to the United States, and especially in respect to slavery in such territory. Nor is this all. They involve not only the authority of Congress, under the Constitution, to regulate the domestic concerns of the persons inhabiting or occupying the public domain beyond the limits of the States, but they may affect for an indefinite period the social and political condition of entire communities. They may vitally concern the prosperity of the future millions who are to fill the valleys and cover the hills of Oregon; and it is due to the magnitude of the subject that it should be discussed with calmness and without asperity either of feeling or of language. Conducted in such a spirit, discussion, even if it were unnecessary, could not do harm, however widely we may differ, or however delicate the questions with which it has to deal. Indeed, it is always possible the very conflict of opinion may strike out light and truth, and furnish a basis for an amicable adjustment of differences, which would otherwise have been irreconcilable. It may be a vain hope to expect to harmonize those who are now so wide apart; but if it prove a delusion, it may nevertheless be profitable to indulge it. It may, at least, serve to moderate the tone of discussion.

In the course of the debate on this and other kindred topics, various propositions have been advanced; and they have been sustained with distinguished ability. Some of these propositions are repetitions of the same general assumption under different phases. For instance, it has been assumed that the citizens of any State in the Union have a right to go into any territory belonging to the United States, and take with them whatever is recognized as property by the local law of the State from which they migrate. It is also assumed that the inhabitants of a territory cannot, by any legislative enactment, prevent the citizens of any State in the Union from coming into the territory with whatever the local law of such State recognizes as property. These are little else than verbal modifications of the same proposition; or, at least, the one is a necessary consequence of the other. On the other hand, it is contended that the inhabitants of a territory belonging to the United States have an inherent right to regulate their own domestic concerns for themselves, wherever the jurisdiction of the soil they inhabit may reside, and without being overruled by the sovereign political power to which they are subordinate.

There is a question which lies beyond all these propositions, and which, if it can be satisfactorily answered, must be decisive of them all, because it includes them all. Has Congress the right, under the Constitution, to legislate for the territory of the United States, organize governments for the inhabitants residing in such territory, and regulate within it all matters of local and domestic concern? I believe this question can be satisfactorily answered in the affirmative; that the power, to this unlimited extent, can be sustained: 1st, by contemporaneous exposition of the meaning of the Constitution and the intention of its framers; 2d, by judicial interpretation; and 3d, by the whole practice of the government, from its foundation to the present day.

This is the fundamental question I propose first to discuss. I shall lay aside all consideration of subordinate propositions. These necessarily fall, if the other can be established. My purpose is, to attempt to establish it; and in all I have to say I shall endeavor to be strictly argumentative.

The power of regulating all matters concerning the public domain I think may fairly be considered a necessary incident to the power of acquiring territory; and this not only in respect to the disposition which may be made of the naked soil, as it has been denominated, but in respect to the classes of persons who are permitted to occupy it, and the conditions of the occupation. I consider this unrestricted power as an inseparable incident of sovereignty, to be exercised by the supreme authority of the organized community or state in which it resides. The power of acquisition is itself unrestricted by the terms of our social compact, so far as the objects of acquisition are concerned. It is incidental also. It is derived from the power of making war and treaties; and the limits to the exercise of these powers are to be found in fundamental rules and principles applicable to all organized societies.

But I do not, for the purposes of my argument, place the power on this ground. I assign to it an origin less likely, I think, to be questioned. I place it on that provision of the Constitution which gives Congress "power to dispose of and make all needful rules and regulations respecting the territory or other property belonging to the United States."

I am aware that this clause of the Constitution has recently received a construction which confines the action of the government in respect to the public domain to the narrowest possible limits,—a construction which leaves to Congress the mere right to regulate the mode in which the public land shall be surveyed, brought into market, and sold, without any power to regulate the political or municipal affairs of those who settle upon it, while they are acquiring the requisites usually exacted as conditions of their admission into the Union. This construction is subversive of every idea of sovereignty in the state (I use the word in its largest sense) as the owner of the soil. It reduces the government of the United States to the condition of a mere individual proprietor of land, without a single attribute of political power. Such a consequence could never have been contemplated by the framers of the Constitution as likely to be drawn from the clause in question. On the contrary, I am satisfied they regarded it as conferring a power of the most plenary nature. I shall endeavor to make this apparent to the Senate; and in doing so it will be necessary to look at the history of the clause of the Constitution referred to.

On the 18th of August, 1787, Mr. Madison introduced into the Federal convention, then engaged in framing the Constitution, a series of propositions, in order to be referred to the Committee of Detail. Among them were these: To authorize Congress

"To dispose of the unappropriated lands of the United States.

"To institute temporary governments for new states arising therein."

On the 22d of August, Mr. Rutledge, from the Committee of Detail, made a partial report on Mr. Madison's propositions, and on others submitted by Mr. Pinckney on the 20th. Mr. Madison's propositions, above quoted, providing for the disposal of the unappropriated lands and the institution of temporary governments for new states arising therein, were not reported by the committee. But, on the 30th of August, Mr. Gouverneur Morris introduced the clause respecting the territory belonging to the United States, which, with a few immaterial verbal alterations, is now a part of the Constitution. After Mr. Luther Martin had offered an amendment, which was rejected, the clause was adopted, Maryland alone dissenting.

It may not distinctly appear at first glance what Mr. Madison designed by the institution of temporary governments for "new states arising within" the unappropriated lands. It might be supposed that he intended to provide for their temporary government as states after their erection or formation. But those who are familiar with the parliamentary phraseology of that day, will have no doubt that the term states was used as we now employ the term territories.

But be this so or not, it is certainly not fair to say, as has been said, that it shared the fate of the proposition to confer upon Congress the power to grant charters of incorporation, to establish a university, and to construct canals, &c. These propositions were distinctly presented to Congress, and formally and decisively negatived by a direct recorded vote, as may be seen by referring to the proceedings of the convention on the 14th of September.

It was not so with Mr. Madison's proposition in respect to the unappropriated lands of the United States. The most that can be said is, that the committee were not in favor of it in its original form. There was no vote on it in that form in convention — no rejection. The proposition of Mr. Morris, which is now a part of the Constitution, was manifestly, from its terms as well as the circumstances and the subject-matter, intended as a substitute for it. It was adopted almost without opposition. The power it is construed to confer has been exercised from the earliest period in our history. The attention of the convention was distinctly drawn to the subject by Mr. Madison; and it is difficult to believe that an authority so general as that of making "all needful rules and regulations" respecting the territory belonging to the United States (the term regulations being used at that time much as we now use the term laws) could have been conferred, without question, if it had been intended to withhold the power of providing for the government of the individuals inhabiting it until they were admitted into the Union.

On the 13th of July preceding, the Congress of the Confederation had passed the celebrated ordinance of 1787, in relation to the territory northwest of the Ohio river. This fact could hardly have been unknown to the members of the convention. Congress, it is true, was sitting in New York, while the convention sat in Philadelphia. I believe the proceedings of both were with closed doors; but the members of the latter were doubtless made acquainted with the proceedings of the other. This fact — the coincidence in point of time — may have some slight bearing upon the intention of the clause giving Congress power to dispose of and make needful rules and regulations respecting the territory belonging to the United States.

The opinion of Mr. Madison has been quoted to prove the illegality of the ordinance of 1787. This being conceded, it cannot by any supposed consequence or analogy have any bearing on the power of legislation by Congress, under the Constitution, in respect to the prohibition of slavery in the territories of the United States. The ordinance, as we know, was passed by Congress under the articles of confederation, though it was ratified by the first Congress which assembled under the Constitution. Any inference from the proceedings of the one, so far as the question of power is concerned, would be wholly inapplicable to the other. But I hold, and shall endeavor to show, that the very argument in which Mr. Madison denied the authority of Congress, under the articles of confederation, to pass the ordinance of 1787, had for its object to prove the necessity of such a power in Congress under the Constitution, and that it proceeded upon the supposed existence of the power.

The usual reference to prove the illegality of the ordinance is to the opinion of Mr. Madison, in the 38th number of the "Federalist," which was written by him. I will read an extract from it referring to the Western territory.

> "We may calculate, therefore, that a rich and fertile country, of an area equal to the inhabited extent of the United States, will soon become a national stock. They have begun to render it productive. Congress have undertaken to do more: they have proceeded to form new States; to erect temporary governments; to appoint officers for them; and to prescribe the conditions on which such States shall be admitted into the Confederacy. All this has been done, and done without the least color of constitutional authority."

What was the object of this reference? Was it to pass a useless comment upon the conduct of Congress in exceeding its powers? By no means. He adds: —

> "I mean not by anything here said to throw censure on the measures pursued by Congress. I am sensible they could not have done otherwise. The public interest, the necessity of the case, imposed upon them the task of overleaping their constitutional limits. But is not the fact an alarming proof of the danger resulting from a government which does not possess regular powers commensurate to its objects?"

The whole article, taken together, and not judged by a single extract, appears to me to lead almost irresistibly to the conclusion that Mr. Madison regarded the new system of government, the Constitution, as supplying defects which had led to abuse and usurpation under the old, the Confederation; that he considered the former as remedying the very defects which had imposed on Congress the necessity of overleaping the constitutional limits of their power; that he viewed the provision of the Constitution authorizing Congress "to dispose of, and make all needful rules and regulations respecting, the territory" of the United States, as conferring the power which, in his opinion, Congress had usurped, and as giving legality, under the Constitution, to proceedings which he condemned, under the Confederation, as void of constitutional authority.

Happily, sir, we are not left to mere inference in respect to the opinions of Mr. Madison on this point. If we turn to the 43d number of the "Federalist," also written by him, we shall find a direct reference to the clause in the Constitution concerning the territory of the United States. If there were any doubt before, I think this would dissipate it. He is speaking of certain powers conferred on Congress by the Constitution. He says: "The eventual establishment of new states seems to have been overlooked by the compilers of that instrument [Articles of Confederation]. We have seen the inconvenience of this omission, and the assumption of power into which Congress have been led by it. With great propriety, therefore, has the new system supplied the defect."

He next quotes the clause giving Congress "power to dispose of, and make all needful rules and regulations respecting, the territory" of the United States; and adds, "This is a power of very great importance, and required by considerations similar to those which show the propriety of the former." By the former, is meant the power of admitting new states into the Union, — a power which he had adverted to as supplying a defect in the Articles of Confederation, and as avoiding the evil of usurping the exercise of an indispensable authority. Would he have denominated it a "power of very great importance," if he had regarded it as limited to a mere sale of the public lands? Would he have said that it was "required by considerations similar to those which show the propriety of the former," — the admission of new states, — unless he had considered it as having "supplied a defect," as in the other case to which he had referred, and empowered Congress to do what it had done in respect to the Northwestern territory without authority? There were other territories beside that northwest of the Ohio to be provided for. South Carolina had at that very time ceded to the United States her interest in the territory east of the Mississippi, now comprised in the States of Mississippi and Alabama; North Carolina and Georgia were expected to cede what now constitutes Tennessee, and the residue of Mississippi and Alabama. Mr. Madison, in the 38th number of the "Federalist," written a year after the ordinance of 1787 was adopted, obviously alludes to those two last cessions as reasonably to be expected. How were these territories, and that which South Carolina had ceded, to be provided for; how were temporary governments to be erected; how were officers to be appointed for them; how was the authority of the United States to be extended over them? Was it not under the clause of the Constitution authorizing "all needful rules and regulations" to be made? Was it not in contemplation of these organic arrangements for the communities which were to arise within the territory then acquired, and expected to be acquired, that Mr. Madison pronounced that clause as conferring "a power of very great importance"?

The reasonings contained in these two numbers of the "Federalist," (the 38th and the 43d,) are directly connected by Mr. Madison himself; and when considered in conjunction with his subsequent participation in legislative acts, by which the ordinance of 1787 was enforced and similar provisions applied to other portions of the public domain, his interpretation of the Constitution, in respect to the powers of Congress over the territory of the United States, cannot well be doubted. But if any lingering doubt should remain in respect to Mr. Madison's opinion as to the right of Congress to regulate municipal concerns of the persons residing upon the territory belonging to the United States, it will be removed by his declaration in Congress in 1790, that, though Congress was restricted by the Constitution from taking measures to abolish the slave-trade, yet there was a variety of ways in which it could countenance abolition, "and regulations might be made in relation to the introduction of them [slaves] into the new States to be formed out of the western territory."

I have been thus particular in explaining Mr. Madison's opinion, not only on account of the high authority which it carries with it, but because, from the manner in which it has been cited, it might seem to support conclusions which, in my judgment, derive no strength from it whatever.

Let me now call the attention of the Senate to the acts of Congress by which this construction of the Constitution is supported, for the purpose of exhibiting the force it derives from legislative precedents.

I. The ordinance of 1787 was recognized by chapter 8, 1st session, 1st Congress. The preamble recites that " it is requisite certain provisions should be made," &c., in order that the said ordinance " may continue to have full effect." There was no division in either House upon its passage. There seems to have been no objection to it. Mr. Madison's name occurs on the Journal of the proceedings of the day on which the bill passed the House, of which he was a member. He was doubtless present, and concurred in the measure.

This first precedent which I cite, has all the force of contemporaneous exposition. It is coeval with the birth of the new government. It may almost be denominated the work of the framers of the Constitution. It is recorded among the earliest acts by which that instrument was put in operation. It is one of the first footsteps by which the movement of the new government is to be traced out of the darkness in which its dawn was enveloped, into the clear, broad sunlight of its stability and strength. The act was signed by General Washington.

That the ordinance was not deemed by its framers, or by the Congress which continued it in force, incompatible with any degree of freedom from restraint, which may be justly claimed as essential to political liberty, is apparent from the terms of the instrument itself. The articles, of which the sixth and last prohibited slavery, were expressly declared to be adopted, "for extending the fundamental principles of civil and religious liberty, which form the basis whereon these republics, their laws and constitutions, are erected; to fix and establish those principles as the basis of all laws, constitutions, and governments, which forever hereafter shall be formed in the said Territory; to provide also for the establishment of States, and permanent government therein, and for their admission to a share in the Federal councils on an equal footing with the original States, at as early periods as may be consistent with the general interest."

Several considerations suggest themselves in connection with this subject.

1. Neither the framers of the ordinance nor the first Congress considered the perpetual prohibition of slavery in the Northwestern territory inconsistent with the admission of the States to be formed out of it into the Union on "an equal footing with the original States." Neither the actual tenure of slaves, nor the right to hold them, could have been considered essential to the full fruition of the political liberty which the States possessed as members of the Union.

2. The prohibition was not considered inconsistent with the terms of cession of the territory by Virginia in 1784, which required that the States to be formed out of it should be "republican States, and admitted members of the Federal Union, having the same rights of sovereignty, freedom, and independence." These rights of sovereignty, freedom, and independence, therefore, which the members of the Federal Union enjoyed, were by the Congress of the Confederation, and the first Congress, deemed fully possessed, although the right to hold slaves was prohibited. Virginia

concurred in passing the ordinance in the Congress of the Confederation in 1787, and in continuing it in force in the first Congress under the Constitution in 1789.

Whatever doubt there may be as to the original validity of the ordinance, I believe, its authority has always been respected by responsible tribunals. I will read a decision from the Supreme Court of Louisiana, in the case of Merry *v.* Chexnaider, 8 Martin's Reports, (new series,) 699: —

> "On appeal from the Court of the First District, Porter, J., delivered the opinion of the court. The plaintiff sues in this action to recover his freedom, and from the evidence on record is clearly entitled to it. He was born in the Northwestern Territory since the enactment of Congress, in 1787, of the ordinance for the government of that country, according to the 6th article of which there could be therein neither slavery nor involuntary servitude. This ordinance fixed forever the character of the population in the region over which it is extended, and takes away all foundation from the claim set up in this instance by the defendant. The act of cession by Virginia did not deprive Congress of the power to make such a regulation.
>
> "It is therefore ordered, adjudged, and decreed, that the judgment of the district court be affirmed with costs."

This decision was pronounced in 1830, and it fully sustains the view of the subject I have taken.

II. On the 7th of April, 1798, an act was passed for an amicable settlement of limits with the State of Georgia, and authorizing the establishment of a government in the Mississippi territory. This act authorized the President to establish therein a government in all respects similar to that in the territory northwest of the Ohio river, excepting the sixth article of the ordinance of 1787. It then prohibited the importation of slaves into the Territory from any place without the limits of the United States. This act was passed ten years (less a few months) before Congress was authorized by the Constitution to prohibit the importation of slaves into the States which were originally parties to the Federal compact. This provision of the Constitution applied only to the then existing States. It did not extend to the States thereafter to be formed, or to the territories of the United States, — a fact of the highest importance, if it is to be regarded as a limitation of a vested power. The exercise by Congress of the power of prohibiting the introduction of slaves into the Mississippi Territory from foreign countries appears to have passed without opposition. I find no division in either House on that clause of the bill. This fact shows the undisputed interpretation put at that day on the Constitution of the United States in respect to the powers of Congress over every matter of domestic concern in the territory belonging to the United States, and especially over the subject of slavery, the most delicate of all. There was a direct exercise by Congress, in respect to the territories, of a power which was positively prohibited in respect to the States existing at the adoption of the Constitution. This act passed under the administration of the elder Adams.

III. At the first session of the 6th Congress, chap. 41, laws of 1800, an act was passed to divide the territory belonging to the United States northwest of the Ohio river into two separate governments. This act created a territorial government for Indiana in all respects similar to that provided by the ordinance of 1787 for the government of the Northwest territory. This precedent reaffirms the principles contained in the ordinance. The act was signed by the elder Adams.

IV. On the 26th of March, 1804, an act was passed dividing Louisiana into two territories, and providing for the temporary government thereof. All that part of the territory south of the 33d parallel of latitude, now the southern boundary of Arkansas, was erected into the territory of Orleans.

The 10th section of the act had three provisions in respect to slavery in the Territory: 1. The importation of slaves, from any place without the limits of the United States, was prohibited; 2. The importation, from any place within the limits of the United States, of slaves imported since the 1st May, 1798, was prohibited; and, 3. The importation of slaves, except by a "citizen of the United States removing into said Territory for actual settlement, and being at the time of such removal *bona fide* owner of such slaves," was prohibited.

When this section was under discussion in the Senate, a motion was made to strike out the last clause, and it was negatived by a vote of 19 to 9. Among the votes in the negative were John Breckenridge and John Brown of Kentucky, Jesse Franklin of North Carolina, James Jackson of Georgia, Samuel Smith of Maryland, Thomas Sumpter of South Carolina, William H. Wells and Samuel White of Delaware; 8 of the 19 from slaveholding States.

The House Journal does not show any opposition to this section. The vote on the final passage of the bill was 66 yeas and 21 nays. Of the latter, only 7—one third of the whole number—were from slaveholding States.

The territory of Orleans appears to have remained subject to these restrictions—certainly all but the first—until 1812, when it was erected into a State, with the name of Louisiana. At least I can find nothing to the contrary. On the 2d March, 1805, an act further providing for the government of the Territory was passed, by which the ordinance of 1787 was applied to it, except the sixth article, prohibiting slavery forever, and so much of the second paragraph as regulated the descent and distribution of estates. But, by the eighth section of the act, the act of March 26, 1804, dividing the territory of Louisiana, which was limited in its operation to one year and to the end of the next session of Congress thereafter, was continued in full force until repealed, excepting so far as it was repugnant to the act of 1805. The restrictions on the importation of slaves were not repugnant to that act, and they must have been continued in operation. I state this fact because it has been supposed and asserted that the act of 1804 was repealed the next year; as though Congress had passed it inconsiderately, and had thus early become convinced of the illegality of the restrictions upon slavery which it contained. But the language of the act of 1805 cannot be held to repeal these restrictions. There is no authority for such a construction. On the contrary, I find a decision of the supreme court of Louisiana, showing that they were continued in force. I will read an extract from it to the Senate: —

"Formerly, while the act dividing Louisiana into two territories was in force in this country, slaves, introduced here in contravention to it, were freed by operation of law; but that act was merged in the legislative provisions which were subsequently enacted on the subject of importation of slaves into the United States generally." — *Gomez v. Bonneval*, 6 *Martin's Rep.* 656, (*Sup. Court of La.*) 1819.

The general law referred to went into operation on the 1st of January, 1808. If, therefore, there was, as this decision shows, a merger in 1808, there could have been no repeal in 1805.

There cannot be a stronger case to show the control Congress has exercised over the subject. Slavery existed in Louisiana when it was ceded to the United States. Congress did not impose any restriction on the tenure of slaves then held in the Territory: that might have impaired vested rights of property under the local law, which the United States had covenanted in the treaty of cession to maintain and protect. But Congress not only proceeded, at once, to prohibit the importation of slaves from foreign countries, but to prohibit their introduction from the States of the Union, excepting when accompanying and belonging to citizens of the United States moving into the Territory to become residents. This was to impose restrictions upon its extension, even within the Territory in which it existed. It was a direct prohibition of the domestic slave-trade. It was an exercise of power, in respect to the territories, which Congress did not possess in respect to the States. It was an anticipation, by four years, of the time at which Congress was authorized to prohibit the importation of slaves into the original States. This act was signed by Jefferson.

V. On the 11th January, 1805, an act was passed establishing the territory of Michigan, with a government "in all respects similar to that provided by the ordinance of Congress, passed on the 13th day of July, 1787, for the government of the territory of the United States northwest of the river Ohio."

VI. On the 3d of February, 1809, a similar government was established for the territory of Illinois. These two last acts also passed under Mr. Jefferson's administration.

VII. On the 4th of June, 1812, an act was passed "providing for the government of the territory of Missouri," and the laws and regulations in force in the district of Louisiana were continued in operation.

VIII. On the 3d March, 1817, a government was formed for the territory of Alabama, and the laws then in force within it as a part of Mississippi were continued in operation. These two acts were passed under Mr. Madison.

IX. On the 2d March, 1819, the territory of Arkansas was formed from the territory of Missouri, and a government established for it.

X. On the 6th March, 1820, the inhabitants of Missouri were authorized to form a constitution and state government, and slavery was prohibited in all that part of the territory of Louisiana north of 36° 30′ north latitude. In this exercise of legislative power the greatest latitude is given to the authority claimed under the clause of the Constitution respecting the territory of the United States.

XI. On the 30th March, 1822, an act was passed for the establishment of a territorial government in Florida, containing provisions making it unlawful "to import or bring into the said Territory, from any place without the limits of the United States," any slave or slaves.

These three acts were passed under Mr. Monroe's administration.

XII. On the 20th April, 1836, an act was passed "establishing the territorial government of Wisconsin," securing to the inhabitants "the rights, privileges, and advantages" secured to the people of the Northwestern territory by the ordinance of 1787, subjecting them to the "conditions, restrictions, and prohibitions" contained in said ordinance, and extending the laws of the United States over them. This act was signed by General Jackson.

XIII. On the 12th June, 1838, a territorial government for Iowa was established, and the laws of the United States extended over it. This act was signed by Mr. Van Buren.

And here, Mr. President, I close this rapid specification of legislative precedents, commencing with the first Congress, and running, with a current of authority uninterrupted and almost unopposed, through more than half a century, down to the present day.

By looking through these acts, it will be found that the power of governing the persons occupying the territory belonging to the United States has been exercised by Congress in almost every form, and for a great variety of purposes, municipal as well as political. Officers have been appointed, their qualifications prescribed; the right of suffrage fixed, limited, and extended; the descent and distribution of estates regulated; courts organized and their powers defined; personal rights secured; and, in general, the whole power of legislation has been controlled by Congress through the supervision it has retained over the laws passed by the legislative assemblies of the territories.

Let me now see how far this exercise of legislative power has been sanctioned by judicial interpretations. I quote from decisions of the Supreme Court, the highest judicial tribunal in the United States. That court, in reference to the clause of the Constitution giving Congress power to dispose of, and make all needful rules and regulations respecting, the territory belonging to the United States, say:—

"Perhaps the power of governing a territory belonging to the United States, which has not, by becoming a State, acquired the means of self-government, may result necessarily from the facts that it is not within the jurisdiction of any particular State, and is within the power and jurisdiction of the United States. The right to govern may be the inevitable consequence of the right to acquire territory. Whichever may be the source whence the power is derived, its possession is unquestioned." — *Chief Justice Marshall; the American Insurance Company* v. *Canter*, 1 *Peters*, 542.

"The power given in this clause is of the most plenary kind. Rules and regulations respecting the territory of the United States: they necessarily confer complete jurisdiction. It was necessary to confer it without limitation, to enable the new government to redeem the pledge given to the old in relation to the formation and powers of the new States." — *The Cherokee Nation* v. *The State of Georgia*, 5 *Peters*, 44.

"The term 'territory,' as here used, is merely descriptive of one kind of property, and is equivalent to the word 'lands,' and Congress has the same power over it as over any other property belonging to the United States; and this power is vested in Congress without limitation, and has been considered the foundation upon which the territorial governments rest. In the case of McCulloch *v.* the State of Maryland, 4 Wheaton, 422, the Chief Justice, in giving the opinion of the court, speaking of this article and the powers of Congress growing out of it, applies it to the territorial governments, and says all admit their constitutionality. And again, in the case of the American Insurance Company *v.* Canter, 1 Peters, 542, in speaking of the cession of Florida, under the treaty with Spain, he says that Florida, until she shall become a State, continues to be a territory of the United States, governed by virtue of that clause in the Constitution which empowers Congress to make all needful rules and regulations respecting the territory or other property of the United States." — *The United States* v. *Gratiot et al.* 14 *Peters*, 537.

I might refer to other decisions of the court, in which the same principle is recognized, though less directly perhaps, but sustaining the same interpretation of the Constitution, and giving validity to the legislative precedents I have cited. Writers on constitutional law (Rawle, Sergeant, Story) concur in this construction. In short, it is believed that no power exercised under the Constitution of such magnitude as that of governing the territories belonging to the United States has been more uniformly acquiesced in from the formation of the government to the present day, and in all its departments, legislative, executive, and judicial. No system of rules would be safe, if its authority could be disputed and overturned, in the face of such comprehensive and long-continued sanctions. Government, law, social and political order, would become unstable, uncertain, and worthless, as safeguards either to property or life, if their foundations could be thus sapped and undermined by logical subtlety and refinement, by new versions of the Constitution at war with its ancient interpretations, and running counter to the whole course of the public administration from the earliest periods of time.

And here, Mr. President, I dismiss the question of power. If, as I think, the affirmative is sustained, something, nevertheless, remains to be considered. A power may be possessed, and yet it may not be right to exert it. Its exercise must be justified by considerations of public or private advantage: it must not work either public or private wrong. I propose to consider it under this aspect.

And, in the first place, I intend to say nothing in regard to private interests excepting this, that there is no proposition before us to interfere with slavery where it exists, no restriction on the exercise of private or personal rights within the sphere of the local laws under which they arise. The question before us is, whether slaves shall be permitted to be introduced into Oregon, or whether their introduction shall be prohibited. It is a remote territory, generally conceded (though in this I do not concur, as I shall hereafter explain more fully) as not likely to be occupied by slaves, if they were allowed to be carried there. The fact that it is generally admitted to be unfit for slave labor must divest the question of all practical infringement of private rights, even in the estimation of those who take extreme views of the subject. I shall therefore consider it only in its bearing upon great public interests.

Mr. President, I consider this question, in the form it has assumed, as involving the extension of slavery. I consider it so under the motion to strike out the twelfth section, which substantially prohibits the introduction of slaves into Oregon. But it is made so more particularly by the amendment offered by my friend from Mississippi,[1] which provides —

> "That nothing contained in this act shall be so construed as to authorize the prohibition of domestic slavery in said territory whilst it remains in the condition of a territory of the United States."

I understand this as an assertion of the right to carry slaves into Oregon, both against the interference of Congress and the desire of the inhabitants to exclude them. I understand it as maintaining the right to introduce domestic slavery into Oregon. This is extension, and against the wishes of the inhabitants who have prohibited its introduction. Let me, then, present some considerations concerning this whole subject of extension.

Those who oppose the extension of slavery to wider limits believe that such extension promotes the multiplication of slaves. On the other hand, it is contended that it makes no addition to their numbers, but merely spreads them over a broader surface. This position is believed to be wholly inconsistent with all the received laws of population. The tendency of the human race is to increase in a compound ratio of the extent and productiveness of the surface on which it is sustained. The highest possible impulse is given to this increase in an unoccupied country, distinguished for its fertility, and offering certain rewards for the products of labor. This is the character of our own soil. Wherever slave labor can be carried, it will, for a time, be productive. Missouri affords a strong illustration of the truth of this proposition. That State lies wholly north of 36° 30′, north latitude, excepting a strip about thirty miles wide on the Mississippi, running down to the thirty-sixth parallel; and yet, though so far north, slavery made rapid

[1] Mr. Davis.

progress there after her admission into the Union. By the census of 1820, there were 10,222 slaves; in 1830, 24,820, an increase of one hundred and forty per cent. in ten years; and in 1840, 58,240, an increase of one hundred and thirty-five per cent. in ten years. For several years, the slave population increased more rapidly than the free. In all new and fertile soils, where the demands for labor are urgent, this will be the inevitable result. The multiplication of the human species is governed by laws as inflexible and certain as those which govern the reproduction of vegetable life. In both, the stimulus, whatever it may be, constitutes the law of the increase. I am aware that the ratio of increase in Missouri, both in respect to the white and the black race, was materially modified by immigration; and to that extent the result is independent of the application of the principle I have stated. But it can hardly be denied that surface, productive surface, is the great element in our extension. It is this alone which has carried the ratio of our increase far beyond that of any other people. If we had been restricted to the area of the thirteen original States, how different would have been the result of our decennial enumerations! The same principle governs the white and the black races. The laws of labor, subsistence, and population act on both, though not everywhere with the same intensity.

If these conclusions are just, an enlargement of the surface over which slavery is spread carries with it, by force of invincible laws, a multiplication of the race held in bondage: in other words, a substantial increase of the number of slaves. Extension in respect to surface is multiplication in point of number. The two propositions cannot be legitimately separated either in reasoning or in practice. In this view of the subject, the extension of slavery is a reproduction of the original responsibility of introducing it; and in this respect it has a moral bearing, to which the great mass of the community cannot be indifferent.

Mr. President, in providing for the government of our territories, while they continue subject to the exclusive regulation of Congress, no view of the subject would be complete which overlooks the part we are performing in the great movement of civilized society, on both sides of the Atlantic. Let us turn our attention to some of the considerations which suggest themselves in connection with this point. It requires no powers of prophecy to foretell that we are destined to spread ourselves over the greater portion of the American continent on this side the great lakes, — south to the densely peopled portions of Mexico, and west to the Pacific. Nor is it an idle dream of the imagination to foresee in our political organization the foundations of an empire increasing more rapidly, and destined to expand to broader limits, than the Roman republic: not an empire, like the latter, founded in war, and propagating itself by brute force, but an empire founded in peace, and extending itself by industry, enterprise, and the arts of civilization. Rome, in receiving into her bosom the surrounding population as she conquered them, instructed them in the art of war, and made them the instruments of new aggressions. We receive into ours the surplus population of the Old World, to instruct them in the arts of peace, and to accelerate the march of civilization across the western continent. There is nothing in the history of human society so calculated to exalt it as the spectacle we present, — receiving into the bonds of friendship, and admitting to the rights of citizenship, the surplus of the over-peopled and over-governed countries of Europe. These annual additions constitute an element of no inconsiderable force in the ratio of our progression. In the last quarter of a century — about the period we take for a duplication of our numbers — we have received, from the United Kingdom of Great Britain and Ireland alone, nearly a million of immigrants, and from continental Europe we have had large additions. These drains, on the one hand, and accessions, on the other, are not only likely to continue, but to increase in force. A surplus population, provided for by emigration, is certain to be regularly reproduced. Europe, therefore, will not be numerically weakened by these annual drains, even though they should be indefinitely augmented; and every addition to our numbers from abroad renders the force of immigration more intense, by relaxing the ties which bind to their native soil the kindred multitudes left behind.

For an indefinite period, then, we may calculate on large and constantly increasing additions to our population by immigration; and the natural multiplication of our own people, under the impulse of the powerful stimulants contained in a soil of extraordinary fertility, and in the superabundant supply of food, will doubtless maintain our past rate of increase, and give us, at the close of the present century, a hundred millions of inhabitants.

One of the most interesting and important problems, both for the American statesman and philosopher, is to determine of what race or races this vast population shall consist; for on the solution which future generations shall give to it, will essentially depend the prosperity of the community or communities they will constitute, and their ability to maintain such a form of government as shall secure to them the blessings of political liberty and an advanced civilization. In a general survey of the races by which the earth is peopled, though the varieties are infinite, there are but four grand divisions — the Asiatic, the Caucasian, the Ethiopian, and the Indian. The whole surface of Europe, with some inconsiderable exceptions, is occupied by the Caucasian race, — by the descendants of the energetic and independent tribes, which, from the shores of the Caspian, have, in different eras, spread themselves over Germany and western Europe, and laid the foundations of nearly all the civilization the world contains. From this Indo-Germanic or Caucasian race we are ourselves descended; and we are doing for the New World what they did for the Old, — spreading ourselves over and subduing it, not, indeed, by arms, but by the arts of peace. In whatever portion of Europe emigration to the United States takes its rise, it brings with it homogeneous currents. The same blood fills the veins of all. If shades of variety exist in the intellectual and physical characteristics of the multitudes who come among us, it is to be traced to the influences which diversities of soil, climate, and government have exerted upon them in the different sections of Europe where their lot has been cast. In the great outlines of their physiognomy, animal and moral, they are identical; and they are distinguishable from all other races by peculiarities not to be mistaken.

I believe it to be in the order of Providence, that the continent of North America, with the exception, perhaps, of some inconsiderable districts, is ultimately to be peopled by the same race which has overspread Europe, and made it what it is in science, in art, in civilization, and in morals. We may, by a misapplication of the means at our command, thwart for a season the divine purpose; we may postpone the consummation of the end we have to accomplish; but the deeply-seated causes which are at work will ultimately triumph over all obstacles. Years, possibly centuries, (and what are centuries in the history of nations and empires?) I say possibly centuries may be necessary to complete this process; but it must in the end be completed. I believe it may be satisfactorily shown that the free black population in the Northern States does not increase by its own inherent force. I doubt whether it is fully reproduced. In four of the New-England States — Vermont, New Hampshire, Rhode Island, and Connecticut — the black population, from 1820 to 1840, materially decreased. In New York, Massachusetts, and Maine, there was an increase during the same period; but this was doubtless due to the immigration of manumitted blacks from the South, finding their way to the principal commercial States. Without these accessions, the result in these States would probably have been the same as in the four New-England States referred to. Under the most favorable circumstances it is, and must continue to be, an inferior caste in the north. It counts nothing in the estimate, physical or intellectual, of the strength of the body politic. Even where the forms of its admission to the privileges of freemen are complete, it is an excluded class. Let the liberal and the humane do what they may, they cannot change the unalterable law of its destiny. Public opinion at the North — call it prejudice, if you will — presents an insuperable barrier against its elevation in the social scale. My own State has recently, by a majority of about one hundred and thirty thousand votes in two hundred thousand, refused to place blacks on the same footing as whites in the exercise of the elective franchise. Illinois and Connecticut have, I believe, done the same thing by decided votes. A class thus degraded will not multiply. This is the first stage of retrogradation. The second almost certainly follows. It will not be reproduced; and in a few generations the process of extinction is performed. Nor is it the work of inhumanity or wrong. It is the slow but certain process of nature, working out her ends by laws so steady, and yet so silent, that their operation is only seen in their results. I am not sure that this fact is so supported by statistical data that it can be considered settled beyond doubt. If it were, it might solve a great problem in population in the United States, — a problem full of consequence and of instruction for our guid ance, — that manumitted blacks, as a class, do not multiply and perhaps are not reproduced.

Is it the part of wisdom or humanity to promote the ex tension or increase of a race, which has its destiny written in characters not to be mistaken or effaced, — an extension adding nothing to the public prosperity or strength, and enlarging the basis of human degradation and suffering?

What is the true policy of the country, looking to its

rapid growth and to the steady extension of our people over the unoccupied portions of this continent? Sir, there is grave cause for reflection in the unexampled increase of our population by its inherent force, and still more in the vast accessions annually made to our numbers by immigration. The public order and prosperity depend in some degree in giving to these accessions, foreign and domestic, a uniform and homogeneous character. We could not divert the current of immigration if we were disposed to do what every dictate of humanity repels and condemns. It is in the vast and fertile spaces of the West that our own descendants, as well as the oppressed and needy multitudes of the Old World, must find the food they require, and the rewards for labor, which are necessary to give them the spirit and the independence of freemen. I hold it to be our sacred duty to consecrate these spaces to the multiplication of the white race. Our part is to see, also, as far as in us lies, that this new material is made to conform to the political organization of which it is to become an integral part. I have always believed this object would be best accomplished by a liberal policy. The Federal governments can do nothing in this respect. The State governments must do all, — rather perhaps by acting upon future generations than the present, — by establishing schools, by the removal of restrictions upon the application of labor and capital, and by emancipating industry, under all its forms, from the shackles of privilege and monopoly

If we were to look to the rapid increase of our own population alone, without reference to external accessions, — accessions annually increasing and with a constantly accelerated force, — I should hold it to be our duty to promote, by all just and constitutional means, the multiplication of the white race, and to discourage, as far as we properly can, the multiplication of every other. Reason and humanity, acting within the limits of the Constitution, will define the mode and extent of the agency we may exert over our destinies in this respect. With regard to the policy of peopling this continent by the highest race in the order of intellectual and physical endowment, there can be no difference of opinion. No man can hesitate to say whether the condition of this continent, in all that concerns its government, morals, civilization, prosperity, strength and productiveness, would be most likely to be promoted by peopling it with the race from which we are sprung, or with the descendants of the Ethiop and the Caffre. There may be portions of the Southern States in which the climate and objects of cultivation require the labor of blacks. I pass by all considerations of this character for an obvious reason. If there are portions of the Union, which can only be cultivated by the African race, they are embraced within the territorial boundaries of organized States, over whose domestic condition and relations the Federal government has no control. The question concerns only them, and I forbear to touch it. But conceding the necessity of slave labor there, the concession furnishes no argument in favor of permitting slavery to be extended to territories in which no such necessity exists.

The character of the population, by which this continent is to be occupied, is a subject of vital importance to every section of the Union. The strength of the whole is concerned, and with its strength its security from external aggression and intestine disorder and violence. The nearer the great body of our people — those especially who till the earth — approach the same standard in intelligence and political importance, the more likely we shall be to maintain internal tranquillity in peace, and bring to the common support in war the united strength of all. A degraded class is always, and must be, by force of immutable laws, an element of insecurity and weakness. I will not say that the North is as much interested in this question as the South. But we have a very deep interest in it. Manumitted slaves come to us in considerable numbers. They will continue to do so in spite of any discouragements we may oppose, and without the aid of compulsory legislation on the part of the States in which they are manumitted. All such additions to our numbers are in the highest degree undesirable. They add nothing to our strength, moral or physical; and, as we fill up, their tendency is to exclude whites to the extent that they contribute to supply the demand for labor. If the fifty thousand free blacks in New York were to be withdrawn, their places would be filled by an equal supply of white laborers. Our strength and our prosperity would be proportionably increased by substituting white citizens for a class laboring under civil disqualifications, and excluded, by the force of opinion, from all share in the concerns of government. We desire and need independent, not dependent classes. We have, then, a deep interest in this question, first as a member of the common Union, and next as a community in some respects independent and sovereign. In both relations it concerns our permanent welfare, and we can never consent or contribute — by any act, by inaction, by acquiescence, express or implied — to the extension of slavery to regions in which it does not now exist.

It is generally conceded that there is nothing in the climate or productions of Oregon, which requires the labor of blacks. If this be so, slavery, if introduced, would gradually give way in the competition with free labor. Notwithstanding this inherent tendency in slavery to wear itself out in districts to which it is not indispensably necessary, it will be profitable for a time in new countries, where there are lands to be brought under cultivation, and where there is an urgent demand for labor. But for a temporary purpose, — with the assurance that it must eventually be eradicated, — would it not be unjust and unwise, considering the question in its political bearing alone, to decline to exclude it, and to make the prohibition absolute?

Gentlemen have said this is not a practical question, —

that slaves will never be taken to Oregon. With all deference to their opinions, I differ with them totally. I believe, if permitted, slaves would be carried there, and that slavery would continue at least as long as in Maryland or Virginia. The Pacific coast is totally different in temperature from the Atlantic. It is far milder. Lines of equal temperature — isothermal lines, as they are technically denominated — traverse the surface of earth in curves of varied eccentricity in reference to the parallels of latitude. These curves are nowhere, perhaps, greater than on this continent. In the latitude of Nova Scotia, which is bound for nearly half the year in fetters of ice, snow on the Pacific does not lie more than three or four weeks. In the valley of the Wilhamette, above the 45th degree of north latitude, — the parallel of Montreal, — grass grows the whole winter, and cattle are rarely if ever housed. Green pease are eaten at Oregon city, in the same parallel, at Christmas. Where is the corresponding climate to be found on this side of the continent? Where we sit — near the 39th? No, sir, far to the south of us. The latitude of Georgia gives on the Pacific a tropical climate.

When I say this is a practical question, I do not rely on reasoning alone. The prohibition of slavery in the laws of Oregon was adopted for the express purpose of excluding slaves. A few had been brought in; further importations were expected; and it was with a view to put a stop to them that the prohibitory act was passed.

Shall we, then, refuse to ratify this prohibition? Are we unwilling to extend to the inhabitants of Oregon a privilege they ask for themselves? Shall we, by our judgment solemnly pronounced here, declare that the territory of Oregon shall be open to the introduction of slaves, unless the people, through their legislative assembly, reënact the prohibition? I might go further, and ask, in reference to a proposed amendment, whether we are prepared to say, against the wishes of the inhabitants, that the introduction of slaves into Oregon shall not be prohibited?

Mr. President, I desire it not to be understood, in putting these inquiries, that I am in favor of leaving to the inhabitants of territories the decision of a question not only affecting them, but of vital importance to the prosperity of the whole community. I have always regarded it as one of the high duties of the Federal government to give direction and shape to the institutions of the inhabitants of a territory while preparing themselves for admission into the Union. This temporary subordination was deemed necessary for the northwest territory, even though settled by the unmixed population of the thirteen original States, trained to self-government and to the exercise of political rights under institutions of the most faultless character. How much more necessary is such a supervision now, when territories are becoming annexed to the Union inhabited by the most heterogeneous races, and wholly unused to the enjoyment or exercise of rational freedom?

An honorable Senator from North Carolina[1] denominated this submission of power to the inhabitants of the territories a republican measure, or as in accordance with the genius of our republican institutions. Sir, it was not so considered in former times — in the earlier and better days of the Republic. Let me state some historical facts touching this question.

In 1805, an act was passed for the government of the territory of Orleans. While the bill was under discussion in the Senate, certain amendments were offered, the effect of which would have been to give the inhabitants of the territory of Orleans the management of their own domestic concerns, uncontrolled by Congress. The Journal of the Senate does not show by whom the amendments were offered; but on searching the records of that period, I find the manuscript copy indorsed, "Mr. Tracy's motion to amend

[1] Mr. Badger

bill." I think this may be regarded as the original, to which subsequent attempts to emancipate the territories from the control of the Federal government, before they have the population necessary to give them a representation in Congress, may be referred. Whatever the doctrine may be considered at the present day, it derived little support from republican sources then. It was brought forward by Mr. Tracy, an able and respectable Federalist from Connecticut. On the division, which was called on his motion to strike out for the purpose of inserting his amendments, it received but eight votes, including his own. They were given by Timothy Pickering and John Quincy Adams, of Massachusetts; Uriah Tracy, the mover, and James Hillhouse, of Connecticut; James A. Bayard and Stephen White, of Delaware; Simeon Olcott, of New Hampshire; and James Jackson, of Georgia. With the exception of Mr. Jackson, all these gentlemen were Federalists, for it was not until several years later that Mr. Adams acted with the Republican party. Some of them were among the brightest ornaments of the Federal party of that day, both in respect to talents and private character, and all were strenuous opponents of Mr. Jefferson's administration. Against these eight ayes were twenty-four noes, given by the great body of Mr. Jefferson's supporters and some of his opponents. Among the former were Baldwin of Georgia, Giles of Virginia, and Smith of Maryland. The supporters of the measure were, with one exception, Federalists, and opponents of Mr. Jefferson's administration. Its opponents were chiefly Republicans, and supporters of his administration.

At the same session of Congress, memorials were presented to both Houses from the inhabitants of the territory of Orleans, and from the District of Louisiana. The former prayed to be admitted immediately into the Union, and insisted that they had a right to such admission under the treaty of cession. The latter asked for a territorial government; the whole territory, or District of Louisiana, as it was called, lying north of the 33d parallel of latitude, having been virtually subjected, in respect to the administration of its legislative, executive, and judicial powers, to the Governor and judges of the Indiana territory. In both cases the inhabitants prayed for the privilege of importing slaves. These memorials were referred, in the House of Representatives, to a committee of which Mr. John Randolph was chairman.

On the 25th of January, 1805, Mr. Randolph made a report, which will be found at page 417 of vol. 20, American State Papers, printed by Gales & Seaton, concluding with a resolution, "that provision ought to be made by law for extending to the inhabitants of Louisiana the right of self-government." This resolution was agreed to, on the 28th of January, without a division.

Mr. Randolph's report, while asserting that "every indulgence, not incompatible with the interests of the Union," should be extended to the inhabitants of Louisiana, and while declaring that the object of the committee was "to give to Louisiana a government of its own choice, administered by officers of its own appointment," maintained at the same time, that, in "recommending the extension of this privilege to the people of that country, it [was] not the intention of the committee that it should be unaccompanied by wise and salutary restrictions. Among these may be numbered a prohibition of the importation of foreign slaves, equally dictated by humanity and policy, [here follows an enumeration of other restrictions,] to which may be added, (for further security,) that such of the laws as may be disapproved by Congress, within a limited time after their passage, shall be of no force and effect."

The report of Mr. Randolph asserted, to the full extent, the right of Congress to provide for the government of the territories, to impose on them such restrictions as were demanded by the interests of the Union, and to prohibit the introduction of slaves from foreign countries, as a measure of humanity and policy.

Such was the action of the two Houses of Congress on this subject, involving the question of yielding to the inhabitants of territories the control of their own domestic affairs, and exempting their legislation from the supervisory and repealing power of Congress. If we regard it as a party measure, all the republican sanctions of that day were against it. And if we consider it as a political question, to be determined, with regard to its complexion, by a reference to the genius of our institutions, it is singular that those who were most deeply imbued with the spirit of republicanism should have been arrayed against it.

Let me now examine for a moment the question immediately before us. A motion is made to strike out the twelfth section of this bill. The section provides: 1st. That "the inhabitants of the said territory shall be entitled to all the rights, privileges, and immunities heretofore granted and secured to the territory of Iowa, and to its inhabitants."

2d. That "the existing laws now in force in the territory of Oregon, under the authority of the provisional government established by the people thereof, shall continue to be valid and operative therein, so far as the same be not incompatible with the provisions of this act, subject, nevertheless, to be altered, modified, or repealed by the Governor and Legislative Assembly of the said territory of Oregon."

3d. That "the laws of the United States are hereby extended over and declared to be in force in said territory, so far as the same or any provision thereof may be applicable."

In order to see what rights, privileges, and immunities the people of Oregon are to acquire, we must refer to the act organizing the territory of Iowa. The twelfth section of this act provides, "that the inhabitants of the said territory shall be entitled to all the rights, privileges, and immunities heretofore granted and secured to the territory of Wisconsin and its inhabitants," &c.

We must next have recourse to the act organizing the territory of Wisconsin. The twelfth section of this act provides, "that the inhabitants of the said territory shall be entitled to, and enjoy, all and singular the rights, privileges, and advantages granted and secured to the people of the territory of the United States northwest of the river Ohio, by the articles of the compact contained in the ordinance for the government of the said territory, passed on the 13th day of July, 1787; and shall be subject to all the conditions and restrictions and prohibitions in said articles of compact imposed upon the people of the said territory."

It will be seen that there is an essential difference in the language of the two sections. The twelfth section of the act organizing the territory of Iowa secures the rights, privileges, and immunities secured to the territory of Wisconsin and its inhabitants, including the ordinance of 1787; but it does not expressly impose the conditions, restrictions, and prohibitions contained in that ordinance. Now, I suppose the exclusion of slavery from the northwest territory by the ordinance is to be referred rather to the class of restrictions and prohibitions than to that of privileges and immunities. Under such a construction of the act, slavery would not have been excluded from Iowa by the twelfth section of the act establishing a government for that territory, nor would it be excluded from Oregon by that portion of this bill which secures to the inhabitants "the rights, privileges, and immunities heretofore granted and secured to the territory of Iowa and its inhabitants."

I know there is a difference of opinion in respect to the true construction of the twelfth section of the act organizing a government for the territory of Iowa. The Senator from Maryland,[1] whose legal opinions are entitled to great weight, is of opinion that the slavery restrictions contained in the twelfth section of the act organizing a territorial government for Wisconsin, from which territory Iowa

[1] Mr. Johnson.

was taken, are embraced in the twelfth section of the act establishing a government for the latter. The Senators from North Carolina and Georgia[1] consider the conditions, prohibitions, and restrictions, imposed by the ordinance of 1787, on the one hand, and the rights, privileges, and advantages, secured on the other, as distinct, substantive propositions, of which the latter only are embraced in the twelfth section of the last-named act. And although I will not undertake to decide between them, I confess this seems to me the most reasonable construction. Practically, this question was of no importance as to Iowa, as slavery was excluded from that territory, which was a part of Louisiana, by the Missouri compromise.

Let us now look at the next provision of this section, which I consider the most important. It declares that the laws now existing in Oregon shall continue to be valid and operative, &c.

One of these laws contains a prohibition of slavery. I will read it; it is article one, section four, of the organic laws of Oregon: —

> "There shall be neither slavery nor involuntary servitude in said territory, otherwise than for the punishment of crimes, whereof the party shall be duly convicted."

This prohibition is adopted by the section I am considering; and the exclusion of slavery will, for the time, be as complete as though it were expressly prohibited by an adoption of the amendment offered by the Senator from New Hampshire, and subsequently withdrawn by him. That amendment subjected the territory of Oregon to the restrictions and prohibitions of the ordinance of 1787. It would have been a perpetual exclusion of slavery; and in this respect it differs from the twelfth section as it stands. For instance: under this section the inhabitants of Oregon might rescind or repeal the law prohibiting slavery; this act of repeal would go into immediate effect, and slaves

[1] Mr. Badger and Mr. Berrien.

could be introduced into the territory. The sixth section, however, provides that all laws passed by the governor and legislative assembly shall be submitted to Congress, and if disapproved, shall be void and of no effect. If such an act of repeal should be passed, it would bring the question again before Congress for its approval or disapproval. Such an act is certainly very unlikely to be passed by the legislative authority of the territory. Still, the positive prohibition contained in the ordinance of 1787 is preferable as making a final disposition of the question; and it is in accordance with the whole legislation of the country in respect to territories situated like this. I shall, therefore, at a proper time, unless some other Senator does so, offer an amendment to that effect.

I regret exceedingly, Mr. President, to have taxed the patience of the Senate so long; but I believed I was performing a duty to high principles, and to the State I have, in part, the honor to represent; and no consideration could induce me to shrink from the performance of it.

Before I conclude, I desire to state some positions which I took last winter, in discussing what was termed the three million bill. I thought then, and I think still, that they constitute the only practical and reasonable basis for the settlement of this question. They were these: —

1. All external interference with slavery in the States is a violation of the compromises of the Constitution, and dangerous to the harmony and perpetuity of the Federal Union.

2. If territory is acquired by the United States, it should, in respect to slavery, be received as it is found. If slavery exists therein at the time of the acquisition, it should not be the subject of legislation by Congress. On the other hand, if slavery does not exist therein at the time of the acquisition, its introduction ought to be prohibited while the territory continues to be governed as such.

3. All legislation by Congress, in respect to slavery in the territory belonging to the United States, ceases to be

operative when the inhabitants are permitted to form a state government; and the admission of a state into the Union carries with it, by force of the sovereignty such admission confers, the right to dispose of the whole question of slavery at its discretion, without external interference.

These positions were in substantial accordance, as I supposed, with the declared opinions of the legislature of New York; and they have been recently reaffirmed, so far as the exclusion of slavery from the territory in which it does not now exist is concerned.

I believe this to be the only just, equal, and reasonable basis on which this question can be amicably settled. Such a result may be hopeless. Extreme views on both sides may defeat all adjustment of it on friendly terms. If so, I shall have the consolation of reflecting, that, while my own opinions lie between those extremes, while they have been advanced, as I trust, in language no one can deem offensive, they have been maintained with a steadiness which ought always to accompany settled convictions of right and duty.

Mr. President, I conclude by saying for New York, as I think I am authorized to say by her legislative resolutions, that, while she will adhere steadfastly to all the compromises of the Constitution, and while she will resist all interference with slavery in the States as unauthorized and disorganizing, she will never consent to its extension to territory in which it does not now exist, and especially where it is now prohibited. On the contrary, she will, in every constitutional mode, oppose all such extension, as of evil tendency in government, wrong in itself, and repugnant to the humanity and civilization of the age.

GOVERNMENTS IN THE TERRITORIES.

The following speech was delivered by Mr. Dix on the 26th July, 1848. The bill under discussion embraced the whole subject of organizing governments for the territories acquired from Mexico; but the only material point of disagreement in the Senate was the question of permitting slavery to be established in those territories. The Southern Senators insisted that citizens of the United States had the right, under the Constitution, to carry into those territories whatever was recognized as property in the States from which they emigrated. The free States denied this doctrine, and insisted that, slavery having been abolished in Mexico, it could only be restored by positive enactment. But to remove all doubt on this point, it was contended that the acts organizing governments in these territories should contain an absolute prohibition of slavery in order to save the government from the reproach of reëstablishing it where it had long been abolished by the fundamental law.

Mr. President: It is with great reluctance that I throw myself on the indulgence of the Senate a second time in this discussion. But since I spoke, positions have been taken in the debate, and assertions made, which I cannot pass by without comment; and especially am I unwilling to be silent when the whole subject is presented to us under a new phase by the report of the committee of eight, and brings up a train of considerations having an important bearing upon the question.

Before I proceed to notice, as I shall very briefly, the provisions of the bill reported by the committee, I desire to say something on other topics which have been introduced into the discussion.

The Northern States have been repeatedly charged in this debate, and on many previous occasions, with aggression, and violations of the constitutional compact, in their action on the subject of slavery. With regard to the surrender of fugitive slaves — the case most frequently cited — it is possible that there may have been some action, or inaction, in particular States, not in strict accordance with the good faith they ought to observe in this respect. I know not how this is; but there is an effective power to legislate on this subject in Congress; and I am sure there will be no want of coöperation on our part, in carrying out the requirements of the Constitution, by providing all reasonable means for executing them.

The Senator from South Carolina,[1] in the remarks he addressed to the Senate yesterday, made repeated allusions to me in connection with the suggestion of a superior civilization in the non-slaveholding States. I have made no such suggestion. I have drawn no parallel. I have made no distinction, in this respect, between the North and the South. And in the case to which he particularly referred, and in which I spoke of "spires pointing to the skies," in language perhaps somewhat more flowery than I am accustomed to use, I expressly said that I made no distinction between the two great sections of the Union.

But this is a matter on which I shall not dwell. I am but an individual; and a misapprehension which concerns only myself is comparatively of little importance. But when the Senator, turning from me, assails the State I have the honor to represent, when the misconception does injustice to those who have given me their confidence, he wounds me in a more tender point, and I cannot pass his remarks by without a more extended notice.

Mr. President, I endeavored to get the floor yesterday when the Senator took his seat, and I made repeated attempts afterwards, in all of which I was unsuccessful. I wished to notice, at the moment and on the spot, the imputations which he had cast on the State of New York, in language I regretted to hear from any Senator on this floor.

[1] Mr. Butler.

He said a requisition had been made, some years ago, on the governor of the State by the executive of Virginia, for the surrender of persons convicted of stealing a slave within the jurisdiction of the latter State; that the governor had refused to surrender them, and that this refusal had been sustained by both branches of the legislature; and on this statement he charged New York with a want of "common honesty." Sir, these are harsh epithets — epithets which should not have been applied to us without a full knowledge of the facts. The Senator labors under a great misapprehension. The responsibility, which he charged on the State, rests upon the governor alone. The facts are these:

In 1841 a requisition was made by the executive of Virginia on the governor of New York, for three persons, charged with stealing a slave in the former State. The governor refused to surrender them, for the reason assigned in the following resolution, which was adopted by both branches of the legislature of New York early in 1842: —

"Whereas the governor of the State has refused to deliver up, on the demand of the executive authority of Virginia, Peter Johnson, Edward Smith, and Isaac Gansey, alleged fugitives from justice, charged with the crime of theft, viz: stealing a slave within the jurisdiction and against the laws of Virginia: and whereas the governor has assigned, as the reason for such refusal, that the stealing of a slave within the jurisdiction of and against the laws of Virginia, is not a felony or other crime within the meaning of the second section of the fourth article of the Constitution of the United States:

"*Resolved*, That, in the opinion of this legislature, stealing a slave within the jurisdiction and against the laws of Virginia, is a crime within the meaning of the second section of the fourth article of the Constitution of the United States.

"*Resolved*, That the governor be requested to transmit the foregoing preamble and resolution to the executive department of Virginia."

These resolutions, as I have said, passed both branches of the legislature. I am unable to state the vote; but I was then a member of the assembly, and I remember that it passed that body by a very decided majority.

Thus it seems that the legislature of New York, in both its branches, representing the people of the State in a double capacity, — for the Senate was at that time the High Court for the Correction of Errors, the highest judicial tribunal in the State, — disclaimed and condemned the act of the governor, and left the responsibility to rest on him alone. Beyond this it could not go. The act to be performed was executive, and the legislature had no control over him to compel the performance.

But the Senator did not stop here. His speech was replete with reproachful allusions to New York, too indefinite to be met with a distinct reply; and he concluded by saying that he expected nothing good from her. Sir, there have been periods, in the history of the country, when she was neither inactive nor inefficient in her efforts for the public good. In 1837, when the whole banking system throughout the Union exploded, — when the President of the Bank of the United States was putting forth manifestoes and employing the whole strength of that institution to continue the suspension of specie payments, — and when, I believe I may say, most other portions of the Union were disposed to yield, — New York stood almost alone in opposing it. She compelled her own banks to resume the discharge of their obligations under the penalty of a forfeiture of their charters; she became the centre of all that was sound in commerce and finance; and through the influence and the power of her example the country was saved from years of dishonor and pecuniary embarrassment.

In 1814, when the whole Southern coast was at the mercy of the public enemy, and portions of it ravaged and laid waste, when the administration here was too weak to defend the capital, and when the very edifice in which we sit was given to the flames by British vandalism, New York stood again almost alone and unassisted, and carried on the contest upon her own frontier chiefly with her own means. She raised money and men, and contributed to sustain the honor of our arms in a series of the most desperate engagements ever fought on this continent.

Of her institutions, social and political, I need say nothing, — the monuments she has reared to science, and to the arts, her great artificial channels of intercourse, and above all, her system of common-school education, embracing every child that is born or is brought within her limits. These are well known to all who hear me; and they say for her more than any words of mine can speak.

Less than a year ago two noble-spirited bands stood, side by side, on one of the bloodiest battle-fields of Mexico. They were led on by chivalrous men, animated by the single resolution of upholding their country's honor and their own. They were the New York and the Palmetto regiments. The blows they gave fell upon the ranks of the enemy with equal force; those they received were sustained with equal firmness. More than a third of these gallant combatants fell together. The grass, which has grown up rich and rank upon that battle-field, can tell where their blood was poured out in common streams. The noble leader of the Palmetto regiment was among the slain,[1] — borne from the field of carnage, perhaps, by the united hands of those whom he led, and those who, though coming from a distant part of the Union, fought by his side with the same devotion as his own followers. Sir, there should be something in these sacred memories to disarm reproach — at least of its injustice. Let me commend them to the calm reflection of the Senator from South Carolina, who has so deep an interest in the glory and the grief of that battle-field. He is neither ungenerous nor unjust. Let me ask him to think of these things, and say whether some good may not come from New York.

But I pass to a charge more immediately connected with the subject under discussion — the application of the principles of the ordinance of 1787 to the territories of the United

[1] Colonel Butler here alluded to was the brother of the Senator to whom Mr. Dix was replying.

States. This charge concerns the whole North; and I am ready to meet it.

In 1846 and 1847, most of the non-slaveholding States, on high considerations of moral and political principle, declared, that no new territory ought to be acquired without a fundamental provision excluding slavery. These declarations had an express and an exclusive reference to acquisitions from Mexico, where slavery had long been abolished, both by executive and constitutional acts. They amounted practically to declarations against the extension of slavery to free territory, and no more. New York did not take the lead in these declarations. The first legislative resolutions received here came from the State of Vermont, and were presented to this body on the 28th January, 1847. The New York resolutions were presented on the 6th February ensuing; those of Pennsylvania on the 8th; of Rhode Island, on the 10th; of Ohio, on the 16th; of New Hampshire and New Jersey, on the 19th; of Michigan, on the 1st of March; and of Massachusetts, on the 3d, — the last day of the session. Connecticut passed resolutions on the 24th of June; but Congress had then adjourned, and they were presented at the commencement of the subsequent session. Delaware, a slaveholding State, followed, and requested her Senators to vote for the exclusion of slavery from territory thereafter to be acquired. Here are eleven States which have passed resolutions on this question. It was a spontaneous movement on the part of the non-slaveholding States, neither led on by New York nor set on foot by her, but arising out of indications in Congress of an intention to acquire territory from Mexico, and leave it open to the introduction of slaves; and every one knows they will be carried wherever they are permitted.

On looking at the dates of these several resolutions, I find New Hampshire, Vermont, Rhode Island, and Pennsylvania preceded New York, in the order in which I name them, in acting on this subject in their respective legislatures.

Three of the small New-England States, which the Senator from Virginia, who spoke first on this question,[1] would have us believe New York was seeking to seduce, and in the end to swallow up, were actually the pioneers in this movement. Pennsylvania was next in the field. New York did but follow and sustain them in their declarations against the extension of slavery to territory in which it does not exist.

Such is the history of this movement, commencing as far back as July, 1846, almost coeval with the war with Mexico, and originating in a charge of intending to conquer territory for the purpose of planting slavery upon it. And these public declarations may perhaps be properly regarded in a twofold light, so far as motive, on the part of the legislatures, is concerned: first, to exonerate themselves from the imputation; and, second, to array their influence against such a design, if it should be entertained in any quarter.

Let me now take a somewhat larger view of this whole subject of Northern aggression. It was said, I think, by a Southern member of the Federal convention, though it may have been in Congress after the adoption of the Constitution, that no slaveholding State would thereafter be admitted into the Union; that there were eight States interested in abolishing slavery, and five interested in maintaining it, and that they would act accordingly in voting for the admission of new States. This prophecy had no foundation in truth. The members of Congress from the North have voted as freely and readily for the admission of slaveholding as for non-slaveholding States into the Union. If we look around us upon this floor, we shall find all prognostics founded upon the supposed prejudices or the unkind feeling of the North utterly falsified. Sir, there are ten Senators here representing slaveholding States formed from territory acquired since the Constitution was adopted. How many are there representing free States formed from new territory? Not a single one! But for a domestic difficulty

[1] Mr. Mason.

in Iowa, it is true, that State would have been represented here, and we should then have had two Senators from free States against ten from slaveholding States formed out of territory purchased by the common treasure and maintained by the common blood of the whole Union. We have given up the territory constituting these States to the South. We have reserved no portion of them to Northern emigration, excepting the misshapen strip of Texas north of 36° 30′, which, so far as extent and productive value are concerned, is, for all purposes of a fair and equitable division, the merest mockery. The area of these five States is equal to two thirds of the entire area of the thirteen original States. This the North has done for the maintenance of slavery, — sir, I might say for the extension of slavery and the multiplication of slaves; for this vast surface was almost uninhabited when it was acquired, and it is now filled up with a slaveholding population. There are more than half a million of slaves in these five States, not one tenth part of whom would have been there, if the right to exclude them had been insisted on. But we have stood on the ground of non-interference. Where we have found slavery, we have left it. We have not countenanced any measure of abolition or emancipation. On the contrary, we have uniformly opposed all interference with slavery in the States. With the single exception of the Louisiana territory, we have left it to spread itself over the areas on which it existed only nominally. We have almost gone, at the North, to the extreme of mobbing abolitionism, when it contemplated interference with the question of slavery in the States, and of instituting a scrutiny of the public mails to arrest the circulation of incendiary publications. And now, after all this active coöperation in the promotion of the objects and interests of the slaveholding States, how are we met? By charges of aggression, of hostility, and of violating the constitutional compact.

Sir, we stand firmly upon the compromises of the Constitution. We have ever done so. We shall continue to do so. We have gone further. We have opposed all interference by Congress with slavery in the District of Columbia, over which Congress is empowered by the Constitution to "exercise exclusive legislation in all cases whatsoever." Beyond this we cannot go. I deny that any compromise in framing the Constitution, or any guaranty arising under its provisions, extends, or was designed to extend, to the regulation of slavery in the territories. What were the compromises of the Constitution? They were three: 1. That the small States should be equally represented in the Senate with the large States; 2. That the slave population in the States should constitute a part of the basis of representation in Congress; 3. That the importation of slaves into the States then existing should not be prohibited prior to 1808. These were the three great compromises on which the adoption of the Constitution may be considered as having turned. In settling them, some reference was naturally had to the distribution and regulation of the powers vested in the Federal government and reserved to the States and the people respectively.

Now, sir, what was the security sought for by the South in the adoption of these compromises? Was it that Congress should impose no restriction on the extension of slavery to the territories? No, sir. That power I have no doubt was left, so far as it was contemplated at all, to be exercised by Congress, according to its own views of humanity and justice. I humbly think this construction sustained by what I said on a former occasion. It is shown also by the deed of the cession by North Carolina of western territory now constituting the State of Tennessee, in which it was provided, "that no regulations made, or to be made, by Congress shall tend to emancipate slaves," — a prohibition implying a right to regulate, restrict, and exclude them.

The Senator from Florida[1] read to the Senate yesterday

[1] Mr. Westcott

the *fac-simile* of an original paper found among the manuscripts of Mr. Monroe, and in his handwriting, by which it appears, that when the Missouri compromise act, as it is called, was passed, he took the opinions of the members of his Cabinet, in writing, in respect to the constitutionality of that act. The Senator from South Carolina[1] was one of the Cabinet; and as I took, and endeavored to sustain, on a late occasion, the position that Congress possesses the right to prohibit slavery in the territories of the United States, I am naturally desirous of fortifying it with all the authority I can command; and I shall be particularly gratified, if it shall be found that the distinguished Senator alluded to, though now denying the right, was then in favor of it. I will read to the Senate all of this paper which relates to the subject: —

(From Mr. Monroe's manuscripts.) — A paper indorsed "*Interrogatories, Missouri; March* 4, 1820. *To the Heads of Departments and Attorney-General:*"

Questions (on opposite page):

"Has Congress a right, under the powers vested in it by the Constitution, to make a regulation prohibiting slavery in a Territory?

"Is the eighth section of the act which passed both Houses on the 3d instant, for the admission of Missouri into the Union, consistent with the Constitution?"

With the above is the original draught of the following letter, in President Monroe's handwriting, on half a sheet of paper, but not indorsed or addressed to any one. There are interlineations, but the text, as left by the writer, is as follows: —

"DEAR SIR: The question which lately agitated Congress and the public has been settled, as you have seen, by the passage of an act for the admission of Missouri as a State, unrestrained, and Arkansas likewise, when it reaches maturity, and the establishment of the 36° 30′ north latitude as a line, north of which slavery is prohibited, and permitted to the south. I took the opinion, in writing, of the Administration as to the constitutionality of restraining Territories, [*and the vote of every member was unanimous and*[2]] which was explicit in favor

[1] Mr. Calhoun. [2] The words in Italics are erased in the original draught.

of it, and as it was that the 8th section of the act was applicable to Territories only, and not to States when they should be admitted into the Union. On this latter point I had at first some doubt; but the opinion of others, whose opinions were entitled to weight with me, supported by the sense in which it was viewed by all who voted on the subject in Congress, as will appear by the Journals, satisfied me respecting it."

This letter has been supposed to have been written to General Jackson, though there is no evidence of the fact.

Mr. Foote. Were these interrogatories sent? or was it merely a statement for his own private convenience?

It is impossible to say, except so far as the paper may be considered as indicating the use made of them. I state the facts as they have been related to me. The paper was found among Mr. Monroe's manuscripts, and is in his handwriting. It was read to the Senate yesterday by the Senator from Florida,[1] for another purpose, and the evidence of its authenticity I understand to be in his possession.

Mr. Calhoun. If the Senator will give way, it will be perhaps better that I make a statement at once respecting this subject, as far as my recollection will serve me. During the whole period of Mr. Monroe's administration, I remember no occasion on which the members of his administration gave written opinions. I have an impression — though not a very distinct one — that on one occasion they were required to give written opinions; but for some reason, not now recollected, the request was not carried into effect. He was decidedly opposed to the imposition of any restriction on the admission of Missouri into the Union, and I am strongly of the impression that he was opposed in feeling to what was called the Missouri compromise.

Mr. Johnson, of Maryland. Is this the original letter?

I understand it to be a *fac-simile* of the original. As a long period (nearly thirty years) has elapsed since the act to admit Missouri into the Union was passed, it is quite natural that the Senator from South Carolina should have forgotten the circumstances attending the discussion of it in the Cabinet. Having heard, some days ago, of the existence of such a paper, and being very desirous of ascertaining the facts, I wrote to Mr. Charles Francis Adams, of

[1] Mr. Westcott.

Boston, a son of the late ex-President, inquiring of him if his father's diary contained anything on the subject. In reply to my inquiry, I received an extract from the diary of the father, certified by the son, which I will now read, and which confirms fully the statement contained in Mr. Monroe's letter:

Extracts from the Diary of John Quincy Adams.

"MARCH 3, 1820. — When I came this day to my office, I found there a note requesting me to call at one o'clock at the President's House. It was then one, and I immediately went over. He expected that the two bills, for the admission of Maine and to enable Missouri to make a constitution, would have been brought to him for his signature; and he had summoned all the members of the Administration to ask their opinions in writing, to be deposited in the Department of State, upon two questions: 1, Whether Congress had a constitutional right to prohibit slavery in a Territory? and 2, Whether the 8th section of the Missouri bill (which interdicts slavery *forever* in the territory north of 36½ latitude) was applicable only to the territorial state, or would extend to it after it should become a State? As to the first question, it was unanimously agreed that Congress have the power to prohibit slavery in the Territories."

This is the first extract; and before I proceed to the others, I will state that, in respect to the second question, there was a diversity of opinion, — Mr. Adams contending that a State would be bound by such a prohibition after its admission into the Union, and the other members of the Cabinet, that it was only operative during the territorial term. In order to secure unanimity in the answers, the second question was modified, as will appear by the remaining extracts which I proceed to give: —

"MARCH 5. — The President sent me yesterday the two questions in writing, upon which he desired to have answers in writing, to be deposited in the Department of State. He wrote me that it would be in time, if he should have the answers to-morrow. The first question is in general terms, as it was stated at the meeting on Friday. The second was modified to an inquiry whether the 8th section of the Missouri bill is consistent with the Constitution. To this I can without hesitation answer by a simple affirmative, and so after some reflection I concluded to answer both. . . . .

"MARCH 6. . . . . I took to the President's my answers to his two constitutional questions, and he desired me to have them deposited in the department, together with those of the other members of the Administration. They differed only as they assigned their reason for thinking the 8th section of the Missouri bill consistent with the Constitution, because they considered it as only applying to the territorial term; and I barely gave my opinion, without assigning for it any explanatory reason. The President signed the Missouri bill this morning."

These extracts are certified to be

"a true copy from the original by me,

"CHARLES FRANCIS ADAMS."

Mr. CALHOUN. Has any search been made in the State Department for these written opinions?

The State Department has been examined, — how thoroughly I do not know, — but they have not been found.

Mr. WESTCOTT. I made an examination, as I stated yesterday, myself, but could find none. This letter is in Mr. Monroe's handwriting, and from its tenor is supposed to have been intended to be addressed to General Jackson. I understand that, upon examination of General Jackson's papers, a letter was found from Mr. Monroe, containing everything which is contained in this draught, except that part which relates to the action of the Cabinet. The letter was also dated the same day. I presume, therefore, that, upon writing the letter to General Jackson, ultimately, unless it was intended for some one else, Mr. Monroe left out that portion relating to the action of the Cabinet in relation to the "Missouri compromise."

I have examined the letter referred to, as addressed to General Jackson, and find that it was written in 1821, while the paper containing the interrogatories was dated the 4th of March, 1820; and the former has only two of the last paragraphs of the letter before us; all the rest being different.

Mr. CALHOUN. If any written opinion was ever given by me, it has entirely escaped my memory; and I feel satisfied, if ever given, it was very little more than an assent or dissent to the course adopted by the Administration. Mr. Adams had the advantage of keeping a diary, which no doubt may be relied upon, as far as he is individually concerned; but which, of course, is liable to mistakes, as far as it represents the views and acts of others. In this case there may be some explanation, if all the facts were known, which would reconcile his statement with my recollection. But of one thing I feel perfectly sure, that I could never have directed my attention and formed an opinion on so important a subject, as a member of his Cabinet, and reduced it to writing, for the purpose of being preserved, without recollecting it.

Mr. JOHNSON, of Maryland, was understood to say, that, on examining the letter, he did not think it sustained the fact the Senator from New York was endeavoring to prove. He observed that Mr. Monroe had first stated that the opinion of the Administration was *unanimous*, and that he had erased the word unanimous, and substituted the word *explicit*, which had quite a different meaning.

Mr. CALHOUN. I feel justified in saying, from all the circumstances of this case, including the facts stated by the Senator from Maryland, and the absence of any written opinion on the file of the State Department, that, notwithstanding the certificate from Mr. Adams's diary, no such opinions were given as it states. There is some mistake about it, but how it originated I am at a loss to conceive. Perhaps it may be explained by the vague impression, as I have stated, on my mind, that the opinions were called for, but never formally given in writing, at least not beyond a mere assent or dissent as to the course ultimately adopted. I know well all about the compromise; the cause which led to it, and the reason why, that the Northern men who voted against it were universally sacrificed for so doing. It is quite a mistake, as some suppose, that they were sacrificed for voting for the compromise. The very reverse is the case. The cause I will proceed to state: During the session of the compromise, Mr. Lowndes and myself resided together. He was a member of the House of Representatives, and I was Secretary of War. We both felt the magnitude of the subject. Missouri, at the preceding session, had presented herself for admission as a member of the Union. She had formed a constitution and government, in accordance with an act of Congress. Her admission was refused on the ground that her constitution admitted of slavery; and she was remanded back to have the objectionable provision expunged. She refused to comply with the requisition, and at the next session again knocked at the door of Congress for admission, with her constitution as it originally stood. This gave rise to one of the most agitating discussions that ever occurred in Congress. The subject was one of repeated conversation between Mr. Lowndes and myself. The question was, what was to be done, and what would be the consequence if she was not admitted? After full reflection, we both agreed that Missouri was a State made so by a regular process of law, and never could be remanded back to the territorial condition. Such being the case, we also agreed that the only question was, whether she should be a State in or out of the Union? and it was for Congress to decide which position she should occupy. My friend made one of his able and lucid speeches on the occasion; but whether it has been preserved or not, I am not able to say. It carried conviction to the minds of all, and in fact settled the question. The question was narrowed down to a single point. All saw that if Missouri was not admitted, she would remain an independent state on the west bank of the Mississippi, and would become the nucleus of a new confederation of states extending over the whole of Louisiana. None were willing to contribute to such a result; and the only question that remained with the Northern members who had opposed her admission was, to devise some means of escaping from the awkward dilemma in which they found themselves. To back out or compromise, were the only alternatives left; and the latter was eagerly seized to avoid the disgrace of the former, — so eagerly, that all who opposed it at the North were considered traitors to that section of the Union, and sacrificed for their votes.

Mr. FOOTE. The gentleman referred to, and from whose journal an extract has been read, as is well known, has been always regarded as a most violent partisan of the peculiar views he held in relation to this subject. I beg leave most respectfully to inquire of the honorable Senator from New York, whether this statement or extract read has been sworn to or not?

The statement was, as I have said, taken from the diary of Mr. Adams, certified, but not sworn to, by his son, a gentleman of the highest respectability.

I do not intend to enter into any discussion concerning the Missouri compromise, or the testimony I have presented. I leave it to speak for itself, and to others to say how far it shall be considered to outweigh the recollections of the Senator from South Carolina. I will only add, that there is the strongest possible coincidence between Mr. Monroe's letter and Mr. Adams's diary in all the important facts. Both state the questions to have been "in writing"; both show that they were submitted in the shape in which they were to be answered, on the 4th of March, 1820. The identity of the questions is another striking coincidence. The only material variation is that suggested by the Senator from Maryland. Mr. Adams states, that the opinion of the members of the Cabinet was "unanimous" in favor of the power of Congress to prohibit slavery in the territories of the

United States. Mr. Monroe wrote "unanimous" in the first instance, and then substituted "explicit," — an alteration he might very naturally have made, on reflection, in writing to a friend, in order to avoid giving a clue to the opinions of individual members of his administration. The answers were very brief, as Mr. Adams shows; but from the manner in which the questions were drawn, the answers, whether affirmative or negative, must either have asserted or denied the constitutional power of Congress to prohibit slavery in the territories. But all this I am willing to submit to the candid judgment of others.

Let me now cite a few of the remarks made in the Federal convention on the subject of slavery and slave representation. On the 12th of July, Mr. Randolph, of Virginia, said, "That express security ought to be provided for including slaves in the ratio of representation. He lamented that such a species of property existed; but as it did exist, the holders of it would require this security. It was perceived that the design was entertained by some of excluding slaves altogether; the legislature, therefore, ought not to be left at liberty."

In the convention of Virginia, by which the Constitution was ratified, Governor Randolph entered into an elaborate argument to show that Congress had no right to abolish slavery in the States. It was feared that under the power of prohibiting the slave-trade, or under the power to regulate commerce, or under some implied power, slavery within the limits of the States might be interfered with by Congress.

On the 13th of July, Mr. Butler, of South Carolina, said: "The security the Southern States want is, that their negroes may not be taken from them, which some gentlemen within or without doors have a very good mind to do."

This was the tenor of the discussions in the State conventions by which the Constitution was ratified. They looked to security from abolition or emancipation by Congress within their own limits. Extension of slavery beyond their limits was hardly thought of; and I have no hesitation in saying, from the tone of the debates, that, if it had been fully discussed, it would have been to brand it with general disapprobation.

On the 22d of August, a very full and interesting debate arose in the Federal convention on the question of prohibiting the importation of slaves. The only objects contended for in any quarter were, the right to import them, and an exemption of the States from all interference with slavery within their own limits on the part of the Federal government. It was generally conceded, except by the extreme South, that slavery would ultimately be abolished. And yet the slave population has gone on steadily increasing, from 600,000 to 3,000,000 of souls; and now we are engaged in a struggle to enlarge the area of slavery, or to prevent its exclusion from territory in which it does not exist.

Mr. Calhoun. I must beg the Senator from New York to state me more correctly. We are not contending for the extension of the area of slavery, and if he places us upon that ground, he places us in a very false position. What we do contend for is, that the Southern States, as members of our Union, are entitled to equal rights and equal dignity, in every respect, with the northern; and that there is nothing in the Constitution to deprive us of this equality, in consequence of being slaveholders.

The Senator contends for the right of carrying slaves into the territories. I understand this to be an extension of slavery, and with all deference to him, I can call it by no other name.

In connection with this subject, we were asked by the Senator from Virginia, whether any one believes that State would ever have come into the Union, if the right to exclude slaves from the territories had been insisted on? I answer, yes; and on the strength of the known opinions of her delegates in the convention.

Mr. Madison would not consent "to admit in the Constitution the idea that there could be property in men." He was unwilling to postpone the prohibition of the slave-trade twenty years. "So long a term," he added, "will be more dishonorable to the American character than to say nothing about it in the Constitution." His language and his action then, and on all occasions, were in favor of the restriction of slavery, and not in favor of its extension. The opinion of General Washington, the President of the convention, on the subject of slavery, is well known. I have already referred to the opinion of Mr. Randolph. Colonel Mason was still more decided and explicit. His language may be quoted now with the more effect, when those who have come after him differ with him so widely in opinion: —

"This infernal traffic originated in the avarice of British merchants. The British government constantly checked the attempts of Virginia to put a stop to it. The present question concerns not the importing States alone, but the whole Union. The evil of having slaves was experienced during the late war. Had slaves been treated as they might have been by the enemy, they would have proved dangerous instruments in their hands; but their folly dealt by the slaves as it did by the Tories. . . . . . Maryland and Virginia (he said) had already prohibited the importation of slaves expressly; North Carolina had done the same in substance. All this would be in vain, if South Carolina and Georgia be at liberty to import. The western people are already calling out for slaves for their new lands, and will fill that country with slaves if they can be got through South Carolina and Georgia. Slavery discourages arts and manufactures. The poor despise labor, when performed by slaves: they prevent the emigration of whites who really enrich and strengthen a country. . . . . . As to the States being in possession of the right to import, this was the case with many other rights now to be properly given up. He held it essential, in every point of view, that the general government should have power to prevent the increase of slavery."

To this declaration in the Federal convention, I might add, that, in the convention of Virginia, he alleged, as one of the objections to the Constitution, that it continued the slave-trade for twenty-two years.

The Senator from Virginia wears, with equal dignity and grace, the name of the illustrious statesman I have quoted. It is quite probable that there is a closer bond of connection between them.[1] But how different is their language, and the causes they have espoused, at the distance of more than half a century from each other! The patriot of the revolution denounced the British government for forcing slaves upon Virginia against her remonstrances. The Senator from that State is contending here, in her name, for the right to carry slaves into Oregon, against the wishes and prohibitions of the inhabitants.

But to return from this digression. The four distinguished individuals I have named constituted a majority of the delegation from Virginia; and I believe I am authorized, from their avowed opinions, to say, that if there had been a positive provision in the Constitution authorizing Congress to prohibit the introduction of slaves into territories thereafter to be acquired, it would not only not have been deemed an impediment to the accession of Virginia to the Union, but that it would have met their decided approbation. But in this case, as in many others, the framers of the Constitution fell far short of the reality, when they looked forward to the future progress of the country. The period in which they lived was enveloped in uncertainty and doubt; and it was only reserved to a few of the more sanguine to obtain some partial glimpses of the prosperity and fame to which their country was destined. It was the very limited foreknowledge of her growth and extension, which left so many of the exigencies we have met unprovided for by direct and positive regulation.

Mr. President, it was chiefly in the school of Virginia that the little knowledge I possess of the theory of our institutions, and of the principles of political liberty and justice, was acquired. I have been accustomed to regard Mr. Jefferson as a standard, to which we might safely refer for the settlement of most questions of political power and duty: and it is with something more than ordinary pain

[1] Mr. Dix subsequently ascertained that the Senator was a grandson of Colonel Mason.

and regret that I have seen his principles assailed, and his acts repudiated and condemned.

I was not a little surprised, too, to hear the Senator from Virginia rest the legal justification of slavery upon the right of conquest, and its introduction into that State during her colonial dependence on the common law of England. I had supposed that Blackstone had furnished sufficient evidence of the mistaken pretensions which had been set up on both these foundations to support the fabric of slavery in the American colonies and their successors, the States. I hold in my hand a volume of the English commentator, edited by St. George Tucker, who was a professor of law in the University of William and Mary, and one of the judges of the general court of Virginia. To this volume is appended an article or tract written by him, "On the state of Slavery in Virginia." Sir, it is in this edition of the writings of the great English commentator that many of us of the North have studied the principles of English law, and from the tracts, which are appended to the several volumes, that we have learned to consider Virginia as the great enemy of slavery extension. I propose to read a few extracts from this volume, to show how widely different are the grounds now assumed and those on which the young men of Virginia, and of the country generally, were instructed, half a century ago, in the principles of political liberty and justice.

And, first, as to the origin of slavery. Judge Tucker quotes largely from Blackstone, denying that slavery rests either upon the law of nations, by which, according to Justinian, "one man is made subject to another contrary to nature," or upon captivity or conquest, or upon the civil law, by which a man may suffer himself to be sold "for the sake of sharing the price given for him." He then proceeds: —

"Thus, by the most clear, manly, and convincing reasoning, does this excellent author refute every claim upon which the practice of slavery is founded, or by which it has been supposed to be justified, at least in modern times. But were we even to admit, that a captive taken in a *just war* might by his conqueror be reduced to a state of slavery, this could not justify the claim of Europeans to reduce the natives of Africa to that state. It is a melancholy, though well-known fact, that, in order to furnish supplies of those unhappy people for the purposes of the slave-trade, the Europeans have constantly, by the most insidious (I had almost said infernal) arts, fomented a kind of perpetual warfare among the ignorant and miserable people of Africa; and instances have not been wanting where, by the most shameful breach of faith, they have trepanned and made slaves of the sellers as well as the sold. That such horrid practices have been sanctioned by civilized nations; that a nation ardent in the cause of liberty, and enjoying its blessings in the fullest extent, can continue to vindicate a right established upon such a foundation; that a people who have declared 'That all men are by nature equally free and independent,' [1] and have made this declaration the first article in the formation of their government, should in defiance of so sacred a truth, recognized by themselves in so solemn a manner, and on so important an occasion, tolerate a practice incompatible therewith, — is such an evidence of the weakness and inconsistency of human nature, as every man who hath a spark of patriotic fire in his bosom must wish to see removed from his own country. If ever there was a cause, if ever an occasion, in which all hearts should be united, every nerve strained, and every power exerted, surely the restoration of human nature to its inalienable right, is such. Whatever obstacles, therefore, may hitherto have retarded the attempt, he that can appreciate the honor and happiness of his country will think it time that we should attempt to surmount them."

Such, according to Judge Tucker, is the foundation on which slavery in Virginia and in the other States rests, — not on conquest, not on any right derived from legitimate warfare, but on violence and treachery. I do not cite this authority to create prejudice of any sort. My only purpose is to meet arguments on the other side.

The common law of England utterly repudiated slavery. To use the language of one of her great commentators, "The law of England abhors, and will not endure the existence of, slavery within this nation." In the colonies it was introduced by virtue of the prerogative of the crown, as

[1] Virginia Bill of Rights, art. 1.

the fountain of chartered rights, and as the arbiter of commerce. Nothing, I believe, is better settled in English law than this. Slavery was at one time, it is true, regulated by act of Parliament, rather by recognizing the laws of the colonies than by original legislation; but the common law always rejected it as unnatural and unjust.

Virginia uniformly acted in accordance with the elevated sentiments expressed by Judge Tucker. She imposed duties on slaves brought within her limits as early as 1699, — one hundred and fifty years ago. In 1759, she imposed a duty of 20 per cent. on all slaves imported from Maryland, North Carolina, or other places in America. In 1772, she petitioned the King of England to allow her to prohibit the importation of slaves from Africa. I quote from the petition: —

"The importation of slaves into the colonies from the coast of Africa hath long been considered as a trade of great inhumanity, and under its *present encouragement* we have too much reason to fear *will endanger the very existence* of your Majesty's American dominions.

"We are sensible that some of your Majesty's subjects of Great Britain may reap emoluments from this sort of traffic; but when we consider that it greatly retards the settlement of the colonies with more useful inhabitants, and may, in time, have the most destructive influence, we presume to hope, that the *interest of a few* will be disregarded, when placed in competition with the security and happiness of such numbers of your Majesty's dutiful and loyal subjects.

"Deeply impressed with these sentiments, we most humbly beseech your Majesty to *remove all those restraints* on your Majesty's governors of this colony, *which inhibit their assenting to such laws as might check* so very pernicious a commerce."

Judge Tucker says: —

"This petition produced no effect, as appears from the first clause of our CONSTITUTION, where, among acts of misrule, 'the inhuman use of the royal negative,' in refusing us permission to exclude slaves from us by law, is enumerated among the reasons for *separating from Great Britain.*"

The clause in the constitution of Virginia is in these words: —

"Whereas, George the Third, King of Great Britain and Ireland, and Elector of Hanover, heretofore intrusted with the exercise of the kingly office in this Government, hath endeavored to pervert the same into a detestable and insupportable tyranny, putting his negative on laws the most wholesome and necessary for the public good;" [Here follows an enumeration of other acts;] by prompting our negroes to rise in arms against us, — those very negroes whom, by an inhuman use of his negative, he hath refused us permission to exclude by law."

Judge Tucker adds: —

"The wishes of the people of this colony were not sufficient to counterbalance the interest of the English merchants trading to Africa, and it is probable, that, however disposed to put a stop to so infamous a traffic by law, we should never have been able to effect it, so long as we might have continued dependent on the British government; an object sufficient of itself to justify revolution."

And now, sir, I ask, will Virginia insist on extending to other communities an evil which she deplored, and thus be guilty of an act which she considered, when done by the British king, as a sufficient justification of revolution, — an act enumerated in the first clause of her constitution among the reasons for separating from Great Britain? Mr. Jefferson, as we all know, introduced into the original draught of the Declaration of Independence a clause reprobating the conduct of the British king in forcing slaves upon the American colonies; but it was struck out, to use his own language, "in complaisance to South Carolina and Georgia, who had never attempted to restrain the importation of slaves, and who, on the contrary, still wished to continue it." Sir, are we willing to do towards other communities dependent on us what we condemned in the British king, — what we relied on as one of the grounds of our justification in appealing to the sword for a vindication of our rights and the assertion of our independence? What matters it to the inhabitants of Oregon, or New Mexico, or California, whether slaves are introduced from Africa or from the States of the Union in which they are bred? Sir, let us abstain from injustice and wrong. If we insist on carrying slaves to those territories, — if the arm of the public authority is employed, directly or indirectly, for the purpose of placing them there, and in uprooting, in two of the territories, the fundamental law of Mexico, which declares slavery to be forever prohibited, — it would not be surprising, when those distant communities shall in the progress of events have grown to manhood, if they should declare themselves "free and independent," and among the causes of the separation charge us, as we charged the British king, with forcing slavery upon them against their wishes and their remonstrances. If this was a just cause of separation for us, why would it not be so for them? God forbid that history should record such a passage as this, to confound and shame our descendants!

It has been said, that this territory should be divided, so that a portion of it may be left open to the introduction of slaves; that it has been acquired by the common treasure and the common blood of the whole Union, and that it would be unjust to exclude a portion of the citizens of the Union from it.

In the first place, I do not admit that there would be any exclusion if slavery were prohibited. It would be open to every freeman in the community. But, even on the score of an equitable division, — if the propriety of such a division can be admitted, when the question is, whether laws abolishing slavery shall be abrogated, — I hold that the territory should be, as it now is, free. When Florida was acquired, we did not ask that any portion of it should be set apart for immigration from the free States. We claimed no division. We gave it all up to the South. And yet it was purchased by the common blood and the common treasure of the whole Union. The soil of Florida has been crimsoned by the blood, and whitened by the bones of Northern men sacrificed in the wars waged to secure it. Including the price paid for it, it has drawn forty millions of dollars from the public treasury, to be reimbursed, for the most part, by the toil and contributions of the North. What have we received in return on this principle of an equitable division? Nothing; nothing.

It is the same with Texas. It is true, the Missouri compromise line was drawn across that State, leaving to the north of it a strip, narrow, misshapen, barren, and broken, for northern immigration. For all purposes of an equitable division, it would have been a deception, if it had been pretended. Why, sir, this very war, which has just terminated, grew out of the annexation of Texas. It is part and parcel of the acquisition. What will it cost? At least eighty millions of dollars, when arrears are liquidated, bounty lands set apart, and pensions fully paid. For this acquisition the North has contributed its full share in blood, and, from its greater ability for consumption, will pay the largest portion of the treasure by which it has been purchased. Taking Texas into the account, with its three hundred thousand square miles, and its capacity for production, I hold that an equitable division — if the propriety of it were to be conceded — should leave California and New Mexico free.

Let us look at the money account, and see how that stands. Florida has cost us forty millions of dollars, and Texas eighty millions. For New Mexico and California we are to pay, including claims of our own citizens, twenty millions. Deduct this from the other, and we have a balance of one hundred millions, which we have paid for new territory given up wholly to the South. The blood, the treasure, the surface, — everything taken into the account, — there is an overwhelming balance in favor of the North; and on every principle we are entitled to New Mexico and California. But, sir, I will not put it on this narrow ground. I hold, that, if we acquire territory which is free, it should remain so, and this on high principle, — that the United States shall not be instrumental to the extension of slavery, and stand before the world, in this age of intellectual light and of moral elevation, in the attitude of ministering to the propagation of an evil for the presence of which among us we can only justify ourselves by necessity.

There is one argument on the other side against restriction, — if it may not rather be termed a complaint, or an accusation, — which I cannot pass by in silence. Gentlemen have represented us, who oppose the extension of slavery, as intending to hem their slaves in, to "pen them up," to surround them with "walls of circumvallation," to crowd them together and leave them to perish; and we have been assailed with such outbursts of eloquent indignation as it has never before been my pleasure to hear on this floor. Pens and walls of circumvallation! These are expressive forms of speech, Mr. President. They are not ungrateful to the imagination. They combine the familiar associations of rural economy with those which belong to the nobler occupation of arms. They are redolent of the classics — the *gratum opus agricolis*, and the *nunc horrentia Martis arma*. Why, sir, an innocent by-stander might have supposed, from the expressions of horror and disgust with which we have been visited, that we had devised, in good earnest, some unnatural scheme for penning up or walling in this unfortunate African race. Now, if gentlemen will consider the facts, I think they will find not the slightest occasion for any exuberance of feeling, either in its higher phases of indignant passion, or in its lower tones of commiseration and sympathy. What is the area of the slaveholding States? What is the size of the enclosure in which the negro race is to be shut up by those who oppose the extension of slavery? More than nine hundred thousand square miles, — more than the entire surface of France, Spain, Portugal, Germany proper, Prussia, Switzerland, and Italy, combined, — nearly equal to two thirds of the entire surface of Europe, Russia excluded, — a greater area than that which, in the eastern hemisphere, sustains a population of one hundred and fifty millions of souls! Let us turn to the non-slaveholding States, and see how their surface compares with that of the slaveholding. What is their area, Mr. President? But little more than four hundred thousand square miles, — not half the geographical extent of the slaveholding. Thus, with an area not half as great as that of the slaveholding States, the free States are charged with aggression and injustice, because they will not consent to the extension of slavery beyond its present limits into districts of country in which it does not exist. And, what is more extraordinary, we are accused of inhumanity because we propose, to use the language of our accusers, "to pen up" the African race on an area nearly a million of square miles in extent! Really, this subject is hardly susceptible of being treated with becoming gravity; and I dismiss it.

Let me now look a moment at the provisions of this bill, so far as they profess to offer us a compromise of the question of slavery in the territories. And here I desire to say, that I intend no reflection upon the conduct or motives of the committee, collectively or individually. I deal only with the measure; but of that I must speak freely and frankly.

There are but two direct references to slavery in the bill: they are contained in the twenty-sixth and thirty-third sections, and both are to the same purport. They prohibit the territorial governments of California and New Mexico from legislating on the subject.

There is one indirect reference to slavery. It is contained in the twelfth section of the bill, which declares the laws now in force in Oregon to be valid and operative for three months after the legislative assembly meets; and, as we all know, one of these laws prohibits slavery.

These, then, are the great provisions of this bill. They leave the whole of New Mexico and California open to the introduction of slaves, and prohibit the territorial governments from legislating on the subject, even if disposed to legislate for their exclusion. And, in consideration of this abandonment of all the territory we have acquired from Mexico to slavery, we have received from the hands of the committee the boon of freedom for three months in Oregon.

This is the great concession to the non-slaveholding States; and this is presented to us as a compromise, — a compromise which surrenders everything on one side, and concedes nothing on the other. Let me pursue this subject, by examining some of the propositions with which this bill was ushered into the Senate Chamber by the Senator from Delaware,[1] as chairman of the committee of eight. They are so extraordinary that I cannot forbear to pay them a passing notice. I hold them to be a true exposition of the meaning and the object of the bill by the one who, of all others, is best qualified to interpret it, — the one by whom it was drawn. I give more credence to his interpretation of it because, on a careful examination, I can put no other construction on it myself.

The first proposition is this (I read from his remarks): —

> "While it was admitted on all sides that by far the greatest portion of the Territories was properly adapted to free labor, and would necessarily be free soil forever, yet it was also, *with equal unanimity, conceded* that there was a portion of it where *free labor* could never be introduced, owing to the climate and the peculiar productions of that portion."

I consider this proposition unsound in all its parts. In the first place, our own experience teaches us that slaves will be carried wherever they are permitted to go; that no soil will be free where they are not excluded by law. They were taken into the territory northwest of the Ohio river. There are now five slaveholding States north of 36° 30′: Missouri, Maryland, Delaware, Virginia, and Kentucky. On a former occasion, I said that slaves would be valuable in any part of the country, in the early stages of settlement, where the demand for labor is urgent. And I have no hesitation in saying, that, if this bill passes both Houses, and becomes a law, they will be carried into every part of New Mexico and California which is habitable. This will be its practical effect. Even if the northern portion shall in

[1] Mr. Clayton.

future years abolish slavery, it will be left with a black population, — a burden and an encumbrance to the white race, and an impediment to its moral and physical development.

But the latter part of the proposition is far more objectionable than the first; and I regret exceedingly to hear that it was conceded with unanimity. I deny that there is any portion of these territories where free labor can never be introduced. I deny that there is any portion of the globe which nature designed for slavery. It would be an impeachment of the character and the purposes of the great Author of the Universe to concede that there is any portion of the earth in which we cannot "stand fast in the liberty" wherewith God has made us free. I deny that there is any portion of Oregon, or New Mexico, or California, to the cultivation of which slave labor is indispensable. The suggestion is as unsound in fact as it is in philosophy. I do not admit that there is any portion of those territories to which African, much less slave labor, is indispensable. There is no portion of it less suited to white labor than the southern portion of Spain,—none which has a more fiery sun than Andalusia,—where slavery does not exist. Besides, there is a free Indian population, natives of the climate, willing to work, singularly docile, and adequate to all the demands for labor for years to come.

I regret exceedingly to have heard the admission that slave labor is necessary in these territories. But I have ceased to be surprised at anything from any quarter. I have heard one of the principles of the Declaration of Independence impugned, and its author charged with error in advocating the exclusion of slavery from the territories of the United States. I have heard negro slavery defended as founded in right, as justified by the laws of God, and lauded as "the mildest species of bondage which labor ever bore to capital on the face of the globe." I confess I have been astonished at these declarations, so different from all I have heard and read of the sentiments of the great men of the

Republic from its foundation to the present day. I have been taught, and taught by the South, to regard slavery as an evil to be got rid of, and not as a good to be communicated to other communities.

The Senator from Delaware, after proposing to organize governments for California and New Mexico, by the appointment of a governor, secretary, and judges, to compose a temporary legislature, without the power to legislate on the subject of slavery, proceeds: "It was thought that by this means Congress would avoid the decision of this distracting question, leaving it to be settled by the silent operation of the Constitution itself; and that, in case Congress should refuse to touch the subject, the country would be slaveholding only where, by the laws of nature, slave labor was effective, and free labor could not maintain itself!"

This proposition is subject to the great and fundamental objection I have taken to the other. It contains a direct admission, that by the laws of nature a portion of the country or territory will be slaveholding. I deny that nature has any such law. It is the law of man, doing violence to all the dictates of nature, that makes a country slaveholding, either by its own voluntary act, or by the act of others forcing slavery upon it.

But the chief and radical objection is, that it contains a further admission that the territories are to be left open to the introduction of slaves,—that they will be slaveholding wherever slaves can be carried. It is an admission that the "silent operation of the Constitution" will be to make the country slaveholding where slave labor will be effective. I consider it an entire abandonment of northern ground. What is the ground taken by the North? It is, that slavery shall be prohibited in the territories. The act contains no such prohibition. It is a complete surrender to the theories and claims of our friends of the South. All they contend for is, that the territories shall be open, and they left to the unrestricted enjoyment of the right they assert to carry their slaves into any territory belonging to the United States. It is the very extent of their demand. It leaves nothing for them to ask or desire. The distinguished Senator from South Carolina[1] commenced his speech with the assertion that all the South desired was — no legislation. This has been conceded — fully conceded. Indeed, something more has been given up. It was not enough to yield all that was asked. The territorial government is prohibited from legislating on the subject of slavery. This I should not object to, constituted as that government is likely to be, but for a single consideration: as a precedent, it may be of importance. It will constitute an argument in favor of extending the same prohibition to the legislative assemblies, when they shall be hereafter created. But I will not look beyond the present. I take it as it is. The territorial government is prohibited from legislating; Congress does not legislate; and slavery will extend itself over the whole of New Mexico and California. It will enter the great basin; it will take possession of the maritime valley of California — the American Italy; and when planted there, neither you, sir, nor I, nor our children, will live to see it eradicated.

And, with this assurance, which no man can reasonably doubt, we are invited to leave this matter "to the silent operation of the Constitution"; when we all know that the Constitution does no more than vest in Congress the power to legislate for the territories. It is an invitation to us to leave this power unexercised, and to let slavery extend itself wherever self-interest can carry it. It is the same argument that was used in the Federal convention against the abolition of the slave-trade. Our fathers were invited to leave the whole subject to the laws of nature. It is the argument which has been employed on all occasions to resist every attempt to prevent the extension of slavery. It was urged against restrictions upon Louisiana, against restrictions upon the territory northwest of the Ohio river, against

[1] Mr. Calhoun.

restrictions upon the territory west and northwest of the Mississippi, when Missouri was admitted into the Union. Did those who have gone before us yield to these persuasions of self-interest? No, sir; they refused to accede to them. They prohibited the introduction of slaves into the territories. They considered it as a political question, proper only to be decided by themselves, and not to be shuffled off upon the judiciary. They met the responsibility like men, and decided it according to the dictates of duty and right. This scheme of the committee, so far as it professes to be a compromise, secures nothing to the North. To the South it yields up all. It concedes all that is asked, all that is desired. It imposes no restrictions; it sets up no barrier; it leaves the whole field open to be entered, and taken possession of, unresisted and unopposed. It is an unconditional surrender; it has not even the grace of a capitulation upon terms.

If gentlemen suppose this proposition will calm the prevailing excitement, they are greatly mistaken. What does it contain calculated to allay agitation in the North? Does it concede anything to the non-slaveholding States? No, sir. It excludes slavery nowhere — not even in Oregon. It only continues her prohibition in force for three months after the first meeting of her legislative assembly. The prohibition is then to cease. From that moment slaves may be introduced, unless the prohibition is reënacted. They will not be excluded then, if Congress shall disapprove the reënactment. Oregon comes here with an organic law prohibiting slavery forever; and we throw it back upon her with a mere temporary vitality. We virtually invite her to reconsider it, as if it had been passed without due reflection, or as if, on further deliberation, she may think it advisable to receive slaves into her bosom. Indeed, it is not necessary for her to do any act. She has only to be passive. We virtually repeal the prohibition. And this the committee give us to calm excitement! Sir, I consider this whole scheme of legislation unworthy of the high character of the country, unworthy of our fathers, unworthy of ourselves. It is commended to us, that Congress may avoid the decision of the question. It is an evasion of responsibility, which will defeat its own purpose. It is sowing the seeds of a future agitation, vastly more profound and exciting than this. It is a temporary colonization of this controversy, to be sent out to the Pacific to stir up dissension among the first settlers, and then to be brought back here, after a time, to renew agitation among ourselves. It will turn out, like every other device of timidity, which shrinks from one embarrassment only to plunge deeper into another.

But, sir, we have reason to be thankful that our case is not utterly void of hope. We are flattered by the chairman of the committee with the assurance, that Congress will be at liberty hereafter to give us the Missouri compromise, and run out the line of 36° 30′ to the Pacific. He considers the arrangement temporary.

It is not so with the Senator from South Carolina.[1] He has pronounced it permanent. And, what is eminently worthy of attention, the bill was to speak for itself. It was so announced. Well, sir, it has spoken for several members of the committee; and it is so artfully or so inartificially contrived, that it speaks a totally different language in each case.

But let us pause and survey this bow of promise which the chairman of the committee has hung out in the distance for our encouragement and hope — the Missouri compromise. When it presents itself, I shall be opposed to it — utterly, irreconcilably; because it will extend slavery where it does not exist; because it would subvert the laws of Mexico which have abolished slavery, and introduce it where it is prohibited. It bears no analogy to the compromise of 1820. That settlement of the question, which was confined to Louisiana, contracted the area of slavery. This would

[1] Mr. Calhoun.

extend it. The whole of Louisiana was open to the introduction of slaves. Slavery nominally existed there. But beyond the limits of the State of Missouri, north of 36° 30′, the territory was nearly uninhabited. The compromise invaded no right. It was no act of abolition or emancipation; but it prohibited the extension of slavery to areas over which, without such a prohibition, it would have been extended. How widely different is this proposition? It is to extend slavery where, without the sanction of the public authority, direct or indirect, it cannot go or exist. It is a proposition to establish slavery by law in a district of country more than two hundred thousand square miles in extent, equal to the entire area of France or the Spanish peninsula. On every principle of justice and right I shall be opposed to it: justice to ourselves, to our national character, and to the future millions who are to occupy the great Pacific, or maritime valley of California — literally the Italy of America, in all but the monuments and classical recollections of the other. Let us look at this question practically. The proposed compromise would carry out the line of 36° 30′ to the Pacific, and prohibit slavery north of it. Let us see the geographical divisions it would make. It would divide New Mexico just above Santa Fé, leaving that city and two thirds of the entire state or territory to the South. How is the distinction between free and slave territory to be maintained? Are we to have two territories with separate political organizations, or only one with an astronomical line separating the bond from the free? Passing New Mexico, the compromise line would cross the Sierra Madre, or Rocky-Mountain chain, and enter a district but little explored, but, so far as known, barren and almost worthless, — leaving a strip of three parallels of latitude to the South. It would next graze the great basin of California — one of the most remarkable features in the geographical conformation of this continent — represented by Frémont as Asiatic rather than American in its character. It is five hundred miles in extent in all directions, enclosed by mountains, — the Sierra Madre on one side, and the Sierra Nevada on the other, — and has its own systems of lakes and rivers. It is for the most part sterile, but with numerous and in some cases extensive tracts capable of cultivation. Passing the great basin without touching it, the compromise line would cross the Sierra Nevada, and enter the maritime valley of California, five hundred miles in length and one hundred and fifty in width from the summit of the mountain chain, which forms its eastern boundary, to the coast range on the Pacific. This valley — the finest in the western hemisphere — is represented by Frémont as bearing a close resemblance to Italy in extent, in climate, and in its capacity for production. It is the natural region of the vine and the olive, and of the infinite variety of grains and fruits which the earth brings forth in tropical climates. Though much farther north, it has all the mildness of the tropical regions on the eastern face of this continent. The compromise line would sever this noble valley latitudinally, leaving four hundred miles to the North and one hundred to the South. It yields nothing to the production of which slave labor is necessary. Slavery would go there as a bane and a hindrance, rather than as an aid, even to production. Why, then, seek to introduce it, when no good purpose is to be answered, when it can only prove an element of unmixed evil? Why sever a region which nature designed for unity in its geographical conformation, its climate, soil, and capacity for production? How is the social distinction which the compromise line would introduce to be preserved inviolate? Will you have two governments, or one with an imaginary line to define the boundary between slavery and freedom? Sir, this whole scheme of division is wrong in all its elements, — geographically, politically, morally wrong, — and I will have no part in it.

Such, Mr. President, would be the Missouri compromise line, applied to New Mexico and California. Bad as it would be, the bill reported by the committee is still worse.

It leaves all open: it surrenders all. It will dedicate the whole of this noble valley to slavery, and exclude from it the freemen of the North, who will not go where their labor is to be degraded by mingling it with the labor of blacks. Sir, there were gallant bands from the North and West, who "coined their hearts and dropped their blood for drachmas" on the ensanguined plains of Mexico to make this acquisition. They are gone beyond the reach of sympathy on the one hand, or injustice on the other. But against their fathers and their children, you will by this act put forth an edict of perpetual exclusion from an inheritance purchased by filial and paternal blood.

There is another consideration which ought not to be overlooked. We have been accused, for the last two years, of making war on Mexico to obtain territory for the extension of slavery. We have denied the truth of these imputations. We have resented them as doing injustice to our intentions. And yet, sir, the treaty is hardly ratified before we are engaged in a struggle in the American Senate to extend slavery to the territory we have acquired. How can we stand up, in the face of the civilized world, and deny these imputations, if the proposition of leaving these territories open to the introduction of slaves is consummated?

I do entreat our Southern friends earnestly, solemnly, not to press this measure upon us: I mean that of insisting on the right to carry slaves into New Mexico and California. I say to you in sincerity and with the deepest conviction of the truth of what I say, that the Northern feeling can go no further in this direction. I appeal to you, through the memory of the past, to do us the justice we have rendered to you. You asked for Florida. You said it shut you out from the Gulf of Mexico. It was an inlet for political intrigue and social disorganization. It was necessary for your safety. We united with you to obtain it. Our blood, our treasure was freely shared with you in making the acquisition. We gave it up to you without reserve. You asked for Texas. It was said to be in danger of falling under the control of your commercial rivals. It was necessary to your safety. You said it would become a theatre for the intrigues of abolitionism. Your slave population might be endangered without it. We united with you again, and gave you back, by legislation and arms, what you had lost a quarter of a century before by diplomacy. We have now acquired free territory. We ask only that it may remain free. Do not ask us to unite with you in extending slavery to it. We abstain from all interference with slavery where it exists. We cannot sanction its extension, directly or indirectly, where it does not exist. And if the authority of the United States is exerted for this purpose, — if slavery is carried into and established, as it will be by this bill, in the territory we have acquired, — I am constrained to say, — I say it in sorrow, — the bond of confidence which unites the two sections of the Union will be rent asunder, and years of alienation and unkindness may intervene before it can be restored, if ever, in its wonted tenacity and strength. Not that I have any present fears for the integrity of the Union. I have not. It is capable of sustaining far ruder shocks than any possible settlement of this question can give. But what I fear is that the current of reciprocal kindness and confidence, which runs through every portion of the community, pervading, refreshing, invigorating all, may be turned out of its course, and forced into channels to which the common feeling is alien, and in which it may be converted into a fountain of bitterness and strife. I conjure you, then, to avoid all this. Ask us not to do what every principle we have been taught, and taught by your fathers, to venerate, condemns as unnatural and unjust.

TRADE WITH CANADA.

THE following speech was delivered by Mr. Dix on the 23d of January, 1849, in support of a bill providing for reciprocal trade with Canada, in certain enumerated articles. The subject had been for several years before Congress, and though the proposition did not finally succeed until some years later, the light shed upon it by the debate of 1849 no doubt contributed largely to its success.

MR. PRESIDENT: Since this bill was taken up for discussion I have been unable, from indisposition and other causes, to bestow upon it the reflection which is due to the importance of the subject. But I will proceed, nevertheless, with such preparation as I have been able to make, to explain the objects of the measure and its probable effects; and I will endeavor, at the same time, to answer some of the leading objections which have been made to it.

If I entertained the belief that the operation of the bill would be prejudicial to the interest of any portion of the Union, I should not be its advocate. The first object of all public legislation is to advance the general welfare of the country; but this object ought certainly not to be sought for at the expense of any particular section, or indeed of any single interest. I believe this bill is entirely free from objection in this respect, that it will be eminently advantageous both to the United States and Canada, and do no wrong or injury in any quarter.

Before I proceed to examine the practical operation of the measure upon the commercial interests of the two countries, I wish to notice a preliminary objection which has been raised.

It is supposed that the privileges conferred by this bill upon Canada will be extended, by virtue of certain reciprocity treaties into which we have entered, to the foreign states with which those engagements have been contracted. I take a totally different view of the subject. I believe Senators have put an erroneous construction upon the obligations of the compacts to which they refer.

We have reciprocity treaties with Russia, Denmark, Hanover, Prussia, Mecklenburg-Schwerin, the Hanseatic republics, and several other foreign countries. They are treaties with sovereign states, and, by every fair rule of construction, their stipulations, so far as they guarantee reciprocity, must be deemed to relate to engagements with other powers equally independent. The commercial arrangement proposed by this bill is with a European colony adjoining us, — one of those dependencies which the states of the Eastern hemisphere are accustomed to except in their compacts with us for reciprocity of commerce and navigation. If any of the states with which we have treaties stipulating for the same privileges which we confer on others had dependencies situated like Canada in respect to us, those states might perhaps acquire in respect to such dependencies the same privileges we shall confer on Canada if the bill passes; but I do not admit that they would acquire those privileges for their metropolitan possessions, and for the reason that colonies have always been made practical exceptions to the general rule of international intercourse. Possibly a special reservation may be necessary in every compact, from the provisions of which it is designed to exclude them; but I do not, as I shall show, consider it a matter of any consequence in this case. This we know in respect to Canada, that it is not only expressly excluded from the terms of our commercial intercourse with Great Britain, but it is the subject of distinct stipulations; and yet the British Legation, in accordance with the wishes of the Canadians, has urged this measure upon us under instructions from home, without the least idea that they would gain for Great Britain under our reciprocity treaty with her the privileges they desire us to confer on Canada.

The honorable Senator from Maryland[1] said that we had "given a construction to these reciprocal provisions worthy of notice;" and he alluded to our treaty with Portugal in 1840, by which it was expressly agreed that the stipulation in our treaty with France in 1831, in regard to French wines, should not be interfered with. This construction is perfectly consistent with the view of the subject I take. These two treaties were with independent powers; they were with continental powers in Europe almost bordering on each other; and a general stipulation in respect to equality of duties necessarily required an express reservation to authorize us to make the duties on any of their products unequal. This, however, is a totally different thing from a commercial arrangement between us and a European colony adjoining us.

But in coming to the conclusion that our commercial relations with Russia, Prussia, and other powers, under the reciprocity treaties we have formed with them, will not be affected by this bill, I put it on other grounds.

These treaties relate to commerce and navigation, and are intended to regulate the commercial intercourse carried on by those countries with the United States on the ocean. They have certainly not been understood as referring to inland trade and exchange between countries bordering on each other. The right to regulate their interior intercourse with adjoining states has not been supposed to be at all impaired by these commercial engagements. If it were otherwise, if these treaties restrained the states which are parties to them from admitting articles free of duty from a neighboring country, except upon condition of extending the same privilege to the other contracting parties, we should at this very moment be entitled, in our intercourse with Prussia, to

[1] Mr. Pearce.

all the benefits of the custom-house exemptions of the Zoll-Verein, of which that kingdom is a leading member. Prussia borders on a number of the Zoll-Verein States. These states interchange with her their common products free of duty under the Zoll-Verein compact, or Customs Union. They have stood to each other in the same relation in which we stand to Canada. They had duties on their respective products as we have. They have abolished them, as we propose to do in respect to Canada on a part of ours.

Now, will it be contended that we are entitled to the same freedom of intercourse with Prussia which she shares with those states, because she has stipulated to impose no higher duties on our products than on those of other countries? Surely not; and for the very reason that the stipulations of our treaty with her are intended to apply to external intercourse by sea, and not to inland arrangements between bordering states. The intention of our treaties of reciprocity is stamped upon them in characters not to be misunderstood. The first stipulation (for those of latter years are of much the same import) limits the reciprocal liberty of commerce and navigation which the treaties were formed to secure to "the ports, places, waters, and rivers of the territories of each party, wherein foreign commerce is permitted." The second stipulation regulates the duties to be imposed on the vessels of the contracting parties engaged in that commerce. The third regulates the duties to be paid on the importation or exportation of their respective products. I admit that, by the letter of these treaties, this bill might affect our commercial relations under them. But I insist that all compacts are to be construed according to their manifest intention, not by one stipulation alone, but by all which relate to the same subject-matter; and I might apply these observations with great force to my first position, and say that those treaties did not contemplate commercial relations with colonial dependencies like Canada. But the whole tenor of their stipulations shows them to have been designed to regulate commerce on the sea, and not the interior traffic carried on by the inhabitants of countries separated from each other by a mere statistical boundary or an astronomical line. They are treaties of commerce and navigation — not of one alone, but of both combined.

When this measure was first proposed, I inquired of the State and Treasury Departments whether it would affect our commercial relations with foreign states under reciprocity treaties, and a decided answer was given by both in the negative. My own examination of the subject has brought me to the same conclusion, whether upon the same grounds I do not know.

If this construction be erroneous, if the privileges proposed to be conferred on Canada will be extended to the foreign states referred to, then, I repeat, we shall, on the same principle, become entitled to the privileges of the Zoll-Verein, in Prussia, and perhaps gain access for our products, through her, to all the other states of that political association, comprehending, I believe, twenty-eight out of the thirty-seven states of the Germanic Confederation. This would, *prima facie*, be an immense advantage, though it is not clear that it would be of any practical benefit. But no one dreamt, when our reciprocity treaties were formed, that they conferred any such privileges on us; and I venture to say it will never occur to any of the states which are parties to those treaties that the proposed arrangement with Canada will confer any new privileges on them.

But if it were otherwise, the privileges the bill confers are reciprocal. We concede nothing which we do not gain in return. If Hanover, Prussia, and Mecklenburg-Schwerin should acquire the privileges conferred on Canada by this bill, we should acquire in respect to them the privileges the bill confers on us. There would be entire reciprocity. Our chances of profiting by the arrangement would be as good as theirs. The Hanse-Towns might send us a few more hams; but there is scarcely an article enumerated in the bill which can be brought to us with advantage from the states on the German Ocean and the Baltic. We are too distant for agricultural exchanges. Besides, we are essentially as agricultural as they. Wheat is the only article likely, under any circumstances, to come here, except in the most inconsiderable quantities. In 1837, when flour was ten, eleven, and twelve dollars a barrel, we received over a million of bushels of wheat from Germany, not half the quantity we sent in 1847 into Canada, Nova Scotia, and New Brunswick; but in the former year, under the influence of these enormous prices, England herself sent us over seven hundred thousand bushels, — nearly as much as Germany; and yet she imported in 1847 over eighty-six millions of bushels of grain. But such occasions very rarely occur; and when they do occur, the tendency of importation is decidedly beneficial. Its influence is to check prices when they reach the high point of extravagance.

Senators have expressed the apprehension that, if this bill passes, we shall, under the construction they give to it, be deluged with wheat from the Baltic. Let us see how much ground there is for this apprehension. On the 1st of February, wheat will pay but one shilling sterling a quarter in Great Britain, — about three cents a bushel. She imports from us: we export to her. The price of wheat there must, therefore, always be as much higher than the price here, when she has a deficiency and we a surplus, as the cost of carrying wheat to her from the United States; and this cost, I am told, is about twenty cents the bushel. When it is a dollar here, it must be $1.20 there. Now, let us see what a vessel laden with wheat from the Baltic would be likely to do in such a case. She must, to come here, sail directly by the ports of Great Britain, where she can get a dollar and twenty cents a bushel, deducting the three cents duty which she must pay. She gets, then, a dollar and seventeen cents. Suppose she continues her voyage to the United States, how will the account stand? Admitting, for the sake of the argument, that the wheat she brings will come in free of duty under our reciprocity treaties, she will get one dollar a bushel; but from this amount she must deduct twenty cents for cost of transportation from Great Britain here. She will get eighty cents here instead of one dollar and seventeen cents in England, — thirty-seven cents a bushel less; and this, on a cargo of several thousand bushels, will amount to no inconsiderable sum. The Northern Germans have the reputation of being rather heavy, but they are, so far as I have had the opportunity of observing them, the Yankees of the Continent in bargaining; and I think they will be found altogether too astute to engage in any such enterprises as honorable Senators apprehend. They will carry on a severe competition with us in supplying England with wheat; but they are just as unlikely to compete with us in our markets as we are to compete with Newcastle in supplying London with coal.

Under the construction, therefore, which Senators give to the bill, I am satisfied its operation would be as beneficial to us as to the states with which we have reciprocity treaties. But I contend that these treaties will not be affected by this arrangement. If I am mistaken, the privileges we confer will also be acquired by us, and we cannot, in any event, be losers.

Let me now turn to considerations which directly concern the commercial intercourse of Canada and the United States.

In order to understand the subject in all its bearings, it will be necessary to see what Canada is, and what she has done for us in the removal of restrictions upon our commerce with her.

The population of Canada (I use a general term, as the two provinces are now united) is 1,527,757 souls, or, in round numbers, a million and a half. With less variety and fertility of soil than the United States, a more rigorous climate, and with colonial restrictions calculated, under the most favorable view of the subject, to impede the development of her resources, to shackle the operations of industry, and to abridge the freedom of individual enterprise, which is always the most powerful stimulus to exertion, it is not to be expected that her progress will keep pace with our own in population or in social and physical improvement. The policy of Great Britain has, within a few years, undergone some important changes, favorable to her in a commercial and political view. Canada, it is true, has lost some exclusive privileges by a relaxation of the colonial system of the mother-country, but the latter has extended to her some new facilities, by surrendering the control of the custom-house, so far as respects the imposition of duties ; and she has also conceded the principle of the responsibility of ministers which exists at home, so that when the Governor is not sustained in his policy by the Provincial Parliament, he is bound to change his advisers, or, in other words, his Executive Council, which may be considered as the ministry of the colony. The Canadian government is thus assimilated to that of Great Britain in the essential feature of its responsibility to the popular voice, — a concession which has been gained after a long and patient struggle on the part of a few able and patriotic men in Canada.

Almost contemporaneous with this fundamental change in the political administration of the affairs of Canada was another of equal importance in respect to her commercial independence. In 1846, an act of Parliament was passed giving the legislative authority of the British colonies the right to regulate their own duties of customs in respect to British as well as foreign products. At that time there were no duties imposed by British acts on British goods imported into Canada, although there were duties imposed by such acts on foreign goods ; but there were acts of the Canadian legislature, made for revenue, imposing additional or cumulative duties on foreign goods, and a duty of five per cent. on British goods. There was also an act of Parliament declaring that no goods should, " upon importation into any of the British possessions in America, be deemed to be of the growth, production, or manufacture of the United Kingdom, unless imported from the United Kingdom."

The effect of this condition of the law was to prevent the importation of British goods into Canada through the United States, and to impose on the productions of the United States and other countries duties which were protective as to those of Great Britain and Canada.

As early as 1843 the duty on the importation of wheat and flour, of the growth of the United States, going through Canada to the United Kingdom, was reduced to three shillings provincial duty, the quarter of eight bushels, and one shilling British duty, without reference to the sliding-scale, by which the importation of breadstuffs from other countries was regulated. The consequence was, a large importation of wheat and flour from the United States into England through Canada.

The corn-laws being repealed, Canada loses this advantage, — the advantage of being a carrier for us, — and it is now as beneficial to export Canadian wheat to England through the United States (the expense being equal) as direct from Canada. In other words, the wheat of Canada and the United States has equal advantages in the British market.

In 1847, the Parliament of Canada, acting under the authority granted by the imperial government, repealed the differential duties, and the new table or tariff of duties then enacted applies equally to goods of all kinds, whether coming from England or the United States. We are, in this respect, placed on the footing of the mother-country.

This equality was effected by a double operation of law: first, by reducing the rate of duty on goods of the United States; and, secondly, by increasing the rate on British goods, thus bringing both to the same standard or scale. There can be no better evidence of the liberality of the Canadians, and of their earnest desire to put their commercial intercourse with us on the most friendly footing.

The consequence of this change of the law has been to create a considerable importation of British and foreign goods into Canada through the United States, and also to cause a large importation of the productions of the United States into Canada for consumption. The cotton fabrics of Lowell are received on the same terms as those of Manchester. The same remark is true of many other products of our industry, of which we carry large quantities into Canada for consumption. The value of our productions annually introduced into Canada, under these new provisions of law, is stated, on high authority, to amount to more than two millions of dollars. It is natural that the Canadians should desire to send their produce to New York and Boston, to meet the trade which has thus been opened to us, — that they, having put this trade upon the most liberal footing in respect to us, should wish to export, on equal terms, such means of payment as they possess in the products of their own labor.

Will the terms of exchange — perfect equality — proposed by the bill be disadvantageous to us? I propose to consider this question somewhat in detail, although it would seem but fair that the liberality which has been manifested by Canada toward us — a liberality by which we have greatly profited, a liberality voluntarily extended to us, without equivalent — should be reciprocated, without stopping to weigh, with over-scrupulous exactness, the precise balance of advantages and benefits.

In the first place, I believe it will be apparent, by looking at the list of enumerated articles which are proposed to be mutually received free of duty, that ashes, flour, and lumber are the only ones ever likely to be brought into the markets of the United States in considerable quantities. Ashes we want, and at the cheapest price. In respect to lumber, there is nothing to be apprehended. We shall unquestionably receive some lumber in New York, but I believe our timber districts do not fear the competition. Besides, it will come to us chiefly in the form of saw-logs for manufacture. New York is almost the only State this competition can affect; and if there is any risk, we are willing to take it, in consideration of the general advantage and convenience the measure promises to confer. It was apprehended by our friends in Maine, that their interests might be injuriously affected in this respect. But the bill is so shaped as to avoid all interference with them. It applies only to the direct trade with Canada. Articles coming through New Brunswick or the other British provinces will continue on the old footing. The lumber interest in Maine, therefore, will not be touched by the bill; and in all other respects that State will in all probability be as much benefited by it as any other. When the railway between Portland and Montreal is completed, the free commerce secured by the bill must be of the greatest advantage.

Flour, in fact, is the only Canadian product likely to come into competition with our own. Of all the others — animals, hides, cheese, meats, &c. — we shall export more largely into Canada than she will export into the United States. The same remark is applicable to corn, and indeed to most if not all the breadstuffs, except wheat.

It is possible that in certain years — years of scanty production in the United States, provided they are years of abundance in Canada — we may receive some wheat from her. But I do not believe that the amount will even in those years (which are very unlikely to occur) be sufficient to influence prices in the United States in a perceptible degree. If the importation, however, shall in such extraordinary cases prevent the price of grain from becoming extravagantly high, it will be a public benefit, by relieving the poor from the necessity of eating dear bread. In years of ordinary abundance I do not believe prices in the United States will be at all affected by the importation of wheat from Canada. The production of wheat in the United States yields a surplus. Whenever prices abroad are sufficient to sustain exportation, our wheat finds its way to foreign markets; and in these cases it is the price in those markets which fixes the price at home. I believe it may be stated as a principle that the price of a product, which is exported in any considerable quantity, is regulated in the markets of the exporting country by the price in the markets of the country to which the export is made. Our own experience proves the truth of this proposition. In 1847, when we were exporting breadstuffs, the price of flour in New York, the chief port of exportation, rose and fell with the fluctuations of price in the British markets with as much certainty as the mercurial column in the thermometer rises and falls with the variations of external temperature. This fact should relieve us from all apprehension as to the influence of this bill on competition with Canada in the production of wheat. She may send her flour to foreign markets now, either by the St. Lawrence, or through the United States, in bond, under the act of 1846, allowing a drawback of duties in certain cases. It enters into competition with ours in those markets now. The bill gives no new facility or advantage in this respect, except to relieve her from custom-house formalities. I hold, then, that the wheat of Canada can only have an influence on the price in the United States in very extraordinary years, not likely to occur, and in years of exportation, by competition with us in the foreign market, and that, in the latter respect, this influence is as sensibly felt now as it would be under the provisions of this bill. These considerations become the more significant, if it be true, as I suppose, that wheat is henceforth to be one of our regular exports.

What, then, are the advantages to be expected from the proposed free interchange of products? The first is, to relieve the inhabitants of both countries, and especially those on the frontier, from the inconvenience of the custom-house in respect to necessaries of common production and daily use. The next is, to enable the Canadians to export their produce through the United States to foreign markets without paying duty at the frontier, and with a deduction of two and a half per cent. on the drawback at the place of exportation. The custom-house formalities seem to have been a great obstacle to the use of our canals and internal channels of communication by the Canadians. From December 1, 1846, to July 1, 1847, we received from all the British North American Provinces 929 bushels of grain of all kinds, and no flour, while we sent them more than two millions of bushels of wheat during the year. During the previous five months we received from all the rest of the world 309 bushels of wheat and 54 cwt. of flour, — equal to 27 barrels. The last year the Canadians have used our canals more extensively. The returns are not yet printed, but I understand that at least 70,000 barrels of flour have been exported through the United States. Whether the experiment will succeed remains to be seen.

Mr. Clarke. Will the Senator from New York state where he obtained this information?

I have ascertained the fact from some statistical statements published in a newspaper at Oswego, containing the transactions at the collector's office. This information is given in an official form in the annual report on commerce and navigation received yesterday; but I have not been able to examine it. From the source I have before referred to, I learn that 50,000 barrels of flour were received at Oswego. At Buffalo the amount was probably less.

The bill will undoubtedly lead to a free interchange of products among the frontier inhabitants. If, in the course of these exchanges, we receive any Canada wheat for consumption, it must be in the few individual cases in which the sellers of our products to the Canadians are able to consume it more freely. To a very limited extent it may possibly reach a new class of consumers, who will become exporters on a small scale, under this bill. For instance, one of our frontier inhabitants who, under the proposed arrangement, can carry half a dozen sheep into Canada without paying the duty of forty cents a head now exacted by the Canadian tariff, and bring back as many bushels of wheat without paying the twenty per cent. duty imposed by our tariff, will save between three and four dollars in an exchange of products of the value of twelve or thirteen dollars, — a monstrous tax! — and he may thus be enabled to eat wheat bread for a while, instead of living exclusively on the coarser breadstuffs. This must be the only effect in ordinary years, when we produce more wheat than we require for our own consumption. We can take none from other countries, unless we consume it more freely; and our increased consumption under this bill must not only be extremely limited, but of such a nature as not to interfere with our own production. But these are very small matters, hardly worthy to be taken into the account in an estimate of large transactions.

Let me now test the truth of my position — that we have nothing to fear from competition with Canada in wheat-growing — by a resort to arithmetical demonstrations. The population of Canada is about half the population of New York. That part of the province which was once politically known as Upper Canada, and which, for distinction, I shall still call so, is the wheat-growing region. The Lower portion does not produce enough for its own consumption. It always draws largely upon the Upper. The least failure of the crops in the Lower would be sure to absorb the whole surplus of the Upper. If there were any just ground of apprehension in respect to our wheat-growing districts, looking to general considerations, it would be removed by the custom-house statistics of Canada for the year 1847, — the great year of exportation for American breadstuffs, by reason of the famine in Europe. I take for illustration the most unfavorable year for my purpose, — the year in which, from unusual causes, the export of wheat by Canada was greatest. I do so that those from whom I differ may have every advantage they can ask in the argument. The quantity of flour imported in that year into Canada was about 84,000 barrels, and the quantity exported about 676,000; the quantity of wheat imported 562,000 bushels, and the quantity exported 668,000 bushels. The imports, of course, were from the United States. The excess of exports over imports was 592,000 barrels of flour, and 106,000 bushels of wheat. This entire export was probably to Great Britain, her American islands, and her Atlantic provinces, Nova Scotia and New Brunswick. Notwithstanding this export of flour from Canada, New Brunswick received from us, in the same year, over 100,000 barrels of flour, and Nova Scotia nearly as much more.

The result of my inquiries is, that in ordinary years the upper portion of Canada produces a surplus of about 2,000,000 bushels of wheat, and that a considerable part of this surplus is consumed by the lower portion, including Quebec and Montreal, and the demands for their shipping. In 1847 Canada produced 4,560,967 bushels of wheat, and imported 982,468 bushels, (including flour, and estimating one barrel of flour to be equal to five bushels of wheat,) making an aggregate of 5,543,435 bushels produced and imported. In the same year she exported 4,047,366 bushels, making a balance of 1,496,069 bushels consumed at home. This is less than a bushel for each inhabitant, — probably not more than half her consumption in ordinary years. But the price of wheat being extravagantly high, the consumption must have been greatly diminished, for the purpose of exportation, by resorting to the coarser grains for domestic use. The statistical tables of earlier years prove the export of 1847 to have been extraordinarily large. From 1838 to 1843 the annual export varied from 50,000 to 350,000 barrels; but in this last amount was included a large import from the United States. It is not probable that her export is essentially different when there are no unusual causes to stimulate exportation. Taking one year with another, and deducting from the entire export of wheat from Canada an amount equal to that which we send to her, to Nova Scotia, and New Brunswick, and I doubt whether there will be much of a balance left. In 1847, which was an extraordinary year, while Canada only exported 3,064,898 bushels of wheat over her imports, we carried into the British North American Provinces alone, in the same year, 2,279,068 bushels. While Canada produces less than three bushels of wheat for each inhabitant, we produce more than five and a half bushels for each inhabitant; while she consumed in 1847 less than one bushel of wheat for each inhabitant, we consumed nearly four bushels and a half for each inhabitant, notwithstanding the temptation of high prices to export and to consume cheaper breadstuffs; while her entire product of wheat in 1847 was four millions and a half of bushels, ours was over one hundred and fourteen millions of bushels.

Against an export of less than six hundred thousand barrels of flour from Canada in 1847, (her excess over imports,) we exported nearly four and a half millions of barrels; and against an export of one hundred thousand bushels of wheat from Canada, (excess over imports,) we exported nearly four millions four hundred thousand bushels. In the same year we exported twenty million bushels of Indian corn and meal, while she exported none. The idea that a million and a half of people, about half the population of New York, with a soil far less favorable to the growth of wheat than our own, can successfully compete with us either in the foreign or the domestic market, and injuriously affect production with us, with twenty millions of people, seems to me a very idle apprehension. It has been stated, on high authority, that the entire trade of the British North American colonies, with three millions of people, does not equal that of Connecticut, with only three hundred thousand inhabitants. The more numerous, active, and enterprising must always have the advantage in exchanging on equal terms. The very fact that we send into New Brunswick every year at least one hundred thousand barrels of flour, and probably as large an amount into Nova Scotia, seems to indicate that we might enter into successful competition with Upper in supplying Lower Canada, if all duties were to be removed. At least our surpluses will, to some extent, meet there.

Looking to the wheat culture alone, therefore, I should have no fears. But if we consider the subject in connection with the export of cattle, corn, salted meats, and other articles, there can be no reasonable ground to apprehend that we shall be losers. We must be gainers. Large quantities of cattle and corn are now exported to Canada, with a specific duty, equal to about twenty per cent. against them. We sent into Canada in 1844 thirteen thousand barrels of pork, and in 1847 about the same quantity, with a specific duty of one dollar and twenty cents the cwt. against us. The removal of these duties cannot but have a most decided influence in increasing the traffic of the northwestern States with Canada.

It has been suggested that the proposed measure, by removing the duties on the enumerated products, will destroy the protection which those duties secure to our agricultural industry. The answer to this suggestion is, that the proposed arrangement is founded upon a mutual abolition of duties, and that the protection extended to like articles of the production of Canada will also be removed. There can be no necessity of protecting our products against Canada, when she ceases to protect her products against us. But the measure will, in truth, be of infinite advantage to our agriculture. Canada sends few products to us; we send many to her. We produce corn, which she needs, and which she cannot raise in sufficient quantity for her own consumption. Her winters are longer than ours; and, as the expense of keeping cattle from autumn to spring is greater, she will always rely on us for her supplies, both for the slaughter-house and for farming purposes. There is now a duty of

$4.40 a head on cows, and seven dollars a head on oxen, on importation into Canada. The removal of these duties will be a great advantage to us. In short, under all its aspects, this measure will, on examination, be admitted to be of infinite benefit to our agriculture. It will, in most cases, remove duties on our products, which operate as a direct discouragement to their exportation, while the removal of the duties on the like articles of the production of Canada cannot affect us, as those duties are chiefly on products which will not come into competition with ours, and are therefore not protective. In a word, I can fancy no measure more likely to be beneficial to our agriculture than this. The highest species of protection to industry is that which opens new markets for its products. In this point of view this measure is eminently protective; it is just, legitimate, effective protection; and if gentlemen desire (as I have no doubt they do) to advance the agricultural interests of the country, they ought to sustain it.

Let me now state a few further statistical facts to the Senate, for the purpose of showing how little influence any increased interchange of products with Canada under this bill is likely to have on our aggregate exchanges with foreign countries.

The duties on merchandise collected in all the inland frontier districts, commencing at Burlington, on Lake Champlain, and terminating at Chicago, on Lake Michigan, are as follows: For 1845, $57,818.55; for 1846, $66,828.80; for 1847, $66,019.80;—making an average of $63,555.71 per annum for the three years.

Estimating the rate of duty at 33⅓ per cent., the whole value of the articles imported from Canada into the United States, and paying duty at the custom-houses, averages $190,667.13 per annum. A portion of the duties was, in all probability, refunded in 1847, under the law allowing a drawback on reëxportation of the articles on which the duties were paid. I learn that the amount of goods entered at Buffalo and Oswego for the benefit of drawback was greatly increased during the last year, as the returns, when we receive them, will undoubtedly show; but the amount refunded will be proportionably increased, so that the treasury will not be affected by the augmented collections from this cause.

Our entire imports from the British North American colonies in 1845 were of the value of about two millions of dollars. Of this amount more than nine hundred thousand dollars consisted of gold and silver, and more than eleven hundred thousand, including specie, were free of duty. The remaining nine hundred thousand dollars are to be divided between Canada, Nova Scotia, and New Brunswick; and from the nature of the articles it is manifest that the quantity received from Canada was but a small portion of the amount. For instance, fish constituted nearly four hundred thousand dollars of the nine hundred thousand; and this came from the Atlantic provinces. The year 1847 gives nearly the same aggregate result. Our entire imports from all the British North American colonies constitute a very inconsiderable part of our commercial transactions with foreign states; and no change we can make in our intercourse with Canada can have any material influence upon them.

Notwithstanding this small import from the British North American colonies, our commercial intercourse with them, including Canada, is as beneficial for its extent as that with any portion of the world. We sent into them, in 1847, products of the value of nearly eight millions of dollars,— about five million eight hundred thousand domestic, and over two millions foreign. The foreign exports were probably, to a great extent, sent through the United States on foreign account. Our imports directly from those colonies, the same year, were of the value of about two millions and a quarter. The remaining five millions and a half (deducting some hundred thousand on foreign account) must have been paid by bills on England. A large portion of our exports into Canada is probably paid for in this way. She sends her lumber and flour to England, and with the proceeds pays us the excess of her imports from us over her exports to us.

But it is only a small portion even of these exchanges which this bill can affect. It is only that portion which embraces the enumerated articles. Now, I have ascertained that in 1847 we did not import of those articles from all the British North American colonies an amount equal in value to one hundred thousand dollars. From Canada it must have been quite inconsiderable. The intercourse this bill is destined to affect is, therefore, not only limited in its extent, but it is essentially local in its character. No apprehension is expressed in any quarter as to its practical operation, except as respects competition in the production of wheat. I trust I have shown that even this apprehension is without foundation. But if it were not so, the States on the frontier are those most likely to feel the influence of the competition. Ohio is the largest wheat-growing State in the Union. She produces a little less than seventeen millions of bushels, — nearly four times as much as Canada. Next in order is New York, with a product of fourteen millions and a half of bushels, — more than three times as much as Canada. Michigan, in 1847, with a population not one fourth of that of Canada, produced nearly twice as many bushels of wheat. These are the States which should object to the free exchange proposed by the bill, if objection could reasonably be made in any quarter; and yet they are the very States in which the measure is most earnestly desired. It is, in truth, a measure which exclusively concerns the inhabitants of the frontier; and I earnestly hope Senators representing States which are far removed from it, and which cannot be affected by the proposed measure, will consent that the wishes of the parties immediately interested shall furnish the rule of their intercourse with each other.

I have endeavored to show, Mr. President, that the Canadian government has acted with great liberality towards us; and that by reciprocally removing the duties on the agricultural productions of both countries, enumerated in this bill, we do no injury to any interest, but create a mutual benefit.

I was very much surprised to hear the Senator from Maryland[1] say that there was no reciprocity in the proposed arrangement; that "the bill is delusive. If it pass, not a dollar's worth of any of these products will be exported from the United States to Canada." The Senator could not have examined this subject with his accustomed care. Let me convince him that he has not done so. In 1847 we exported to Canada 83,983 barrels of flour, and 562,553 bushels of wheat, with a duty of about seven and a half cents a bushel on the importation; we also sent her 64,378 bushels of other grains.

Mr. Pearce. I will thank the Senator to state whence he derives his information. I do not find it in the public documents.

I have obtained the information from the custom-house statistics of Canada, to which I have referred, furnished at my request by the officers of the Canadian government.

We also sent into Canada 943,280 pounds of tallow, with a duty of one per cent. (the very large export probably resulting from the very low duty); 28,000 pounds of butter, with a duty of $1.50 per cwt.; 1458 oxen, with a duty of $7 a head; 14,701 bushels of potatoes, with a duty of ten per cent.; 49,099 bushels of apples, with a duty of ten cents per bushel; 16,809 barrels of salted meats, chiefly pork, with a duty of $1.20 the cwt.

The duty on sheep is nearly prohibitory. It is, at ordinary prices, forty per cent. Nearly the same may be said of the duty on most other animals. Now, I do not hesitate to say, that the export of most of the enumerated products

[1] Mr. Pearce.

may be very greatly increased by the removal of the duties upon them; and I am satisfied that the Senator from Maryland will find, on a more careful examination of the subject, that he has entirely misapprehended the operation of the bill upon the agricultural interest of the country.

And now I wish to notice, in the briefest manner, the amendment proposed by the Senator from Vermont.[1] The effect of the amendment, if adopted, must be to defeat the measure. It cannot be accepted by Canada. The articles the amendment proposes to make reciprocally free are hats, boots, shoes, and other manufactures of leather; cotton and woollen fabrics. These are all manufactured articles. The bill contemplates a free exchange of certain agricultural products. The amendment changes the whole character of the bill. It extends to a class of imports on which Canada must rely for revenue. It would be just as unreasonable in her to ask us to receive her furs free of duty.

But the duties on these articles, though revenue duties, are exceedingly moderate. They come within the range of those proposed by General Hamilton in his celebrated report on manufactures, made shortly after the organization of the Federal government. The duty on hats is $7\frac{1}{2}$ per cent.; on boots, shoes, and manufactures of leather of all kinds, an average duty, I think, not exceeding 10 per cent.; and on manufactures of cotton and wool, $7\frac{1}{2}$ per cent. These duties are not only moderate, but low; and without reference to the departure of the amendment from the general policy of the bill, it is unreasonable to ask their abolition.

Besides, the same duties are imposed on like products of British manufacture. The mother-country has no advantage over us in this respect in Canada, and we ought not to ask an advantage over her.

It is quite manifest that the amendment must defeat the bill; and I entreat Senators not to give it their support. If the bill is not acceptable to them, I trust they will, at

[1] Mr. Phelps.

least, consent to manifest their opposition to it by a direct vote.

I now come to an objection to the bill which I consider it proper to notice, though I regret to be under the necessity of making any reference to it. The Senator from Virginia[1] terms this bill a measure "of *quasi* annexation, because the advantages which are urged as arising from it seem to relate to some such project in the future." Mr. President, if this measure had any such object, and there were no other ground of objection, we might reasonably count upon the support of the Senator from Virginia. It is but four years since every Democratic vote in this body from the Northern, North-eastern, and Northwestern States was cast for the annexation of Texas. If Canada should desire to unite herself to us, are we not to expect the same unanimity among our Democratic friends in another quarter? or are we to understand that annexation is only to be countenanced when it can be made at one extremity of the Union, and to be opposed at the other? — that even freedom of intercourse is to be discouraged and repelled, because it may by possibility lead to such a result in the future? I hope the intimation of the Senator from Virginia is not to be so understood. If it is, it is well that we know now in what manner our coöperation in the annexation of Texas and the acquisition of Florida is likely to be reciprocated.

Mr. Hunter. The gentleman from New York is mistaken if he supposes I urged this view of the bill as an objection to it. I stated the fact without comment on it, or intimating either an approval or condemnation of it. I said that such must be its purpose, for that the best arguments urged in its favor seemed to be based upon some such prospect in the future.

I am aware that the Senator did not comment upon the intimation he made, though I understood him to make it by way of objection to the bill. But I am happy that he does not wish it to be so received. While on this subject, I

[1] Mr. Hunter.

desire to say, that, so far as I am concerned, so far as concerns those with whom this measure originated, no such design was even imagined until it was suggested by those to whom it seems to be unacceptable. I believe (though I am not sure) this proposition came originally from Canada, — from the liberal party in Canada, — though it was cordially acquiesced in on our side by those who supposed they had a direct interest in it. Among the first by whom it was publicly suggested, if I remember right, was the Secretary of the Treasury. He has twice recommended it; and undoubtedly because he regarded it as a commercial arrangement which would be beneficial to both parties.

I know personally many of the prominent men in Canada. I know they are strongly opposed to a separation from the mother-country. They desire union with England first, independence next, annexation to the United States last of all. They desire a free exchange of products with us, because they believe the existing restrictions upon our commerce are prejudicial to both countries; and they desire nothing more. What the feeling is with the great body of the people in Canada, I have no means of knowing. That they desire free intercourse with us, there is no doubt. Beyond that, I know nothing of their opinions or wishes.

For myself, I have heretofore spoken freely on this subject. I would neither be forward in courting the annexation of adjacent states, nor backward in acceding to it. I would neither make overtures nor repel them, without good cause. I believe we are large enough for all the purposes of security and strength; but I do not fear further extension, nor would I decline it when circumstances render it convenient to ourselves or others.

Mr. President, this consideration has been urged, and urged directly, as an objection to commercial freedom between the United States and Canada. I have recently heard it from the anti-liberal party in Canada, who are for new restrictions on our commerce. They are in favor of existing restrictions, as well as new ones, upon the ground that free intercourse may lead to a political union between Canada and the United States. The Board of Trade in Montreal, in a petition to the Queen, on the 18th December last, prayed for a renewal of the discriminating duty on American grain in favor of colonial grain; and one of the reasons assigned was, that the recent changes in the commercial relations of Canada had led to "a growing commercial intercourse with the United States, giving rise to an opinion, which is daily gaining ground on both sides of the boundary line, that the interests of the two countries, under the changed policy of the Imperial government, are germane to each other, and under that system must sooner or later be politically interwoven."

Whether this view be just or not, I do not believe the result is to be defeated in either of the modes proposed, — by a continuation of existing restrictions, or by the imposition of new ones. I believe the tendency of such measures will be to hasten and to consummate the very end they are intended to defeat. Let us see if it be not so. A man at Champlain, New York, or Swanton, Vermont, wishes to sell an ox to his neighbor in Canada, living in sight of him, and take wheat in exchange. On making his entry at the Canadian custom-house, he is taxed seven dollars on the importation of his ox. He brings back thirty-five bushels of wheat, at one dollar a bushel, and, on entering them at our custom-house, he is taxed twenty per cent. *ad valorem*, (seven more,) — fourteen dollars tax to the two governments for the privilege of exchanging his commodity with his neighbor, separated from him in one case by a narrow sheet of water, and in the other by an astronomical line. Now, I venture to assert that these impositions will not long be submitted to on either side; and if they are not removed by the two governments, the inhabitants of both countries will look to annexation as the only practicable measure of relief. Sir, a liberal policy is always the most wise, as well as the most just; and I say again, that the people of the two countries will not submit to such a system as I have described, — a system executed by an army of custom-house officers on each side of the boundary line, placed there to enforce exactions which absolutely prohibit commercial intercourse, or to fill their bags of plunder out of the hard earnings of the frontier inhabitants. And I cannot believe that those who advocate the doctrines of free trade will sustain a state of things so utterly at variance with their own principles; that they will be found acting in unison with the anti-liberal party in Canada, upholding commercial restrictions, which do no good, against commercial freedom, which works no injury; throwing impediments in the paths of those who are marked out by the great features of the districts they inhabit for friendly intercourse, and creating these embarrassments for the avowed purpose of making them alien to each other.

Notwithstanding the opinion of the Senator from Maryland, there is another consideration in favor of this bill, which I consider of vital importance to us. We have earnestly desired, since the American Revolution, the free navigation of the St. Lawrence. In 1826 it became the subject of diplomatic correspondence between the two countries. The discussion exhibits the high value we have attached to this privilege. Indeed we claimed it as a right; and it was asserted as such by Mr. Clay in a letter of great power and eloquence. The right was not admitted by Great Britain, and the matter was dropped. But there has been no period when we would not have been willing to grant an equivalent for a privilege in which, according to Mr. Clay, nine States have an interest. Canada is now desirous of granting it without equivalent. She stands ready to pass a bill opening the free navigation of the St. Lawrence to our vessels. Her Parliament is in session. The liberal party, which is now in power, is about to bring the measure forward; and I am happy to say that Lord Elgin, the Governor, — a gentleman distinguished for an enlightened and liberal statesmanship, —

is in favor of the measure. Its success is certain, if we do not decline the reciprocity asked for by this bill.

When the Senator from Maryland said that the navigation of the St. Lawrence was useless to us, he could hardly have been aware that ship-canals have been constructed around the falls of Niagara, and other points below, to connect the great lakes with the Atlantic Ocean by way of the St. Lawrence, and that vessels of three hundred and fifty tons pass freely through these internal channels of communication. During the last summer, two of our revenue vessels passed from Lake Erie and Lake Ontario, through the St. Lawrence, to the Atlantic. When our ships can go to Quebec by sea and meet vessels from our northwestern States, there can be no doubt that large quantities of the products of those States will be carried, in summer, spring, and autumn, in this direction, by our own vessels, to Europe. If this bill becomes a law, I have no hesitation in predicting that vessels at no distant day will be laden with wheat in Chicago, Green Bay, Detroit, and Cleveland, and unlade in Liverpool. Ship-owners, producers, all will be greatly benefited by this free commerce, which will have an advantage in avoiding transshipment between the point of embarkation and the sea, or the foreign market. If the result is to affect in any way producers in the Middle States, as Kentucky in the West, and Maryland and Virginia on the Atlantic, it will be to relieve them from competition in our own markets with the wheat-growers of Ohio, Illinois, Michigan, and Wisconsin; and I greatly err if gentlemen from the wheat-growing States do not find themselves acting in direct contravention of the interests of their constituents in opposing this measure. In any point of view under which the subject can be considered, the opening of the St. Lawrence will be of incalculable benefit. It is, indeed, the only outlet of the Northwest to the sea for vessels of any magnitude, — the only outlet of this kind they can ever have; for, with all the facilities for internal communication

New York possesses, a ship-canal through her territory is opposed by physical obstacles too serious to be overcome.

I believe the adoption of this great measure — the free navigation of the St. Lawrence — depends on the passage of this bill. If the reciprocity it provides for is refused, we cannot expect that Canada will grant us what she considers as a boon, what we claim as a right, and what all must concede to be a privilege of inestimable value. On the contrary, if the liberal course she has pursued is met by an illiberal spirit in us, I fear she will be compelled, in self-defence, to resort to her old system of differential duties, and to continue the restriction on navigation. There is a strong party in Canada in favor of this course. I have already alluded to the anti-liberal party. I have quoted their recent petition to the Queen, in favor of discriminating duties on our products. And, sir, I greatly fear, if this bill is defeated, that we shall put a weapon into their hands to be wielded to our serious annoyance and injury. To withhold, therefore, a just measure of reciprocity mutually advantageous, as I verily believe, to both parties, would not only be exceedingly narrow in policy on our part, but, like all selfishness, it would defeat itself, and result in a loss of benefits we already enjoy. These benefits, as I have already shown, are: first, equal duties in Canada on American and British goods; and, second, a market for at least three millions of dollars in value of the products of our industry.

Mr. Dayton. Will the Senator allow me to interrupt him? The statement of facts he makes is important; and I desire to know on what authority he says that our manufactured articles are received in Canada on the same terms as those of Great Britain.

I state it on the authority of the Canadian tariff, which I shall be happy to show the Senator from New Jersey; and I will add, that large quantities of our manufactures are carried into Canada for consumption, — iron castings, coarse cottons, and a variety of articles sent from the New-England States, New Jersey, and Pennsylvania. To these

States the increased intercourse proposed by this bill will be of great importance. The prospective benefit which we should reject by a narrow policy is the free navigation of the St. Lawrence, — one of the highest prizes offered to the commercial enterprise of the country for many years. It will also carry with it the application, which we have always contended for, of a principle of the greatest value in international intercourse, — a principle generally conceded in Europe since the report of Baron Von Humboldt, — the right of riparian states to an outlet to the sea by the water-courses on which they border. These seem to me to be advantages which far outweigh in importance any considerations of pecuniary profit to be drawn from a close computation of the number of bushels of wheat which may be reciprocally received and exported; though, even on this narrow ground, I trust I have shown that we are not likely to be losers by the competition.

There is another view of the subject, which, I confess, weighs greatly with me. The liberal party in Canada has been struggling for years to obtain the measure of political and commercial freedom to which they believe every community of men to be fairly entitled. Commercial freedom they have secured, — not fully, but so far as to give them the regulation of the impost; political freedom, so far as to give the popular voice a control over all cardinal subjects of internal administration and external intercourse. The first use they have made of this partial independence of the mother-country is to tender to us the most liberal terms of commercial exchange. They have extended to us these benefits without equivalent. We have enjoyed them for nearly two years with great advantage. They now ask equality in exchanging a few agricultural productions common to both countries. Sir, I should deeply regret that the United States, powerful and populous as they are, should withhold from a comparatively weak and dependent neighbor a privilege claimed on grounds so fair in themselves, and so entirely in accordance with the liberal principles by which we profess to be governed. It would be but a poor encouragement to a country adopting our political maxims to some extent, and carrying them into the administration of her own commercial affairs, to be driven from the liberal policy she has espoused into the old system of exclusion; to be thus checked at the very outset in her attempts to cast off the shackles which she has regarded as the greatest impediment to her prosperity; to be forced to this alternative, too, by us, the country, above all others, most interested in the establishment and maintenance of an enlightened policy in government and in commerce.

TERRITORIES ACQUIRED FROM MEXICO.

THE speech which follows — the last made by Mr. Dix in the Senate — was delivered on the 28th February, 1849, three days before the adjournment of Congress. The question before the Senate, presented in a variety of forms, was the institution of governments for the territories acquired from Mexico, — a question embarrassed throughout by the determination of the Senators from the slave States to extend slavery to those territories, and by a majority of the Senators from the free States to guard, by an express prohibition, against what they deemed a moral and political evil, and the national dishonor of restoring it where it had been formally abolished.

I REGRET to be under the necessity of asking the indulgence of the Senate at this late period of the session; but I feel it my duty to make some remarks upon the amendment offered by the Senator from Wisconsin,[1] and the general subject to which it relates. I regret also to be under the necessity of discussing the question of providing a government for California, in the form under which it is presented to us, — in an amendment to an appropriation bill. Independently of this objection, I have considered it from the beginning a measure of too great importance to be disposed of in this incidental manner. The proposition of the Senator from Tennessee,[2] also in the form of an amendment to this bill, was almost ruled out of this body, upon the ground that it was incongruous and out of place. It received in the end but four votes. I consider this amendment equally irrelevant and misplaced.

The amendment of the Senator from Tennessee proposed to admit California and New Mexico into the Union as a State. The amendment of the Senator from Wisconsin arms the President with extraordinary powers to govern these terri-

[1] Mr. Walker. [2] Mr. Bell.

tories. On the score of congruity, in respect to the general purposes of the bill upon which they were proposed to be ingrafted, I see no difference between them; and I do not understand how one proposition should be resisted on the ground that it is incongruous, and the other entertained as unobjectionable in this respect. Although I did not concur in the propriety of the proposition of the Senator from Tennessee, and although I considered his argument not very happily adjusted to the conclusion it aimed to enforce, yet I must say that I decidedly prefer his proposition to the one before us. I would rather admit California and New Mexico into the Union as a State, wholly unfit as I think they are, than to arm the President with despotic powers to govern them, — not from any distrust of the individual by whom those powers would be exercised, but because I consider such a delegation of authority to any individual utterly indefensible.

The proposition of the Senator from Tennessee is disposed of, and I have therefore not a word to say in respect to it. But there are three other propositions before this body: first, the bill introduced by the select committee, of which the Senator from Illinois[1] is chairman; second, the amendment of the Senator from Wisconsin, now under immediate consideration; and, third, the territorial bill which was received from the House yesterday, and referred to the Committee on Territories this morning. The first creates a State out of a portion of California, and admits it into the Union; it also creates the State of New Mexico *in futuro*, and leaves it out of the Union. The amendment of the Senator from Wisconsin vests in the President all the power which a state or territorial government ought to possess over both territories. It authorizes him to prescribe and establish all proper and needful rules and regulations, in conformity with the Constitution of the United States, to carry into operation the laws referred to in the first part of the proposition, for the preservation of order and tranquillity, and the establishment

[1] Mr. Douglas.

of justice therein, — not an executive, but a creative power, — and from time to time to modify or change said rules and regulations, in such a manner as may seem to him desirable and proper. It authorizes him to establish offices, and to appoint and commission officers, for such terms as he may think proper, and to fix their compensation. It is literally arming him with dictatorial powers. It appears to me to delegate to him, nearly in the language of the Constitution, the power under which the authority to establish governments for the territories has been claimed. And, sir, if the President elect, on taking into his hands the reins of government, should find himself, in respect to the States, a less absolute ruler than he was at the head of his army, he will, in respect to these territories, be amply indemnified for any diminution of authority he may have sustained by exchanging a military for a civil station. He will find himself in the possession of larger powers than he ever before possessed. I repeat, my objection is not founded on any distrust of the individual by whom these powers are to be exercised. I believe him to possess honesty and truth, — the highest ornaments of exalted station. But I will not consent to delegate to any individual, whatever confidence I may have in him, the powers this amendment proposes to confer, — "mighty powers," as the mover himself pronounced them.

I forbore, Mr. President, to take any part in the debate while the Senate was in Committee of the Whole, except to urge that all such amendments might be withdrawn. I forbore to make any proposition, by way of amendment, to that offered by the Senator from Wisconsin, because I believed all such propositions to be out of place. But when this amendment had been adopted by a deliberate vote of the Senate, I prepared a bill — a full territorial bill — with a view to establish a government in California, on the basis of law, with powers clearly defined for the governing, and rights clearly defined for the governed. When the territorial bill was received yesterday from the House, I resolved not to offer mine as an amendment to the bill before us, extremely averse as I am to all of these propositions, in the manner in which they are presented. But I hold a territorial government the only proper one to be created for these territories, under a system like ours, excepting for the merest temporary purposes. The object of the amendment of the Senator from Wisconsin is more than temporary, whatever its language may import. It has no limitation in point of time. The powers it confers are equally unlimited in scope and duration. And, Mr. President, I am constrained to say, with all deference to the majority of the Senate, that I consider it the most objectionable proposition I have been required to vote upon since I have been a member of this body.

Precedents have been cited to sustain this amendment: one in the case of Florida, and the other in that of Louisiana. Now, sir, let me refer to dates to see how far the precedents are applicable to it. The treaty with Spain for the cession of Florida was ratified here on the 22d of February, 1819, and it was to be ratified in six months, or sooner if possible, by the King of Spain. This was the short session of Congress; and the six months would have brought us to the 22d August, 1819, when Congress was not in session. The act of the 3d March of that year was therefore passed, authorizing the President to take possession of the territory. It was to expire at the end of the next session of Congress. But the treaty was not ratified by the King of Spain until the 24th of October, 1820, and I believe Florida was not taken possession of under this act at all. The treaty as ratified by Spain was sent to the Senate on the 14th February, 1821, as the ratification was not within the time limited. It was ratified by the Senate on the 19th February of that year. The act of the 3d March, 1821, was then passed, reënacting substantially the act of 3d March, 1819. This was also to expire at the close of the next session of Congress. The Senator from New Jersey stated that Florida was governed about three years under the act of 1819. Am I mistaken?

Mr. Dayton. Two years.

The territorial government of Florida, as I have stated, was established on the 30th March, 1822,—one year and twenty-seven days after the passage of the last act authorizing the President to take possession of the territory.

The Louisiana treaty was ratified by the Senate on the 20th October, 1803. An act was passed on the 31st of the same month, eleven days afterwards, authorizing the President to take possession of the territory; and this act was to expire at the close of the same session of Congress. On the 26th March, 1804, a territorial government was established, to take effect the 1st October, 1804. The power was exercised in this case eleven months. In both cases, the duration of the act was limited to the close of the same or the ensuing session of Congress. The powers conferred were to expire at a certain period. The want of such a provision in this amendment constitutes one of the strongest objections to it. But even this omission sinks into insignificance when compared with the magnitude of the powers which the amendment confers.

I cannot believe this amendment can receive all the constitutional sanctions necessary to give it the validity of law. I shall, therefore, proceed to examine the other propositions before the Senate, as we may be called upon to act on them when it is too late for discussion. I wish to avail myself, for a very short time, of the privilege which has been taken by other Senators, of speaking upon the different propositions before us.

The 14th May, 1787, was the day fixed for the meeting of the Federal convention by which the Constitution of the United States was framed. A majority of the States was not convened until the 25th of the same month; and nothing was done, with the exception of organizing and adopting rules for the orderly transaction of business, until the 29th, when Governor Randolph, of Virginia, to use the language of the Journal, "opened the main business of the session"; or, as he expressed himself, "the great subject of their mission."

He spoke of the difficulty of the crisis, the necessity of revising the Federal system, the properties such a government ought to possess, the defects of the Confederation, the dangerous situation of the States, and the remedy. His propositions for the correction and enlargement of the Articles of Confederation, so as to accomplish the objects of their institution, were stated in a series of resolutions, one of which declared that provision ought to be made for the admission of States, lawfully arising within the limits of the United States, whether from a voluntary junction of government and territory, or otherwise. He was immediately followed by Mr. Charles Pinckney, of South Carolina, who presented a plan of a Federal Constitution, in which it was provided that the Legislature should have power to admit new States into the Union on the same terms with the original States, provided two thirds of the members present in both Houses agree. We all know in what manner these propositions were modified in the subsequent proceedings of the convention, and the limitations by which the exercise of the power was guarded by the framers of the Constitution. How far the extension of our political jurisdiction beyond the existing boundaries of the States and their territories was in contemplation at that time, I do not stop to inquire. We have given a practical construction to this provision of the Constitution. We have admitted into the Union six States beyond the limits of the thirteen original States and their territories,—one an independent nation, and the others colonial dependencies at the time of their acquisition.

The debates in the Federal convention, which seem to have had an exclusive reference to the admission of new States from territory we then possessed, show that, even in these cases, the extension of the proposed system, so as to include new members, was deemed a matter of the utmost delicacy and importance, not only as affecting the proper balance of its parts, but in respect to the moral influence of such extension upon the character of the whole. This disposition in the original States to surround the system with all the safeguards necessary to insure its stability, and to perpetuate the principles in which its foundations were laid, had even an earlier date than the era of the Federal Constitution. It is shown in the ordinance of the Congress of the Confederation, providing for the territory northwest of the Ohio river. The ordinance prescribed rules for the government of that territory, in its moral as well as its political relations; and it imposed upon the admission of the States to be formed out of it, in respect to representation, conditions more onerous than those which were annexed by the Federal convention to the representation of the thirteen original States. These exactions and conditions all had for their object to maintain the purity of the system, the homogeneousness of its parts, and the harmony of its movements. They looked to training and discipline in the school of representative government before the communities which were to be incorporated into the Union were raised to the dignity and equality of sovereign States.

Sir, I hold to this prudence and caution in the founders of the Republic. I believe it to be due to ourselves, to the institutions they framed, and to the future millions whose destiny for good or for evil is in some degree to be wrought out in our political action.

I deduce, then, from the organization of the government, this practical principle, which I hold to be fundamental: that no State ought to be admitted into the Union which has not been prepared by a familiar knowledge of the theory and practice of our political system, and by such a training in the discipline of free institutions as to render its participation in the administration of the general concerns an aid and an advantage, not an embarrassment and an obstacle, to the steady action of the system.

This requirement, which I consider absolute, is not fulfilled by the condition of California. The bill reported by the select committee admits that territory into the Union at once as a sovereign State. That, too, was the purport of the amendment of the Senator from Tennessee, though it embraced New Mexico also. This proposition is directly opposed to all the practical rules and usages of the Republic, from its foundation to the present day. It is in palpable violation of the principle I have stated as inherent in the organization of the Federal government. It discards all the prudential considerations which entered into the reasonings of the framers of the Constitution concerning the extension of our political system.

Let me state some of the leading objections to it, as they relate to the condition of California. 1. Its present inhabitants are, to a considerable extent, Indians or Mexicans of mixed blood. 2. They are, for the most part, uneducated. 3. They are not sufficiently familiar with the business of self-government. 4. They do not even speak our language. 5. They would not come into the Union with an enlightened understanding of the principles of our political system, or with the general cultivation and intelligence essential to such a fulfilment of the duties and responsibilities of the American citizen as to render them safe participants in the administration of the government. I need not enlarge upon these propositions. Those who are familiar with the condition of California and the character of the people will assent to their truth. I hold these objections to the immediate admission of California into the Union as a State — objections drawn from the character and condition of the people — to be insuperable. I know very well that territory is rapidly filling up, and that it is receiving from us thousands of citizens, active, enterprising, and of unexceptionable character. But we know also that it is receiving multitudes of adventurers from almost every quarter of the globe, — from both hemispheres, from Oceanica, from the European continent and islands, — some for a permanent abode, but more for mere temporary purposes. I wish to see this heterogeneous mass pass through the process of fermentation, to which it is destined, and settle down into something like consistence, before we undertake to endow it with all the attributes of self-government.

This view of the subject is sustained by the uniform practice of the government. 1. Our alien laws have always prescribed a period of probation for individuals who come among us for a permanent abode, and to unite their fortunes to ours. This period has always been of several years in duration. The most liberal (and of these I have always claimed to be one) have never proposed to dispense altogether with this probationary term. The only question is as to its proper extent. It proceeds upon the principle, admitted by all, that no man shall become a member of our political association until he has been taught by experience to appreciate its advantages, and to take part in its deliberations with some knowledge of its requirements. 2. The same principle which has governed in cases of individual immigration has been applied to territories acquired by treaty and to large masses of persons. When Louisiana was ceded to us by France, we stipulated that the inhabitants should be incorporated into the Union, and admitted as soon as possible, according to the principles of the Federal Constitution, to the enjoyments of the rights, advantages, and immunities of citizens of the United States; and in the mean time that they should be maintained and protected in the enjoyment of their liberty, their property, and in the exercise of the religion they professed.

Louisiana was acquired in 1803. The inhabitants made repeated applications for admission into the Union; they protested against the tardy action of Congress; they appealed to the treaty in vindication of their right to such admission. Yet Congress refused to admit Louisiana into the Union as a State until 1812. Nine years were deemed necessary to prepare the inhabitants for the exercise of the highest political rights, though there was a strong infusion of our own citizens among them.

Florida was acquired in 1820, and in the treaty with Spain there was a stipulation nearly identical in language with that which was contained in the treaty with France for the cession of Louisiana, in respect to the admission of the inhabitants into the Union. Yet Florida was not admitted as a State until 1845, — a quarter of a century after its acquisition. I know that numbers had something to do with this delay; but other considerations doubtless had their influence also. These territories were both foreign; and, when acquired, their inhabitants were presumed to have but little knowledge of the theory or practice of our political institutions.

But even with our own territories and our own people we have dealt with the same caution and the same prudent regard to the privileges which an admission into the Union confers. Instead of curtailing the period of probation, where Congress had a discretion, we have rather been disposed to insist on a rigid fulfilment of the prescribed conditions, both in respect to numbers and time.

The ordinance of 1787, by which the division of the territory northwest of the Ohio river into States, and the ultimate incorporation of those States into the Union, were provided for, fixed on sixty thousand free inhabitants as the number necessary to their admission; but it was provided also that, so far as it should consist with the general interest of the Confederacy, such admission might be allowed at an earlier period, and with a less number of inhabitants. Yet Ohio was not admitted into the Union until 1802. It must have had sixty thousand inhabitants; and it was admitted with a single member of Congress. At the same time the ratio of representation in Congress was one member for thirty-three thousand inhabitants.

Indiana was admitted in 1816, Illinois in 1818, Michigan in 1837, and Wisconsin a year ago. These territories were settled chiefly by our own people. The settlers came from the old States. They were nurtured in the love of liberty, and trained to the exercise of political rights. All their associations were of a character to render them safe depositaries of the priceless treasure of freedom. Yet they were subjected to a protracted probation. They were held in political subjection, not only in respect to the appointment of their chief executive officers, but in the more delicate relation of supervising and overruling them in the exercise of the power of legislation.

Such, Mr. President, has been our practice, not only in respect to territories acquired by treaties with foreign powers, but in respect to our own people occupying territories held by a tenure coeval with our political independence. The bill reported by the select committee proposes to overthrow and reverse the uniform practice of the country in this essential particular. This practice assumes that some familiarity with the duties and privileges of citizenship is necessary for the inhabitants of a territory as a preparation for the independent management of their public affairs. It supposes that a territorial government, founded upon principles and administered according to laws analogous to those which govern the State administrations, should precede the admission of a territory into the Union. It holds the privileges, the responsibilities, the rights incident to an independent membership of the political association, into which the States have entered, to be of too great a value to be communicated to other communities without a just regard to their capacity for assuming and exercising them with advantage to others as well as to themselves.

The bill discards all these considerations. California has not yet been acquired a single year; nine months ago it was foreign territory. Its population is foreign; its interests, associations, usages, laws, and institutions are, in some degree, alien to our own. The people do not even speak our language; they cannot read our Constitution or laws without translating them into a foreign tongue. Yet the committee propose to admit it into the Union on the footing of the original States, and to give it a weight in this body equal to that of Virginia, or Pennsylvania, or New York. With a population, perhaps, of twenty thousand souls, it is to wield here an influence equal to that of New York, with three millions.

I cannot consent to cheapen, in this manner, an independent membership in the union of the States. I believe it to be unjust to the present members of the Union, hazardous to the stability of the government, a departure from a wise and well-considered policy, and unjust, as I shall endeavor to show, to California herself.

Her physical and social condition is as unsuited to the independent management of her own concerns as her intellectual and moral. Her population is scattered over a vast surface; her improvements are not such as to give stability to her political organization; she has no commerce; she has hardly emerged from the pastoral state and risen to the grade of an agricultural community. She has not the strength to uphold an independent sovereignty. The recent discoveries of gold have made a bad condition worse; they have dissolved, for the time being, the very bonds of society. It will require months, if not years, to restore order, to bring back her people to the sober pursuits of industry, and to qualify them for any deliberative purpose. I believe there never was a community less fitted than California is at this moment, and under existing circumstances, to organize a government and put it in operation. All the influences which are at work with the minds and passions of men are to the last degree unfavorable to the high duty the bill imposes on them. When all the obligations which bind men to the performance of their duty appear to have lost their force; when ships are abandoned by their crews; when soldiers desert by platoons and companies; when villages and towns are depopulated; and when the whole community is possessed by the frenzy of gold-digging, and lose sight of all other objects; we call upon them to meet in solemn conclave and perform the highest and most responsible of all deliberative acts — that of framing a constitution for their own government, — a work of deliberation and soberness and calm reflection. I have been, from the beginning, opposed to this whole scheme. I believe, if ever there was an occasion, since the foundations of this Republic were laid, when it was incumbent upon Congress to establish a temporary government for a territory, to provide for its wants, to give direction to its action, and to sustain it by the collective wisdom and strength of the whole community, until it shall have passed through the period of probation to which all our territories have been subjected, — a period rendered doubly perilous there by the prevailing disorganization, — that occasion is presented in the condition of California.

I am in favor, then, of a territorial government, endowed with the energy to control and remedy existing embarrassments and evils. I believe the course proper in all similar cases is preëminently proper in this. I shall concur in no other, unless it be for a mere temporary purpose. And it was with great regret that I heard honorable Senators say there was no hope of giving California a territorial government. I do not concur in opinion with them. I will not relinquish hope until the last moment. The most certain mode of giving effect to a feeling of hopelessness is to despair of the battle before it is fought, and resort to other devices to supply our own want of constancy and courage.

The objections I have stated to this bill are insuperable; they are fundamental, and therefore not to be obviated. There are objections of detail, which might be remedied; but I will merely state, without enlarging upon them, — as no variation in the details can reconcile me to the general purpose of the bill, — the immediate admission of California into the Union as a State.

Of these objections I consider the dismemberment of California one of the most serious. I would keep that territory as it is until the spread of population and the growth of improvement shall indicate where the division line can be drawn with least prejudice to the parties concerned. The bill proposes a chain of mountains as the eastern boundary. Sir, physical obstacles are not always the most appropriate or convenient for statistical divisions. Moral obstacles are more powerful to repel, and moral affinities more powerful to attract, than physical. Identity or diversity of race, association, or condition often does more than rivers, and mountains, and plains to bind men together or force them asunder. What is there, for instance, in the class of natural obstacles more appropriate for a statistical demarcation than the Alleghany mountains? And yet they have not sufficed to divide Virginia into two distinct communities. Nor have they sufficed to divide Pennsylvania into two States. What is there more suitable for such a purpose than the Chesapeake bay? And yet Maryland lies on both sides of it. If we were to look to physical obstacles as constituting the most appropriate boundary for California on the east, we ought to stop at the Sierra Nevada, which is more elevated than the boundary of the committee, "the dividing ridge separating the waters flowing into the Colorado from those flowing into the Great Basin," or we ought to go on to the Sierra Madre, and leave the territory with its present limits. We need not consider geographical extent as an objection to the organization of a territorial government. When Louisiana was acquired, we placed all that part of it north of the thirty-third parallel of latitude under the direction of the governor and the judges of the Indiana territory, for the purposes of government and the administration of justice; and it had a more extended area than California.

Let us leave statistical divisions to be fixed by events. The movement of population, physical development, social progress, and their incidents, — these are the great causes which mark out permanent boundaries between separate states. Let us leave California to be filled up, and the races which occupy it can better determine than we who shall live apart and who together.

The disposition the bill makes of New Mexico, I consider, if possible, still more objectionable. She was known long before the era of Von Humboldt as having a distinct organization. In connection with Durango and Chihuahua, she constituted an independent member of the Mexican confederation, under the constitutive act of 1824, and a separate territory under the constitution of that year. The consolidation of the confederated states into a central republic, under the constitution of 1836, made her a separate department, with an independent organization for the management of her local concerns. We have held commercial intercourse with her under laws applying only to herself and another member of the Mexican republic. She has had an individual name, existence, and organization. So far as I am concerned, they shall be respected. I will neither consent that she shall be dismembered nor merged in a more extended organization. Subjection by conquest is the greatest humiliation that can befall a community. The magnanimity of the conquerors should spare the subjugated state the further humiliation of dismemberment, or the obliteration of its identity in a useless extension. I will neither consent to play towards New Mexico the part of Austria, Russia, and Prussia towards Poland, nor the part of the Holy Alliance towards Genoa. I will neither agree that she shall be divided nor swallowed up. She has petitioned to us to save her from dismemberment. I am for exercising our power over her with humanity as well as forbearance, — for conforming, as far as we can, to the wishes of the vanquished. I believe she is now, considering all circumstances, as well fitted to come into the Union as California. I will not consent to dilute what fitness for self-government she possesses by a territorial expansion of which I can neither comprehend the object nor foresee the result.

But it is not quite clear, from the language of this bill, what is to be the fate of New Mexico, — whether she is to be merged wholly or in part in Texas, or merely drawn out to the Pacific. If the latter, — and I suppose this to be the intention of the committee, — she will be stretched out some two or three hundred miles westward on the north, and eight or nine hundred on the south. But the New Mexico created by the bill is to be bounded on the east by the summit of the Rocky Mountains and the State of Texas. The Rocky Mountains, or the Sierra Madre, a continuation of them, are now the western boundary of New Mexico. I am not sure whether they would not under this bill become the western boundary of Texas. I am not sure that New Mexico would not be merged in Texas by the mere designation of a boundary line. The bill seems to me, by a literal construction of its terms, to accomplish these three objects, alike objectionable in my mind: 1. The annexation of New Mexico to Texas. 2. The dismemberment of California. And, 3. The creation of a new State of New Mexico, wholly within the limits of California, and wholly without the limits of the present New Mexico.

Nor is this all. While the bill introduces California into the Union, it leaves New Mexico out of it. We consent that it shall become a State of this Union, with the name and style of the State of New Mexico, as soon as it shall have the proper number of inhabitants. What is the proper number of inhabitants? Louisiana was admitted into the Union with about eighty thousand; (I speak in round numbers;) Ohio, with about sixty thousand; Illinois, with forty thousand; Michigan, with one hundred and fifty thousand; and Florida, with perhaps thirty thousand white persons. Where is the criterion of proper numbers to be sought for? Is it in the ratio of representation in Congress? Why not say so, if it be intended? The greater portion of the territory is nearly unpopulated. It is not likely, either from its position or physical character, to be populated rapidly. What is to be its political condition until it has the proper number of inhabitants? It cannot be admitted into the Union until then. What is to become of it in the mean time? To what political category is it to belong? It is not to be a territory. The bill makes no provision for it as such. We merely cut it off from California, and leave it to the uncertain progress of events, and the still more uncertain phraseology of our own statute. We cast it away, to use a barbarous law-phrase, "*a flotsam*" on the ocean of politics, — "*incertum quo fata ferant*," — to reclaim it ourselves at some future day, if we can find it first, and agree afterwards on the meaning of our own enactment.

I am opposed to this whole scheme; it seems to me to have been dictated by a desire to avoid embarrassing questions. I trust I appreciate rightly the motives of honorable Senators. But I hold that there is always more embarrassment in postponing or evading troublesome questions than in meeting them boldly, and disposing of them promptly when they present themselves. I propose to myself but two inquiries in reference to the course we ought to adopt. 1. What does the interest of the country, and, 2. What does the interest of California and New Mexico require? The answer seems to me to be too clear to be mistaken. I have already given it. Both considerations point to a territorial government, framed on proper principles.

What shall these principles be? This is the only question which remains to be considered. Recognizing, as I do, to the fullest extent, the democratic doctrine of instructions, I am not altogether a free agent in this matter. During the last three years, resolutions have been as many times passed by the legislature of New York, and presented here by myself, declaring that in any territories acquired from Mexico slavery ought to be prohibited. I have endeavored to carry out the instructions by which those resolutions were accompanied. I have done so with the more cheerfulness, because, apart from all obligations of obedience, I believe them just.

I hold, then, that territorial governments ought to be organized for California and New Mexico, and that the act establishing them should contain a prohibition of slavery. I believe there never was an occasion in which such a prohibition was demanded by higher obligations than the present. I shall endeavor to make it apparent to the judgment of the Senate, and for this reason I shall be under the necessity of entering into a brief review of the origin and progress of slavery in the United States; and I shall begin with the condition of the American colonies before the establishment of their independence.

Slavery, I believe, was never originally established by law in any State in this Union, nor was it so established in the British colonies in America. The relation of master and slave, in modern times and in civilized states, usually springs up in the transactions of commerce, without positive authority, and the law afterward comes in to regulate it. It was so in the American colonies. It is a curious fact, that the same year (1620) which witnessed the landing of the Pilgrims on the Rock of Plymouth saw the first ship enter the waters of the Chesapeake bay and the James river with Africans to be sold into slavery. It is still more curious that the ship freighted with freemen and the ship freighted with slaves commenced their voyages from the same country — Holland. In the same year the monopoly of the London company was overturned, and the commerce of the colony of Virginia was thrown open to free competition.

The introduction of slaves into that colony was one of the first fruits of this commercial freedom, — not necessarily, but as one of those incidents which the chances of life bring with them to illustrate its uncertainties and its contradictions. There was no law in Virginia at that time authorizing the existence of slavery; nor was there any such law in England. It gained a foothold without law. Indeed, the early enactments of the colony of Virginia had for their objects to restrain the introduction of slaves, and to limit the control of their masters over them. Before the Revolution, she petitioned the British king to sanction the measures she had adopted for the suppression of the slave-trade. The appeal was vain. It was the interest of British traders, who derived a mercenary profit from this detestable traffic, that it should continue; and, down to the period of the Revolution, every effort on the part of Virginia and the other colonies to put a stop to it was fruitless. Slavery was thus forced upon us by Great Britain; we are not responsible for its origin. In the North it has been abolished; in the South, peculiar circumstances have continued it in existence. I make no inquiry into those circumstances, or their necessary influence upon the result. The responsibility which rests upon us is to see that it is not further extended, that it shall not, as far as depends on us, be planted where it has never existed, or where it has been abolished.

After the termination of the war with Great Britain, when the American colonies, to use the language of the Declaration of Independence, had "assumed among the Powers of the earth the equal and separate station to which the laws of Nature and of Nature's God entitled them," the attention of the great men of the country was turned to the subject of slavery, not only with a view to its exclusion from the unoccupied portions of the Union, but with a view to its extinction in the States where it existed. The definitive treaty of peace with Great Britain, acknowledging our independence, was signed in September, 1783. In March, 1784, Mr. Jefferson introduced into the Congress of the Confederation a plan of a temporary government for the territory northwest of the Ohio river, containing a provision abolishing slavery after the year 1800 in that territory, now comprising the States of Ohio, Indiana, Illinois, Michigan, and Wisconsin.

The anti-slavery clause received the votes of six States out of the ten present in Congress. Under the Articles of Confederation the delegates voted by States; and by the same Articles a majority of the thirteen States was requisite to carry any proposition. Mr. Jefferson's proposition, having received only six votes, was not adopted.

I hold in my hand, Mr. President, a copy of his plan for a temporary government for the Northwest territory, made from the original, which I found a few weeks ago, among the archives of the Confederation, in the State Department, where they are deposited.[1] The original is in the clear, careful handwriting of Mr. Jefferson; and it settles the question of authorship. It divides the territory into ten States instead of five, as was finally determined; and it contains the anti-slavery clause to which I have referred, and which has heretofore been attributed to him. I will read it for the information of the Senate. Like some other propositions of a kindred character, and of later date, it is in the form of a proviso: —

> "After the year 1800 of the Christian era, there shall be neither slavery nor involuntary servitude in any of the said States otherwise than in punishment of crimes whereof the party shall have been duly convicted."[2]

I am happy to have had it in my power to refer this declaration to the author of an earlier declaration in favor of human freedom, — I mean that of our independence, — and to have found it in his own handwriting. Without this testimony, no one could doubt, on reading the whole paper, that it was written by him. It contains internal evidences of authorship which, to any one familiar with his style of composition and his peculiarity of thought, must be conclusive. Let it be known henceforth as the Jefferson proviso. As such, it will at least escape the imputation of selfish motives, from which, in the prevailing heat of party contention, no follower in the same field can hope to be exempt, however unjustly they may be attributed to him. I have already said that this proposition failed for the want of a single vote. It was renewed in 1785 by Rufus King, then representing the State of Massachusetts, and it was

[1] Appendix, No. 1.

[2] Appendix, No. 2.

referred to a committee, though it was not finally acted upon at that time. The reference was made by the votes of eight States out of eleven present, one State being absent, and another represented by a single delegate, and therefore not entitled, according to the Articles of Confederation, to vote.[1]

Thus things remained until 1787, when the ordinance of that year was passed, establishing a government for the Northwestern territory, and prohibiting slavery within it forever, except for crimes. This ordinance was reported by a committee of which Mr. Edward Carrington, of Virginia, was chairman, and Mr. Nathan Dane, of Massachusetts, a leading member. It received the votes of all the States present. It was a unanimous vote as to States, and unanimous, with a single exception, as to delegates. There were only eight States present, viz: Massachusetts, New York, New Jersey, Delaware, Virginia, North Carolina, South Carolina, and Georgia. The five absent States were New Hampshire, Connecticut, Rhode Island, Pennsylvania, and Maryland. The first four — New Hampshire, Connecticut, Rhode Island, and Pennsylvania — voted for Mr. Jefferson's proviso in 1784, and Maryland voted to refer Mr. King's proposition in 1785.[2]

Thus, I think, it may be fairly asserted that if all the States had been represented in Congress, the vote would have been equally unanimous. The ordinance would have been adopted by the votes of the thirteen States.

The South united with the North in excluding slavery from this territory. It was a unanimous verdict of the whole country against the extension of slavery. It was the first great movement of our revolutionary fathers to rid themselves of the responsibility and the country of the evil of slavery. And I take great pleasure in awarding to a Southern man, to Thomas Jefferson, the conception of this great measure of justice and humanity.

While the Congress of the Confederation, sitting in New

[1] Appendix, No. 3. [2] Appendix, No. 4.

York, was framing the ordinance of 1787, the Federal convention, sitting in Philadelphia, was framing the Constitution of the United States. While the former body was devising measures for the exclusion of slavery from the Northwestern territory, the latter was engaged in providing for the suppression of the African slave-trade. Thus, the representatives of the new-born Republic, legislating for the old government, and framing a new system for the better administration of their common concerns, — sitting in different places, and acting in separate capacities, — were jointly engaged in eradicating what they considered a great public evil and reproach. While the former declared that slavery should thenceforth be forever prohibited in the Northwestern territory, the latter virtually declared (though in the form of a restriction on the exercise of a power) the American slave-trade should cease after the year 1807. It would have been abolished at once but for the opposition of South Carolina and Georgia, the only States which were at that time desirous of continuing it.

In the Federal convention, Virginia was among the foremost in her opposition to the slave-trade. Madison, and Mason, and Randolph were distinguished for the ability and zeal with which they advocated its immediate suppression. They were unwilling to wait twenty years for its abolition. But their efforts were unavailing; and, for fear South Carolina and Georgia would not come into the Union, a compromise was agreed on, and the traffic was tolerated until 1808. On the first day of January of that year, the very first day Congress had power to make its prohibition effective, the slave-trade was abolished forever by an act passed ten months before.

I have stated these historical details, Mr. President, for the purpose of showing two facts: 1. That the policy of the founders of the Republic was to get rid of slavery, by preventing its extension, and by suppressing the African slave-trade; and 2. That some of the Southern States were among the foremost in advocating both measures, with a view to the accomplishment of the ultimate object. One of the avowed objects of the abolition of the slave-trade was to prevent the extension of slavery into the territories. The same policy prevailed for many years. The inhabitants of the Northwest territory, or a portion of it, (that portion, I believe, which now constitutes the States of Indiana and Illinois,) petitioned Congress for the privilege of importing slaves from the States; and they had sufficient influence to obtain two reports in favor of a temporary suspension of the sixth article of the ordinance of 1787. But their prayer was not granted. The inhabitants of Louisiana, before the abolition of the slave-trade, petitioned for the privilege of importing slaves. Their prayer was denied. Wherever Congress had the power, it was exercised to prevent the extension of slavery beyond the States and territories in which it existed.

I have always been opposed to interference with slavery where it exists. The Federal government has no control over it, directly or indirectly, within the limits of the States. It is a civil relation over which they have exclusive jurisdiction. It must ever rest with them to determine whether it shall be continued or abolished within their limits. But it is not so with the territories. Congress has always exercised the power of regulating their civil as well as their political relations. The territorial governments are the creatures of Federal legislation; they have no powers except such as are conferred on them by Congress. Congress stands to the inhabitants of the territories in the relation in which the State legislatures stand to the people of the States. The power of regulating the internal concerns of the inhabitants of the territories has been exercised under every administration since the adoption of the Constitution.

Sir, I hold the exercise of this power for the exclusion of slavery from California and New Mexico to be even of higher obligation than it was in respect to the Northwestern territory. Slavery existed in that territory at the time the ordinance of 1787 was framed and passed. The tenure of slaves owned by the inhabitants of the territory and held within it was sanctioned by the courts. The prohibition was construed to extend only to persons born or brought into the territory subsequently to the adoption of the ordinance.

The situation of California and New Mexico is entirely different. Mexico long since abolished slavery throughout her limits. The abolition was first publicly proclaimed by President Guerrero in 1829, in pursuance, as the decree declares, of extraordinary powers vested in him. It was again declared to be abolished by an act of the sovereign Congress in 1837, and again by the Constitution of 1844. Though, as a nation, but imperfectly civilized, struggling against the embarrassments of bad government, and distracted by internal dissensions, arising, in a great degree, out of the heterogeneous character of her population, Mexico has, nevertheless, placed her institutions on the broad foundation of human liberty, by declaring all within her limits to be free.

To permit slavery to be carried into California and New Mexico would be to annul this declaration, and to reëstablish slavery where it has been abolished. I cannot consent to any settlement of this question which can by possibility have such a result.

Mr. Berrien. I desire to inquire of the Senator from New York if he intends to assert that the proclamation of President Guerrero was issued under any power specially delegated to him in reference to this subject?

I will answer the Senator with pleasure. I take the decree as I find it. I said that the first public declaration was made by President Guerrero in 1829, in pursuance, as his decree stated, of extraordinary powers conceded to him. I am under no obligation to inquire further in relation to the matter, or to look behind the act for the authority on which it was founded.

Mr. Berrien. I ask the question with a view of ascertaining whether the Senator was disposed to contend that slavery was abolished in New Mexico by virtue of any other power than this proclamation?

I suppose it was abolished by virtue of the authority on which the decree was made. I have the decree, and will read it, if the Senator from Georgia desires it.

Mr. Berrien. The Senator is not aware, perhaps, of the fact, that the power granted to the President was given him for the purpose of repelling invasion, and had no other object. I would propound another question: If slavery was abolished by force of the proclamation of President Guerrero, in 1829, what slavery remained in Mexico to be abolished by the act of the sovereign Congress, and whence did the sovereign Congress derive the power to do that which belonged to the municipal authorities of the several States exclusively?

I prefer not to answer the inquiry of the Senator; it will require a diversion from the course of my remarks, which I do not care to make.[1] I repeat, the first public declaration that slavery was abolished was made in 1829; the next by the Congress of 1837; and they were virtually reaffirmed by the constitution of 1844. I do not design now to go beyond the limits of these executive, legislative, and constitutional acts, to inquire into the authority upon which they rested. I stated, when I was interrupted, that the effect of carrying slavery into California would be to subvert the prohibition contained in these acts. This is the first great objection. The second is, that it would be unjust to the community at large, by promoting the multiplication of a race which adds neither to the intellectual nor physical power of the body politic, and which excludes free labor as far as it extends the labor of slaves. I consider this one of the greatest objections to it. It should be our object to promote, in every constitutional way, the extension of free labor, and the most effectual is to devote the unoccupied spaces of the West to the white race. The third objection is, that it would be unjust to California and New Mexico. They have no slaves. I believe I am authorized to say, they desire none.

[1] See Appendix, No. 5.

Mr. Foote. I would inquire of the Senator from New York, if he considers that any injustice will result to California and New Mexico, by allowing the people of those territories to do with this matter as they please?

I am in favor of doing what the fathers of the Republic did in relation to the Northwestern territory, — of preventing the extension to California of what they considered, and what I consider, a great evil. If we carry slavery into New Mexico and California, we shall do it against the wishes of the people there. They have no slaves now, and we should plant slavery where it does not exist. We should stand before the world in the same relation in which Great Britain stood to her American colonies. She allowed slavery to be carried into those colonies against their wishes, and, in some instances, against their earnest remonstrances.

The introduction of slavery into California and New Mexico, as I conceive, would be the more indefensible, as there is nothing in the soil and climate which renders the labor of the African race necessary, — nothing that makes it unsafe or oppressive for whites to be employed in productive industry under any of its forms. New Mexico consists, for the most part, of mountains, with narrow valleys between, which require to be watered by artificial means. There is no need of the African race. A large portion of California is elevated and broken. It yields nothing to the production of which slave labor is even claimed to be indispensable. Much of the value of that territory consists in the maritime valley which lies on the Pacific. It is about five hundred miles long, and one hundred and fifty wide, with an area of some seventy-five thousand square miles. The breezes from the Pacific moderate the temperature, and the mountains on the east, rising to the height of thousands of feet, collect and precipitate the moisture of the atmosphere, and pour it down in fertilizing streams into the valley below. It is said by Frémont to bear a strong resemblance to Italy in soil, climate, and capacity for production. It is perhaps the finest region of the same extent in the western hemisphere. The vine, the olive, and the fig, the infinite variety of fruits and grains which are produced within the tropics, are to be found in California. Nature has, in a word, lavished upon it her choicest gifts. In the recent discoveries of gold, there is much to be deplored. Let us hope that it will soon become exhausted, and that the steady pursuits of agricultural, commercial, and mechanical industry, by which alone nations are made prosperous, may constitute the sole objects of application. There is no need of blacks in California; the white race can labor there without difficulty. The productions are such as to require the care and intelligence of the more intellectual race. It would be a perversion of the purposes of nature, in more senses than one, to carry slaves there.

I believe this will be the effect of the amendment of the Senator from Wisconsin, but not by virtue of any right conferred by the Constitution. I do not acknowledge the existence of any such right. I speak of practical effects. Slaves have been carried, and always will be carried, wherever they are not prohibited. Ohio, Indiana, Illinois, and Missouri are in the same range of States. The fortieth parallel of latitude divides them all. The influences of soil and climate are much the same in each. From the first three, slavery has been excluded by the ordinance of 1787. The last has been overrun with slavery for want of a prohibition. The fate of California in this respect will be settled by similar laws. I believe we shall, by the amendment under consideration, lay the foundation of a contest among the inhabitants of California, far more disastrous than their present disorganization. I hold it to be our duty to settle this question ourselves, instead of sending it out to the Pacific to distract our countrymen in laying the foundation of a new government.

I have but one more consideration to present in connection with this topic; and I submit whether this ought not to weigh much with us all? When the war with Mexico was commenced, we were charged with the intention of acquiring territory with a view to carrying slaves into it. The charge was denied. We repelled the imputation, as doing injustice to our motives. Yet, in the very first attempt to establish a government for that territory, the right is insisted upon — the purpose is confessed. Whether the Mexican government was aware of this imputation, I do not know; but in the negotiation with Mr. Trist, the Mexican commissioners wished us to stipulate not to carry slavery into the territory which was proposed to be ceded.

Mr. FOOTE. Will the honorable Senator from New York allow me to propound a question to him? That question is this: Who, from the South, either here or elsewhere, has avowed any such purpose? Had Southern Senators insisted upon anything but that Congress shall not legislate on the subject of slavery in the territories at all? Have we asked Congress to legislate for the introduction of slavery, or avowed any purpose of doing anything except to resist unconstitutional encroachment?

I was speaking of an avowed purpose to carry slaves into California; and I thought I understood the Senator from Mississippi not only as asserting the right, but as supporting his argument by contending that a portion of the country was likely to become a slaveholding region.

Mr. FOOTE. I said this, on that point: It is well known that slavery is adapted to only a small portion of this territory. Believing this to be the case, I urged that the moderation and forbearance of the South, in order to establish a territorial government affording protection to the people of these territories, is strikingly exhibited in her not urging her right, in any shape or form, to be authorized specially by law to carry slaves there. We ask nothing but to *be let alone.*

I cannot consent to go into this discussion now. I said, that whether the Mexican government was aware of the imputation cast upon us, I did not know; but that in the negotiation with Mr. Trist, the Mexican commissioners wished us to stipulate that we should not allow slavery to be established in any territory they should cede to us. I will read a brief extract from a letter addressed by Mr. Trist to Mr. Buchanan upon this subject, while the negotiation was pending. It is dated the 4th September, 1847, and is contained in a document printed by order of the Senate.

"Among the points which came under discussion was the exclusion of slavery from all territory which should pass from Mexico. In the course of their remarks on the subject, I was told, that, if it were proposed to the people of the United States to part with a portion of their territory in order that the *Inquisition* should be therein established, the proposal could not excite stronger feelings of abhorrence than those awakened in Mexico by the prospect of the introduction of slavery in any territory parted with by her."

I could make no comment on this correspondence, if I were disposed, which would be half so eloquent as the facts. These Mexicans, whom we have been accustomed to consider half-civilized, vanquished in the field, driven from their capital, compelled to make peace with us almost on our own terms, and forced to cede a portion of their territory, implore us not to carry slavery into it. Sir, I ask how should we stand before the world, liberal and enlightened as we are, proclaiming to mankind the principle of human liberty as one of the inalienable rights of our race, if we were to disregard these entreaties?

Mr. Mason. Does the Senator refer to the petition which has been presented from New Mexico?

No, sir; I refer to Mr. Trist's negotiation in Mexico, and the representations made to him during an interview with the Mexican commissioners.

Mr. Rusk. I wish to ask the honorable Senator whether he does not know that the Mexican commissioners negotiated the treaty under the influence of an agent of the British government?

I suppose there can be no doubt that the treaty is in strict accordance with the feelings and wishes of the Mexican people on this subject. Their repeated declarations in respect to the abolition of slavery prove it, under whatever influences the treaty may have been framed.

Mr. President, two years ago, when I first addressed the Senate upon this subject, under the instructions of the State of New York, I said that, by no instrumentality of hers, should slavery be carried into any portion of this continent which is free. I repeat the declaration now: by no act, by no acquiescence of hers, shall slavery be carried where it does not exist. I said at the same time, that, in whatever manner this question should be settled, if it should be decided against her views of justice and right, her devotion to the Union and to her sister-States should remain unshaken and unimpaired. Speaking in her name, and for the last time within these walls, I repeat this declaration also. She does not believe in the possibility of disunion. I am thankful that her faith is also mine. My confidence is founded upon the disinterestedness of the great body of the people, who derive their subsistence from the soil, and whose attachment is strong in proportion to their close communion with it. They have incorporated with it the labor of their own hands. It has given them back wealth and health and strength,—health to enjoy, and strength to defend what they possess. In seasons of tranquillity and peace they are unseen, too often, perhaps, forgotten; but it is in their silent and sober toil that the public prosperity is wrought out. It is only in the hour of peril that they come forth from a thousand hills and valleys and plains to sustain with strong arms the country they have made prosperous. In them the Union will find its surest protectors. They are too virtuous and too independent to be corrupted. They are spread over too broad a surface for the work of seduction. It is in towns and public assemblies, where men are concentrated, that the tempter can with more assurance sit down, as of old, in the guise of friendship, and whisper into the unsuspecting or the willing ear the lesson of disobedience and treachery. From this danger the great body of the people are secure. And let us be assured that they will never permit the banner which floats over them at home, and carries their name to every sea, to be torn down, either by internal dissension or external violence. Such is my firm, my unalterable conviction. But, if I am mistaken in all this, — if the spangled field it bears aloft is destined to be broken up, — then my prayer will be, that the star which represents New York in the constellation of States may stand fixed until every other shall have fallen!

APPENDIX, No. 1.

THE following is a copy of Mr. Jefferson's plan: —

The committee appointed to prepare a plan for the temporary government of the Western Territory, have agreed to the following resolutions:

Resolved, That the territory ceded or to be ceded by individual States to the United States, whensoever the same shall have been purchased of the Indian inhabitants, and offered for sale by the United States, shall be formed into distinct States, bounded in the following manner, as nearly as such cessions will admit, — that is to say: northwardly and southwardly by parallels of latitude, so that each State shall comprehend, from south to north, two degrees of latitude, beginning to count from the completion of thirty-one degrees north of the equator: but any territory northwardly of the forty-seventh degree shall make part of the State next below; and eastwardly and westwardly they shall be bounded, those on the Mississippi by that river on one side, and the meridian of the lowest point of the rapids of Ohio on the other; and those adjoining on the east by the same meridian on their western side, and on their eastern by the meridian of the western cape of the mouth of the Great Kanawha; and the territory eastward of this last meridian, between the Ohio, Lake Erie, and Pennsylvania, shall be one State.

That the settlers within the territory so to be purchased and offered for sale, shall, either on their own petition, or on the order of Congress, receive authority from them, with appointments of time and place for their free males, of full age, to meet together for the purpose of establishing a temporary government, to adopt the constitution and laws of any one of these States, so that such laws nevertheless shall be subject to alteration by their ordinary legislature; and to erect, subject to a like alteration, counties or townships for the election of members for their legislature.

That such temporary government shall only continue in force in any

State until it shall have acquired twenty thousand free inhabitants; when, giving due proof thereof to Congress, they shall receive from them authority, with appointments of time and place, to call a convention of representatives to establish a permanent constitution and government for themselves: *Provided*, That both the temporary and permanent governments be established on these principles as their basis: 1. [That they shall forever remain a part of the United States of America;] 2. That, in their persons, property, and territory, they shall be subject to the government of the United States in Congress assembled, and to the Articles of Confederation in all those cases in which the original States shall be so subject; 3. That they shall be subject to pay a part of the Federal debts contracted or to be contracted, to be apportioned on them by Congress according to the same common rule and measure by which apportionments thereof shall be made on the other States; 4. That their respective governments shall be in republican forms, and shall admit no person to be a citizen who holds any hereditary title; 5. That after the year 1800 of the Christian era there shall be neither slavery nor involuntary servitude in any of the said States, otherwise than in punishment of crimes, whereof the party shall have been duly convicted to have been personally guilty.

That, whensoever any of the said States shall have, of free inhabitants, as many as shall then be in any one of the least numerous of the thirteen original States, such State shall be admitted by its delegates into the Congress of the United States on an equal footing with the said original States: after which the assent of two thirds of the United States in Congress assembled shall be requisite in all those cases wherein, by the Confederation, the assent of nine States is now required: *Provided*, The consent of nine States to such admission may be obtained according to the eleventh of the Articles of Confederation. Until such admission, by their delegates into Congress, any of the said States, after the establishment of their temporary government, shall have authority to keep a sitting member in Congress, with right of debating but not of voting.

That the territory northward of the forty-fifth degree, that is to say, of the completion of forty-five degrees from the equator, and extending to the Lake of the Woods, shall be called SYLVANIA.

That of the territory under the forty-fifth and forty-fourth degrees, that which lies westward of Lake Michigan, shall be called MICHIGANIA; and that which is eastward thereof, within the peninsula formed by the lakes and waters of Michigan, Huron, St. Clair, and Erie, shall be called CHERRONESUS, and shall include any part of the peninsula which may extend above the forty-fifth degree.

Of the territory under the forty-third and forty-second degrees, that to the westward, through which the Assenisipi or Rock river runs, shall be called ASSENISIPIA; and that to the eastward, in which are the fountains of the Muskingum, the two Miamies, of the Ohio, the Wabash, the Illinois, the Miami of the Lake, and Sandusky rivers, shall be called METROPOTAMIA.

Of the territory which lies under the forty-first and fortieth degrees, the western, through which the river Illinois runs, shall be called ILLINOIA; that next adjoining to the eastward SARATOGA; and that between this last and Pennsylvania, and extending from the Ohio to Lake Erie, shall be called WASHINGTON.

Of the territory which lies under the thirty-ninth and thirty-eighth degrees, to which shall be added so much of the point of land within the fork of the Ohio and Mississippi as lies under the thirty-seventh degree, that to the westward, within and adjacent to which are the confluences of the rivers Wabash, Shawanee, Tanissee, Ohio, Illinois, Mississippi, and Missouri, shall be called POLYPOTAMIA; and that to the eastward, further up the Ohio, otherwise called the Pelisipi, shall be called PELISIPIA.

That the preceding articles shall be formed into a charter of compact, shall be duly executed by the President of the United States in Congress assembled, under his hand and the seal of the United States, shall be promulgated, and shall stand as fundamental constitutions between the thirteen original States and those newly described, unalterable but by the joint consent of the United States in Congress assembled, and of the particular State within which such alteration is proposed to be made.

This paper is indorsed as follows, in a different handwriting, supposed to be that of a clerk: "Report — Mr. Jefferson, Mr. Chase, Mr. Howell."

WASHINGTON, *February* 20, 1849.

I certify, that, at the request of my father, and with the permission of Mr. Buchanan, Secretary of State, the foregoing copy of "a plan for the temporary government of the Western Territory" was made by me from the original, deposited in the State Department among the archives of the Congress of the Confederation; and that I compared the copy with the original, with the assistance of Lund Washington, Jr., Esq., and found it correct. MORGAN DIX.

APPENDIX, No. 2.

THE following is the vote on the anti-slavery clause of Jefferson, above given, April 19, 1784: —

New Hampshire	Mr. Foster,	ay	ay.
	Mr. Blanchard,	ay	
Massachusetts	Mr. Gerry,	ay	ay.
	Mr. Patridge,	ay	
Rhode Island	Mr. Ellery,	ay	ay.
	Mr. Howell,	ay	
Connecticut	Mr. Sherman,	ay	ay.
	Mr. Wadsworth,	ay	
New York	Mr. De Witt,	ay	ay.
	Mr. Paine,	ay	
New Jersey	Mr. Dick,	ay	*
Pennsylvania	Mr. Mifflin,	ay	ay.
	Mr. Montgomery,	ay	
	Mr. Hand,	ay	
Maryland	Mr. McHenry,	no	no.
	Mr. Stone,	no	
Virginia	Mr. Jefferson,	ay	no.
	Mr. Hardy,	no	
	Mr. Mercer,	no	
North Carolina	Mr. Williamson,	ay	div.
	Mr. Spaight,	no	
South Carolina	Mr. Read,	no	no.
	Mr. Beresford,	no	

[*Journals of Congress*, (*Way & Gideon*,) Vol. IV. p. 373.]

APPENDIX, No. 3.

THE following is a copy of Mr. King's proposition: —

"That there shall be neither slavery nor involuntary servitude in any of the States described in the resolve of Congress of the 23d of April, 1784, otherwise than in punishment of crimes whereof the party shall have been personally guilty; and that this regulation shall be an article of compact, and remain a fundamental principle of the Constitution, between the thirteen original States and each of the States described in the said resolve of the 23d of April, 1784."

On the question for commitment, the yeas and nays being required by Mr. King, the vote was as follows: —

New Hampshire	Mr. Foster,	ay	ay.
	Mr. Long,	ay	
Massachusetts	Mr. Holten,	ay	ay.
	Mr. King,	ay	
Rhode Island	Mr. Ellery,	ay	ay.
	Mr. Howell,	ay	

* The asterisk opposite the name of Mr. Dick, of New Jersey, indicates that the vote was not counted, as a State could not be represented by less than two members or delegates. (See sect. 2, art. 5, of the Articles of Confederation.)

State	Delegate	Vote	State vote
Connecticut	Mr. Cook,	ay	ay.
	Mr. Johnson,	ay	
New York	Mr. W. Livingston,	ay	ay.
	Mr. Platt,	ay	
New Jersey	Mr. Beatty,	ay	ay.
	Mr. Cadwalader,	ay	
	Mr. Stewart,	ay	
Pennsylvania	Mr. Gardner,	ay	ay.
	Mr. W. Henry,	ay	
Maryland	Mr. McHenry,	no	ay.
	Mr. J. Henry,	ay	
	Mr. Hindman,	ay	
Virginia	Mr. Hardy,	no	no.
	Mr. Lee,	no	
	Mr. Grayson,	ay	
North Carolina	Mr. Spaight,	no	no.
	Mr. Sitgreaves,	no	
South Carolina	Mr. Bull,	no	no.
	Mr. Pinckney,	no	
Georgia	Mr. Houston,	no	*

[*Journals of Congress*, Vol. IV. p. 481.]

The vote was taken on the 16th of March, 1785.

APPENDIX, No. 4.

The sixth article of the ordinance of 1787 is inserted here to show how far it conforms in language to the anti-slavery proposition of Mr. Jefferson, in 1784, and that of Mr. King in 1785:—

"That there shall be neither slavery nor involuntary servitude in the said territory, otherwise than in the punishment of crimes whereof the party shall have been duly convicted: *Provided always*, That any person escaping into the same, from whom labor or service is lawfully claimed in any one of the original States, such fugitive may be lawfully reclaimed, and conveyed to the person claiming his or her labor or service as aforesaid."

On the 13th July, 1787, the ordinance of which the above is a part was passed by the following vote:—

State	Delegate	Vote	State vote
Massachusetts	Mr. Holten,	ay	ay.
	Mr. Dane,	ay	
New York	Mr. Smith,	ay	ay.
	Mr. Haring,	ay	
	Mr. Yates,	no	
New Jersey	Mr. Clarke,	ay	ay.
	Mr. Scheurman,	ay	

Delaware	Mr. Kearny,	ay	ay.
	Mr. Mitchell,	ay	
Virginia	Mr. Grayson,	ay	ay.
	Mr. R. H. Lee,	ay	
	Mr. Carrington,	ay	
North Carolina	Mr. Blount,	ay	ay.
	Mr. Hawkins,	ay	
South Carolina	Mr. Kean,	ay	ay.
	Mr. Huger,	ay	
Georgia	Mr. Few,	ay	ay.
	Mr. Pierce,	ay	

[*Journals of Congress*, Vol. IV. p. 754.]

APPENDIX, No. 5.

THE answer which Mr. DIX declined making to Mr. BERRIEN, from an unwillingness to be further interrupted in the course of his remarks, he now proceeds to give.

The decree of President Guerrero will be found, as indicated below, in the collection of laws and decrees of the General Congress of Mexico. It is classed among the decrees made by the government by virtue of extraordinary powers, and the original is in the following words : —

ABOLICION DE LA ESCLAVITUD.

El Presidente de los Estados Unidos Mejicanos a los habitantes de la republica, sabed :

Que deseando señalar en el año de 1829, el aniversario de la independencia con un acto de justicia y de beneficencia nacional que refluyia en beneficio y sosten de bien tan apreciable ; que afiance mas y mas la tranquilidad publica ; que coopere al engrandecimiento de la republica, y que reintegre à una parte desgraciado de sus habitantes en los derechos sagrados que les dió naturaleza y proteje la nacion por leyes sabias y justas, conforme à lo dispuesto por el art. 30, de la acta constitutiva ; usando de las facultades extraordinarias que me estàn concedidas, he venido en decretar :

1. Queda abolida la esclavitud en la republica.
2. Son por consiguiente libres los que hasta hoy se habian considerado como esclavos.
3. Cuando las circunstancias del erario lo permitan, se indemnizarà a los proprietarios de esclavos en los terminos que dispusieren las leyes.

Mejico, 15 de Setiembre de 1829. A. D. José Maria de Bocanegra.

[Coleccion de Leyes y Decretos, etc., en los años de 1829 y 1830, pag. 147.]

[Translation.]

ABOLITION OF SLAVERY.

The President of the United Mexican States to the inhabitants of the republic:

Desiring to signalize, in the year 1829, the anniversary of Independence by an act of national justice and beneficence, which may tend to the benefit and support of so important a good; which may strengthen more and more the public tranquillity; which may coöperate in the aggrandizement of the republic; and which may restore to an unfortunate portion of its inhabitants the sacred rights which nature gave them, and protect the nation by wise and just laws, in conformity to the provision of the 30th article of the constitutive act; exercising the extraordinary powers which are conceded to me, I do decree:

1. Slavery is abolished in the republic.

2. Those who until to-day have been considered slaves, are consequently free.

3. When the condition of the treasury will permit, the owners of the slaves will be indemnified in the manner which shall be provided for by law.

MEXICO, *15th September*, 1829. A. D.

JOSE MARIA DE BOCANEGRA.

[Collection of Laws and Decrees, &c., in the years 1829 and 1830, page 147.]

The following addition, not contained in the above collection, will be found at page 147 of the "American Annual Register" of 1829–30:—

And, in order that the present decree may have its full and entire execution, I order it to be printed, published, and circulated to all those whose obligation is to have it fulfilled.

Given in the Federal Palace of Mexico, on the 15th of September, 1829.

VINCENTE GUERRERO.

LORENZO DE ZAVALA.

The publication of this decree in the general collection of the Laws and Decrees of Mexico would seem to afford, *primâ facie*, sufficient evidence of its authority. But there are higher evidences. In the law of 5th April, 1837, of which an extract is given below, it is recognized in the following terms:—

"Los dueños de esclavos manumitidos por la presente ley ó por el decreto de 15 de Setiembre de 1829, serán indemnizados," etc. [Coleccion de Leyes y Decretos, etc., tomo 8, pag. 201.]

[Translation.] — The masters of slaves manumitted by the present law or by the decree of the 15th of September, 1829, shall be indemnified, &c. [Collection of Laws and Decrees, &c., Vol. VIII. page 201.]

The extraordinary powers, by virtue of which this decree was made, do not appear to have been conferred, as Mr. BERRIEN supposes, for the purpose of repelling invasion. The decree does not show that they had such a purpose at all. They were vested in the Executive by an act of the Third Constitutional Congress, in the following words: —

FACULTADES EXTRAORDINARIAS AL GOBIERNO.

ART. 1. Le autoriza al ejecutivo de la Federacion para adoptar cuantos medidas sean necesarias à la conservacion de la independencia, del sistema actual de gobierno, y de la tranquilidad.

2. Por el articulo anterior no queda el gobierno autorizado para disponer de la vida de Mejicanos, ni para espelerlos del territorio de la Republica.

3. Esta autorizacion cesará tanluego como el Congreso General se reuna en sesiones ordinarias.

[Coleccion de las Leyes y Decretos expedidos por el Congreso General, etc., de 1829 y 1830, pag. 55.]

[Translation.]

EXTRAORDINARY POWERS TO THE GOVERNMENT.

ART. 1. The Executive of the Confederation is authorized to adopt whatever measures may be necessary for the preservation of independence, of the present system of government, and of tranquillity.

ART. 2. By the preceding article the government is not authorized to dispose of the lives of Mexicans, or to expel them from the territory of the republic.

ART. 3. This authority shall cease as soon as the General Congress shall meet in ordinary sessions.

[Collection of Laws and Decrees made by the General Congress, &c., of 1829 and 1830, page 55.]

The powers conferred by the first article are only limited by the provisions of the second and third, excepting so far as they may be considered restrained by the purposes for which they were conferred. These purposes are very extensive, — so much so as to comprehend nearly all the great ends of government. The decree of President Guerrero, as will be perceived, has reference to the very purposes for which the extraordinary powers were delegated, — to support "independence" and strengthen the "public tranquillity." The extraordinary powers referred to were conceded on the 25th August, 1829, and the government was required to report to the Congress to assemble in January, 1830, the necessity that existed in the cases in which it had exercised the powers conferred by the first article. The Congress met in January, and continued in session, ordinary and extraordinary, with brief intermissions, till the 29th December, 1830. During this period, the decree of Guerrero was untouched. But on the 15th February, 1831, a resolution was passed by Congress declaring that the laws, decrees, rules, orders, and provisions, which belong to the legislative authority, and which the government had made by virtue of the extraordinary powers referred to, were subject to the qualification of Congress, and were to be without effect until revised by the Chambers. There were, however, exceptions to the rule. How far the decree of Guerrero was affected by this declaration, — whether it was an authority executed and not to be revoked, or whether it was suspended in its operation until 1837, — it is not necessary to inquire. The subsequent recognition of the decree by legislative and constitutional enactments disposes of the question of authority. It is hardly admissible in us to dispute the validity of an act of the Mexican government thus recognized in Mexico; or to assert, in the face of that recognition, that the power of abolishing slavery belonged to the municipal authorities of the several States.

The act of Congress of 1837, referred to by Mr. Dix, is in the following words: —

"Queda abolida, sin escepcion alguna, la esclavitud en toda la república: Abril 5, de 1837." [Coleccion de Leyes y Decretos, etc., tomo 8, pag. 201.]

[Translation.] — Slavery is forever abolished, without any exception, in the whole republic: April 5, 1837. [Collection of Laws and Decrees of the General Congress of the United Mexican States, Vol. VIII. page 201.]

The constitution of 1844 (of Tacubaya) reiterates the prohibition of slavery in the following words: —

"Slavery is forever prohibited." — *Thompson's Mexico,* page 180.

It will be perceived that the constitution of 1844 does not abolish slavery: it prohibits it. From the difference between the phraseology of the decree of 1829 and the act of Congress of 1837 and that of the constitution of 1844, is it not fairly to be inferred that the latter designed to prohibit in the future what the two former acts had abolished in the past?

On the strength of these authorities, Mr. Dix asserted that Mexico had long since abolished slavery throughout the republic.

END OF VOL. I.

www.ingramcontent.com/pod-product-compliance
Lightning Source LLC
LaVergne TN
LVHW021122110826
845150LV00005B/915

9781425551636